POLICE AND THE LIBERAL STATE

Critical Perspectives on Crime and Law

Edited by Markus D. Dubber

EDITED BY MARKUS D. DUBBER
AND MARIANA VALVERDE

Police and the Liberal State

STANFORD LAW BOOKS
An imprint of Stanford University Press
STANFORD, CALIFORNIA

Stanford University Press
Stanford, California

Printed in the United States of America on acid-free, archival-quality paper

Library of Congress Cataloging-in-Publication Data

Police and the liberal state / edited by Markus D. Dubber and Mariana Valverde.
p. cm.—(Critical perspectives on crime and law)
Includes bibliographical references and index.
ISBN 978-0-8047-5932-8 (cloth : alk. paper)
1. Police power. 2. Police. 3. Criminal law. 4. Police power—United States. 5. Police—United States. 6. Criminal law—United States. I. Dubber, Markus Dirk. II. Valverde, Mariana, 1955- III. Series.
K3220.P65 2008
363.2—dc22 2008011549

Typeset by Newgen in 9.75/13 Janson

Contents

Contributors

Markus D. Dubber is Professor of Law and Director of the Buffalo Criminal Law Center, SUNY Buffalo.

Mark E. Kann is Professor of Political Science and History, University of Southern California.

Ron Levi is Assistant Professor, Centre of Criminology, University of Toronto.

William J. Novak is Associate Professor of History, University of Chicago, and Research Fellow, American Bar Foundation.

Peter Ramsay is Lecturer in Law, London School of Economics and Political Science.

Jacqueline E. Ross is Professor of Law, University of Illinois College of Law.

David Alan Sklansky is Professor of Law, University of California at Berkeley.

Christopher Tomlins is Research Professor, American Bar Foundation.

Mariana Valverde is Professor, Centre of Criminology, University of Toronto.

Preface

This book first took shape in the summer of 2006, when a group of scholars from different disciplines and countries came to Buffalo to explore a range of topics from the general perspective of policing as a tool of governance. It advances and expands a project on the police power that began with a workshop in 2004, which yielded *The New Police Science: The Police Power in Domestic and International Governance* (Stanford University Press, 2006).

The police power as a modern technology of governance recommends itself as the focus for interdisciplinary and international exploration for two reasons. First, as a general tool of governance it pervades all aspects and levels of modern government. The police power, understood as the power to maximize the public welfare (or, more colorfully, "peace, order, and good government") as opposed to, say, the power to do justice, is thought to be so essential to the very idea of government that it (1) underlies such diverse technologies of government as liquor licensing and the criminal law; (2) is claimed by city governments as well as county, state, and national governments, and increasingly even governments in the international realm; and (3) appears, in various forms—and under various names—in the practices and theories of governance of many modern liberal states, including not only the United States and Canada but the United Kingdom and Continental Europe (home of the original "police science") as well.

Second, part of the problem of writing, and thinking, about police today is that people do study "it" in different disciplines, and from different angles, but without knowing that this is what they—or for that matter others—are doing. The range of disciplines that address various aspects of the power to police is wide, including social and political theory, legal theory and history, criminology, and feminist studies. This book, by combining contributions by people from different disciplines and places, contributes to the rediscovery of police as a common topic of interest and inquiry.

We are grateful to the Baldy Center for Law and Social Policy at SUNY Buffalo for its continued support of our work. The 2004 and 2006 meetings were cohosted by the Baldy Center, the Canada–United States Legal Studies Centre at SUNY Buffalo, and the Buffalo Criminal Law Center. We are also happy to acknowledge the important contributions to this book and the larger project by Igor Akrapovic, Rob Crawford, Jeff Davis, Julius Dubber, Sara Faherty, Anne Gaulin, Al Gillen, Ellen Kausner, Gerald Kiska, Laura Mangan, Lynn Mather, Nils Olsen, Swarna Perinparajah, and Joe Schneider.

Markus D. Dubber
Mariana Valverde

POLICE AND THE LIBERAL STATE

INTRODUCTION

Policing the *Rechtsstaat*

MARKUS D. DUBBER AND MARIANA VALVERDE

The legal doctrine of the police power does not have a high public profile, by comparison to such topics as emergency powers or same-sex marriage. On its part, the venerable tradition of police science, developed by publicly minded administrators and lawyers to justify and rationalize the exercise of the police power, is virtually unknown to nonspecialists. Every few years, however, a legislative or judicial pronouncement about the police power of the state manages to stir the general public out of its usual complacency about living in a free country.

A recent example is the U.S. Supreme Court decision in *Kelo v. City of New London*.[1] A lowly case about how a small town in Connecticut might improve its waterfront shook people up across the United States, caused numerous state legislatures to pass new laws restricting eminent domain powers, and even prompted the House of Representatives to enact a resolution disapproving of the decision.[2] Can the state condemn private property under eminent domain powers even beyond the already broad powers granted by the 1950s' nebulous term *blight*? Even if the state can condemn nonblighted property when public works are deemed necessary, is it really constitutional for states and through them municipalities to condemn nonblighted property—explicitly to sell the parcel to more desirable private owners? Is anyone's property safe?

The sharply split decision of the U.S. Supreme Court in *Kelo* has given rise to a vocal debate that is notable not only for the stridency of the property-rights lobby but also, and more pertinently for our purposes, for the unexpected alliance of strange bedfellows generated by the case. Ms. Susette Kelo was represented by the Institute for Justice, a libertarian public interest law firm that subsequently pushed for state laws tightening up the definition of eminent domain: but the justices who found for her included more progressive ones alongside libertarian ones. In the oral argument, the lawyer for the petitioner was very vigorously challenged first by Justice Ginsburg and then by Justice Scalia, the two voices speaking in complete harmony about the validity of a city's efforts to enlist large capital in its revitalization efforts. As Ginsburg colloquially put it at oral argument, "the community had gone down and down and the town wanted to build it up."[3]

Since the decision, the battle to legislatively reverse the Supreme Court's expansive approach to public use has been led by right-wing property-rights activists. However, a hefty amicus curiae brief supporting Ms. Kelo was submitted by none other than the 1960s' new urbanism guru Jane Jacobs (who died soon after). Jacobs's brief stated that if the court deferred to the expansive definition of *public use* deployed by the city of New London, this would spell doom for small folk. The brief's conclusion that "only a categorical ban on economic development takings can prevent the Public Use Clause from becoming a nullity that can be circumvented any time local governments seek to benefit a politically connected private business"[4] was written in such a way as to command support from the libertarian absolute-property-rights movement—as well as from downtown liberals worried about global corporations with allies on city councils.

Nevertheless, Jacobs and her "new urbanist" successors are hardly opposed to the police power of the state as such. They favor height restrictions, zoning measures increasing density, and other conventional municipal regulatory strategies: they just oppose certain uses of the police power that, in their view, would be destructive of established (if somewhat impoverished) communities. Similarly, it is unlikely that those who oppose condemnations and expropriations as a matter of principle (the libertarian property-rights advocates with whom Jacobs uneasily allied in the *Kelo* case) would oppose other uses of the police power—panhandling ordinances, for instance. It could thus be said that all of the arguments swirling around inner city improvement strategies are purely internal to the police power, rather than arguments in favor or against.

Curiously, as a technical matter of constitutional law, *Kelo* was not even a police power case, at least not explicitly. On its face, it concerned an exercise of the power of eminent domain, which authorizes the sovereign to "take" private property for "public use" but also entitles the owner to "just compensation" for the taking.[5] By contrast, regulation—as opposed to taking—of property under the police power, again in the interest of the public welfare, requires no compensation. The distinction between takings and police power regulation of property, however, has eroded over time thanks to such doctrinal innovations as the oxymoronic "regulatory taking."[6] As the dissent in *Kelo* points out, rather meekly, the opinion relied on precedent that had come to "equat[e] the eminent domain power with the police power" and, more specifically, had treated eminent domain's "public use" requirement as "coterminous with the scope of a sovereign's police powers," thereby "conflat[ing] these two categories."[7]

This conflation of eminent domain taking and police power regulation is significant because, by treating a takings question as a police question, the *Kelo* majority firmly locates the issue within the realm of virtually unlimited sovereign discretion. The dissent's point, then, is not that a doctrinal category mistake has been committed but that the majority was wrong to treat the takings issue in the case as a police power issue because doing so implies taking a radical laissez-faire attitude. In the end, then, the case is about the police power after all. Among all their sharp disagreements, majority and dissent are in complete agreement that the police power is essentially boundless and, as such, beyond meaningful constitutional scrutiny. *Kelo* joins the long line of cases, since *Lochner v. New York*,[8] that illustrate the police power's function in constitutional law as an "idiom of apologetics."[9]

The contradictions of inner city revitalization projects led by large capital and facilitated by cash-strapped municipal governments that are neither economically nor politically able to undertake major public works on their own are emblematic of urban governance in our neoliberal era.[10] But the legal powers used to summarily expropriate Ms. Kelo and her neighbors in favor of a large pharmaceutical company promising to further the public welfare (*salus populi*)[11] are very old—indeed, ancient. These powers are crucial not only to urban governance (in planning and zoning powers, loitering and panhandling ordinances, etc.) but to a whole range of other fields of state power. The phrase *eminent domain*, and the sweeping powers that it triggers, is widely understood to be apposite only when legislatures wave the wand of public use and general welfare: but numerous other legal (and policing) acts of state power are also based, more or less visibly, on the police power.

As *The New Police Science*,[12] our previous book on the subject, has made clear, the police power reaches far beyond the disputed terrain of urban renewal, or city government more generally. It is deeply rooted in constitutional rhetoric and law not only in the United States[13] but also throughout the former British Empire and, at least in the United States, is recognized as the black-letter foundation of criminal law. And while the police power has traditionally been defined in the common law as a—quite literally—domestic power, that is, patriarchal power of the sovereign to order his kingdom to ensure the health, welfare, and morals of the population, Teddy Roosevelt already envisioned an international police power to order the Western hemisphere as if it were the (or perhaps more accurately, his) domestic realm. The exercise of international police power over the entire globe as a megahousehold without a householder as a matter of institutional form, if not of *Realpolitik*, has been the subject of much concern in the post-Yugoslavia and post-Rwanda era.[14]

In fact, the two areas of current legal debate that we mentioned at the outset as having a higher profile than the doctrine of police (emergency powers and same-sex marriage) are both rooted in other aspects of police. As for the first area, insofar as the power of police can be regarded as one aspect of the sovereign's power to order his kingdom, the control of boundaries and the management of threats to the internal security of the kingdom are closely related to (and even coterminous with) the police power.[15] As Chris Tomlins shows in Chapter 2, the late nineteenth-century cases regarding Indian nations and colonial possessions (the Insular Cases) have not been traditionally seen as at all related to the exercise of the police power, but doctrinally they are closely related—an observation with important implications for today's debates on emergency powers, especially in regard to noncitizens.[16] In regard to same-sex marriage, the 2003 Massachusetts case that first legalized same-sex marriage in the United States framed the issue not in terms of family law but in terms of the state's obligation to issue licenses to citizens on a basis of equality. Licensing, however, as Mariana Valverde's work has shown, is integral to police and policelike powers in the common law.[17] Moreover, the regulation of marriage as a social relation traditionally has fallen under the rubric of the police power.[18] For instance, the police power was invoked to justify the criminalization of interracial marriages in the United States.[19]

Spanning a wide variety of otherwise separate legal and political realms, the police power has tended to resist definition. It has been suggested that the core characteristic of police power is precisely its indefinability; insofar as one of its functions is to preclude efforts to constrain the discretion of the sovereign invoking it, any definition would be unwelcome.[20] At any rate, the police power is many things to many people. Nonetheless, some common themes can be traced through contemporary discussions of the police power, including those in *The New Police Science*. Before we go on to describe in more detail the individual contributions in this book, let us recapitulate some points of convergence on the meaning of police.

Police powers and policelike powers (such as the peace, order, and good government, or POGG, powers of the Canadian federal government[21]) act as a kind of hinge articulating the past-oriented punishment of wrongdoing with the future-oriented governance of risks and dangers. *Police* thus links the two temporalities of law—but without abolishing the tension between them. Those who contravene laws and ordinances that were passed to ensure the king's peace or the general welfare can be fined or in some cases imprisoned (not to mention executed) for acts committed in the past; but the police power also underlies such future-oriented risk-management measures as environmental regulations, zoning ordinances, and rules and guidelines regarding security searches.

Police powers have often taken a rather despotic form, the *Kelo* case being a useful reminder that, according to the doctrine of police, all land in the kingdom is ultimately the king's. However, as Bill Novak's chapter shows, the police power was also crucial to the development of Progressive Era and New Deal measures to defend the "general welfare" of the community, including the working class, in the face of the power of capital. Thus, police can be a powerful tool of sovereign oppression; but it can also be deployed in a more communitarian direction. Indeed, some of today's examples of police-type measures (e.g., the UK's Anti-Social Behaviour Order and the gang congregation ordinances analyzed by Peter Ramsay and Ron Levi, respectively, in this book) have been criticized as deeply illiberal and discriminatory. Unlike older police measures such as vagrancy statutes, however, today's public order measures often are defended not from the standpoint of the security of the sovereign but rather from the more or less communitarian perspective that speaks about working-class communities defending themselves against disorder and fear.

Police powers are thus neither despotic nor democratic—they can be both, even at the same time. They also work simultaneously to punish and to prevent, although without eliminating that fundamental binary division of legal powers. One can thus begin to understand why a police power case like *Kelo* could reveal some surprisingly strong agreements among groups (and judges) on opposite sides of the political spectrum.

* * *

Political and legal theory, at least in the Anglo-American world, tends to spend little time trying to capture, never mind to understand, the actual operation of government. Too tempting are deep questions about the principles and rules, the norms and the ideals, that frame state action through law. The mechanics of government, the inner workings of state control, largely escape theoretical investigation and instead are tagged for empirical studies, usually to be performed by specialist social scientists whose tabulations then can safely be ignored. Likewise, everyday participants in the institutions of state government are considered to be too far removed from the realm of theoretical inquiry, too wrapped up in their doctrines and their rituals, to produce useful insights.

This book is part of a broad interdisciplinary and international project to refocus scholarly attention through the lens of the police power on the scope and functioning of government in its myriad manifestations, from the family to the prison to the workplace, from the city to the state to the international community, that first bore fruit in *The New Police Science*. *The New Police Science* recovered the age-old project of studying the police power (hence the "new police science"); *Police and the Liberal State* takes the further, and logical, steps of refining the conceptual apparatus of the police power project and applying the general approach to a more specific set of questions—notably in criminal law.

The book begins to move the police power project from the realm of theory and agenda and drives home the point that it provides a fruitful framework for research in several disciplines—in any discipline, in fact, that concerns itself with problems of government, including law. The more explicit focus on questions of criminal justice is important since criminal law in particular is in dire need of a sophisticated conceptual framework that connects it to research agendas in other disciplines, including criminology, criminal justice, political science, and history.

The chapters in this book approach the phenomenon of government in general, and of police government in particular, from a variety of disciplinary perspectives and tackle a wide range of topics. Police is a broad—some might say boundless—rationality of government that manifests itself in any number of formal and substantive ways, without regard to place or time, institution or academic division of labor. For that reason, it is both a formidable subject and one perfectly suited for the sort of interdisciplinary and international approach illustrated by these chapters.

Apart from their recurring interest in the multifaceted concept of police—police as sovereignty, police as welfare, police as uniformed constabulary, and so on—the chapters in this book also share a deep historical sensibility, without which inquiries into the police power must appear pointless. To think about the police power today is impossible without some historical digging; much of the recent history of the police power since the Enlightenment has been one of denial and displacement. It's no accident that the police power makes no appearance in *Kelo* until the O'Connor dissent. Once the frequent subject of constitutional analysis—if not necessarily scrutiny—the police power has fallen into desuetude as a category of U.S. constitutional law. It might have all but disappeared in name, but it survives in function, as a synonym for lax judicial oversight of the exercise of state power by the legislature and the executive. There is thus no need to invoke the police power, nor is there an occasion—cases that fall under the police power are by definition, or at least by universal consensus, inappropriate for judicial scrutiny. With its limited modern docket, the U.S. Supreme Court has no time for pointless police power analysis. The only question that may arise is one of classification, and only in federal cases, where constitutional orthodoxy requires adherence to the fiction that only the states have police power. Although legal textbooks and court decisions continue to assert that in U.S. law the police power is wholly a state power, this claim ignores and erases the considerable police powers exercised by the federal government not only under the commerce clause but also through drug laws, border security, and other realms in which coercive measures are justified through appeals to "the general welfare."[22]

Anyone who looks beyond the absence of police power in contemporary black-letter law soon discovers a rich literature on police as a key ordering concept in the theory and practice of government, not only in the United States but elsewhere as well. One need not follow the thread of police government to the *oeconomics* of the Athenian householder to stumble across the police science that flourished in Europe (notably in France and Germany) in the seventeenth and eighteenth centuries, Adam Smith's Lectures on Justice, Police, Revenue and Arms, or the Blackstonian definition of police as "the due regulation and domestic order of the kingdom: whereby the individuals of the state, like members of a well-governed family, are bound to conform their general behaviour to the rules of propriety, good neighbourhood, and good manners: and to be decent, industrious, and inoffensive in their respective stations,"[23] quoted over and over again in U.S. texts and opinions as late as the 1960s.[24]

All of the chapters in this book thus take a broader, historical, view of their subject matter. The more explicitly historical, or rather genealogical, chapters appear at the beginning. The reference to genealogy is deliberate—Foucault made a significant contribution to the rediscovery of the concept of police in his searching inquiries into the genealogy of core concepts of power. No attempt to reinvigorate the concept of police for contemporary work on law and government can ignore Foucault's treatment of police, which attracted considerable interest in social and political theory, particularly within the broader context of his discussions of what he came to call "governmentality." It is only fitting, therefore, that the book begin with Mariana Valverde's analysis of Foucault's considered view on theories and practices of governance, based on a careful reading of Foucault's recently published College de France lectures. Valverde's chapter makes a significant contribution to our understanding of Foucault's thought on police and on police's relation to law and government in particular, which the lectures set out in a usefully concentrated form. Valverde develops an original argument about the importance of Foucault's analysis of modern state formation in a contribution that will interest Foucault specialists, while at the same time providing an accessible introduction to the uninitiated. Valverde sounds several themes that will recur throughout the book, including the contrast but not incompatibility of liberal and police government (as illustrated not only by licensing schemes[25] but also by formal criminal police offenses[26]) and the connection between police government and the project of urbanization and even the very idea of a city (as exemplified, for instance, by Patrick Colquhoun's comprehensive program for the policing of early nineteenth-century London[27]).

Tomlins's chapter begins to shift focus from general theoretical approaches—a way of doing theory, rather than a theory itself—to history, and it expands the genealogy from selected French materials to U.S. constitutional law. In an influential earlier work, Tomlins highlighted the contested relationship between police and law in the early American Republic.[28] Now he traces U.S. constitutional history from its prerevolutionary origins through *Lochner* from the perspective of the police power. This approach locates American state sovereignty on a continuum of sovereignty transfers from one governmental entity to another, rather than as a revolutionary reinvention of political power. It also highlights and connects such apparently disparate—and often neglected—loci of American governance as the treatment of Indians, immigrants, and the new American colonies (most importantly, Puerto Rico), all of whom—or which—joined the great mass of the policed, the plebeian rubble that the American Revolution threatened to sweep into power, a thought that struck fear into the Founders once they turned to the business of governing the new republic.[29]

As Tomlins shows, the police power also played a central role in the constitutional structure of the American nation-state—with the police power ostensibly reserved for the states to mark their continued sovereignty, but de facto wielded by the nation under various headings (such as the commerce power).[30] The myth of the police-powerless federal government (and the nonexistence of a nation-state above and beyond "the States") became increasingly difficult to maintain as federal law and regulation continued to increase in heft and bite. Still, the U.S. Supreme Court continues to police the distinction between the (illegitimate) federal police power and the (explicit) federal commerce power with considerable vigor.[31]

The police power also figures prominently in the emergence of the modern U.S. administrative state (Tomlins's bureaucratic-administrative state of sovereign police), as Bill Novak argues in Chapter 3. Building on his groundbreaking study of the police power in nineteenth-century America, *The People's Welfare*, Novak chronicles the dramatic expansion of federal power in the name of public welfare during the late nineteenth and early twentieth centuries, which drew on an unbounded conception of police power far beyond the vague, but still formally constrained, nuisance power familiar from English common law against which the police power was often defined in the early nineteenth century.[32] The police power became a tool for progressive reform on a grand, national, scale. Proponents of the police power stood for the public welfare, for rationality and modernity in government; its detractors sought to tie the hands of "the public" through their insistence on anachronistic formalities of process and definition and reactionary anxiety about the protection of private property in an active, progressive, modern state, epitomized by the tendentious, meddling, and ultimately anachronistic reading of the due process clause in *Lochner* steeped in passé eighteenth-century ideas of the social compact. The future belonged to the police power; and the future was the comprehensive national administrative state.

Beginning with Chapter 4, the book shifts focus from constitutional and administrative law to criminal law, where it will remain. This is a shift in focus only, from one manifestation of the police power to another. We've already noted that it is black-letter law in the United States that the state's power to criminalize is based on its power to police, that is, to protect the public welfare in all of its aspects. Though not explicitly framed in terms of police, Foucault's most influential book, *Discipline and Punish*, captured criminal punishment's transition from physical to psychological sanctions and the attendant replacement of violent public displays of sovereign power to the establishment of a carceral web, at the node of which was the correctional prison rather than the vindictive gallows. Nothing more vividly illustrates the police power's oppressive potential than the intentional interference with the property, liberty, and even the life of those whom the state deems to have committed an "offense" against its sovereignty.[33]

Mark Kann, in Chapter 4, presents a compelling account of the failure of American criminal law to rethink the patriarchal foundations of English criminal law in light of the liberal principles of the Revolution. Despite the Revolution's rights rhetoric, criminal law remained grounded in the state's sovereignty, with the public peace simply replacing the king's peace as the formal object of protection. The police power was the king's (and later the public's) patriarchal power to regulate, in Blackstone's words, "the individuals of the state, like members of a well-governed family." The king's power to keep the peace in turn traced itself back to the householder's peace of medieval law and, eventually, to the power of the Roman *paterfamilias* over his *familia* and the Athenian *oikonomikos* over his *oikos*. Prisons, which emerged as the predominant American penal sanction, were organized like households, under the discretionary authority of the warden-householder. Drawing on prisoners' memoirs, among other sources, Kann powerfully evokes the experience of objects of penal police in the early Republic, placing the prison household within a structure of patriarchal government ranging from the family and the plantation, the workplace and the church, the military and the city, to the macro household of the (invisible) American state.

The police power has shaped not only the execution of penal sanctions in so-called correctional facilities but the American penal process in its entirety, Dubber argues in Chapter 5. As a police matter, American penal law never underwent the basic critique in light of the principles that ostensibly drove the American Revolution and that continue to shape American political self-understanding and ideology. While the Enlightenment (even in England, thanks to the efforts of Bentham and others) drew into question the very legitimacy of punishment in a state self-governed by autonomous persons, American political and legal thought largely perceived, and ignored, the problem of punishment as an administrative police issue.

Contemporary American penal law, then, appears as a police system—albeit a fairly primitive and inefficient one—for the identification and disposal of human threats, with little regard to hallowed principles like *actus reus* and *mens rea* that are little more than anachronistic remnants of the common law without any obvious connection to more fundamental questions of legitimacy. Focusing on what he takes to be the ultimate source of legitimacy in a modern democratic state and in the American Republic in particular—autonomy, or self-government—Dubber sharpens the features of this police model of the penal process by contrasting it with an alternative model that would submit itself to, rather than avert, the sort of legitimacy critique that a purported commitment to the protection of the "life, liberty, and property" of citizen-offenders in a *Rechtsstaat* would seem to demand.

David Sklansky, in Chapter 6, turns his attention to the application of norms of substantive criminal law to particular cases at the outset of the penal process rather than at its end, when sanctions imposed in court are inflicted (most notably in prisons). Sklansky, in other words, discusses the police as an institution, the limited sense in which the concept survives in common parlance, long after the comprehensive scope of the original notion of police has largely been forgotten (though even today "to police" means something else besides *to act as police* in the institutional sense). More specifically, Sklansky explores the connection between the government of American police departments and the ideal of democracy. The police, it turns out, is governed much like other quasi-familial institutions, including factories, the military, and—most interesting—prisons (as Kann shows in Chapter 4). In other words, the police itself is a prime locus of police; more pointedly, police officers manifest the *subject* of police power, the state, in its interaction with the objects of its police power (qua police force or—less pointedly and more obscurely—arms of the law) and at the same time are themselves *objects* of police power on their side of the thin blue line, in their patriarchal departments, stations, units, squads. Ironically, police departments therefore resemble a prison, another patriarchal institution modeled after various households (family, military, factory, slave plantation). Bringing democracy to police departments, then, is a project not unlike once notorious—and long since abandoned—experiments in prisoner self-government in the United States, all of which ultimately failed in the face of the rigid patriarchal hierarchy characteristic of quasi-familial police institutions.[34] Sklansky's discussion suggests that attempts to institute internal police autonomy stand a better chance of success, apart from whatever effect these reforms might have on the legitimacy of the police's exercise of state power against "civilians" in the penal process.

Jacqueline Ross and Peter Ramsay broaden the book's approach along another, comparative, dimension beyond the historical one found throughout all the chapters. In Chapter 7, Ross contributes an original discussion of German police law (*Polizeirecht*), a branch of law explicitly devoted to the legalization of policing. Unlike Sklansky, Ross focuses on the regulation of police activities in the exercise of the police's official function, rather than on the internal government of police departments. The attempt in German law to place legal limits on police activities turns on a distinction between preventive functions (to prevent harm, whether criminal or not, of human origin or not) and repressive functions (to enforce provisions of criminal law). Preventive police acts are governed by police law, repressive acts by penal law (both procedural and substantive criminal law). Police law is state law; penal law is federal (national) law. (At the same time, intelligence agencies are prohibited, according to the principle of separation, from performing any repressive law enforcement functions and police departments are prohibited from gathering intelligence.)

Drawing on an extended empirical study of German undercover policing, Ross shows how the distinction between preventive and repressive policing—or between policing and law enforcing—has proved untenable in practice as police activities naturally and continuously shift from law enforcement to prevention. Police, in other words, tends to drive out law, as early intervention in the form of preventive incapacitation makes retrospective punishment for violations of criminal norms unnecessary.

Peter Ramsay, in Chapter 8, subjects the British Anti-Social Behaviour Order (ASBO) to a thoroughgoing analysis from the perspective of police. Placing the ASBO in historical perspective by exposing its similarities to the age-old practice of binding over, Ramsay shows the ASBO to be firmly rooted in the traditional police power, "whereby," to quote Blackstone once again, "the individuals of the state, like members of a well-governed family, are bound to conform their general behaviour to the rules of propriety, good neighbourhood, and good manners: and to be decent, industrious, and inoffensive in their respective stations."[35] The ASBO, in fact, was specifically designed to overcome the apparent crudeness (and unconstitutionality) of the bind over as a police instrument. Much like possession offenses in the United States proliferated as traditional vagrancy statutes encountered constitutional difficulties (notably on vagueness grounds),[36] so the ASBO was to serve the bind over's policing function without wearing the potential for arbitrariness, oppression, and exclusion on its sleeve. Whether either attempt succeeds in legalizing a police project, instead of merely providing a formal or procedural cover for long-standing practices, is another question.

In the final chapter, Levi returns to, and expands on, some of the themes set out in Valverde's chapter at the beginning of the book while continuing Ramsay's inquiry into the special part of criminal law (dealing with specific offense definitions, rather than general principles of criminal liability). In particular, Levi turns his attention to the resurgence of vagrancy as a policing tool in American cities. Rather than rely only on a multitude of possession offenses (most importantly, drug and gun possession, with severe penalties, including in some cases, life imprisonment without the possibility of parole), Chicago in the early 1990s passed a revised vagrancy ordinance targeted at gang loitering. Analyzing the ordinance from the perspective of police, rather than as a matter of constitutional law, Levi reveals its operation as a tool for policing the city. As an urbanization measure, the ordinance concerned itself directly with the health of the city, rather than its inhabitants. It served to ensure proper circulation among the human resources that constitute the city household; idleness, on this view, interferes with city government's effort to maximize the city's welfare and for that reason is to be prevented and suppressed. As a liberal policing tool, the ordinance failed, where possession offenses, the ASBO, and licensing succeeded—it was struck down by the U.S. Supreme Court as unconstitutionally vague because it did not differ sufficiently from vagrancy, its inartful police predecessor.

In the end, the chapters in this book show police to be a rich and flexible concept that can elucidate the operation of governmental institutions and practices by placing them into a broader functional context. Police analysis can reveal connections across the history of government, across systems of government within a given state, and comparatively, across states and levels of government, from the familial to the global. Its comprehensive scope and boundless ambition, the very characteristics that tend to endear it more to those who wield it than to those who are governed by it, make the police power a particularly useful platform for interdisciplinary and international inquiries into fundamental questions of government and law.

ONE

Police, Sovereignty, and Law

Foucaultian Reflections

MARIANA VALVERDE

Introduction

During the 1970s progressive activists and scholars were centrally concerned—one could almost say obsessed—with a set of questions revolving around a megaentity known as the state. The international debate about how progressives who were moving beyond orthodox Marxism ought to theorize the state—a debate involving such central figures as Louis Althusser, Nicos Poulantzas, Ernesto Laclau, and Ralph Miliband—was constitutive of a certain politic whose influence reached well beyond the academy, for a few years at least.

Michel Foucault, who died suddenly in 1984, lived and worked in a milieu in which theorizing the state was highly valued. But instead of participating in the existing debates, he built his own path. His research projects tackled the key questions of the philosophical debates of his day—the individual and the question of agency, the state and the question of power—but indirectly or at an angle, since he always began by putting in question concepts that others took as starting points. Thus, his work on sexuality addressed the question of subjectivity that had been central both to the existentialism of the 1960s and to the poststructuralism of the 1980s, but it did so by sidelining philosophical position-taking in favor of historical inquiries into the techniques that brought into being the subject of Western philosophy. Similarly, instead of attempting to theorize the state, he pursued historical inquiries into practices developed in a variety of sites (from monasteries to physicians' consulting rooms) that were later used and adapted by state as well as nonstate institutions.

Many of Foucault's readers, habituated to theoretical edifices built out of large-scale concepts (bureaucracy, social cohesion, forces of production), read Foucault's work as if the protagonists of his genealogies were modes of power-knowledge such as sovereignty and discipline, seen as succeeding each other in the same manner that capitalism replaced feudalism. Thus, many if not most readers missed the radical methodological revolution brought about by focusing on practices of governance rather than on quasi-epochal generalizations.[1] The misreading was not solely the reader's fault, however: in some of his works Foucault, who like other empirically inclined scholars did not set out on research projects with a fully worked out theory, gave the impression that he was putting forward an alternative grand theory of modernity. *The Order of Things* contrasted the classical *episteme* to the modern *episteme*, and *Discipline and Punish* contrasted sovereignty to discipline: both of these works contain many warnings against taking these large-scale concepts as more real than the practices that constituted them; nevertheless, the epochalist misreading was not wholly without basis.

The methodological revolution involved in highlighting practices, techniques of governance, rather than epochs (or even generalized modes of power-knowledge) is more clearly apparent in the recently published College de France lectures than in some of the better known books. This justifies a close reading of these volumes, in my view.[2] But Foucault's method was always site specific, always closely linked to—and therefore varying with—the specific object of inquiry. Thus, Foucault's work does not contain a static method that can be explicated in the manner of American sociology, and I present here a reading of the recently published lectures (focusing mainly on the 1978 lectures, on security and governmentality) that highlights the methodological innovations but simultaneously explains how the substantive claims made about the history of modern practices of power-knowledge amount to an admittedly incomplete genealogy of the state. It will become clear that, contrary to the general view among scholars, Foucault did make a very important contribution to the question preoccupying progressive theorists in the 1970s—the question of the state—but he did so not by giving alternative answers to the same questions (What is the state? Is the state independent from capital?) but rather by completely changing the terms of the debate.

Sidelining or bracketing the basic concepts of philosophy and political theory—the subject, the state—was a move that had also been performed by sociologically inclined students of institutions (e.g., Erving Goffman) who demonstrated that social power relations do not leap ready-made from structural economic relations, but rather are made and remade every day in the encounters between individuals and groups that make up and are enabled by institutions. However, in contrast to the sociological and political science studies so popular in the late 1970s, Foucault's approach also bracketed institutions. Citing Robert Castel's book *L'ordre psychiatrique* as a methodological model, he critiqued the limitations of what he called "institutional-centrism."[3]

For Foucault, institutions are secondary objects of analysis because they are only coagulations or densifications of certain assemblages of practices that are also found in other institutions. Behind and before the institution, he continues, lie practices that are rarely unique to particular institutions, practices that can be seen as enabling and making up a certain technology of power. While institutional analyses trace the origins of institutions, genealogy maps the ascent of cross-institutional technologies of power.[4]

Even this very brief discussion of power, subjectivity, and institutions shows that Foucault borrowed insights and research tools from both philosophy and empirical social science; but he used them in such a way as to put in question the basic methodological assumptions of both, simultaneously. His focus was neither on the static concepts of philosophy nor on the institutions that captivated 1970s' critical social science, but rather on practices—practices of power-knowledge—with institutions as well as forms of subjectivity and agency being regarded mainly as effects of governing practices.[5] And in distancing himself both from philosophy and from the critical social science of his day, Foucault moved closer to the enterprise of history. His earlier work had been more philosophical and somewhat structuralist, but in later years his prose became much more straightforward and descriptive. The protagonists of his later, more descriptive writings, however, were neither the individuals of traditional history nor the structures of Marxist history, but rather the shifting practices used to govern people, populations, and spaces. As Foucault's friend and influential colleague put it, "The Foucault-style genealogy-history thus completely fulfills the project of traditional history; it does not ignore society, the economy, and so on, but it structures this material differently—not by centuries, peoples, or civilizations, but by practices."[6]

Assemblages of governing practices are in turn treated in a radically anti-functionalist manner, that is, as ever-changing, contingent, site-specific, pragmatically put-together collections of governing techniques whose success or failure depends on their usefulness not to society but rather to contenders in particular battles or struggles. The focus on power struggles was borrowed in turn from Nietzsche, as the first lecture in the *Society Must Be Defended* collection makes perfectly clear; but Foucault was a much keener student of history than Nietzsche and on the whole eschewed the German philosopher's weakness for making statements about power in general. Despite some incautious remarks in interviews that some people took as a theory of power in general, in Foucault's published writings and in his lectures, power relations are always of a particular sort. The scholar's task is thus not to philosophize about power in general, since such a thing does not exist, but rather to map the historical fortunes and misfortunes of the different forms of power (with their associated knowledges). A comment in one of the 1978 College de France governmentality-security lectures put the main conclusions of his research of the 1970s in deceptively simple form: governmentality is to the state what disciplinary techniques are to prisons and what biopolitics is to medical institutions.[7] And in each case, it is the practices that are regarded as primary objects of analysis, with the state, correctional institutions, and medical institutions being regarded as coagulations of practices.

The studies of sixteenth- and seventeenth-century political theory, eighteenth-century police science and police regulations, physiocratic economics, and early liberal economic policies that together gave rise to the idea of governmentality remained unpublished during Foucault's lifetime, being presented only in lectures—the 1979 Tanner lectures, given in the United States, as well as the College de France annual series of lectures—and in a few ephemeral publications. Foucault's contribution to understanding the mechanisms of modern state power and modern political thought thus remained largely unacknowledged, not only during his life but for more than a decade afterward. This has been noted for some time. In the influential 1991 introduction to a volume featuring the fourth of the 1978 College de France lectures (published in English under the simple title "Governmentality"), Colin Gordon, who was familiar with the unpublished lectures, stated,

> We are only gradually becoming aware of, and are still far from having fully documented access to, the astounding range of Foucault's intellectual enterprises, especially in the later years from 1976 to 1984. The governmental theme has a focal place in Foucault's later philosophy; an effort needs to be made to locate this as accurately as possible.[8]

What Gordon did not say, however, is that *not* publishing much about the state, sovereignty, and law may well have contributed to Foucault's posthumous fame. This is because, shortly after Foucault's death, *civil society* began to overshadow *the state* as the key concept in critical political theory, with the demise of the cold war and the general optimism (shared not only by neoliberals but even by many post-Marxist leftists) about nonstate initiatives. If avoiding talk of the state helped marginalize Foucault's thinking about power in the 1970s, especially within political theory, by the 1990s his emphasis on extrastate flows of power (such as the expertise- and profession-based power of medicine) appeared very timely and helpful.

In other words, Foucault's work may have become tremendously influential in the late 1980s precisely because it gave critical thinkers tools for understanding "political power beyond the state," as a very influential article by two English Foucaultians put it,[9] at a time when the state had in any case lost its centrality even in political science. Books such as *Discipline and Punish*[10] and *The History of Sexuality, vol. 1*[11] were certainly concerned with power, and even with politics, but they deliberately decentered the state. Even the "Governmentality" lecture published in English in 1991,[12] which launched a thousand ships, mainly of a sociological character but with some resonance within political science,[13] was read and used to understand modern Western society more than as a way to return to the questions of sovereignty and the state.

But the "Governmentality" lecture, as Gordon noted long ago, was not a one-off experiment with a neologism. It was, rather, the fourth in a tightly structured series of lectures devoted to understanding the processes giving rise to modern state knowledges and powers. This set of lectures continued the task Foucault had set for himself in the previous set of College de France lectures (given two years earlier, in 1976). The main aim of the 1976 lectures had been to understand law and sovereignty by closely examining not the traditional canon that begins with social contract theory but rather the now-forgotten texts of those aristocratic writers of heroic narratives of blood and honor who were defeated or marginalized by monarchical regimes fostering centralized legal systems. These noble chroniclers, whose writings did not count as theory then or now, are set off against the thinkers who, even when they sought to define the limits of the monarch's power (as Locke did), still treated the monarch as the central figure. The 1976 lectures thus turned the theorizing of sovereignty on its head, simply by looking closely at minor writers who had been written out of intellectual history.[14]

The 1978 lectures continued the story of sovereignty into the nineteenth century. The lectures develop the novel notion that the pastoral techniques pioneered first by Jewish patriarchs and later by Christian church fathers, techniques designed to provide individualized guidance to sheep in danger of straying from the flock, are an important element in the makeup of modern states. While early modern states treated subjects largely as an undifferentiated mass subject to the sovereign's top-down authority, nineteenth-century states (in part due to the influence of philanthropy) developed techniques to know and understand and guide citizens—young citizens in particular (through public education) but also adult citizens, particularly those at risk. Pastoralism, as Foucault calls the mode of governance that characterizes not only spiritual gurus but also social workers and therapists, can strengthen the state's hold on people even as it helps them.

In the 1979 Tanner lectures given in Stanford,[15] Foucault had said (rather mysteriously) that modern states' demonic power lies in the combination of pastoral power—previously held mainly by spiritual leaders working quite outside state structures—and the sovereign authority of state institutions. But what was not stated in the Tanner lectures (although it had been an important part of the 1978 College de France lectures) is that sovereignty, as developed in practice and in theory by centralizing monarchs such as Louis XIV, would not have survived into the contemporary era in the absence of techniques for governing the people of the state, now construed as a set of populations, in a differentiated manner. Sovereign law unifies the subjects; but modern conditions and what we would now call modern risk factors require differentiated governance.

Urbanization and commerce, in particular, require governing mechanisms that facilitate certain activities (whereas sovereign law can only prohibit and coerce). Urbanization and commerce also require the differentiation of space and time. This is where the police power finds its field of action. And in the 1978 lectures, having developed the analysis of pastoralism in the first part of the course, Foucault moves on to *police* as he begins to describe the rise of modern state apparatuses. The lectures argue in great detail that police (police regulations, police powers, and police science) enabled the sovereign power of states to begin to govern differently, in the eighteenth century, than had been the case earlier. (Foucault does not mention that police regulations had existed in medieval cities, but he would likely say that it was only in the eighteenth century that police became central to the exercise of state power.)

What Foucault does not quite say but which follows from his analysis is that police enabled sovereignty to survive into the era of constitutional monarchies and republicanism. Instead of merely securing territories and maintaining the loyalty of subjects, modern sovereign power, concerned more about security than about the absence of treason, and therefore constantly worried about the future, sets out to govern risks—risks to the state itself and risks to what was coming to be conceived as a population, not merely an aggregate of souls or subjects. Foucault's account—which is mainly based on French history—ends before democracy or even republicanism, thus leaving the impression that liberal political economy came to replace police; but fortunately, a recent Foucaultian account of the transformation of police that took place during the French Revolution has filled in the picture and made it perfectly clear that, while police mechanisms were cleansed of some of their more absolutist features (e.g., through the elimination of direct state surveillance of organizations or the abolition of press censorship), police governance was by no means diminished by republican regimes.[16] Indeed, Foucault's analysis suggests (though this is not stated explicitly) that it would be quite wrong to look at the field of police quantitatively, as if we could compare two regimes and decide which one had more or less police power; police mechanisms differ qualitatively and so cannot always be compared by asking which regime has more or less police—or more or less freedom.

Having given an overview, let us go through the elements for a genealogy of contemporary state powers and knowledges that Foucault provided in his lectures.

The Shepherd-Flock Game

Because Foucault refused to identify governing with the state, when looking back to the ancient world for elements of a genealogy of modern arts of government, he paid little attention to the Greek polis and its descendants, spending a great deal of time instead on a form of power unknown to political science: pastoral power. Sovereignty centrally involves controlling a territory, but pastoral power is unconcerned with space: it is wholly focused on the flock, wherever it may wander.[17] The good shepherd of the Old Testament, who according to Foucault also figures in Egyptian and Assyrian political cultures, is furthermore not merely concerned to preserve his power (as is the sovereign): his power lies precisely in the fact that he devotes himself to the care, and in particular the spiritual care, of every one of his sheep.

Plato's ideal polis has space for pastoral power, Foucault claims, but pastoral power is quite separate from making decisions about the polis. Magistrates and other functionaries may well exercise care and concern for individuals and guide them; but they are magistrates rather than lawmakers precisely because they deal with individuals, rather than making laws of general application. "If the state is the political form of a centralized and centralizing power, let us call pastorship the individualizing power."[18] With the spread of Christianity in the West, pastoral power flourishes, as Foucault shows through a long exegesis of texts by church fathers: but it grows and develops as a strictly spiritual project, with political power (the city-citizen game) developing its own sets of practices quite autonomously, even when the same person was exercising both political and pastoral power.[19]

In the Tanner lectures pastoral power is described very briefly; but in the much longer discussion in the College de France lectures, Foucault explains that pastoral power is necessarily individual and particular, and indeed constitutive of individuality as such. And the pastor's sacrifice generates a sense of debt and loyalty in the follower as well as a knowledge of the sheep's individual vices and virtues in the mind of the shepherd—thus achieving both obedience and agency. Pastoral practices, Foucault states, pioneer both subjection and subjectification or agency: "assujettissement, subjectivation."[20]

In the ancient world, and in the Europe of the Roman Empire and after, these largely spiritual practices of power remained separate from the city-citizen game. However, much later on (Foucault does not say when, but one thinks of the practices pioneered by philanthropic reformers in the nineteenth century and perfected by the "psy" professions—i.e., psychiatry, psychology, and psychoanalysis—in the twentieth), pastoralism undergoes a veritable renaissance. With the rise of governmental rather than merely sovereign projects, modern states acquire not only the interest in shaping the souls of citizens one at a time but also the capacity to do so. In that sense, he says, "pastoralism is the sketch or prelude of that which I have called governmentality."[21]

The College de France 1978 lectures thus provide us with a much fuller sense of the meaning and the implications of the much-quoted sentence: "Our societies proved to be really demonic since they happened to combine those two games—the city-citizen game and the shepherd-flock game—in what we call the modern states."[22]

Sovereignty

The theories of sovereignty that circulate in treatises of the John Rawls and Ronald Dworkin type are for Foucault beside the point; what needs to be documented in a genealogy of state practices and state knowledges are not doctrines but rather practices of sovereignty.

A detailed Foucaultian analysis of practices of sovereignty remains to be carried out. In *Discipline and Punish*, where some practices of sovereignty are described, the emphasis is on the rise of discipline, and so practices of sovereignty are discussed only where the description is useful as a foil for explaining discipline's innovations. Thus, certain sovereign practices of punishment are given pride of place, most famously the gory execution of the regicide that opens the book. As is well known, the details of the execution are shown to have worked to symbolize and perform the absolute power of the sovereign, a power thought to be in need of reiteration after the crime had been committed. But little or no attention is given to other arguably more important and more constantly acting practices of sovereignty, from tax collecting to the establishment of royal courts of justice. Comments scattered through *Discipline and Punish*, the Tanner lectures, and the 1976 race wars lectures (*Society Must Be Defended*) suggest that sovereign practices seek mainly to affirm control over a territory and secure the loyalty of subjects, in a somewhat static manner, in contrast to the future-oriented, resource-maximization logic of modern disciplinary and biopolitical practices. These scattered comments also suggest that sovereign power works mainly through binary prohibitions rather than through normalization, prescription, and risk management. These comments do not amount to a genealogy or even a full description, however. One might have thought that the 1978 lectures would provide us with a fuller picture of sovereign power, but that is unfortunately not the case.

The 1978 course begins with three lectures setting up a three-way contrast differentiating sovereignty from discipline from governmentality (which is first called security and only becomes governmentality in the fourth lecture, the one published in *The Foucault Effect*). Sovereign techniques for governing the problem of bread prices, for instance, include rigid controls on what crops can be grown and what prices can be charged; more governmental, liberal techniques developed in the early nineteenth century did not prohibit anything but rather incentivized certain economic activities.[23] Similarly, sovereign city planning emphasizes clear sight lines and monumental state architecture, techniques that together incite loyalty to a sovereign,[24] whereas what Foucault calls cities of security are more concerned with managing public health and other risks. But as Foucault hits his stride, at about the fifth lecture, sovereignty is left very much in the background, making a cameo appearance only as a foil that brings governmentality into sharper focus. For example, when discussing the birth of what Foucault calls properly political discourses—that is, post-Machiavellian writing on the workings of the state and the art of governing—he makes statements such as "by contrast to the juridico-theological problem of the foundations of sovereignty, political thinkers are those who attempt to think the form and the rationality of government for itself."[25] Political thinkers are here associated more with policy than with the polis,[26] through a move that emphasizes the practical work of public administrators and politicians and marginalizes the justificatory work of theorists.

The relative dearth of content provided for *sovereignty* in the various texts canvassed points to a much larger theoretical issue. *Sovereignty* has very little content other than as a name for a family resemblance linking a variety of theological, monarchical, and juridical projects of rule. But this does not mean that *sovereignty* is a highly abstract and indeterminate concept. Sovereign practices and sovereign rationalities are everywhere, and they are just as concrete and multifarious as any other kind of governing practice. These practices can be described and understood, however, only if one carefully situates them in the particular struggle or war within which they developed.

There is no Foucaultian theory of sovereignty, in other words (just as there is no general theory of discipline). There are only accounts of particular moves within which sovereign practices emerge as weapons in a battle that is shaped, as all battles are, by the position-taking that goes on in the face of a particular antagonist. The Renaissance-era sovereignty that defeated feudal narratives of heroism and blood (as told in the 1976 race wars lectures) is not the same as the sovereignty that Louis XVIII sought unsuccessfully to defend against the Jacobins, which is in turn not the same as the constitutionalized sovereignty that faced the challenge of the suffrage movement in nineteenth-century Britain. And these examples do not even begin to consider how European fascism and Stalinism revisioned and revised old practices of sovereignty, in struggles that were waged not against feudalism or republicanism but against liberalism.[27]

Sovereignty, then, is not a concept to be theorized. It is rather a name that loosely gathers, for the sake of making large-scale contrasts and generalizations that are inherently unjust to reality, an indefinite set of practices whose concreteness can be understood only relationally, or more accurately, agonistically.

Police

After several lectures on security and several devoted mainly to pastoral power, Foucault moved on to the topic of police in the lecture of March 29, 1978. The lecture was somewhat delayed because Foucault, as he breathlessly explains, was stuck in a traffic jam. This contretemps could not be more apt, since the regulation of all manner of traffic in the service of the smooth circulation of people, goods, and wealth was one of the key objects, if not the key object, of the new arts of governance pioneered by physiocrats in France and by *Polizeiwissenschaft* experts in Germany, as this lecture (and the next, and last, one) tells us.

By the eighteenth century, *police* had acquired a fairly settled meaning as one of the key dimensions of state power. The diplomatic-military dimension was routinely distinguished from the revenue function of the state, and both of those were in turn distinguished from police—the regulatory and preventive governance of the internal order of the kingdom. Urban space was the site par excellence of police regulations, as legal historians have shown.[28] Commenting on various treatises that attempted to collate the multifarious, highly detailed regulations that made up the field of police in the eighteenth century, Foucault concludes that "to police and to urbanize are one and the same thing"; even more strongly, "police is the condition for the existence of the urban."[29] Transportation was also a crucial arena for the development of what in the United States came later to be called the police power of the state, with harbors, rivers, markets, and roads all being important sites for both central and local regulatory measures that often interfered very significantly with private property rights.

If the *content* or object of police governance is generally to ensure that movement (of people, things, and wealth) is orderly and efficient, police also takes a distinctive *form*. Foucault points out that Catherine the Great's police regulations manual states that law or right is composed of general rules, whereas police works on details. Indeed, as legal historians have documented, police regulations are in fact nothing but lists of details, with little by way of overriding rationale. Police power being largely discretionary and often unenumerated, authorities acting under the banner of police are always seeking particular solutions to specific and ever-changing problems of order and security.[30] Highly theorized, largely static legal frameworks are suitable for declarations of sovereignty in the Hobbes tradition, and also for declarations about the limits of sovereignty and the rights of man in the revolutionary tradition. By contrast with both of these highly theorized discourses on sovereignty, the police power is usually exercised through detailed regulations—regulations that are sometimes of general application but that often (typically, one could say) seek to act on specific groups of people or specific activities, spaces, and times. Vagrants, itinerant sellers, prostitutes, and Jews were some of the main groups identified and governed through specific rules in the older police regulations. In the nineteenth century, while vagrancy laws certainly persisted, many of the other special groups were no longer governed through special regulations: however, the police power flourished because the differentiation of space and the differentiation of time increased in importance as regulatory strategies, beginning with maximum hours of labor for child workers and continuing into the twentieth century through myriad mechanisms of municipal, administrative, planning and zoning, and eventually, environmental regulation.

That the differentiated risks posed by capitalist labor, urban space, transportation, moral and social threats, and later, sites and substances identified as dangerous to public health were the main sites giving rise to police innovations and regulations is well known.[31] But what is distinct about Foucault's account is the analysis of the crucial location of *police* as a rationality of governance that articulates sovereignty with biopolitics and discipline. Police projects, from modest proposals about street cleaning and pub licensing to large-scale efforts to organize the labor force and create nationwide transportation systems, are exercises of sovereign power; but in police projects, unlike in projects of criminal punishment, sovereignty's aims are to a greater or lesser extent aligned with the interests of the people taken as an aggregate. Police, Foucault comments, reconciles or aligns the welfare of the people in general—the public interest in prosperity, public health, and public order—with the concern to preserve and enhance state power.[32] Tearing down someone's warehouse without compensation to make way for a port (the classic police-power-of-the-state situation) is an exercise of sovereign power. But unlike more purely coercive moves, such expropriation is justified through—and may well actually serve—the general interest of the commercial and consuming publics, which is what U.S. law calls *salus populi*, or general welfare.

Perhaps because he uses French, German, Italian, and Russian sources much more than English sources,[33] Foucault's account of police stresses the absolutist uses of police power. "Police is the direct governmentality of the sovereign as sovereign," Foucault states; "police is the permanent coup d'etat."[34] Police rationalities, and the law of the police power, have indeed authorized numerous absolutist exercises of state power. But by emphasizing how sovereign projects are operationalized through police means, Foucault neglects other dimensions or other uses of police power. Perhaps because he was not very familiar with the common law, he misses the paternalistic dimension of police, the dimension that Markus Dubber's work on patriarchy and police has emphasized.[35] In the 1978 lectures, then, *police* is generally presented as quite separate from pastoral power, whereas one could easily have argued (particularly if one considered the English and common law contributions to the doctrine and the practice of police) that police combines and synthesizes sovereignty and pastoral power.[36]

Along similar lines, because the sovereign and specifically absolutist dimension of police science and police power is so heavily emphasized, the liberal revolution in law and in economics is presented as a negation of police, rather than as a revision or modification of police techniques. At the end of the final 1978 lecture, Foucault had run out of time and did not develop the analysis of liberalism that had been foreshadowed in the first few lectures; but he concludes his account of the governmentalization of modern states by stating that liberal governmentality opposed itself in every respect to the governmentality developed within the idea of a police state (*un Etat de police*).[37] This is somewhat misleading. It is of course true that writers such as Adam Smith furthered their own arguments about freeing the natural processes of the marketplace by denouncing the regulatory constraints of the old police economy. However, in the moral and social fields, as distinct from the economic, Smith certainly did not believe in abandoning police mentalities and practices, and neither did liberal legal authorities on the other side of the Atlantic. And in any case, even in the economic field, while certain police practices for regulating the economy (e.g., sharp curbs on where and when markets could be held) disappeared with free enterprise and free trade, the state did by no means lose its sovereign power to interfere with private property rights—and not just in somewhat unusual fields such as eminent domain. I have argued elsewhere that the legal technology of business licensing is one that enables police aims—including moral-ordering aims—to be pursued without imposing a direct surveillance of private spaces and private lives by state agents.[38] No doubt other examples could be found, within the common law tradition, of techniques that happily combine liberal philosophical and economic rationalities with the police objective of maximizing order, prosperity, and efficiency and that exercise much coercion in the name of the general welfare or public interest. The relation between police and liberalism is not necessarily a negative one, as Foucault almost claims here.

A final feature of the discussion of police in the 1978 lectures is well worth discussing here, especially because Chris Tomlins's chapter speaks directly to this. Departing from the conventional view of police as the purely domestic ordering of the kingdom, Foucault tells us (with very few references, unfortunately) that police is not a strictly domestic governmentality. The European equilibrium of states established by the Treaty of Westphalia, Foucault argues, is also a site of and for police. Each of the European states—and Europe is defined as a plurality of states in equilibrium, a diagram of power elsewhere contrasted to the unitarian and expansive logic of empire[39]—has to treat the internal order and economy of the other states as integral to its own welfare. "Equilibrium is only maintained to the extent to which each of the states is capable of increasing its own strength [but] at a rate that does not threaten other states."[40] Therefore, each state must be assured that other states are effectively minding their own order, their own police. "The European equilibrium thus functions as a sort of inter-state police or inter-state law [*droit*]. The European equilibrium gives the community of states the right to make sure that police matters are in good order in each of its states."[41] This quasi-international-law doctrine of intervention in what were not yet called failed states was formalized, Foucault claims, in the 1815 Treaty of Vienna.

Clearly, these comments on international police are highly relevant to today's international law and international police discussions—much more relevant now than they were in the cold war, two-superpower world of 1978.

Governmentality and Security

What Foucault meant by *governmentality* has been the subject of so many discussions that a brief and general overview of the term and its implications has become almost impossible. In any case, a recent annual-review essay covers much of this ground for a sociolegal audience.[42] Referring readers who want more background on the governmentality literature to that essay, I will here address only a feature of the 1978 lectures that is not found elsewhere in Foucault's available work. This is how governmentality emerges, briefly in the second lecture and in full-dress form in the fourth lecture, as a replacement for what in the course summary and the title of the lecture series Foucault had earlier called security.

In regard to security, the first thing to note is that the meaning of the English word does not coincide exactly with that of the French word *securité* as Foucault uses it. *Securité* is the future-oriented management of risks; by contrast, security forces would fall under the rubric of *sûreté*. Machiavelli, Foucault tells us, is certainly keen to defend the *sûreté* of the sovereign but is not yet able to think in terms of security.[43] In keeping with this, in Canada today the Quebec provincial police's official title is Sûreté du Québec, whereas in discussions of social security or food security, the term is *securité*. Security in this latter sense is somewhat detached from (or is not contained by) the project of sovereignty. One way of characterizing it is by saying that security is positioned as the larger, overarching rationale within which police mechanisms do a great deal of their work. Elsewhere Foucault states that governmentality (i.e., what had in the first three lectures been called security) arises from a novel combination of three existing elements: pastoral power, diplomatic-military strategies, and *la police*.[44]

Security, as Jeremy Bentham pointed out, is the necessary complement of liberty; it secures liberty, literally, being essentially future oriented and risk driven. But it is, or at least it becomes, an end in itself as well as a means to the end of liberty. Security, as Hobbes as well as Bentham put it long ago, is the ultimate end of law—security is what sovereignty is *for*. Maintaining security is difficult for modern states not only because people are keen to pursue liberty but also because economic change brings with it new security needs. With the rise of modern economic and social practices and modern knowledges, new entities, such as labor markets, that were unknown to princes concerned only with territories and loyal subjects have to be secured.

Foucault explains the difference between the logic of sovereignty and that of security in the first lecture with an example: while a theft is treated by the system of sovereign criminal law as an act to be punished, assemblages of security (what Foucault calls *le dispositif de securité*) insert the phenomenon of theft—turned into an aggregate—into a series of probable events and set out to govern the general problem of future thefts as it affects not individuals, or the sovereign, but rather the population.[45] Indeed, security only begins to exist as a goal and a rationality of governance as the population emerges from older entities, such as subjects and souls.

This is a relatively familiar argument and so need not detain us here. What is worth pointing out—aside from the interesting contrast between security in the sense of social security and security in the sense of the sovereign's security, *sûreté*—is the fact that *governmentality* (*gouvernmentalité*) was a neologism with which Foucault began to experiment only as he was actually delivering the lectures. And frustratingly for governmentality scholars, he does not explain why he changed terms. He simply walks in one day (February 1, 1978) and declares that if he were able to go back and correct the theme and title of that year's lectures, he would no longer use the advertised title, "*Sécurité, territoire, population*," but rather "Lectures on Governmentality." Then he goes on to talk about techniques of governmentality, with security quietly receding into the background.

One possible explanation of the shift from assemblages of security to governmentality may lie in the fact that security had strong statist and authoritarian connotations for Foucault's audience, even after he distinguished it from *sûreté*. Given that Foucault sought to emphasize the contrast between police (and reason of state) rationalities, on the one hand, and (liberal) governmentality on the other, *security* was perhaps not the best term. Security definitely includes police as a discursive field and, at the level of practice, relies heavily on police techniques. The neologism *governmentality*, by contrast, had no authoritarian, security-force associations and was thus better suited to Foucault's project in the 1978 lectures, which was to highlight the novel features of what he called the governmentalization of the state.

If Foucault had not changed his mind and had kept "security" as the title of the lecture that found its way into *The Foucault Effect*, the central role of police practices and rationalities in modern liberal states would have been clearer. On the other hand, the innovations of neoliberalism would have become less visible if "security" had remained the overarching title. Graham Burchell, for instance, contributed an important essay gathering the elements of Foucault's not wholly critical analysis of liberalism, an essay that emphasized even more than Foucault's own lectures did the break between the state of police and liberalism.[46]

Foucault's tactical and hence somewhat shifting conceptualization is compatible with somewhat different accounts. Burchell looks to Foucault for inspiration for his own quite positive account of liberalism (an account in which persistent sovereign practices and negative biopolitical projects are left out of the picture altogether). Many other scholars, however, including me, use Foucault to further their critical understanding of capitalism and liberalism.[47]

Be that as it may, with the benefit of hindsight we can now see that there might have been some value—especially to us today, since we are drowning in neoliberalism rather than in 1970s Marxism—in keeping the original term *security*. Among other things, this term might have made it more difficult for Foucault's work on governmentalization and subsequent governmentality studies to be seen as highly friendly to neoliberalism by Burchell and others. The dispersed discussions of governmentality in the 1978 lectures tend to identify governmentality with liberal political economy: we are repeatedly told that governmentality incentivizes rather than prohibits, it engages in cost-benefit analyses rather than forbidding anything, and so forth.[48] The persistence into the present, in fully liberalized states, of governmental mechanisms based on older police rationalities is simply ignored. By focusing on the rise of physiocratic economics and associated state policies—rather than on morals laws, colonial strategies, national security, or other illiberal dimensions of modern state activity—Foucault tends to reproduce liberal political economy's own identification of liberal economic practices with freedom from state coercion as such.

Discipline

Discipline and Punish is probably the best known of Foucault's works. Therefore, the general understanding of Foucault's innovative terms—*surveillance* and *discipline*—is very much tethered to that book's central argument, which contrasts sovereign practices for punishing offenders with disciplinary techniques for reforming and rehabilitating deviants. The brilliance of that work was to show that disciplinary techniques needed their own history, a history that ought not to be reduced to the history of a particular institution (the army, the prison, the school). Thus, just as the security-governmentality lectures perform an anti-institutional reading of state practices, so too *Discipline and Punish* foregrounds practices of governance, seeing institutions merely as temporary sites on which various practices were tried out and articulated with other practices. Governing strategies being by nature flexible and adaptable, and thus to some extent site specific, our current understanding of *discipline* is perhaps overly influenced by the specific context of Foucault's discovery—that is, the criminal justice system, and punishment in particular. (Army training camps and schoolroom practices are discussed as well, but most of Foucault's research was conducted in the archives of the French prison system.)

The security-governmentality lectures stay away from the realm of punishment and document disciplinary practices being developed elsewhere, most importantly in the economic realm. The control of grain prices, grain growing, and grain exports and imports are discussed at some length in the initial lectures, as a way of showing how disciplinary techniques (pioneered by mercantilist economic writers) differed from the sovereign practices of the feudal economy, on the one hand, and from the liberal free-trade practices of the later nineteenth-century economy. City building and city planning provide Foucault with another way to demonstrate shifts in practices: for sovereignty, cities (royal cities, preferably) need to "capitalize" a territory and constantly pose problems of loyalty (a point well borne out by the English history of the municipal corporation, not mentioned by Foucault); whereas disciplinary cities need to architecturalize space and create symmetry and beauty. On their part, cities of security are less concerned to establish visually appealing grids of authority and instead work with probabilities, rates, and risks.[49]

The comments about discipline in the 1978 lectures are brief and undeveloped, and it would not be appropriate to make them do too much work, given Foucault's decision to not publish these lectures or even to reuse them (as he reused the material on pastoral power and on police for the Stanford Tanner lectures). But what can be said is that *Discipline and Punish* explores only one face of discipline. Discipline is not a concept—something that becomes clearer when one considers that the original title of the well-known book is *Surveiller et punir*, a two-verb combination that resists turning the new form of power-knowledge under study into a thing. *Discipline* (in my view) is an umbrella term for a family of techniques of governance that resemble each other but whose specific features vary from one location to another and from one time period and one political moment to another. The normalization of bodies and the normalization of souls and desires are certainly key features of disciplinary projects from the penitentiary to the self-esteem workshop; but discipline as such is not exhausted by the sovereignty versus discipline contrast set out in *Discipline and Punish*. Spaces too can be normalized (as in the discussion of royal vs. disciplinary cities); and even the price of bread can be said to be subject either to sovereign controls (a set price) or to disciplinary measures that seek to govern markets in a normalizing manner but without arbitrary, top-down price setting.[50] The terms of Foucault's analysis remain always flexible and open ended and change as the research develops. There is no one master genealogy, of discipline or of anything else.

Conclusion

It should be clear by now, I hope, that the 1978 lectures at the College de France can be read with profit by those interested in questions of law and sovereignty, including the more specific question of police. In reading and using these texts, it is important to constantly keep in mind that Foucault does not present either contributions to existing theoretical debates or alternative theories. He uses terms tactically, usually using terms borrowed from history itself (e.g., *police*) but sometimes developing neologisms (*governmentality*, *biopolitics*) to stress that his own analysis runs counter to the received epistemology of power. What we have in the lectures is a series of insights and conceptual innovations that must be borrowed carefully, since the tactical context in which they were developed (most importantly, the dominance of Marxist epistemologies) is no longer immediately visible. In borrowing and adapting insights, bits of research, and philosophical decisions, we will have to strive to be as keenly aware of our own intellectual-political context as Foucault was of his.

TWO

The Supreme Sovereignty of the State

A Genealogy of Police in American Constitutional Law, from the Founding Era to Lochner

CHRISTOPHER TOMLINS

Introduction

I recall a conversation more than twenty years ago when I was awaiting publication of my first book, *The State and the Unions.*[1] An acquaintance—an American historian—asked me which state the book was about. Michigan? Maryland? When I told him it was about "the" state he replied that there was no such state in America.

Fortunately for me, that was the year the state began to be brought back in.[2] "Back into what?" one might ask. In real life it had never left. My acquaintance's belief that there was no state in America supplies the answer: back into scholarly awareness. His supposition that there was no U.S. state worth consideration as such was grounded on decades of scholarly practice in the United States. Since the mid-nineteenth century, historical practice has, as Thomas Bender has described, "sustain[ed] the project of making the modern nation state" by producing national histories and certifying national literatures and cultures, not least those of law and constitutionalism.[3] As it did so, however, historical practice created a framework that largely occluded the state.[4] Later twentieth-century scholars added new layers of invisibility.[5]

Two decades of research in American political history have somewhat remedied the defect.[6] Scholars now ponder not the state's absence but the extent and effects of its capacious presence.[7] At first content to conceptualize the state as an effect of the socioeconomic, scholars have more recently begun to explore it as a phenomenon of governance in itself, a phenomenon of *police.*[8]

Police enters the American political and legal lexicon in the 1770s and 1780s, when both popular debates and many of the first state constitutions make explicit reference to "the police" and the "internal police" of the state.[9] The concept is far older—indeed ancient—in origin, but throughout its history *police* has articulated the essence of prevailing governmentalities; the forms it takes track successive governmentalities' conditions of existence.[10] It is therefore of little surprise that *police* should well up explicitly in the first throes of late eighteenth-century U.S. self-definition. Nor, however, given its much older roots, is it a surprise that, expressed in slightly different language, a discourse of police should have accompanied Europeans in America from their earliest intrusions.

Here I attempt a genealogy of police in its relationship to American constitutional law. I argue that police is manifested in state and federal juridical discourse both as an expression of unrestricted and undefined powers of governance (internal police) exercised by the states and as an increasingly vociferous insistence that the federal nation-state enjoys similarly undefined capacities—the power "to do all acts and things which independent states may of right do"—all rooted in a discourse of sovereign succession and state necessity.[11] This requires drawing together several distinct strands of constitutional law: domestic regulatory law, notably the commerce power; constitutional doctrine with regard to indigenous peoples and immigrants; and the legalities attending continental and transoceanic expansion.[12]

Because this is a genealogy of constitutional law, let us first consider police in the context not of history but of *founding*, that is, the moment of profound rupture with the past when the federal state was first defined and enabled. Where is police in this moment?

At the Founding: Police and Popular Sovereignty

Akhil Amar recently noted that "a general commitment to Enlightenment values . . . pulsated through the Constitution."[13] His observation is something of a throwaway. Amar does not explicate Enlightenment values or where, precisely, they pulsated. But the Enlightenment itself can guide us—a grand prescription for human perfectibility built on the rejection of (religious) dogma and hereditary inequalities, the purposeful exercise of scientific reason in the service of human improvement, and the development of a science of government and administration intended to facilitate self-determination and the maximization of human resources. If such values pulsate anywhere in the Constitution, it is in the preamble, which Amar calls "the foundation for all that followed."[14] He is not alone in so identifying the preamble; it is virtually a cliché of American political thought that the Constitution's animating spirit is "for the ages," and implicates all humankind.[15] "We the People" ordain and establish the Constitution to secure the blessings of liberty, "to ourselves" but also to "posterity." The preamble registers the people's commitments to improvement: to form a "more perfect" Union; to remedy injustice and disorder by establishing justice and domestic tranquility; and to pledge security and commonality ("the common defence . . . the general Welfare") for all and for generations to come.

Discourses of perfection, protection, and welfare—of improvement and safety and happiness—are quintessentially discourses of police.[16] Elsewhere I have argued that it is indeed possible to detect in the genealogy of police an implication of democratized state capacity, of "government as a means, informed by constitutional declarations of communal as well as individual rights, to maximize opportunities for the sovereign people to participate in the framing of the collective good."[17] This, indeed, is what Amar finds in the preamble. "These words did more than promise popular self-government. They also embodied and enacted it." He identifies the process of ratification as the concrete fulfillment and expression of the preamble's embrace of *popular* sovereignty.[18]

Peel off the promise of radical democratization, however, and police discourse appears in its American incarnation a rather more conventional instantiation of successor state capacities.[19] For in certain important regards the words of the preamble echo those of the imperial predecessor. Take "domestic Tranquility." Blackstone called police an expression of the "due regulation and domestic order" produced by the visitation of good government upon "the individuals of the state."[20] Such continuity in the discursive expression of police is a commonplace of postcolonial Anglophone governmentality. For example, the unenumerated and residual peace, order, and good government (POGG) powers of Canada's federal government are derived from section 91 of the 1867 British North America Act establishing the Dominion of Canada, which retained for the Crown full power, with the advice and consent of the Dominion Parliament, "to make laws for the Peace, Order, and good Government of Canada."[21] Mariana Valverde has described the process of Canadian state formation initiated in 1867 as a colonial governmentality "infolded" into the postcolonial successor state. The POGG powers exhibit the "more or less paternalist legal and political technologies used to promote what eighteenth-century police science called 'the general welfare.'"[22]

The Canadian example is in no sense unique. POGG discourse turns up in the founding documents of colonies, in British legislation bestowing forms of "responsible" government on colonies, in postcolonial successor-state constitutions, and in the discourse of postcolonial judiciaries throughout the British imperium.[23] Wherever some form of decolonization occurred, that is, POGG-like discourse becomes the practical postcolonial expression of colonial police's continuity.

What has this to do with the U.S. case? Police discourses of security and improvement, though refined in the Enlightenment, are not an Enlightenment invention. Powers to establish "settled and quiet Government" were embedded in the founding documents of Anglo-American colonizing from the moment of their first formal-legal expression in the first Virginia charter (1606).[24] Indeed, ideologies of security and improvement are pervasive in European colonizing discourse.[25] After independence, the same governmentalities were re-embedded by the successor-state constitutions, rendered explicitly in the language of authority over the state's internal police and echoed in the federal preamble.

Police and Sovereignty: The States

Infolding was decidedly a feature of state succession in postindependence America. The origins of the states' authority over their internal police were articulated precisely as such in Massachusetts Chief Justice Lemuel Shaw's opinion in *Commonwealth v. Alger* (1851), the first and most famous elaboration of the derivation of "police powers" in American constitutional law. Shaw explained the police power of the nineteenth-century state by tracing its descent through prior regimes of governance from the earliest moment of colonizing. Specifically, Shaw built Massachusetts's power to police—"the power vested in the legislature by the constitution, to make, ordain and establish all manner of wholesome and reasonable laws, statutes and ordinances, either with penalties or without, not repugnant to the constitution, as they shall judge to be for the good and welfare of the commonwealth, and of the subjects of the same"[26]—on a string of conveyances of *sovereignty*: the Charter of New England (1620), which had clothed colonial government with so much of the royal prerogative as necessary to maintain and regulate the rights of the Crown's subjects in the colony ("agreeable to the Laws, Statutes, Government and Policie of this our Realme of England"); the Provincial Charter (1691), which had reconfirmed those powers after the Dominion of New England; and the Declaration of Independence (1776), which as acknowledged by the Treaty of Paris (1783), had vacated such powers of dominion and regulation as had remained in the Crown after 1691. Notably, in Shaw's genealogy the power to police—of "dominion and regulation of the public right"—was not created by the state constitution but reinvested; it existed as an instantiation of a prior governmentality and never fell out of existence: "this right of dominion and controlling power . . . when relinquished by the parent country, must vest somewhere." Because the states had not relinquished their inherited sovereignty to the Union except in specified instances beyond the realm of internal police, "it is settled that [the power to police] vested in the several states, in their sovereign capacity, respectively." Further, what had vested was not just the prerogative exercised by the Crown to the extent allowed at common law but "all the powers of dominion and sovereignty" of the British parliament, unlimited by common law; that is, "all the power which exists anywhere." This rendered all "social and conventional rights . . . subject to such reasonable limitations in their enjoyment . . . as the legislature, under the governing and controlling power vested in them by the constitution, may think necessary and expedient."[27]

Shaw undertook no exploration of police as an expression of *popular* sovereignty. His references to the constitution meant, at least implicitly, the sovereign people, for in instituting government "for the common good, for the protection, safety, prosperity, and happiness of the people," in declaring government's purpose to be the security and protection of the body politic and "safety and tranquility" for its members, the Massachusetts constitution (1780) had defined the exercise of government to be under the supervision of and accountable to "the people."[28] Other early state constitutions made pithier statements of the relationship. In the Delaware Declaration of Rights (September 1776), "people [*sic*] of this state have the sole exclusive and inherent Right of governing and regulating the internal police of the same."[29] Pennsylvania (September 1776), Maryland (November 1776), North Carolina (December 1776), New York (April 1777), and Vermont (July 1777) followed suit, more or less verbatim.[30] As each state re-created itself as a jurisdictional successor to a colony, it lodged sovereignty in its people and in their name vested its inherited jurisdiction over internal affairs and arrangements (its internal police) in its legislature. In each case, the legislature's exercise of that jurisdiction expressed the power to govern inherited from the king in parliament.[31]

But like cognate mid-nineteenth-century state decisions, *Alger* underscored the essential irrelevance of the sovereign popular claim to a *constitutional* point of origin when it came to the police power. State court decisions instead emphasized the virtually unlimited extent of police powers, their roots in a long history of *state* necessity, and the absence of restraint on their exercise. In so doing, courts articulated the routine actuality of governance prevalent throughout pre- and postrevolutionary British America: "a plethora of bylaws, ordinances, statutes, and common law restrictions regulating nearly every aspect of early American economy and society."[32] These routines of local and regional governance well satisfied, indeed overspilled, the Blackstonian conception of "the public *police* and *oeconomy*" as a species of "due regulation and domestic order" within the state's *criminal* jurisdiction.[33]

They expressed not discrete instances of government within a particular jurisdiction but governance itself as a practice and condition of life.

Three years after *Alger* had outlined the lineage of the state's power to police, Chief Justice Isaac Redfield of the Vermont Supreme Court offered an extensive statement of what that power to police had come to mean by the mid-nineteenth century.[34] First, said Redfield (like Shaw), it was fundamental to the political organization of American states that their legislatures had "the same unlimited power in regard to legislation which resides in the British parliament, except where they are restrained by written constitutions."[35] Second, while "all legislative power" was "of course" originally possessed by the people, they had chosen to commit it "in the most *general and unlimited* manner" to the state legislatures. Citing with approval U.S. Chief Justice Roger Taney's observation in *Charles River Bridge v. Warren Bridge* (1837) that "the continued existence of a government would be of no great value, if by implications and presumptions it was disarmed of the powers necessary to accomplish the ends of its creation," Redfield held that "no claim in any way abridging the most unlimited exercise of the legislative power over persons, natural or artificial, can be successfully asserted, except upon the basis of an express grant, in terms, or by necessary implication." Indeed, "the general control over the police of the country, which resides in the law-making power in all free states, and which is by the fifth article of the bill of rights of this state, expressly declared to reside *perpetually and inalienably* in the legislature, which is, perhaps, no more than the enunciation of a general principle applicable to all free states . . . cannot, therefore be violated so as to deprive the legislature of the power, even by express grant."[36]

Having established that legislative capacity was effectively unlimited, Redfield proceeded to emphasize the absence of restraint on the actual exercise of that capacity. The state's responsibility to police extended in two directions; first, to "the protection of the lives, limbs, health, comfort, and quiet of all persons, and the protection of all property within the state" and, second, to such measures as would "secure the general comfort, health, and prosperity of the state" (that is, of the state itself). These, as Shaw had noted in *Alger*, were distinct modes of police. The former secured persons and property from injurious interferences of *others*; the latter rendered "persons and property" *in general* subject "to all kinds of restraints and burdens" for the good of the *state*.[37] That the legislature had a "perfect right" to undertake such a general police of persons and property, population and resources, in the interests of the common or general security and welfare, Redfield insisted, was incontrovertible, an expression of the state's "invincible necessity."[38] Treatise writers would confirm the message. The state's power of police was "multifarious and far-reaching"; it was "more general and pervading than any other." It took in "all the operations of society and government"; all constitutional provisions "*presuppose* its existence"; none "preclude its legitimate exercise."[39] In 1904 Ernst Freund found the police power "without authoritative or generally accepted definition." It was conceptually uncircumscribed. "It means at the same time a power and function of government, a system of rules, and an administrative organization and force." Police had no logic or organization or coherent content as a single department or division or classification of law: to present it otherwise was a matter of "convenience," not principle. Indeed "the general tendency is to identify it with the whole of internal government and sovereignty, and to regard it as an undefined mass of legislation."[40] As Freund encountered it, that is, police was an expansive discourse of state power, productive and prolific.

So far, what we have observed is substantive continuities in the routines and discourse of governance, restated in light of revolutionary constitutionalism's appropriation of sovereignty to the people but not in practice deflected thereby. This notwithstanding, something was changing in the middle decades of the century: the explicit articulation in state supreme courts of police as the virtually unlimited power of the state rendered police the signal instance of governance as an autonomous rationality.[41] Police becomes increasingly the expression of the fullness of state sovereignty, both inside and outside constitutional boundaries. And over the next half century, slowly but surely, the last remaining restraint—that police was a domestic or internal power, a power of the states, falls away.

Police and the U.S. Nation-State

The U.S. Constitution's seven articles articulate no federal police power as such. Nor, because they enumerate specific federal powers, do the articles recognize any unallocated residuum equivalent to Canada's POGG powers. On the other hand, as a matter of practice, particular enumerated powers, notably the commerce clause, have become proxies for federal police powers. Arguably, moreover, in identifying the fundamental purposes of constitutional governance, the preamble declares *all* federal power is directed to "police" ends—improvement and security for all. It was "impossible to deny," Freund noted in 1904, "that the federal government exercises a considerable police power of its own."[42]

Freund found that a federal police power rested chiefly on Congress's enumerated powers—notably the commerce clause but also powers over coinage, weights and measures, and patents and copyrights; over taxation and tariffs; over post offices and post roads; and (most important for our purposes here) over territories—but was also to be detected in the way enumerated powers were mobilized in the general assertion and projection of sovereignty.[43] The last in particular saw the most extensive nineteenth-century expressions of federal police power, which occurred in the arenas of Indian affairs and immigration regulation. Here the Supreme Court consistently showed extreme deference to federal power: its plenary powers doctrine recognized in Congress an exclusive authority to act in certain realms judged essential to the maintenance of sovereign statehood, undisturbed by the claims or checks of other branches or departments or levels of government.[44] As Stephen J. Field put it in *Chae Chan Ping v. United States* (1889; the *Chinese Exclusion Case*), "The government, possessing the powers which are to be exercised for protection and security, is clothed with authority to determine the occasion on which the powers shall be called forth; and its determinations, so far as the subjects affected are concerned, are necessarily conclusive upon all its departments and officers."[45] According to plenary powers theory, it was not within the Court's purview "to pass upon political questions, the final decision of which has been committed by the Constitution to the other departments of the government." In such matters "the judicial department cannot properly express an opinion."[46]

The idea of plenary federal powers echoes the preamble to the U.S. Constitution to the extent of identifying the fundamental purpose of governance as protection and security. Over the course of the nineteenth century, however, the concept completely departed the preamble in locating the origins of those powers to a very considerable extent not in the Constitution at all, where as we have seen no plenary residuum as such exists, but in the very idea of the sovereign state. Plenary powers are those that are expedient to the necessities and purposes of the state. They are inherent in its "state"-ness.[47] Ultimately, we shall see, powers expedient to preserving the existence and achieving the purposes of a sovereign nation-state came to be derived in the U.S. case more or less independently from those powers delegated by the sovereign people in their act of "constituting" the state.[48]

Indians, Immigrants, Islands

The infolding, or succession, of sovereign powers, we have already seen, is essential to the transmission of police. In the U.S. case, *Alger* is the best extended example of infolding as an intellectual strategy. But the question of sovereignty and its attendant powers had already been considered in early nineteenth-century Marshall Court cases. Infolding would also make its appearance in the Marshall and Taney Courts' native peoples jurisprudence.[49]

In *The Schooner Exchange v. M'Faddon* (1812), Marshall held that the most salient indicator of a nation-state's sovereignty was "[exclusive and absolute] jurisdiction . . . within its own territories," to which exception might be had only by "consent of the nation itself," a matter hence of political rather than legal determination—"for diplomatic rather than legal discussion."[50] Marshall's opinion was notable less for itself than for the way it inserted the United States into a conventional discussion of nation-states exercising sovereignty, each by dint of its stateness possessed of the same capacities, each governed by the same conventions. The Founders, that is, had not established a state distinct in any way (when it came to the matter of sovereign authority and its deployment) from other nation-states.[51] Sovereignty in the U.S. case would express itself in the same fashion as elsewhere.

INDIANS

So too, in the Indian trilogy, the decisive issue in Marshall's jurisprudence was the derivation of U.S. sovereignty over indigenous lands from its status as sovereign successor to European colonial powers. Colonizing powers claiming title by discovery and conquest had ceded title to postcolonial successor states, which had in turn ceded their unsettled territories to the United States. Indigenous occupants were at best third-party observers of title transfers. Such Indian title as was recognizable consisted in occupancy for use, on sufferance of the successor state. Within the discussion lurked the familiar discourse of improvement and security and of plenary powers vested in the sovereign successor as the means to their realization. "To leave them in possession of their country, was to leave the country a wilderness; to govern them as a distinct people, was impossible . . . [they] were ready to repel by arms every attempt on their independence."[52] To claim title by conquest, Marshall admitted, was an extravagant pretension, yet, echoing *The Schooner Exchange*, when it came to the claims of the sovereign "the Courts of the conqueror" were required to recognize them. "If the property of the great mass of the [conqueror's] community originates in it, it becomes the law of the land, and cannot be questioned."[53] When the Taney Court took up the matter in *United States v. William Rogers* (1846) it stated the same conclusion more bluntly, with no concession of the conqueror's pretensions. Indigenous occupants had never been acknowledged as independent nations who owned their territories. Colonizing powers had simply divided and granted the continent "as if it had been vacant and unoccupied." As the successor state the United States "insisted upon the same powers and dominion." Should "the right and the propriety of exercising this power" be held open to question in any respect, it would be a matter for "the law-making and political department of the government, and not for the judicial" to determine. Such a question was *a political question* to be resolved not by courts but by the exercise of the sovereign's plenary power.[54]

The apogee of the sovereignty trajectory at the federal level was reached in the later nineteenth and early twentieth centuries, finding full expression in Supreme Court decisions on congressional regulation of Indian tribes, of immigration, and of transoceanic territories. Court decisions discovered that the requisite (and exclusive) powers of legislative and administrative regulation were inherent in the exercise of sovereignty. In the matter of Indian tribes, *United States v. Kagama* (1886) found Congress had complete authority to legislate unilaterally to control Indian tribes rather than treat with them as previously and to abrogate treaty terms formerly negotiated and recognized. "Indians are within the geographical limits of the United States. The soil and the people within these limits are under the political control of the government of the United States, or of the states of the Union. There exists within the broad domain of sovereignty but these two." Congress having declared it would no longer conduct its business with the tribes by treaty, it was quite within its competence to extend the operation of the laws of the United States where formerly they had not been put in effect.[55] This purposeful wiping out of anomalous pockets of tribal autonomy internal to the territory of the United States, even though "recognized" in prior treaty provisions, and the proclamation in their stead of total and exclusive congressional power over tribal relations and lands was confirmed in *Lone Wolf v. Hitchcock* (1903).[56]

IMMIGRANTS

The immigration cases, decided concurrently, asserted the same plenary capacity in Congress to exercise absolute control over territory, countervailing treaty provisions notwithstanding. In *Chae Chan Ping* the Court considered whether, on presenting themselves for reentry, Chinese laborers entitled under previously negotiated treaties to reenter the United States after interrupting a period of residence could nevertheless be excluded by new legislation. The appellant did not contest "the inherent right of a sovereign power to prohibit . . . the entry into its territories of the subjects of a foreign state" but contended that "the United States, while a sovereign government, is yet one which can exercise only those powers of sovereignty which are enumerated in and delegated by the instrument which created it" and that the exclusion legislated in this instance did not qualify.[57] The Court held otherwise.

"When once it is established that Congress possesses the power to pass an act," stated Justice Field, "our province ends with its construction and its application." Congress might legislate to exclude as it pleased. Jurisdiction over its own territory was an incident of every independent nation and an attribute of sovereignty, here exhibited and affirmed as the power of the state to police population.[58]

Field's account of the powers of the national government and their distribution still made reference to the ultimate authority of the people and of the Constitution. His colleagues were less inhibited. In *Nishimura Ekiu v. United States* (1892), for example, the power to police the entry of foreigners was termed "an accepted maxim of international law . . . inherent in sovereignty." In the U.S. case the power was exercised by the political department of the national government because that was where the Constitution placed control of international relations.[59] The Constitution did not create powers, in other words; it simply distributed already inherent powers. In *Fong Yue Ting v. United States* (1893), the Court cited successive "leading commentators on the law of nations" in holding that congressional exercise of the power to exclude, inherent in sovereignty, extended unproblematically to a power to expel, equally inherent in sovereignty. With relish the majority also cited the 1869 assertion of Ulysses Grant's secretary of state, Hamilton Fish, that "the control of the people within its limits, and the right to expel from its territory persons who are *dangerous to the peace of the State*, are too clearly within the essential attributes of sovereignty to be seriously contested."[60] Justice Brewer dissented, denouncing the notion that the U.S. government enjoyed powers "inherent in sovereignty" derived from the law of nations as a doctrine "indefinite and dangerous" with no obvious limits. Other national governments might enjoy "elastic powers," but "ours is fixed and bounded by a written constitution."[61]

ISLANDS

The argument became full-blown in the so-called Insular Cases. The Insular Cases were a long drawn-out sequence of decisions extending through 1914, the most important of which were handed down between 1901 and 1904.[62] In 1898 the United States annexed Hawaii and began the Spanish-American War. In 1899 the Treaty of Paris saw Spain cede the islands of Cuba, Puerto Rico, the Philippines, and Guam to the United States. The Insular Cases debated the role of Congress and the Constitution vis-à-vis these new colonial territories. The decisive group of cases, all concerning Puerto Rico, was heard and decided in the first half of 1901. Turning on the specificities of congressional regulation of interstate and foreign commerce, the Court addressed at length the bases of national governmental power. Its decisions revealed deep division.

First, in *De Lima v. Bidwell* (1901) the Court held (5–4) that, as a result of the Treaty of Paris, Puerto Rico had ceased to be a foreign country under U.S. tariff laws. Puerto Rico had become domestic territory. No act of Congress was required to effect this transformation. Nor did any failure of Congress to act somehow preserve Puerto Rico as foreign. No intermediate status was available under American constitutional law.[63] The minority disagreed, vehemently. No treaty could impair congressional discretion over ceded territory. The U.S. government was free to determine the status of Puerto Rico in virtually any fashion it pleased.[64]

The minority was unavailing in *De Lima* but prevailed in the companion case *Downes v. Bidwell* (1901), in which the Court held (5–4, Brown being the only justice to vote with the majority in each case) that, although the Treaty of Paris had indeed made Puerto Rico a territory of the United States, its precise status as such remained a matter for positive congressional determination.[65] In particular, Congress might determine how, or whether, to bring territory within article 1, section 8 of the Constitution requiring uniform duties, imposts, and excises throughout the United States, it being long established that "the Constitution is applicable to territories acquired by purchase or conquest only when and so far as Congress shall so direct."[66] As a result of the Treaty of Paris, Puerto Rico had clearly become territory subject to the jurisdiction of the United States, but the treaty alone could not make it part of the United States. Hence, Congress might impose a duty on goods shipped from Puerto Rico to the United States and otherwise legislate its status, as it had in the Foraker Act (1900).[67]

The lead opinion in *Downes* echoed the *De Lima* minority in its enthusiastic embrace of the United States as a great and imperial power, to which it added an extraordinarily broad reading of congressional capacity to make it so. For there existed, Brown stated, no constitutional limitations on the powers of Congress in acquiring or governing new territories.[68] Nor, Justice White added, in his separate concurrence, were there any grounds to insist that territory once acquired became so far incorporated into the United States that "every provision of the Constitution which would apply under that situation is controlling in such acquired territory." So to insist was to acknowledge the power to acquire and simultaneously deny the acquirer its benefit. In justification, White cited innate rights of imperial acquisition: "The general principle of the law of nations . . . is that acquired territory, in the absence of agreement to the contrary, will bear such relation to the acquiring government as may be by it determined." To concede that the United States had the right to acquire but not to control the outcome of acquisition "is, in effect, to say that the United States is helpless in the family of nations, and does not possess that authority which has at all times been treated as an incident of the right to acquire."[69]

Cumulatively, then, the majority in *Downes* reproduced the position of the minority in *De Lima*. As a nation-state the United States exercised broad powers in no wise different from those enjoyed by comparable sovereign states. Beyond indicating that those powers were lodged in the political department of the state, the Constitution had no relevance to their exercise. It stayed out of the way. The *Downes* minority emphasized precisely the opposite, stressing that Congress had no powers beyond those expressly granted by the Constitution. In a dissent joined by Justices Peckham and Brewer, Chief Justice Fuller argued that the national government was "a government of enumerated powers, the exercise of which is restricted to the use of means appropriate and plainly adapted to constitutional ends." Though a separate, independent, and sovereign nation, the U.S. derived none of its powers from international law, "which, though a part of our municipal law, is not a part of the organic law of the land" but only from the Constitution. "The government, as to our internal affairs, possesses no inherent sovereign power not derived from that instrument."[70] Congress had "no existence" outside the Constitution, Justice Harlan added in a separate dissent, and could exercise "no authority" other than granted therein. It was not empowered to deal with new territories "just as other nations have done or may do." To argue otherwise was to endanger constitutional governance. "The idea prevails with some . . . that we have in this country substantially or practically two national governments; one, to be maintained under the Constitution, with all its restrictions; the other to be maintained by Congress outside and independently of that instrument, by exercising such powers as other nations of the earth are accustomed to exercise." But the Constitution was not a convenience, to be obeyed or put aside as circumstances might warrant. "The People have decreed that it shall be the supreme law of the land at all times. When the acquisition of territory becomes complete, by cession, the Constitution necessarily becomes the supreme law of such new territory, and no power exists in any Department of the Government . . . to declare that constitutional provisions may be ignored."[71]

Between them, *De Lima* and *Downes* created the trajectory for the remainder of the early Insular Cases. In tariff questions, half the Court—Fuller, Brewer, Harlan, and Peckham, in addition to Brown—followed *De Lima* in holding that acquired territories ceased at the moment of acquisition to be foreign for purposes of U.S. tariff laws.[72] In questions of administration of acquired territories, the other half of the Court—White, Shiras, McKenna, and Gray, in addition to Brown—held that Congress had virtually complete discretion in deciding whether, and to what extent, the Constitution should influence policy.[73] Changes on the bench—the replacement of Horace Gray by Oliver Wendell Holmes, of George Shiras by William Day—made no difference; both joined the *Downes* majority.[74]

The broad invocation of state capacity in *Downes* and the majority's concern to avoid any imputation of restraint that might endanger "the development of . . . the American Empire" were of a piece with the "preventive, ordering, and safekeeping technology of government" marshaled contemporaneously in the international sphere by Theodore Roosevelt with particular regard to the police of the Western Hemisphere.[75] In both one encounters the exaltation of state power to create regimes of stewardship, the one through acquisition and reorganization of the territorial object, the other invoking the "duty of civilized nations to secure the welfare of foreign states *by ensuring that they are orderly and well administered in their domestic affairs*," directly expressed in the Roosevelt Corollary to the Monroe Doctrine.[76]

But governance as the expression of a "preventive, ordering, and safekeeping technology" was as much a characteristic of contemporaneous state action in the domestic sphere, both Rooseveltian in particular and progressive in general. In the police of the domestic, indeed, we encounter during the years from 1900 through the New Deal a pronounced reproduction of the disputes that characterized the Insular Cases.

Commerce as Proxy

Increasingly aggressive U.S. expansionism, both transcontinental and transoceanic, underlay the confrontation between the popular sovereignty of the Constitution and the conventional sovereignty of the nation-state that climaxed in the Insular Cases. When it came to the exercise of police capacities within the United States, the question whether the federal state had regulatory powers to exercise was complicated by the jurisdictional borders of the nation and the states, and by the availability of the commerce clause to serve as a federal police power proxy. Throughout the nineteenth century, and beyond, the question was not whether police powers might be exercised but rather by whom.

As in its early sovereignty jurisprudence, the Marshall Court embraced an expansive view of the federal commerce power. Congressional authority to regulate commerce, the Court stated in *Gibbons v. Ogden* (1824), was "complete in itself," and might be exercised "to its utmost extent." It penetrated the borders of the states, acknowledging "no limitations, other than are prescribed in the constitution." Like all powers granted Congress, it was exclusive, which is to say no other body might enter upon its exercise.[77] The Court did not recognize in Congress "direct power to regulate the purely internal commerce of a State, or to act directly on its system of police." The point was, states had no concurrent authority within congressional jurisdiction. Conflicting state legislation was thus preempted, even when passed in service of "the acknowledged power of a State to regulate its police, its domestic trade, and to govern its own citizens."[78]

In *New York v. Miln* (1837), one of the first decisions handed down after Marshall's death, the successor Taney Court substantially redrew the frontier between the federal commerce power and state police powers by allowing that within its borders a state might act within the jurisdictional realm supposedly given over to Congress, though its action might affect commerce, if its activity was demonstrably an exercise of its acknowledged police powers. Reading *Gibbons* against the grain, the Court averred that a state law that was a regulation of the state's domestic commerce would survive where it could be shown not to "collide" with federal legislation. But *Miln* did not confront *Gibbons* directly, preferring to rest on three "impregnable" positions. First, "a state has the same undeniable and unlimited jurisdiction over all persons and things, within its territorial limits, as any foreign nation" except where restrained by the federal constitution. Second, within that jurisdiction it was a state's right and duty "to advance the safety, happiness and prosperity of its people, and to provide for its general welfare." Third, that all "municipal" powers of "internal police" conducive to those ends were retained by the states, in relation to which "the authority of a state is complete, unqualified, and exclusive."[79] Justice Story dissented, arguing *Gibbons* had rendered the federal commerce power both preemptive and exclusive; Justice Smith Thompson dissented, arguing the Court should confront *Gibbons* directly. States, he claimed, could legislate as they chose within the realm of commerce where Congress had not; where Congress had acted, state laws would stand concurrently where there was no collision.[80]

The Fourteenth Amendment

The Taney Court's restatement of federal commerce jurisdiction provided running room for the broad sovereignty-based state-police-powers discourse developed in *Alger* and *Thorpe*.[81] Its influence extended well into the 1870s, when the Waite Court maintained the broad regulatory capacity of the states in matters of internal police and commerce notwithstanding new and expansive claims of limitation based on Fourteenth Amendment due process protections.[82] Change came only in the 1880s, when as we have seen the Court was fully engaged in a rapid sovereignty-based expansion of federal plenary powers in the realms of indigenous affairs and immigration. That expansion was replicated in the unambiguously domestic realm in the form of a substantial extension of "the exclusive domain of Congress" in matters of commerce.[83] Then, in *Chicago, Milwaukee and St. Paul Railway Co. v. Minnesota* (1890), the Court majority adopted the due process arguments first aired in dissents in *Slaughter-House Cases* (1873) and *Munn v. Illinois* (1877), establishing a second and distinct federal restraint on state police powers.[84] In *Allgeyer v. Louisiana* (1897) Justice Peckham, for the Court, suggested that due process would trump police powers wherever they might be found to have infringed on pursuit of "an ordinary calling or trade, and of acquiring, holding and selling property." These were "an essential part of [a citizen's] rights of liberty and property, as guaranteed by the Fourteenth Amendment." Though denying the decision meant state police powers had been rendered a nullity, the Court announced it would examine the legitimacy of their exercise in "each case as it arises."[85]

In effect, *Allgeyer* announced terms for the next cycle of police power jurisprudence, which—federal exclusivity in matters of commerce now finally established—turned on the extent of state police powers in matters of safety, health, morals, and the common welfare in light of the Fourteenth Amendment. Following closely on *Allgeyer*'s defense of contractual liberty, *Holden v. Hardy* (1898) examined the question (alluded to in *Allgeyer*), to what extent police regulation thus described might permissibly intrude. *Holden* did not controvert *Allgeyer*'s claim that an individual's general right to contract was protected by the Fourteenth Amendment. Nevertheless, the Court found (Peckham and Brewer dissenting) that in exercising the police powers "necessarily inherent in *every* form of government" a state might regulate terms of contracts to be performed within its limits where the regulations were demonstrably for the protection and improvement of the lives, health, and morals of its citizens.[86] Again, in *Jacobson v. Massachusetts* (February 1905), Peckham and Brewer again dissenting, the Court endorsed state police powers exercised "to secure the general comfort, health, and prosperity of the State," in this case by legislating compulsory vaccination. Neither the federal Constitution nor the Fourteenth Amendment prevented compulsions warranted by the general good—and here welled up the supervening language of state necessity, in the most pointed terms possible. A person might indeed have the right to "live and work where he will," yet still he might be compelled, "by force if need be, against his will and without regard to his personal wishes or his pecuniary interests, or even his religious or political convictions, to take his place in the ranks of the army of his country and risk the chance of being shot down in its defense." It was quite in order, then, to compel public obedience of "reasonable regulations established by the constituted authorities, under the sanction of the State for the purpose of protecting the public collectively."[87] One must note that the example employed (compulsory military service) necessarily acknowledged that the federal state no less than the state of Massachusetts claimed authority to mobilize and dispose of population in the collective interest.

Lochner

A riposte was not long in coming. In *Lochner v. New York* (April 1905), the Court held (5–4) that the New York state legislature could not justify regulatory intervention in the contractual relationship between bakery workers and their employers as a legitimate exercise of the state's police powers. Long considered the poster child for judicial overstretch, Peckham's majority opinion is remarkable for its attempt, albeit clumsy, to redirect the trajectory of police powers jurisprudence. Though vague and indistinct, police powers had been found over time to be expressed in legislation safeguarding the "safety, health, morals and general welfare of the public." The Court had chosen to uphold their exercise in many cases properly considered borderline by this criterion, but particularly in light of the Fourteenth Amendment, there were necessarily limits to the police power's scope—else "the legislatures of the States would have unbounded power," and "police power" would simply mean "the supreme sovereignty of the State." Measures invoking police powers should therefore be scrutinized to ensure that they were "fair, reasonable and appropriate" in their impact on individual rights and liberties, not "unreasonable, unnecessary and arbitrary."[88]

Peckham, it appears, was attempting both to "enumerate" the states' police powers (safety, health, morals, and general welfare) and—because the courts had never been able to define what these categories encompassed—to set a standard ("fair, reasonable and appropriate") that police measures had to meet. Applying his tests, Peckham found the New York statute wanting on both fronts. It was neither "within the police power of the State" as enumerated because it could not stand scrutiny as the health measure it purported to be, nor was it (in its full extent) "proper, reasonable and fair."[89] Peckham's antagonism to state police powers appears to have been heightened by the "leakage" to the federal state of capacities to compel broadly implied by the majority opinion in *Jacobson*, for in dicta he debated whether the state might declare a supervening interest in a "strong and robust" population lest its "fighting strength" be impaired and accordingly demand "any legislation which may be said to tend to make people healthy" be held valid "as health laws, enacted under the police power." Were this so, everyone might be subjected to state compulsion, "forbidden to fatigue their brains and bodies by prolonged hours of exercise."[90] Peckham's language condemning police as "the supreme sovereignty of the State . . . exercised free from constitutional restraint" also reiterates the minority's position in *Downes*. In *Lochner*, that is, one can observe the convergence of police discourses alive in both domestic and international spheres of state action.[91]

Lochner bred two dissents. Harlan, joined by Justices White and Day, reiterated the case-by-case approach to police powers articulated in *Allgeyer* but loaded outcomes heavily in favor of affirmation. The states' police powers extended "*at least* to the protection of the lives, the health and the safety of the public." States might not interfere in the lives of their citizens to the extent of actually violating their liberty of contract, but "within certain limits," left undefined, states might enact regulations "designed and calculated to promote the general welfare or to guard the public health, the public morals or the public safety." In considering whether an enactment had exceeded the state's authority, courts were required to interpret that authority broadly. To be void, a statute had to be "plainly and palpably in excess of legislative power." Doubts were to be resolved "in favor of . . . validity."[92]

The other, more famous, dissent, by Oliver Wendell Holmes, proposed to alter police powers jurisprudence no less than Peckham, but in the opposite direction. Peckham saw the police power as the state on the loose—sovereign, supreme, unrestrained. He wanted the Fourteenth Amendment to confine it domestically, just as the *Downes* minority looked to the Constitution to confine it internationally. Holmes agreed that the police power expressed the supreme sovereignty of the state. But where was the problem? Police was synonymous with governance; governance was the job of the state. Judges had no business forestalling "the natural outcome of a dominant opinion," no matter how tyrannical it might appear.[93] In *Lochner*—as before in *Jacobson*, as years later in *Buck v. Bell* (1927)—Holmes thought the police of bakers, no less than the police of bodies, an entirely appropriate matter for a legislative majority.[94]

Lochner *"Era"?*

Like the Insular Cases, *Lochner* attempted to debate the terms of state power. "*Lochner* did what courts, and the public, should do in the American view of law and government: It subjected state action to principled scrutiny."[95] But *Lochner* languished. Distinguished in *Muller v. Oregon* (1908),[96] ignored in

McLean v. State of Arkansas (1909),[97] implicitly set aside in *Bunting v. Oregon* (1917),[98] *Lochner* made a brief comeback in *Adkins v. Children's Hospital* (1923), where the three main protagonists replayed, more or less, the roles of 1905. For the majority Justice Sutherland played Peckham, seeking a general rule to scrutinize legislative interventions limiting freedom of contract. In dissent, Chief Justice Taft played Harlan, mapping police powers (retrospectively) case by case. And Holmes played himself, holding that legislatures might do, more or less, whatever they wanted.[99] *Adkins* momentarily reinvigorated *Lochner*.[100] But it did not thereafter pass the Court's lips except to be vacated, alongside *Adkins*, in the key New Deal case *West Coast Hotel v. Parrish* (1937).[101]

In the debate over *Lochner*, most have preferred Holmes's side. Progressives were appalled by *Lochner*'s disputation of state power, Holmes became their dissentient hero. Over time, constitutional lawyers and historians have tended to agree on *Lochner*'s errors more than they have disagreed.[102] Consider, though, that police means state segregation statutes, state eugenics statutes, state criminalization of interracial marriage, state sodomy laws—all passed in the name of the people's health, morals, and general welfare. Police, more broadly, means the management of population as a resource. Police and the administrative state that New Deal liberals taught generations to revere exist in intimate regard for one another. State action subjected to principled scrutiny? The New Deal needed a demonizing history of the *Lochner* "era."

The New Deal received the first installment of that history courtesy of the young Roscoe Pound, who in his later years would become one of its greatest enemies. None at the time was more effective in assailing judicial interference with state power to manage population. In his 1909 *Yale Law Journal* article "Liberty of Contract," Pound attributed the *Lochner* majority's stance to an exaggeratedly individualistic juridical ideology that denigrated "public right"; to an excessively "mechanical" or conceptualist mode of reasoning that ignored practicalities; to an absence of regard for the societal role of state power; and to the elevation of legal principles over "situations of fact." His ideal was a "sociological" jurisprudence that would "adjust[ ] . . . principles and doctrines to the human conditions they are to govern."[103] Pound was so successful that any promise of meaningful scrutiny of assumed authority that *Lochner* might have suggested would remain unrealized. For that, Pound too became a Progressive hero.[104]

To Conclude

During the nineteenth century, the states' execution of their internal police established networks of local and provincial governance whose extent scholars have begun fully to appreciate only in the last fifteen years. Simultaneously, the federal state adopted the same broad discourse of sovereign capacity to create regimes of police authority additional to the powers explicitly enumerated in the Constitution. Both tendencies comported with the reality of the United States as postcolonial successor to a colonizing metropolitan state. The second in particular served the continuation and intensification of the predecessor's colonizing practices through aggressive programs of Continental expansion and controlled redistribution of population. Relations with indigenous populations turned on enforced transfers to western reservations and their management through the Bureau of Indian Affairs (established in 1824) located in the War Department. As the Civil War ended, management of freed slaves and other refugees was given over to the Bureau of Refugees, Freedmen and Abandoned Lands ("Freedmen's Bureau"). In 1891 administration of immigration became the province of the Bureau of Immigration. In both the states and the Union, sovereign police inspired the bureaucratic state.

The bureaucratic-administrative state of sovereign police strained the constitutional state of popular sovereignty. The founding enactment of popular self-government at the end of the eighteenth century had become, by the end of the nineteenth, merely one source of state capacity—one to be passively avoided, or moved out of the way, or put in its proper place. One might argue, and indeed it has been argued, that an important correlation exists between the ascendancy of the state of sovereign police and the decline of the state of popular sovereignty. Take as one manifestation the rapid erosion of mass political participation that occurred after the turn of the twentieth century. Progressive distaste for rambunctious and unpredictable partisanship was realized in reforms that favored the rapid extension of a functional and bureaucratic administrative state that in its very structure distanced government from popular control. Elite progressivism's clear preference was not for democracy per se but for a politics that would indulge elite expertise.[105] At a time when the state of sovereign police was expanding, the capacity of political parties to serve as vehicles for popular constitutionalism was contracting, replaced by personality-based insurgencies that spoke *for* "We, the People," but in their own language of police.

Theodore Roosevelt, Bull Moose insurgent, typified the new domestic state of police undertaken in the name of the people.[106] As we have seen, Roosevelt also stands at the point of convergence of domestic with international police discourse on display in the Insular Cases, in *Jacobson*, in *Lochner*, and in his corollary to the Monroe Doctrine. Roosevelt is hence a fitting end point to this chapter (just as he is a fitting segue to the converged domestic and international police of our own times), for he embodies the ultimate seamlessness of police. In Anglo-American law, Blackstone's description of police as "the due regulation and *domestic* order of the kingdom" is taken to be the classic statement.[107] But we can detect a discourse of police in the law of nations from the late sixteenth century onward—fittingly, for this is where so much of the justification of European colonial expansion (and its ambitions for the domestic ordering of newly discovered others) rested.[108] To draw a distinction between domestic and international, in short, is unhelpful:[109] the foundations, the flow, and the extensibility of police make the distinction analytically meaningless. Rather, this chapter suggests that the powers claimed for the sovereign state *as such*, whether to order internally or externally, are the place to start.

THREE

Police Power and the Hidden Transformation of the American State

WILLIAM J. NOVAK

Introduction

In the late nineteenth and early twentieth centuries, an unmistakably new kind of American state came into being. That state was not the product of a sudden new moment of constitutional revolution or democratic reform, nor did it involve an overt break with earlier traditions of governance. Rather, it is best understood as something of a hidden revolution in American government—a fundamental shift in the scale, scope, techniques, and legitimating rationales of governance. American governance by 1932 bore little resemblance to nineteenth-century practice, and public policy making had acquired the characteristics that would define the American state for the rest of the twentieth century.[1]

This hidden revolution in governance that forged a distinctly modern state in the United States consisted of several interrelated components, including (a) new conceptions of public good and public purpose; (b) a redefinition of a new active liberalism for an industrial age; (c) an increasingly positivist idea of law, legislation, sovereignty, and the very notion of a state as a legal entity itself; (d) a radical expansion of the ideas of regulation, public management, and administration; (e) new policies and practices of socialization, social police, and social control (including the social control of labor, business, and capital); and (f) an increased governmentalization of political and democratic processes. The resultant transformation of American public law yielded a polity far more rationalized, centralized, and bureaucratized than any anticipated by the Founders, and it laid a new legal-political foundation for the series of policy initiatives through which the modern state apparatus extended its reach into American social and economic life. At the very center of all of these developments was an underlying reworking of traditional notions of police power.[2]

The long genealogy of police is nicely accounted for in other chapters in this volume. As Mariana Valverde suggests, the power of modern nation-states was built directly on early modern developments in the legal, economic, and political theory of police and *Polizei*—the changing conception of state responsibility for the health, safety, and welfare of the population as power slowly shifted from ecclesiastical pastor to secular potentate.[3] In the American context, as Chris Tomlins's survey makes clear, the police power became the central component in an insistently expanding American sovereignty simultaneously legitimated while refusing to be hemmed in by a national mythology emphasizing a popular sovereignty in "we, the people."[4] Beneath the public formalities of constitutional law and the public pieties of democratic theory, the more concealed, subterranean world of police exposes the exceptional coercive power of this supposedly limited government. For as Markus Dubber concludes, the essence of police power is necessity—overruling necessity—the inherently unlimited, extraconstitutional, discretionary prerogative of the sovereign to act quickly and expediently so as to eliminate threats to the health, safety, and security of the people.[5] The links between police power and the state of exception, national emergency power, and military and martial law are direct and inescapable.[6] If we are to understand the inexorable rise of administrative state power and the imperial executive that has accompanied the permanent condition of wartime discipline that has characterized American politics since at least 1941 (in the seamless transitions from a hot war against fascism to a cold war against communism to a perfectly boundless war on terror), we have to trace the trail of the serpent of police over all.

But contrary to some of the new theorizing that surrounds the subject of police, I would contend that the history of police in the United States cannot be separated out from the history of American law. Inspired by the work of Michel Foucault, much current theoretical literature emphasizes police as a separate sphere of governmental action apart from law—in the realm of the preconstitutional or the extralegal or the decisionist political force that knows no law. The notion thus holds out the comforting illusion that law might provide a ready answer or a compelling alternative to the problem of police in the modern world, that is, that law can distinguish "good" police from "bad" police or rein in arbitrary and despotic exertions of police power. The idea draws on a deeply rooted juristic mythology that falsely sees law (or *recht* or *ius*) as the antithesis of power, sovereignty, coercion, violence, and police. It also draws authority from an equally mythical American constitutional history that posits the rule of law primarily as a nay-saying, outside limitation on state power—forever checking, balancing, dividing, and constraining power as the ultimate guardian of natural rights to life, liberty, and property against artificial usurpations by government.[7] Unfortunately for the clear and present distinctions of liberal legal theory, American legal history reveals a much more complicated and obscured relationship between rights and powers, contract and coercion, liberty and force, and law and police.

Indeed, far from being strange bedfellows, American law and police, constitutionalism and sovereignty, the judiciary and the bureaucracy have been frequent fellow travelers. Nowhere is that clearer than in the history of the growth of police power. The police power itself is largely responsible for the strangely self-denying and hidden quality of the extraordinary power exercised by the American state. And at bottom, the American version of police power is a distinctly *legal* idea and practice. Police power originated and was legitimated in law—in the formal delegations of state prerogative in the charters of the municipalities, villages, corporations, and subsidiary associations that so beautifully reflect the intimate interrelationships of the state, the law, and the legitimate power to regulate, expropriate, and punish—to rule and govern others.[8] The official development of the police power as a legal doctrine is almost inseparable from the story of the rise of the judiciary and the common law and American constitutionalism. The original phrase *police power* came from none other than the chief justice of the U.S. Supreme Court, John Marshall, and the concept was most fully worked out by the equally influential Massachusetts Supreme Court Chief Justice Lemuel Shaw.[9] The role of police power in the production of modern legislative and administrative regulation was meticulously traced by the University of Chicago Law School's Ernst Freund.[10] Those cases, arguments, and articles that most clearly denoted the procedural and substantive due process limitations on police power simultaneously legitimated the unprecedented expansion of police power as part of a growing nation-state's legitimate monopoly of violence in the late nineteenth and early twentieth centuries. In short, though we commonly separate the jural state and the police state as necessary antipodes in a normatively charged metanarrative of the rise, decline, and phoenix-like rise of Western civilization, the actual constitutional history of at least the American version of the modern nation-state suggests a close interconnection and interpenetration of sovereignty, police, and the rule of law.

This chapter attempts to trace these three interdependent elements in the great transformation of American statecraft and public law between the end of the Civil War and the start of the New Deal, particularly (a) the reconfiguration of sovereignty around a more positivist notion of a modern state, (b) the redefinition and expansion of the legislative and regulatory authority of that state through a broader conception of the police power, and (c) a realignment in the relationship of the rule of law and administration. Together these intertwined transformations in sovereignty, police, and law created a modern polity that forever changed the relationship of state to citizen and government to civil society in the United States.

Sovereignty and the Nature of a Positive State

Theorists of American political order first began fundamentally rethinking the nature of the American state during the Civil War and Reconstruction. The need to reconstitute the nation was a powerful spur to a more general reconsideration (and reassertion) of governmental authority in the United States. With roots in the nationalistic oratory of Webster and Lincoln, the immediate post–Civil War period was flooded with treatises advocating constitutional defenses of the Union and strong nationalistic theories of the polity. Sidney George Fisher, John Alexander Jameson, Orestes Brownson, John C. Hurd, Elisha Mulford, and others downplayed the original significance of compact, contract, and states' rights and defended the overriding prerogatives of Union, nation, and state.[11] The impact of this nationalistic discourse on ideas of the American state was twofold. First, it articulated an aspiration toward a more powerful, unified, central government in the United States—a testament to and a guarantor of the Union's victory in war. Second, it reflected a more realistic and positivistic assessment of the powers of government needed to forge a new nation and to realize national ambitions. It acknowledged the role of force, coercion, and violence in modern governance and the relationship of necessity to national sovereignty and self-preservation. As Fisher wrote in the heat of battle, "If the Union and the government cannot be saved out of this terrible shock of war constitutionally, a Union and a government must be saved unconstitutionally."[12]

Building on such general wartime considerations of Union and nation, a subsequent generation of theorists and activists constructed a new theory of a positive state in the late nineteenth century. These theorists were more overtly international and cosmopolitan in their influences and vision, drawing on such important intellectual movements as the rise of analytic jurisprudence in England under the leadership of John Austin (inspired by Bentham) and advances in state theory in Germany under the direction of Johann Kaspar Bluntschli (inspired by Hegel).[13] The result was an impressive new set of legitimations and justifications for the expansion, centralization, and rationalization of state power in the United States. Such theories provided an intellectual template for governmental transformation and political action—in what Vernon Parrington artfully dubbed the "conscription of political theory."[14]

John W. Burgess's *Political Science and Comparative Constitutional Law* (1890), Woodrow Wilson's *The State: Elements of Historical and Practical Politics* (1890), and Westel Woodbury Willoughby's *An Examination of the Nature of the State* (1896) were the paradigmatic texts.[15] Together they moved American conceptions of sovereignty and the state beyond Alexis de Tocqueville's and Francis Lieber's emphasis on local authority, self-government, and civil liberty and unambiguously embraced the modern nation-state and its positive sovereign and legal powers.

A key element in this redefinition of the national polity was a new entity theory of the state. The intellectual roots of this idea were a curious blend. Burgess began with Hegel and the German "idea of the state" (*Staatsidee*) as an abstract ethical entity—a rational unity that acts and knows and wills as "the spirit which is present in the world and which *consciously* realizes itself therein." Bluntschli (once characterized as attempting to do for the modern European state what "Aristotle accomplished for the Hellenic") exerted even more influence on American political science through his psychological conception of the state as more of an organism or person.[16] But American theorists were just as likely to draw on the evolutionary social organicism of Comte and Spencer and the analytic jurisprudential categories of Austin and Holland. Willoughby, for example, consciously embraced just such an eclecticism, defending the need to approach the nature of the state as an entity from "a number of viewpoints," ranging from classical conceptions of "*civitas*" and Hegelian conceptions of "being" to the more commonly accepted juristic formulation of the state as "a legal person."[17]

In the end, the intellectual effort to specifically define the existential character or juristic personality of this thing called the state came in for some fairly harsh criticism, as in Morris Cohen's devastating attack on the "Communal Ghosts" of legal and political philosophy.[18] But it would be a mistake to underestimate the force of this reconceptualization of the state as an entity in itself with a juristic personality and agency, ready to wield an ambitious new set of governing powers and rationales. For the collective result of this effort was a reimagining of the American state as something more than an agglomeration of individuals or groups, more than a jurisdiction or territory, more than a governing council or a representative legislature—a notion of the American state not as a mere reflection of underlying social and economic interests but as a prime mover and shaker in its own right, with its own ends, objectives, and functions—a sovereign entity.

This new and increasingly modern notion of the state and its sovereign powers was further buoyed by the rising tide of legal positivism in the United States. The analytic jurisprudence of John Austin found many adherents in the United States, including John Chipman Gray, Henry T. Terry, Albert Kocourek, and Wesley Newcomb Hohfeld, and it helped transform American thinking about the relationship of law and statecraft.[19] The heart of this influence was the emphasis that analytic jurisprudence placed on sovereignty—law as the command of a duly constituted sovereign. As Gray pointed out, according to Austin, "'*The* State' is usually synonymous with '*the* sovereign.' It denotes the individual person, or the body of individual persons, which bears the supreme powers in an independent political society."[20] By making explicit the links between the positive law, sovereignty, and the state, legal positivism provided American jurists with a new model of the state and its positive lawmaking powers. Whereas the nationalistic thinkers of the immediate post–Civil War era remained murky on ideas like sovereignty—John Hurd dedicated his *Theory of Our National Existence* to "the Sovereign: Whoever He, She, or They May Be"—political scientists like Burgess organized their theories of the state around a positivist conception of sovereignty.[21] As Burgess wrote, "The essence of the state is everywhere, and at all times, one and the same, viz; sovereignty."[22]

The themes of positive law, sovereignty, and the state came together particularly well in the synthetic public law treatises of Westel Woodbury Willoughby.[23] Willoughby, one of the most prolific law writers of his time, grafted modern political theories of the state and sovereignty onto a more traditional understanding of American constitutional law. In contrast to antebellum jurists who regularly rejected a Blackstonian or utilitarian argument for the force of law, Willoughby drew the nature of sovereignty and all other forms of governing power strictly from a "conception of law as wholly a product of the State's will."[24] "However confederate in character the Union may have been at the time of its creation," Willoughby declared, "the transformation to a Federal State was effected." The essence of that state was not compact or communal custom or natural rights; rather, it was modern sovereignty—that power that was "the source of all law."[25]

In this way, early nineteenth-century concerns with custom, local self-government, compact, and evolutionary common law gave way to a new emphasis on the positive constitutional powers of a modern nation-state. The reception of analytic jurisprudence speeded a legal movement away from the perceived absurdities, irrationalities, and inefficiencies of common law rulemaking (so vigorously criticized by Bentham) and toward more systematic and rationalized accounts of law as a tool of modern governance—an instrument of a sovereign people and state that could be used to accomplish necessary social ends. Legal positivism thus reinforced a growing tendency to view law and the state, as Rudolf von Jhering put it, as "a means to an end."[26] Imperative legislation, statute law, and administrative regulation assumed greater significance on the basis of stronger claims to legal legitimacy and efficacy. This more positive conception of law, sovereignty, and statecraft underwrote a steady expansion of American governing power—police power—in the twentieth century.

Police and the Modern Legislative State

A second unmistakable indicator of a transformation in the nature and functions of the American state was the explosion of legislation in the United States at both the state and the federal levels between 1877 and 1932. At the first meeting of the American Law Institute in 1923, Elihu Root contributed to a frenzy of concern about the "flood of laws" when he reported that some 62,000 statutes had been added to the federal and state legislative record in just the five-year period before 1914.[27] Charles Merriam counted 18,243 legislative acts and resolutions for the biennium 1899–1900 and 23,403 for 1929–1930. Well before the heightened activity of the Depression and New Deal years, Congress alone was passing between 1,700 and 2,000 legislative acts per session, and larger states like New York were adding approximately 1,000 statutes to their books every two years.[28] By quantitative standards, statute law—the positively enacted law of the duly constituted popular legislature—was becoming a dominant instrument of American legal development.

But quantitative measures can be deceiving (especially given the number of private acts, internal administrative measures, and simple statutory amendments). Even more significant than the number of statutes being passed in this period was the radical character of some of this legislation—what some commentators started to call "the new social legislation" or "industrial legislation." For many of these statutes involved wholesale revisions of American common law and far-reaching social and economic reforms. From price-fixing regulation and corporate antitrust laws to worker's compensation and state and national prohibition laws, this was an era of unprecedented statutory innovation. In 1922 John Maurice Clark offered up a sampling of the broad-based movement for social control through legislation:

> This period of fifty years has seen the growth of effective control of railroads and of public utilities; while electricity and the telephone have developed, first,

> into recognized public utilities, and, second, into businesses which transcend state boundaries and thus become essentially national problems. Irrigation, land reclamation and flood prevention also belong properly in the class of interstate public interests, while radio and aerial navigation have but recently been added to the list. The trust movement and anti-trust laws, conservation, the Federal Reserve system, vast developments in labor legislation, social insurance, minimum-wage laws and the growing control of public health, prohibition, control over markets and marketing, enlarged control over immigration and international trade, city-planning and zoning, and municipal control of municipal growth in general, have all come about within this period.[29]

By 1910 James W. Garner's introductory American political science text could list the following functions of the modern state (beyond the basic maintenance of peace, order, and safety) as subjects of state and federal legislation:

> The operation of the postal service; the construction of dikes, levees, canals, public roads, bridges, and irrigation works, and works of public utility generally; the maintenance of scientific and statistical bureaus; the erection and maintenance of lighthouses, beacons, and buoys; the construction of harbors, wharves, and other instrumentalities of trade and commerce; the care of the poor and helpless; the protection of the public health and morals; elementary education; . . . the conduct of railway traffic; the telegraph and telephone service; the manufacture and distribution of gas and electricity for lighting purposes; the furnishing of water for drinking and other purposes in cities; the maintenance of theaters, pawn shops, bath houses and lodging houses; the encouragement of certain industries by means of bounties, protective tariffs, and subventions; the planting of colonies; the encouragement of immigration; the establishment of experiment stations, liquor dispensaries, banks, universities of learning, hospitals, reformatories, art galleries, museums, zoölogical and botanical gardens; the erection of improved dwellings for working people; the making of general loans to farmers; grants in aid of railroads; the distribution of seeds for agricultural purposes; the conduct of the business of insurance; the granting of old age pensions; the maintenance of employment bureaus; and many other activities too numerous to mention. Under this head may also be included a great volume of regulatory or restrictive legislation dealing with the conduct of certain trades and occupations which are affected with a public interest, such as: railway traffic and means of communication; mining, manufacturing; the relations between employer and employees; the conduct of dangerous, offensive, or obnoxious trades; the censorship of the press, vaccination,

> quarantine, and sanitary legislation; laws regarding the erection of buildings in cities; laws regulating banking, barbering, baking, plumbing, pawnbroking, slaughtering, and many other trades or businesses.[30]

Such lists could be multiplied a hundredfold and still not capture the full scale and scope of the American social and economic legislative record in this critical period. The appearance of such sweeping social and regulatory statutes meshed well with modern positive theories of state power and legal action, but they raised fundamental questions for more traditional ideas about statute law and the extent of state and federal legislative power to regulate in the public interest. The place to best witness this transformation of public law concerning statutes and legislation is in the modern development of the legal doctrine of the police power.

The peculiar language and terminology of *police power* no longer resonates today, as the idea has been fully incorporated (and thus rendered invisible) by a modern acceptance of general legislative lawmaking power. But in the late nineteenth and early twentieth centuries, discussion of the police power was pervasive. Economists, politicians, social reformers, and journalists were all aware of its important consequences for policy making. For the police power was basically the American legal expression for the authority of the government to regulate private interests, property, and behavior on behalf of the public health, safety, morals, order, and welfare. The police power had deep roots in the early American Republic and beyond where it resided exclusively with state and local governments and reflected a common law vision of well-regulated communities.[31] The reason the police power was so ubiquitous in turn-of-the-century jurisprudence and public discourse was that it was undergoing a fundamental transformation. That transformation was twofold. First, the police power was becoming a formal constitutional doctrine that defined a modern conception of positive legislative regulatory power. Second, somewhat less conspicuously, the police power was going national.

One of the chief architects of the transformation of the police power was Ernst Freund. Freund was one of the great hidden revolutionaries in American political and legal history. With German university training, a background in political science, and a long career at the University of Chicago Law School, Freund was well positioned to contribute to the redefinition of legislative, administrative, and regulatory powers under way in the late nineteenth and early twentieth centuries. He accomplished this through a range of national, state, and local reform activities, numerous scholarly articles, and four influential treatises on the key legal issues surrounding the creation of the modern American state: *Police Power*, *Standards of American*

Legislation, *Administrative Powers*, and *Legislative Regulation*.[32] Like Roscoe Pound and Robert Luce, Freund was aware that he was living in a "new age of legislation," and his legal work can be seen as an attempt to create a science of modern legislation, regulation, and statecraft that would clarify the new forces and standards at work. He suggested that the course of Western history consisted largely of the "wresting of legislative power from the executive," except in the case of administrative regulations proliferating through express delegations of legislative authority. The degree to which written statutes and codes increasingly supplanted both unwritten law and executive proclamations reflected the importance in democratic societies of having popular and representative sanction for governmental action.[33] It also reflected an increasingly realist and functionalist approach to the nature and obligations of the state. Freund argued explicitly that modern socioeconomic change, particularly "the growing power, scope, and complexity of private industrial and social action," brought an increasing demand for positive state action in the public interest.[34] That action appropriately took the form of written, legislative enactments in areas of police, revenue, and administration that were increasingly positive and public rather than declaratory and private. These regulatory statutes were the hallmarks of a modern legislative state—a direct consequence of the "increasing complexity of the social and industrial structure" and the expansion of "the functions of government" in pursuit of "the public welfare" and "the public interest."[35]

At the center of this expansion of legislative regulation and the multiplication of the social and economic functions of government stood the police power—the only open-ended source of state regulatory authority in American public law. Together with a bevy of other commentaries in this period, Freund's *Police Power* helped free the conception of police power from the limitations of its common law origins in nuisance-law doctrines like *sic utere tuo ut alienum non laedas* (use your own so as not to injure another) and establish it as an independent constitutional basis of extended legislative regulatory authority.[36] The police power traded in its ancient common law roots in rather murky ideas like overruling necessity and Blackstone's notion of "offences against public police" and became a formal and positive category of the constitutional law of a modern state. Freund began his treatise by noting the great objects of government, most importantly, (1) the maintenance of national existence (the law of overruling necessity) and (2) the maintenance of justice (the redress of right and wrong via the administration of civil and criminal justice). To these more traditional, defensive, and protective functions of government (which reflected a more negative conception of liberty and the role of government), a third was quickly being added in modern states, namely, the positive promotion of public welfare through "internal public policy." As Freund put it, "[T]he care of the public welfare, or internal public policy, has for its object the improvement of social and economic conditions affecting the community at large and collectively, with a view to bringing about 'the greatest good of the greatest number.'" It was here that an expanded conception of police did its work, no longer primarily preoccupied with negative common law protections or the simple maintenance of civil and criminal justice, but reconstituted as an instrument for the positive promotion of public welfare. Freund summarized, "No community confines its care of the public welfare to the enforcement of the principles of the common law. The state places its . . . resources at the disposal of the public by the establishment of improvements and services of different kinds; *and it exercises compulsory powers for the prevention and anticipation of wrong by narrowing common law rights through conventional restraints and positive regulations which are not confined to the prohibition of wrongful acts. It is this latter kind of state control which constitutes the essence of the police power.*"[37]

In this way, Freund traced the transformation of the police power from a more limited doctrine of community self-defense and protection hemmed in by traditional common law maxims and local and customary legal procedures into a more positive and affirmative authority to legislate broadly on behalf of the general welfare. Reinvented as the legislative "power of promoting the public welfare by restraining and regulating the use of liberty and property," the modern police power provided a powerful constitutional foundation for the modern legislative state. Innumerable other commentators reinforced Freund's positivist conception of police power. Lewis Hockheimer proclaimed, "The police power is the inherent plenary power of a State . . . to prescribe regulations to preserve and promote the public safety, health, and morals, and to prohibit all things hurtful to the comfort and welfare of society."[38] And judges and courts also followed suit, linking the police power more directly to the promotion of public welfare. Citing a host of cases upholding police power regulation, Justice McKenna argued in *Bacon v. Walker* (1907) that the police power "is not confined, as we have said, to the suppression of what is offensive, disorderly or unsanitary. It extends to so dealing with the conditions which exist in the State as to bring out of them the greatest welfare of its people."[39]

By linking the police power with the general promotion of public welfare in a positive legislative state, these jurists and law writers paved the way for the explosive growth of police power regulation in the Progressive Era. Some Progressives saw in the police power "almost unlimited opportunities for adopting whatever legislation the augmenting demands of social pioneers may require."[40] The police power thus became the legal foundation for the extensive legislative and regulatory experiments enumerated by Clark and Garner. As Freund noted, the modern police power encompassed the whole range of public and governmental regulatory interests, from the primary social interests of "safety, order, and morals" to the regulation of economic interests in the guise of burgeoning industrial legislation to the nonmaterial or ideal interests in the "cultivation of moral, intellectual and aesthetic forces" to the political interests secured via the increased regulation of the governmental machinery itself. Under these general categories, Freund arranged his 800-page encyclopedic survey of America's new regulatory state.

But legislative police power not only dramatically expanded its scale and scope in this period, it also began a slow and steady ascent up the levels of American government. As Samuel P. Hays among other historians has noted, the period between 1880 and 1920 witnessed a thoroughgoing nationalization and systemization of American social and economic life necessitating a distinctly "upward shift of decision-making" power.[41] Leonard D. White surveyed the extent of such administrative centralization even before the onset of the New Deal in 1933: "The evidence of the last thirty years demonstrates a steady accretion of power and influence by the state governments over the administrative powers of local officials especially in the fields of public finance, education, health and highways, as well as a steady extension of federal influence over the states, particularly in the regulation of commerce."[42] In this respect, perhaps the most important development in the transformation of legislation and police power in this period was the invention of a federal police power—the extraconstitutional centralization of general welfare lawmaking in the United States.

In *United States v. Dewitt* (1870), the U.S. Supreme Court adopted the clear antebellum constitutional consensus that the police power was explicitly a state and local rather than a federal power. Echoing Chief Justice Marshall's analysis in *Barron v. Baltimore* (1833) in refusing to apply the federal Bill of Rights to the individual states, Chief Justice Chase held that, though Congress clearly had the authority to regulate interstate commerce, it did not have a general national power to pass regulations of internal state police in the interests of public health, safety, and welfare. The police power remained with the individual states and localities, and the national government wielded nothing analogous to the general plenary authority of state legislatures to regulate liberty and property in the public interest.[43] But, of course, one of the great stories of the period after 1870 was that Congress increasingly secured the power to do precisely that—obtaining a de facto if not de jure national police power through the creative exercise of its commerce, taxing, spending, and postal powers. As Charles Evans Hughes told the American Bar Association in 1918, the most significant decisions of the recent Supreme Court involved "the extended application of the doctrine that federal rules governing interstate commerce may have the quality of police regulations."[44] In the areas of business, labor, transportation, morals, health, safety, and education, powers and issues that were once the exclusive domain of state and local governments moved up into the purview of the national government in one of the most significant expropriations of political power in American history. And as Ernst Freund argued in 1920, the role of law and the judiciary in that expropriation was pivotal: "The consolidation of our own nation has proved our allotment of federal powers to be increasingly inadequate; and had it not been aided by liberal judicial construction, our situation would be unbearable."[45]

One of the most important advocates of such liberal legal construction was Robert E. Cushman, who, in a series of influential articles in the *Minnesota Law Review*, laid out the Progressive quest for a national police power. As Cushman noted, "The enumeration of the congressional powers in the Constitution does not include any general grant of authority to pass laws for the protection of the health, morals, or general welfare of the nation. It follows, then, that if Congress is to exercise a police power at all, it must do so by a process something akin to indirection." Cushman argued that if Congress wanted to expand Progressive state police power experiments to the national level in an ambitious program to secure the general welfare, it would have to "cloak its good works under its authority to tax, or to regulate commerce, or to control the mails, or the like, and say, 'By this authority we pass this law in the interest of the public welfare.'"[46] That is exactly what Congress did in passing such important national morals, health, safety, and economic regulations as the Pure Food and Drug Act (1906), the Mann Act (1910), the Harrison Narcotics Tax Act (1914), the Child Labor Tax Act (1919), and the National Prohibition Act (1919). Through its spending power and federal grants in aid to the individual states, Congress was able to wield even more national regulatory authority through the incentive power of the public purse.[47] Consequently, the United States achieved a centralization of national legislative police power authority even before the Supreme Court accepted an expansive interpretation of the interstate commerce clause at the height of the New Deal.[48]

Administration and the Rule of Law

The third and final factor in the transformation of the American state was the reconfiguration of the role of administration in American public law. As with the police power, the development of administrative law was not wholly an invention of the late nineteenth century. Of the fifty-one major federal agencies and departments with administrative rulemaking powers at the time of the adoption of the Administrative Procedures Act in 1946, eleven traced their origins to statutes enacted before the Civil War.[49] Indeed, national administrative authority was coincident with the very first Congresses and the delegation of extensive administrative powers to the Treasury Department, the Departments of War and the Navy, the Pension Office, the Patent Office, the Customs Office, the General Land Office, and the U.S. Postal Service.[50] But while administration was certainly not invented after the Civil War, it was fundamentally transformed. Like the police power, it traded in early common law origins (and limitations) in the law of public officers and became the modern science of governmental management—public administration.

Many important aspects of the movement for a modern state administration deserve to be discussed in detail: the professionalization of civil service inaugurated by the Pendleton Act of 1883; the Research, Bureau, and Budget movements; the periodic efforts for governmental reorganization at federal, state, and municipal levels; the creation of independent federal regulatory commissions like the Interstate Commerce Commission (1887), the Federal Reserve Board (1913), and the Federal Trade Commission (1914); and the innovations in public management entailed by that quintessential example of the new public service state—the public ownership of public utilities.[51] There is space here only to review the overarching movement toward modern administrative models that transformed public law and aided the construction of the new American state.

The impact of administration on modern governance is perhaps best suggested by Max Weber's conception of modern governmental rationalization as "legal authority with a bureaucratic administrative staff." Weber enumerated the attributes of administrative governance that increasingly characterized governance in modern states: the continuous rule-bound conduct of official business; the rigorous specification of jurisdictional competence; the hierarchical organization of offices; the governance of offices via technical rules or norms; the separation of ownership and control in administrative decision making; the objective rather than subjective nature of rights in an office; the importance of written documentation of administrative acts, decisions, and rules; and the presence of an elaborate administrative staff—officialdom, bureaucracy.[52] The development of this distinctly modern form of bureaucratic organization in modern Western states brought an increasingly formal, rational, impersonal, and functional style of rule that sustained and extended the state's monopoly on the legitimate use of force in a territory. Though the topic of administration is sometimes overlooked in American history, Theodore Lowi captured its absolute centrality to the development of modern power and policy: "The modern method of social control involves the application of rationality to social relations. . . . Rationality applied to social control is administration. Administration may indeed be the *sine qua non* of modernity."[53]

This more general vision of overall governmental rationalization and modernization guided the development of public administration in the United States. It was part of what Woodrow Wilson called the "new meaning of government." As he put it in his pioneering article "The Study of Administration" in 1887, "The field of administration is the field of business. It is removed from the hurry and strife of politics." Public administration involved the application of efficiency, economy, and rational techniques of management and organization to the "detailed and systematic execution of public law."[54] Leonard D. White elaborated, "Public administration is the management of men and materials in the accomplishment of the purposes of the state. . . . The objective of public administration is the most efficient utilization of the resources at the disposal of officials. . . . In every direction good administration seeks the elimination of waste, the conservation of material and energy, and the most rapid and complete achievement of public purposes."[55] Consequently, the development of administration and administrative regulation involved something of a culmination of many of the state-building trends examined thus far: a conception of the state as a modern form of businesslike organization, a more positivist and instrumental conception of rulemaking and lawmaking, and an increased tendency toward the centralization and consolidation of governmental power. Wilson saw governmental organization and rationalization as a necessary accompaniment of the increasing functions demanded of Progressive states. Administration was a vehicle of the "common interest"—a way of making the government a more "sensitive registering instrument" of public need and opinion.[56]

Given the centrality of administration to Progressive reform and modern American politics, political scientists and theorists have spent a considerable amount of time charting the rise of administrative organization and bureaucracy in the late nineteenth- and early twentieth-century United States.[57] But somewhat less attention has been devoted to the important legal consequences of that historical development. The rise of professional administration and administrative regulation posed two fundamental challenges to existing American public law. First, it challenged the traditional role of the officeholder in a common law system formerly oriented around local and participatory self-government.[58] Second, it raised important questions for traditional constitutional ideals like checks and balances and the separation of powers.

Like the common law generally, nineteenth-century conceptions of the legal nature of office holding assumed a general continuity between ruler and ruled, officeholder and citizen in the day-to-day practices of local self-government. The nature of the justice of the peace, the role of the jury, and the proliferation of citizen-officers in the enforcement of regulations all bespeak the fluidity of common law conceptions of the interconnectedness of society, politics, and local administration.[59] In contrast, modern administrative law and theory posited a foundational separation between the administrative officeholder as professional business manager and the social and political life of the citizenry—a separation of political ownership from the administrative control of the American polity.[60] As Woodrow Wilson somewhat aristocratically justified the idea of administrative discretion and the limits of direct popular participation in modern bureaucracy, "Self-government does not consist in having a hand in everything, any more than housekeeping consists necessarily in cooking dinner with one's own hands. The cook must be trusted with a large discretion as to the management of the fires and the ovens."[61] Max Weber captured the departure from more traditional and personal conceptions of office when he characterized the objective formalism at the heart of bureaucratic administration: "It does not establish a relationship to a *person*, . . . but rather is devoted to *impersonal* and *functional* purposes." In place of the subjective, interpersonal, irrational, time-consuming, and case-by-case methods of self-governance, "precision, speed, unambiguity, knowledge of the files, continuity, discretion, unity, strict subordination, reduction of friction and of material and personal costs" were "raised to the optimum point in the strictly bureaucratic administration."[62]

But as much as modern administration posed challenges for common law conceptions of office and self-government, it produced even greater problems for traditional ideas about American constitutionalism. The original constitutional regime of divided and mixed government, carefully counterbalancing executive, legislative, and judicial powers as well as local, state, and national authority did not easily accommodate some of the new omnibus powers entailed in administrative regulation usually at the level of a centralizing executive. Most of the independent regulatory commissions formed in this period wielded a curious and potent blend of quasi-judicial adjudicative power, quasi-legislative rulemaking authority, executive law enforcement capacity, an inquisitorial or investigative function, and a responsibility for overall policy planning. Such powerful, independent, and multifunction governmental entities did not fit comfortably into the existing constitutional schema.

As the writings of Ernst Freund documented the transformation of legislative police power, the texts of Frank J. Goodnow charted the constitutional implications of the rise of the administrative state. Goodnow was one of Freund's teachers at Columbia, the first president of the American Political Science Association, president of Johns Hopkins University, and one of the first and most comprehensive analysts of public administration in the United States—frequently referred to as the father of American administration. From his casebooks on the *Law of Officers* to his treatises on *Principles of Administrative Law* to Progressive advocacy texts like *Social Reform and the Constitution* to his multiple administrative studies of *Municipal Government*, Goodnow laid the intellectual and legal groundwork for the jurisprudential transition from traditional ideas about self-governing officeholders and constitutional limitations to the public law legitimacy of professional administration in a modern bureaucratic state.[63] Like most Progressive reformers, Goodnow started with an acute awareness of "the tremendous changes in political and social conditions" inaugurated by industrial modernization and the enormous social and economic problems attending that "great transformation." And he argued explicitly that solutions to those problems required a legal and political transformation of equal extent. In *Social Reform and the Constitution* and *Principles of Constitutional Government*, Goodnow equaled Charles Beard and J. Allen Smith with a devastating Progressive critique of the constraints of ancient constitutionalism. He proposed that original American constitutionalism was based on an eighteenth-century political theory of social compact and natural right that presupposed "that society was static rather than dynamic or progressive in character." The unfortunate result of this original understanding was "to fix upon the country for all time institutions which . . . were established in the eighteenth century to deal with conditions then existing, but which may in this twentieth century be unsuitable because of the economic, social and political changes which have taken place in the last hundred years."[64] Goodnow endorsed instead a new positive, Progressive, and dynamic approach to the Constitution that would keep public law flexible, responsive to public opinion, and adaptable to the changing needs of modern life. He echoed Theodore Roosevelt's critique of the "false and mischievous" notion of the Constitution as a "strait-jacket to be used for the control of an unruly patient—the people." He opposed the static idea wherein "the United States Constitution is to the country what a coat too small in size is to a man. If he buttons it up in front he splits it open behind." Rather, he endorsed Roosevelt's vision of constitutional dynamism in the public interest: "Our constitutions are instruments designed to secure justice by securing the deliberate but effective expression of the popular will, that the checks and balances are valuable as far, and only so far, as they accomplish that deliberation."[65]

In his works on administrative law, Goodnow made clear the implications of this critical constitutionalism for the Progressive expansion of administrative power. He protested against overly rigid interpretations of federalism and checks and balances, which he claimed "resulted in a constitutional tradition which is apt not to accord to the federal government powers which it unquestionably ought to have the constitutional right to exercise." And he called on courts and judges to abandon "the strict application of the principle of the separation of powers whenever the demand for administrative efficiency would seem to make such action desirable."[66] Here Goodnow agreed with Roosevelt's sometime adversary Woodrow Wilson on the necessity of "large powers" and "unhampered discretion" in public administration, believing that there was "no danger in power, if only it not be irresponsible."[67] Goodnow advocated a centralized and professionalized bureaucratic corps insulated from popular politics, arguing that there was "a large part of administration which is unconnected with politics, which should be relieved very largely, if not altogether, from the control of political bodies. It is unconnected with politics because it embraces fields of semi-scientific, quasi-judicial and quasi-business or commercial activity."[68] In *Politics and Administration*, Goodnow went so far as to suggest that a new system of government had displaced traditional American constitutional notions of federalism and the separation of powers. In place of a traditional understanding of the divisions of judicial, legislative, and executive power, he reduced all practices of modern government to two overriding functions—politics ("the will of the state") and administration ("the execution of that will"). As administration was outside politics per se, it need not be subject to traditional constitutional limitations. Indeed, Goodnow argued that administrative powers should be expanded so as to meet the demands of social reform for increased government ownership, government regulation, and government aid. Through the expansion of administration, "the great centralization of our government" was to be secured.[69]

Conclusion

With the arrival of the New Deal, the modern American state found new prophets and advocates like Felix Frankfurter and James Landis. In a larger sense, they consummated the hidden revolution in governance, regulation, and administration pioneered by the likes of Willoughby, Freund, and Goodnow. As Frankfurter noted in 1936, it was "Frank J. Goodnow and Ernst Freund, as early as the '90s, [who] saw general tendencies towards an administrative law" and a new regulatory state where others saw only unrelated, individual occurrences. In *The Public and Its Government*, Frankfurter synthesized and popularized the several themes worked out by two previous generations of political and legal thinkers and reformers: the demands of modern society on government, the need for a more positive and instrumental conception of law and legislation, the new liberal idea of public service in the public interest, and the need for an expert administration in a constitutional democracy.[70] These were the crucial building blocks of the hidden revolution in governance—the transformation of public law—that created a new state in modern America. Well before James Landis, as former chair of the Securities and Exchange Commission and dean of Harvard Law School, wrote his great defense of the administrative regulatory system, *The Administrative Process*, in 1938, the main lines of modern American state development had already been well established. And as Landis pointed out, that "growth of the administrative process shows little sign of being halted. . . . Its extraordinary growth in recent years, the increasing frequency with which government has come to resort to it, the extent to which it is creating new relationships between the individual, the body economic, and the state, already have given it great stature."[71]

By 1932 the legal rights of the new citizen were increasingly hammered out in relationship to a new state—what Charles Beard had already dubbed the *American Leviathan*.[72] That new state boasted a new institutional identity as a modern governmental organization reflecting an unmistakable centralization of decision-making authority, an expanded positive lawmaking power, a professionalized bureaucratic competence, and an unprecedented administrative regulatory range. As Beard surveyed the "huge complex of wealth, political institutions, military engines, economic undertakings, and technological activities" that made up American government by 1930, he could do no better than to characterize this vast new power through Thomas Hobbes's mythical notion of the state as a "powerful and bewildering Titan."[73] But in the end, this revolution in American governance was about more than just the transformation in traditional public law conceptions of state power, authority, and interest. It turned just as much on the new functions of this governmental apparatus—the new jobs that the new state was constantly being asked to perform. Beard listed just some of the more significant public obligations concerning taxation, finance, and supplies; money and banking; transportation (inland and coastal waters, railways, express, pipelines, highways, aviation); communications (postal service, wire communications, radio); the promotion of business enterprise (tariff, unfair competition, antitrust, trademarks, copyrights, patents); labor and immigration policy; agricultural promotion and regulation; the conservation of natural resources; public health, safety, and morals; measurements and planning (standards, surveying, mapping, statistics); and the nature and conduct of foreign relations. And this was but the tip of an ever-expanding iceberg. Here, in the actual output of the positive state, one gains a better appreciation of the dramatic changes in American life begun by this hidden revolution in governance—the social and economic consequences of the creation of an American leviathan—a leviathan rooted in new understandings of law, sovereignty, and police.

FOUR

Limited Liberty, Durable Patriarchy

MARK E. KANN

One generation fought the American Revolution for liberty; the next generation restricted that liberty. Postwar officials worried that the Revolution unleashed widespread licentiousness, vice, and crime. Setting aside liberal notions of autonomy, consent, and law, American leaders perpetuated the patriarchal power of public officials to police and punish citizens. Their commitment to limited liberty and durable patriarchy was particularly evident in the penal reform and penitentiary movement that emerged in the 1780s and 1790s.

* * *

The new Republic's civic leaders and political officials addressed their fear of public disorder in two ways. First, they called on Americans to invest liberty in virtue. Benevolent individuals heeded the call by founding voluntary organizations to spread the gospel of Christian goodness and good citizenship. Second, they called on local and state governments to limit or deny liberty to those individuals who appeared to endanger public peace. Legislators, judges, and other officials responded by exercising the state's police power to detain, prosecute, and punish wrongdoers.

Markus D. Dubber notes that early American leaders viewed the state's authority to punish citizens as "an entirely unproblematic exercise of sovereign power over offenders."[1] The Revolution simultaneously freed Americans from the king's police power and freed American officials to exercise police power.[2] For the most part, officials' authority to wield police power was considered self-evident; it was necessary for maintaining social order and promoting public welfare.[3]

The idea of police power was rooted in ancient notions of the patriarchal householder who had the authority to manage his household and address all contingencies, threats, and opportunities. Similarly, the American version of police power considered the state as a patriarchal householder that was superior to citizens, wielded broad discretionary authority over them, and did so to promote their safety and welfare. The state's police power existed in tension with liberal law, which involved relations between equal citizens, common law and formal statutes, and justice in the service of individual rights.[4] In the post-Revolution period, with the new Republic's survival uncertain, police power "expanded rather contracted." Public officials claimed the discretionary authority to employ coercion against anyone who threatened the "repose" of the community. Citizen rights were secondary. Dubber suggests that government officials' exercise of police power was "obviously legitimate to Americans," who would not deny their leaders the power of self-preservation.[5]

The state's exercise of patriarchal police power and its restraints on citizens' liberty were manifested in a postwar penal reform and penitentiary movement. Penal reformers wanted to replace traditional punishments (such as public hangings, beatings, and humiliations) with long-term incarceration in "penitentiaries." These houses of penitence and correction were to be administered by personnel whose job was to maintain order among inmates and rehabilitate them into law-abiding citizens who could be safely discharged into free society.[6]

* * *

Penal reformers sought to make imprisonment in state penitentiaries the primary punishment for felons. What was most punishing about penitentiaries was that they deprived inmates of liberty for many, many years. Benjamin Rush was Philadelphia's most prominent reform advocate. He observed, "Personal liberty is so dear to all . . . that the loss of it . . . is a punishment so severe that death has often been preferred to it." Edward Livingston, in his proposed revision of Louisiana's criminal code, suggested that Americans' love of liberty made "its privation in different degrees . . . the fittest punishment for faults which disturb social order." Englishman Patrick Colquhoun wrote to New York reformer Thomas Eddy that Americans' devotion to liberty should not interfere with police restraints on the liberty of "evil doers." Such restraints "can never disturb the proceedings of the peaceful citizen in the general intercourse of society."[7] Overall, penal reformers were convinced that the state's denial of convict liberty was an extremely painful but just and appropriate punishment.

Critics agreed that liberty denied was an extremely painful punishment, but they also complained that it was a cruel punishment, more fit for a monarchy than a republic. In the 1790s the Duc de Warville, while touring America, condemned what was becoming the typical practice of long-term incarceration. "Prisons," he wrote, "are fatal to the health, liberty, and morals of men." They plunged convicts into "grief and mortification" by depriving them of fresh air, exercise, good food, and ties to loved ones. They were unnatural institutions, and they were ineffective institutions. They did not rehabilitate people. If they did not kill inmates, they robbed them of the sense of dignity essential to citizenship. Incarceration twice betrayed the Revolution, first by stripping people of liberty and then by treating them in perverse ways.[8]

The harshest critics of penal reform and penitentiaries were former inmates who published prison memoirs. Inmate-author William Stuart noted that liberty was so important in the new Republic that Americans generally distrusted and limited the state's authority to regulate citizen behavior. For example, "the spirited drinker" may have been destined for a life of crime but liberty-loving Americans, "jealous of what they think to be their rights," refused to enact or enforce laws against excessive drinking. Following the same logic, Stuart indicated, Americans should have refused to allow reformers and officials the authority to so readily deny individuals' liberty by sending them to prison.[9]

Stephen Burroughs was imprisoned in Massachusetts in 1785, the same year that state reformed its penal practices. Burroughs contrasted the liberty promised by the Revolution and the "slavery" inflicted by the reformed prison system: "It has been abundantly said by the leading men in this state that life without liberty is not worth the possessing. This was abundantly urged to the people in the time of war and it was urged with great truth and propriety. Therefore, that the same characters upon a revision of the criminal code . . . should substitute slavery for death is to me conduct truly enigmatical."[10] Revolutionaries declared liberty more precious than life, but postwar officials increasingly punished offenders by denying them liberty for years.

Burroughs reported that his yearning for liberty increased the longer he was incarcerated. He made several failed escape attempts and asked his readers, "Would any of you, who are walking at your ease, enjoying the sunshine of liberty, if placed in my situation, lie down tamely under the burden and not exert yourselves for freedom when you possessed a faint ray of hope that you may obtain it?"[11] Inmate-author John Reynolds justified virtually any risk to regain liberty because confinement was truly torturous. "Take the purest apartment in heaven and confine a seraph there," he wrote, "and the simple fact that he was a prisoner would make his home a hell. The Devil himself would prefer liberty in the world of woe to imprisonment even in Paradise—freedom with damnation to salvation with restraint."[12]

Imprisoned for forgery, W. A. Coffey "ardently sought a restoration to liberty." He condemned the reformed penal system for taking liberty so lightly: "We are accustomed to affix too small a value to the liberty of a fellow creature." The reformed penal system made it too easy to incarcerate individuals. Traditionally, juries were reticent to hang people because hanging foreclosed the possibility of correcting mistaken convictions. By the early nineteenth century, Coffey claimed, juries were predisposed to prison sentences because, if mistakes were made, the innocent still could be set free. This predisposition was augmented by the widespread belief that "if the accused man is innocent, a short imprisonment will do him no harm; and if he is guilty, it would be injustice to the community to let him go unpunished." Coffey concluded that this belief was "too frequently prejudicial to an accused man's liberty."[13] In a single generation, it seemed, a presumption favoring liberty became a presumption favoring incarceration.

Critics connected incarceration to slavery. Tennessee state representative Louis Reneau claimed that reformers' "pretended humanity" amounted to "taking a man who by the present law can only be sentenced to a few stripes [lashes] and a few weeks imprisonment and shutting him up in the penitentiary, there to be kept at hard labor and to be whipped and driven at the whim and pleasure of his master." The suffering caused by traditional punishments was far less than the misery produced by long-term imprisonment. It was this *surplus* misery that rankled John Reynolds, who described Vermont's Windsor Prison this way: "That prison is called *penitentiary*. As properly might hell be called heaven. The spirit of the penitentiary system finds there no place to lay its head. Not the reformation of the convicts is sought . . . and they are treated just as an intelligent but heartless slaveholder would treat his Negroes—made to work as long as they can earn their living and then cursed with freedom that they may die on their own expense."[14] For Reynolds, citizens subjected to the state's police power were no better off than blacks subjected to the slave master's abuse.

* * *

In addition to supporting imprisonment for convicted felons, American penal reformers and politicians also supported the state's application of police power to deny liberty to delinquents, misdemeanants, vagrants, poor people, and nearly everyone else they suspected of viciousness and criminal tendencies. These were mostly marginal people who had not been accused of criminal acts or prosecuted for committing crimes. The mere fact that civic leaders suspected them of somehow threatening public order was sufficient to subject them to reformers' scrutiny and the state's police power.

Reformers gradually became concerned about the large numbers of undisciplined children who roamed the streets of New York, Philadelphia, Boston, and other cities. Thomas Eddy called for "a suitable prison solely for the confinement of boys under sixteen years of age, considered as vagrants, or guilty of petty thefts or other minor offenses." Child-saver John Griscom was intrigued with the idea of preemptive detention for youths who had committed no crimes but who, without preventive action, were likely to do so. He wanted delinquents remanded to a House of Refuge that would impose penitentiary-like discipline and promote rehabilitation. New York City District Attorney Hugh Maxwell agreed that "vagrant boys" needed early state intervention and detention lest they become "accomplished in iniquity." Reformers paid particular attention to what John Sutton calls "the not-yet criminal child" who was likely to become a criminal unless "rescued" from free society and incarcerated in institutions run by benevolent citizens and paternalistic state officials.[15]

An 1824 New York law granted police magistrates, superintendents of the poor, and House of Refuge managers the authority to take custody of problem children; discipline them; teach them good morals, good work habits, and good citizenship; and if appropriate, bind them out as apprentices or servants. The law reflected a Society for the Prevention of Pauperism recommendation that five classes of children be detained in the House of Refuge. Boys guilty of vagrancy or petty crimes constituted the main population. A second class included juvenile offenders who otherwise would be sent to a state prison. The third category consisted of boys suffering parental neglect or abuse. A fourth group included child convicts discharged from adult prisons who, without intervention, were apt to drift back into crime. The fifth category was "delinquent females" who had yielded to "corrupting influences." Without policing, these problem children would likely engage in theft, prostitution, and worse.[16]

Lawmakers granted broad discretion to public officials. New York's Society for the Reform of Juvenile Delinquents reported, "The legislature has . . . entrusted to its managers powers that have not heretofore been delegated. . . . If a child be found destitute—if abandoned by the parents—or suffered to lead a vicious or vagrant life; or if convicted of any crime, it may be sent to the House of Refuge." Refuge records reported that youths were generally committed for vagrancy and suspicion of theft. The impulse toward preventive incarceration was strong. Between 1826 and 1829, Boston's House of Reformation detained 192 children. Few were criminals. Forty-nine were committed "for being stubborn and disobedient," twenty-nine for being vagabonds, eleven for leading idle lives, and four for lascivious conduct.[17]

Reformers' inclination toward preventive incarceration was equally strong when directed at adult vagrants. As Dubber notes, vagrant men and women were unattached to a household and thus "subject to the patriarchal power of no one." They were "unpoliced" and, civic leaders feared, "peaceless." Vagrancy laws and nuisance ordinances were sufficiently vague to provide officials great discretion in banishing or imprisoning vagrants. Even where there was no statutory law for detaining suspicious strangers, the courts policed them by way of common law misdemeanors. Vagrancy was a status. Vagrants may have committed no criminal acts but they were nonetheless subjected to policing and prison with virtually no legal recourse.[18]

Some reformers wanted to empower public officials to apply summary justice to vagrants and other at-risk adults. Thomas Eddy advocated authorizing police magistrates to incarcerate vagrants, drunkards, disorderly persons, and petty criminals by sentencing them to "perfect solitude . . . on a spare diet" for as long as ninety days.[19] Reformers regarded vagrants as incipient or undetected criminals. They drew no sharp distinction between vagrants and convicts or between workhouses for vagrants and prisons for criminals. Boston's Prison Discipline Society proposed that "the poor and ignorant and vicious at large" be placed in workhouses where they would be exposed to "wholesome regulations and useful principles" developed for penitentiaries. They also recommended that "intemperate persons, vagabonds, pilferers, and the vicious poor" be "brought under wholesome discipline and instruction" in state penal institutions. Conceivably, every county in America could build a poorhouse or prison for detaining and disciplining the disorderly poor.[20]

Benjamin Rush regarded habitual drunkards as more dangerous than most vagrants because, ultimately, alcohol addicts destroyed "the order and happiness of society." He recommended that the state incarcerate drunkards in "Sober Houses" that would be built in every town and city. These men and women would be detained to prevent injury to themselves and to receive treatment for alcohol addiction. Anticipating criticism, Rush claimed that drunkards' incarceration in Sober Houses was not "an infringement upon personal liberty incompatible with the freedom of our governments." Americans did not complain when thieves were imprisoned. Rush estimated that the aggregate evil caused by thieves paled in comparison to the "greater evil" caused by the "immoral example and conduct" of habitual drunkards.[21]

Discussions about preventive incarceration for vagrants, poor people, and alcoholics focused on adults "on the verge between vice and crime." Edward Livingston argued these dangerous individuals needed "inspection and restraint" lest their "idleness and profligacy" lead to crime. He called on legislators to fund the construction of a public House of Industry composed of two departments, one voluntary and one coercive. The voluntary department would be "a place of employment for all those who are capable of gaining, by their bodily exertions, a complete or partial support and for the few who are totally helpless." The coercive department would be a place where the able-bodied poor "shall be forced to labor for their support." Livingston assumed that the poor person with no visible means of support, sooner or later, would commit crimes. This trajectory toward wrongdoing could be diverted if the poor person was incarcerated in an adult reform school, which taught "industrious obedience to the law, a respect for religion, and a love of justice and moral duties."[22]

Livingston linked preventive incarceration to crime reduction. He explained, "As prevention in the diseases of the body is less painful, less expensive, and more efficacious than the most skillful cure; so, in the moral maladies of society, to arrest the vicious before the profligacy assumes the shape of crime . . . to reform them by education and make their own industry contribute to their support, though difficult and expensive, will be found more effectual in the suppression of offenses and more economical than the best organized system of punishment." Preventive incarceration, an exemplary exercise in police power, was good for prisoners and good for society. Livingston was not the least concerned that this exercise of police power involved stripping individuals of liberty.[23]

Indeed, some reformers claimed that stripping people of liberty could be positively good for them—regardless of their legal innocence or guilt. Pennsylvania reformer Franklin Bache applied a "supposition of guilt" to inmates who were accused of a crime but were still awaiting trial. He wanted accused prisoners to undergo solitary confinement to rid them of vice and open them to virtue—even though they had not yet been found guilty of any crime. His colleague, James Mease, claimed that untried prisoners, at the very least, were likely guilty of petty crimes and probably worse. He too recommended solitary confinement in the expectation that this punishment would reduce the chances that they would commit additional crimes. Even if some untried prisoners were eventually acquitted, Mease argued, their time in solitary confinement was still a good thing because it made them more prone to law-abiding behavior. Prison architect Charles Bulfinch joined the chorus by agreeing that the accused should endure solitude to "encourage reflection" and produce "a degree of contrition" in the service of "reformation."[24] Any presumption of innocence or actual innocence was beside the point.

* * *

Did imprisoned Americans have "rights" that protected them against the state's patriarchal exercise of police power? Penal reformers claimed that punishment should be consistent with America's spirit of liberty and popular form of government. For William Bradford, that meant less severity and more proportionate punishment than in the past. Thomas Eddy thought a free society deserved a criminal code marked by "moderation." Nearly all reformers believed that penitentiary incarceration aimed at rehabilitation was proportionate, moderate, and redemptive: it gradually prepared prisoners to regain their liberty.[25] However, reformers did not express this belief as a foundation for establishing, enumerating, or advocating prisoner rights.

Reformers rarely talked about prisoner rights. They considered most inmates to have forsaken liberty long before their imprisonment. Early in their lives, wrongdoers usually habituated themselves to begging, stealing, drinking, gambling, illicit sex, brawling, and other vices that prefigured their future crimes. Slaves to their passions, they never matured into rational, responsible, civil individuals capable of exercising rights or enjoying a disciplined liberty. Reformers' hope and expectation was that long-term incarceration combined with a regenerative regimen of solitude, silence, labor, schooling, and moral counseling would free prisoners from subjection to their passions and prepare them for the responsible exercise of rights and liberty in a free society. Reformers portrayed the penitentiary as a school for liberty; but it was a school in which inmates had no rights against officials' police power.

Some reformers explicitly denied that inmates had rights. New York reformer and politician Stephen Allen claimed that the criminal, by his own illegal actions, deprived himself of the "rights of a free man" and "rights of a citizen." Those who engaged in crime forfeited their rights. Warden Gershom Powers offered a more practical reason for rejecting prisoner rights. He argued that a criminal had to be "brought to a sense of his degradation" if he was to have a chance for rehabilitation. That chance was lost, however, "where the prisoner stands on his rights."[26] Mostly unspoken but widely understood by reformers was the presumption that those in state custody had acted like disorderly children who did not require rights or liberty but who instead needed exposure to patriarchal authority and paternal guidance.

Neither reformers nor prison officials advocated due process rights for inmates. Due process was invoked to legitimize the imposition of punishment, not the application of punishment. For example, the Reverend Moses C. Welch sermonized at the end of one trial, "Having been accused of the crime of shedding human blood, the Grand-Jury of the county, after a due investigation of the case, have indicted you for murder. You have been brought to the bar of the Honorable Superior Court, and assisted in your defense by able and learned counsel. But the evidence was so clear against you as to induce twelve sober, judicious, disinterested jurors, on their oath, to pronounce you guilty."[27] Once convicted and sentenced, however, the individual's due process rights disappeared at the prison's gates. John Reynolds memorialized the consequences: "When any [inmate] was reported to the warden for any crime, he was without any hearing committed to a solitary cell, as dark as a tomb, and confined there on bread and water for a number of days, seldom less than a week, at the pleasure of the keepers."[28] According to inmate-authors, prisoners regularly received capricious punishments and had no right to appeal them.

Lacking rights, inmates were wholly subordinated to their prison superiors. This subordination was crucial to reformer plans to build penal institutions that eliminated everything that might inflame inmate passions. Males and females were separated; masturbation and sodomy were prohibited; alcohol, tobacco, and other stimulants were banned; and silence was mandated. Sean McConville writes, "Prisoners were to become better by being subject to controls on every aspect of daily life: sleeping, eating, working, associating with others, reading—and in religion, dress, and exercise."[29] Penitentiary officers were to have complete control of the convicts and the penal environment to maintain order, neutralize adverse influences, and rehabilitate criminals.

Critics claimed that this extreme subordination of inmates invited institutional abuses. Most famously, Charles Dickens toured Pennsylvania's Eastern Penitentiary and published an exposé of what he considered to be state-inflicted terror. The prison's regimen of long-term solitary confinement constituted "slow and daily tampering with the mysteries of the brain . . . worse than any torture of the body." The prisoner was "a man buried alive." He was told nothing of his wife, children, or friends and saw no one but prison officials. After years of solitude, he suffered bewilderment and confusion at the thought of release. At discharge, he passed into society "morally unhealthy and diseased." Dickens's charges were unoriginal. Many American reformers had criticized the Pennsylvania practice of long-term solitary confinement as "unnecessarily severe."[30] They preferred the New York system of nighttime solitude and daytime silence.

New York Warden Elam Lynds required his inmates to observe total silence and enforced this requirement with the whip, saying, "I consider it impossible to govern a large prison without a whip." Levi Burr, a three-year prisoner at Lynds's Sing Sing prison, called attention to the frequency of floggings by labeling the institution a "Cat-ocracy" and "Cudgel-ocracy." English observer William Crawford agreed that the whip produced "instantaneous and unqualified submission," but prisoners felt degraded and sought revenge.[31] Where penal reformers succeeded in eliminating traditional *public* punishments, which were often physically brutal, reform-minded prison officials reproduced brutality behind penitentiary walls. Along with long-term solitary confinement and whippings, officials enforced prison discipline with denials of exercise, reduced rations, forfeited meals, darkened cells, tranquilizer chairs, straitjackets, iron jackets, iron chains, wooden blocks, and gags. Brutal punishments were apparently tolerable when concealed from public sight and oversight.

* * *

Early American penal reformers were quite inventive in devising new ways to reduce prisoner liberty. Several called for indeterminate sentencing. Caleb Lownes felt that inmates' time in penitentiaries should depend partly on the nature and severity of their crimes as determined by a court of law and partly on inmates' degree of penitence, good behavior, and future prospects for good citizenship as determined by prison officials. William Roscoe recommended giving prison administrators the authority to add extra time to prisoner sentences to ensure "a reasonable and sufficient time for the inculcation of better principles and habits and the effectual reformation of the offender." These suggestions presumed an extraordinary faith in public officials' willingness and ability to exercise broad discretionary authority in fair and effective ways; they also exhibited little concern for the denial of prisoner liberty.[32] Reform-minded officials did in fact find ways to extend court-mandated sentences. The Connecticut State Prison punished disorderly prisoners with solitary confinement on reduced rations and then, "for every day thus passed in solitude, a day is added to the prisoner's sentence." The Indiana State Prison was typical of other penitentiaries that lengthened the incarceration of convicts who had not fully paid their court fines and prison fees. William Stuart reported that he was imprisoned for four months beyond his original sentence so as to work off the remaining costs of his trial and confinement.[33]

Some reformers wanted the state to continue to restrict convict liberty beyond inmates' discharge from prison. James Mease recommended that officials offer to pardon a convict "on condition that he will remove himself to such place, out of the bounds of the United States, as shall be pointed out to him, and not to return." Francis Lieber proposed that prisons release convicts into the countryside and prevent them "from returning to large cities," where temptation and vice often lured offenders back into crime. To the degree that officials could determine a convict's postprison environment, they could indirectly police his behavior.[34]

Reformers and officials experimented with economic incentives to police discharged prisoners' conduct. Where institutions paid convicts for their prison labor, Thomas Eddy suggested that payments be deferred to the moment of discharge. The actual amount paid out was to be based on officials' estimate of whether the freed prisoner would use the money wisely or not.

If inspectors felt the convict would squander his earnings, they would give him "one or two dollars only." If inspectors felt the freed prisoner's prospects were brighter, "a larger sum is allowed." Knowing that officials might misjudge the degree and durability of a convict's rehabilitation, Eddy added, "On the discharge of a prisoner who appears meritorious, a trifling sum is given him, and a promise in writing by the inspectors to pay him the residue of such sum as is agreed upon; provided, that at the expiration of three months after his discharge, he shall produce a certificate, signed by creditable citizens, to the satisfaction of the inspectors, that he has, during that period, behaved orderly, soberly, and industriously; otherwise the promise to be void." Using economic incentives, officials could police the behavior of former convicts for months after they returned to free society.[35]

Edward Livingston, also encouraging officials to police postprison behavior, proposed that penitentiaries reward "convict industry, obedience, repentance, and reformation" with a certificate attesting to "good conduct, industry, and skill." This certificate would help the deserving individual regain society's confidence and attain honest employment. But a certificate was not enough. Livingston recommended that the depth and durability of prisoner rehabilitation be tested by "a proper interval of probation." A convict would be released into free society, where his behavior would be scrutinized. If he passed probation, officials would "assign him a place in society which will enable him to subsist without reproach." If scrutiny revealed backsliding, he would be returned to prison. Livingston also felt that the convict should be discharged into an early version of a halfway house, where he would find temporary shelter and employment and "pass the dangerous and trying period between the acquisition of his liberty and restoration of the confidence of society." Livingston's plan treated discharged prisoners like apprenticed delinquents. They would be released into society but remain subjected to state authority, monitoring, and recall for a considerable period. In effect, they would serve an apprenticeship in liberty to prove they deserved it.[36]

Some reformers contemplated the possibility of extending prison discipline into institutions in free society. Boston's Prison Discipline Society suggested that the New York system of nighttime solitude and silent, daytime congregate labor might be applied in "families, schools, academies, colleges, factories, [and] mechanics' shops"—social institutions where large numbers of people gathered and thereby created a potential for public disorder. Penitentiary regimens would discipline individuals and ensure "order, seriousness, and purity" among them. Boston reformers also thought about imposing penitentiary discipline on at-risk individuals "who are not yet lost to virtue but prone to evil." Included in this group were "large numbers of youth of both sexes . . . exposed to youthful lusts" as well as the "vicious poor." Indeed, "the time is not distant when to a much greater extent than at present, institutions of all kinds intended to reform men or prepare the rising generation for usefulness will provide places, materials, and hours for labor as part of the system." Here, Boston reformers speculated that a significant segment of American society might be remanded to forced labor camps for at-risk children and at-risk adults.[37]

Most reformers were more modest. They suggested that penitentiary discipline be applied to public institutions such as asylums, almshouses, and schools. The idea that patriarchal police power could legitimately employ coercion to incarcerate marginal people—to secure order and prepare disorderly persons for liberty—proved to be remarkably palatable to a people who fought a revolution for independence and liberty.[38]

* * *

Could prison officials be trusted to wield so much power over inmates? John Reynolds called it an "absolute impossibility" to find "proper persons" to staff prisons. None but "the true sons of an uncompromising and iron-hearted severity will consent to perform for any considerable time the unenviable task of inflicting pain on a fellow creature." Prison policies could be "as merciful as they are wise" and prison officers could be "warmed with the pure glow of benevolent and Christian feeling," but wardens and guards regularly evolved into "cruel and heartless" brutes "intoxicated with power."[39] William Stuart agreed: "Prison keepers are usually despots. Their words are law, peremptory and inflexible. Their station very naturally engenders a spirit of tyranny and oppression, which they are apt to manifest unnecessarily. Their feelings of benevolence, when first entering upon their duties, are shocked, in due time blunted, and finally extinguished." The "unfeeling Nero" who commanded nearly every penal institution practiced "unholy, illegal, and secret oppression." Inmate Ann Carson detested the "Nero" who ran Philadelphia's Walnut Street Prison, which she considered "better calculated for a Turkish prison than one in a mild republican government."[40]

W. A. Coffey claimed that penitentiaries were run by "the worst men that society could produce." Their cruelty was especially disturbing because it was concealed by "the umbrage of the law." Coffey traced the original source of cruelty in his prison to the "brutal caprice" of the head keeper, who set the tone for an institution in which sadistic guards "laughed heartily" when whipping convicts. In reformer theory, the legal and moral relationship between the principal keeper and the inmates was supposed to be "very like that between a parent and his children." The warden should have been a "father" to inmates. However, Coffey reported, his warden's inhumanity instead produced resentment among his "children." From prisoners' vantage point, paternalistic rhetoric could not mask the fact that the penitentiary was actually a "college of depravity" rather than what reformers claimed was a school for liberty.[41]

Historian Paul Keve explains why reform-minded officials rarely endured: "A warden who tries to be humane . . . may be perceived as bumbling and too lenient. He is eventually replaced by someone seen as a no-nonsense, tough-minded administrator."[42] Many reformers did call for tough-minded prison wardens. Only rarely did they notice keeper brutality or condemn prison officials for it. It was unusual that New York Commissioner Samuel M. Hopkins accused Sing Sing Warden Elam Lynds of being "a despot" who exercised "the will of an absolute dictator." More predictable, a Senate committee dismissed the charge. Penal reformers' norm and public officials' practice was to presume that prison officials wielded police power properly.[43]

* * *

Reformers were convinced that prison officials needed broad discretionary powers for incapacitating, incarcerating, and rehabilitating criminals. A strong sense of necessity overshadowed any lingering fears of guard abuse. Nevertheless, reformers saw themselves as enlightened participants in an emerging liberal society founded on skepticism of patriarchal political authority. They addressed this skepticism, in part, by infusing the patriarchal exercise of police power with the familiar rhetoric of paternalism. Although the veracity of this rhetoric was disputed by convicts who suffered abuse, it was rarely questioned by an American public that could no longer observe convict punishments, because they had been removed from accessible public venues to controlled environments concealed behind penitentiary walls.

Dubber notes that prison officials' exercise of police power presumed "good faith on the part of the warden, or other correctional officers." Furthermore, prison discipline was "presumed to have been motivated by a concern for the welfare of their object (the prisoner), or at least of the prison community as a whole."[44] This presumption of good faith in the service of prisoner welfare was implicit in reformers' understanding of penitentiaries as houses of penitence and correction that were "organized under a quasi-familial model . . . with the warden occupying the position of head of household, and the guards acting as his overseers."[45] Reformers used benign paternalistic language to promote the idea that wardens and guards were sincere and trustworthy and acted out of a fatherly concern for the good of inmates, their families, and society as a whole.

Boston reformers asserted that the success of penal reform depended on the state's ability to choose "men of great integrity" to govern penal institutions: "Without such men, neither this plan nor any other can save the state from continual fraud."[46] French observers Alexis de Tocqueville and Gustave de Beaumont reported that American prisons were governed by men whose pious caring and compassionate paternalism cushioned the impact of what would otherwise be "the spectacle of the most complete despotism." Accordingly, America's reform-minded wardens were said to communicate their authority as "that of a father over his children."[47] The language of religious benevolence and paternal caring framed police power as comforting, not threatening.

Reformers and legislators defined wardens' mission as paternalistic control and guidance. Robert Turnbull described the administration of the Walnut Street Prison in familial terms. Responding to the question of whether criminals could be rehabilitated, Turnbull noted that if "a profligate son" could be "amended by precepts given in the influxious language of parental instruction," the criminal's vices could be amended in the same way. After all, "a nation is merely a family in large." Ideally, keepers provided paternal instruction to inmates and commanded their respect by speaking authoritatively but mildly to them. A fatherly warden could "boast of being a protector—an instructor—not an iron-hearted overseer!" Turnbull reported that the Walnut Street Prison's first head jailer excelled in the dual role of father and father figure. "Discharging the duties of a tender parent," he nursed his daughter through the yellow fever only to succumb to the disease himself, leaving the prisoners "to regret the loss of a friend and protector."[48]

Reformers regularly used the idiom of fatherhood to legitimize prison officials' discretionary authority. When disciplining prisoners, reformers admonished, wardens were to exercise their authority "with humanity and discretion, without passion, and with such a temper of mind and feeling as will convince the offender that the chastisement is given solely for his good." Reformers expected prisoners to appreciate this paternalistic treatment. Before being hanged, for example, Richard Barrick complimented his jailers for "having treated us [inmates] more like children than criminals." In his prison memoirs, John Reynolds praised the few officials who, "by a kind and fatherly administration," endeared themselves to inmates. Their paternalism, "warmed with the pure glow of benevolent and Christian feeling," drove many a "prodigal child" back to his mother and a "reclaimed" husband back to his wife.[49]

Fatherly wardens, "benevolent, upright, and gentlemanly," were to use their discretionary authority to "break down the obdurate spirit" of inmates, paying "close attention to discover the evil propensities that have led to the crimes" and cultivating "a knowledge of human nature to apply the proper correctives." For Edward Livingston, penitentiary officials were "no longer jailers and turnkeys charged with the custody of the body only"; they were now spiritual guides who ministered to the "diseased minds" and "depraved habits" of their "patients." Their compassion would "tranquilize the tumultuous feelings of despair" and "prepare the mind to receive impressions favorable to future amendment." It was most important, William Roscoe advised, that officials take "a sincere interest in the welfare of the offender" and convince him that his punishment is "inflicted upon him for his own good."[50]

Would paternalistic prison officials actually be seen by inmates as beloved fathers of their prison households? Inmate-author criticisms notwithstanding, Warden Gershom Powers argued that prison officials' perceived status as institutional father figures explained how it was possible for a single unarmed guard to maintain control of fifty or sixty convicts (in a workshop where prisoners had easy access to a number of deadly instruments) when one inmate committed an infraction. He wrote, "As a father would call up a rebellious son," the jailer would call up a disorderly inmate and punish him in the presence of the other convicts. "The delinquent almost uniformly received his punishment submissively" and returned to work. In the rare case that the prisoner resisted punishment or assaulted the guard, "the other convicts have never failed to rush instantly to [the guard's] relief and protection." Powers concluded, "So strongly does this moral and kind feeling pervade the mass of the convicts towards their keepers that the latter feel the most perfect security in their unarmed and exposed condition."[51] Jailers were safe because paternalism generated inmate obedience and loyalty.

When discussing young delinquents, reformers' paternalistic rhetoric escalated. Reformers idealized administrators of houses of refuge as surrogate parents, not prison keepers. The superintendent was "a father to the fatherless." He exhibited "parental goodness of heart." His institution was "strictly paternal." For the New York Committee on Juvenile Delinquents, this paternalistic language reflected a more general obligation of public officials to serve as guardians of youthful virtue. "Every feeling of justice" urged officials to act as "political fathers" of "the unprotected" and of "juvenile culprits." An "energetic parental government" was needed to transform at-risk youths and young criminals into productive citizens.[52]

Child savers were convinced that public officials had an obligation to act in loco parentis to root out childhood corruption. They should help at-risk children by detaining them and guiding them to maturity. Good parenting by their fathers or by fatherly state officials was essential to children's preparation for adulthood and citizenship. Legislators authorized officials to assume paternal authority over both noncriminal and criminal youths. The 1838 case of ex parte *Crouse* legitimized this authority. Pennsylvania's Supreme Court invoked the doctrine of *parens patriae* (the state's right to stand as guardian to minors) to justify state officials' authority to detain noncriminal youth.[53]

It was a relatively short step from justifying officials' paternal guidance of at-risk youths to legitimizing officials' paternal authority over at-risk adults. Suppose that chronological age was a poor indicator of maturity. Could ignorant, impassioned, malicious, vengeful, intoxicated adult white males be treated as if they were at-risk minors who would commit crimes unless they too were deprived of liberty by political father figures who sought to transform them into mature adults? Furthermore, could disorderly women, free blacks, and rebellious slaves—who had little or no *recognized* capacity to make conscientious, rational decisions and whose characters were often considered infantile and incorrigible—also be treated as at-risk minors who needed to be governed by trustworthy father figures?

Benjamin Rush, who recommended institutionalizing criminals, the insane, drunkards, and even school children, was not particularly concerned that public officials who exercised nearly unlimited authority over their subjects would abuse their police power. He compared officials' broad discretion to the paternalism evident in "the best governed families and schools," where "the faults of servants and children are rebuked privately and where confinement and solitude are preferred for correction to the use of the rod." Like servants and children (as well as the insane, alcoholic, and naïve), convicts were to be subjected to paternalistic guidance for their own good.[54]

Echoing Rush's logic, inmate-author William Burroughs criticized his keepers less for exercising patriarchal power than for exercising it without paternalistic caring. Burroughs explained that God the Father loved all mankind, good people and vicious criminals alike. Prison officials should emulate God by exhibiting paternal benevolence toward all convicts. They were to govern inmates the same way that a devoted father governed his family, treating good children and bad children "as equal members of his household" who deserved "compassion." Unfortunately, prison officials often exhibited little paternal "benevolence and compassion" and instead practiced "cruelty and severity."[55] For reformer Rush and critic Burroughs alike, the problem was not patriarchal police power so much as officials' heartless applications of it.

* * *

Reformers' use of paternalistic rhetoric helped make the exercise of police power to strip people of liberty more palatable. Several reformers went further; they sought to make the exercise of police power to strip people of liberty positively virtuous. They portrayed subordination and imprisonment as temporary means to prepare individuals for greater autonomy and disciplined liberty. For them, long-term incarceration was an investment that would benefit both today's law-abiding citizens (by incapacitating wrongdoers) and tomorrow's discharged convicts (who would be rehabilitated into law-abiding citizens).[56]

Thomas Jefferson supported the institution of indentured servitude. Europeans contracted to pay their passage to America by promising to perform service for several years. "So mild was this kind of servitude," Jefferson wrote, "that it was very frequent for foreigners who carried to America money enough, not only to pay their passage, but to buy themselves a farm, it was common I say for them to indent themselves to a master for three years, for a certain sum of money, with a view to learn the husbandry of the country." Meanwhile, poor Europeans who indented themselves to pay their passage to America "are better fed, better clothed, and have lighter labor than while in Europe." What differentiated indentured servitude from both wage labor and slavery was the anticipated outcome. Jefferson expected former indentured servants to "buy a farm, marry, and enjoy all the sweets of a domestic society of their own." Servitude was tolerable, even admirable, if the temporary servant had a reasonable prospect of acquiring his own farm—the economic and cultural foundation of individuals' autonomy and citizens' liberty.[57]

Although Jefferson's initial argument for supporting indentured servitude was that it was founded on participants' voluntary consent to a contract, he did not take this argument very far. Consent was important but not decisive. His stronger argument was that indentured servitude was consistent with robust liberty and public order. Those who traded servitude for the cost of passage to America would eventually become independent family farmers and law-abiding citizens. A few years of mild servitude *today* were well worth the liberty and welfare expected *tomorrow*.

A physician by trade, Dr. Benjamin Rush injected the exercise of patriarchal police power into this analysis. Whether the issue was curing the mentally insane or rehabilitating criminals, Rush believed that the state must use its police power to take subjects into its custody, treat them, and eventually release them to be mature, free citizens. It was necessary for the state to remove subjects from free society, where they were exposed to irregular influences. They were to be sequestered (i.e., imprisoned) in self-contained institutions where authorities would establish "complete government" over them. Following the best practices of an enlightened age, authorities would remove negative influences from their institutional environment and devise positive influences intended to reshape subjects' thought and behavior. Rush wanted patients and prisoners to be prohibited liquor (and sex) but provided solitude and silence. His clinical assessment was that excessive drinking caused madness; his moral evaluation was that liquor "seldom fails of rousing every latent spark of vice into action"; his political analysis was that intemperance was "a greater enemy to the prosperity and liberties of the United States than the fleets of Britain and the armies of Bonaparte." Meanwhile, the inmates of asylums and penitentiaries would be exposed to long periods of solitude and sleep to calm their passions and stimulate their moral reflections.[58]

Rush considered the state's denial of subjects' liberty acceptable for two reasons. First, the loss of liberty needed to be balanced against the benefits. People who were slaves to alcohol, sex, and other passions, once institutionalized, could be set free from their internal demons and thereby become free to develop into productive, law-abiding citizens. Second, this loss of liberty was meant to be temporary. Like children who were denied a will of their own until they matured into adults, institutionalized subjects temporarily lost their liberty in anticipation of transitioning to a more mature, robust liberty. Rush wanted officials to exercise patriarchal police power by assuming the role of institutional father figures who governed minors and adults in the expectation that, one day, they would be fully prepared for freedom. Indeed, every penal reformer gambled that incarceration today would yield greater liberty tomorrow.

Punishment is "the most extreme of the state's powers over citizens" and "the test of its dealings with citizens in all lesser exercises of authority."[59] The idea of punishing free people by depriving them of liberty for many years and, simultaneously, offering to them "hopes of obtaining a restoration of liberty arising from a propriety of conduct" was a dramatic effort to reconcile Americans' revolutionary dedication to liberty with their leaders' postwar fear of licentiousness.[60] This dramatic effort was possible because leaders' commitment to liberty was limited and their attachment to patriarchy was durable; it was plausible because the exercise of the state's police power seemed necessary for the survival of the new Republic; and it was palatable because reformers portrayed public officials as father figures who stripped people of liberty for their own good, ultimately so that they could achieve a more robust and disciplined liberty.

FIVE

Criminal Police and Criminal Law in the *Rechtsstaat*

MARKUS D. DUBBER

Introduction

Modern state government, despite the trappings of principled rule, good governance, and most notably, the rule of law and its variants (the principle of legality comes to mind), bears a genetic resemblance to the ancient practice of household government.[1] The patriarchal origins of state power need to be exposed; it's worth pointing out that the emperor still has no clothes, that state power at bottom today is as naked as was the power of the *pater familias* and the *oikonomikos* before him.

Much work of this sort remains to be done—the exposure of the patriarchal elements of modern state action has only begun. Even criminal law, one small part of the state's arsenal of punitive and quasi-punitive measures, where the deeply heteronomous, hierarchical, discretionary, and oppressive nature of state power is more apparent than in many other forms of state action, still awaits detailed analysis from the standpoint of police.

This chapter, however, takes a different tack. It turns from charting the police apparatus, the inner workings of modern state government as patriarchal power, to studying its veneer of legitimacy.[2] It flips the hypocrisy of the modern state as police regime upside down, or right side up, by taking its declarations of principle, its reach for legitimacy, at face value. It is part of a project that parallels and complements the police project and asks the simple question, What would state government look like if it were to conform to the principles that are said to legitimate it? Let's call this project the law project for now.

It's tempting to think of the law project as an inquiry into the ideal and of the police project as an inquiry into the actual. This would be misleading, however, since the law project is not limited to capturing the ideals invoked in legitimating rhetoric but also considers actual state practice to see how they measure up against these ideals. Both the police project and the law project are instances of critical analysis, in that they combine investigation and description with critique. The law project is more critical than the police project for substantive, rather than formal, reasons. Law recognizes principles against which the legitimacy of state action can be measured. Police does not—or to put it more charitably and perhaps even more accurately, it resists the very sort of legitimacy inquiry that law invites. Police is not without rules and patterns that can be catalogued and refined in an art or even a science of police; at bottom, however, police turns on the discretionary authority of a patriarch who, for all pragmatic purposes, is all-powerful. Police rules are pragmatic guidelines written by and for those wielding the power of police; their enforcement generates efficiency, good governance, not legitimacy.

At the same time, the law project is no more exclusively critical than the police project is exclusively analytic. The legitimacy of practices cannot be assessed without first carefully analyzing them. Moreover, this analysis itself does not occur in a normative vacuum or in a perspectiveless world. In the law project, state practices are regarded from the standpoint of law, much as they are regarded from the standpoint of police in the police project. The very same practice, in fact, may well combine law aspects with police aspects and may even, as a whole, appear as a manifestation of police or law, depending on how it is viewed.

This chapter, then, investigates substantive criminal law, one aspect of the state practice of criminal law, from the standpoint of law, with particular focus on that practice in the contemporary United States. This inquiry complements earlier analyses of that practice from the standpoint of police. The two inquiries are complementary in the sense that law means nothing without police. The concept of law is the Enlightenment attempt to legitimate government by bringing it within principles derived from the discovery of the person as an autonomous—quite literally, self-governing—being. Law government was meant to replace police government. Instead of replacing police, law has for over two hundred years fought for its place within a practice of government that has roots in times immemorial and that remains ingrained in the minds and habits of rulers of micro and macro households and quasi households even in societies with modern ideologies that assign to the rule of law pride of place.

Substantive criminal law here is taken to encompass rules and norms governing the definition and scope of criminal liability, which in turn are often labeled as the "general part" and "special part" of (substantive) criminal law. Other aspects of the state practice of criminal law—including procedural criminal law (criminal procedure) and prison law (correction law, execution law) will be addressed only insofar as they touch on our discussion of substantive criminal law. Cutting up the punishment pie in this way serves only analytic purposes; it also follows general (largely unreflected) convention in the legal literature.

Punishment Theory as State Theory

What, then, is the principle, or set of principles, against which the legitimacy of criminal law is to be measured? Criminal law covers norms that pertain to punishment and, more specifically, to state punishment. Punishment being a form of state action, then, one would expect that theories of the state—political theory in the lingo of the purportedly stateless Anglo-American sphere—might be a good place to start our search for principle.

Simply put, punishment is one way the state—or rather, certain individuals acting under the authority of the state—coerces its constituents. As a particularly egregious form of state coercion, punishment poses a particularly serious challenge to the legitimacy of state coercion, in particular, and state action, in general. If punishment can be justified, so can other, lesser, forms of coercive state action. If it cannot, what's the point of justifying, say, taxation (with or without representation)? If we don't know if it can, what's the point of political theory?

Contemporary political theory, to the extent it concerns itself with the legitimacy of state action at all, has found it difficult enough to divine principles for the distribution of benefits. Theories of justice are theories of distributive justice, not of penal—or *re*tributive—justice. Setting up the rules governing—or rather, the rules governing the setting up of the rules governing—a well-ordered society has occupied the minds of our best political philosophers, with no time left over for not-so-well-ordered societies that require a distinctly nonideal theory. Once we know the rules, the attitude seems to be, we can worry about how to deal with their violation later on. Political theory is, by and large, *ideal* political theory.[3]

Let's get a sense of the norm first, our political theorists say, before we move on to consider deviations from it. This makes a lot of sense as a matter of convenience. It makes considerably less sense as a matter of theory. The state is about power. Punishment is power incarnate. Therefore, a theory of the state that doesn't deal with punishment isn't a theory of the state but of a charitable organization.

It's certainly more pleasant to deal with questions of distributive justice. Distributive justice is about a good institution—the state—handing out good things to good people. Retributive justice is about the state doing bad things to bad people. Whether the state can remain good in doing bad is the question.

In addition, legitimating punishment isn't just dirty work, it's also hard. To put it bluntly, punishment is prima facie illegitimate. In punishing its constituents, the state harms the very people it is supposed to protect, by interfering with the very rights it claims to guarantee, in the name of guaranteeing them.

The deeper significance of the "presumption of innocence"[4] is a general presumption of inviolability: the state has no right to harm those it is meant to protect. On the face of it, state punishment isn't just illegitimate, it's a crime—the statutory threat of punishment looks suspiciously like "menacing,"[5] wiretapping like "eavesdropping,"[6] entrapment like "solicitation" (or even "conspiracy"),[7] searching a suspect's house like "trespass,"[8] searching (or frisking) the suspect herself like "assault,"[9] arresting her like "battery," seizing her property like "larceny," a drug bust like "possession of narcotics" (with or without intent to distribute),[10] indicting—and convicting—a defendant like "defamation,"[11] imprisoning the convict like "false imprisonment,"[12] and executing her like "homicide" ("murder,"[13] to be precise).

No matter how much political theorists might want to wish away the facts of state coercion and noncompliance, punishment and crime are here to stay. Perhaps one day we will all live justly together in a just society, without crime, without punishment, and perhaps without justice. (Marx, for one, apparently thought so.[14]) Until then, however, the task of political theory remains one of subjecting the state's claims to justice to a relentless legitimacy critique, regardless which variety of justice is at stake, distributive or retributive.

Legal theory, by contrast, has lavished considerable attention on the justification of punishment, or so it seems. Retributivists and consequentialists, deontologists and utilitarians have been plowing the field of so-called punishment theory for, not years, not decades, but centuries. Unfortunately, these punishment theorists tend to forget one crucial fact of punishment, namely, that it is a form of *state* coercion. That's not to say that punishment in other contexts may not also be of interest to the legal theorist. For instance, we might wonder whether a parent has the right to punish her child. We might even think that the answer to that question may have something to do with the answer to our question, whether the state has a right to punish a constituent. Even so, the two questions would remain distinct, no matter how related their answers might be.

Moral theory too has shown some interest in the question of punishment. In fact, traditional punishment theory is probably better thought of as an exercise in moral, rather than legal, theory. Certainly, moral theorists should have something to say about punishment. It would be silly to deny that punishment has a moral aspect. The process of judgment in cases of punishment closely resembles that of moral judgment. The particular norms are different, to be sure, but the process of determining whether they have been violated is much the same (through empathic role taking, by placing oneself in the shoes of the person subject to judgment[15]), as are the presuppositions for legal (not just criminal law) and moral accountability.[16]

And yet punishment is not *merely* a moral matter. Moral theorizing can make an important contribution to punishment theory, but it cannot exhaust the subject. Punishment, once again, is the infliction of violence in the name of the state according to the criminal law. As such, it remains in the end a problem of state theory (or political theory). Criminal law is the solution to the problem insofar as it legitimates what otherwise would be an absurd spectacle of the state harming precisely those whom it exists to protect. That effort at legitimation in turn must fail unless it keeps within the confines of personhood unmodified (as opposed to legal or political personhood [citizenship]), which are ultimately set by moral theory.

In U.S. political history, lack of interest in legitimation of punishment has a long tradition. In the Old World, Enlightenment thinkers such as Beccaria, Kant, Hegel, Voltaire, Bentham, and P. J. A. Feuerbach struggled to rationalize punishment in various ways and proposed criminal law reforms with varying degrees of detail and success (ranging from Bentham's wildly fruitless efforts to Feuerbach's influential Bavarian Penal Code of 1813). In the New World, by contrast, the rethinkers of political power, known collectively as the Founding Fathers, showed very little interest in the subject. Thomas Jefferson was the exception to the rule. But even Jefferson did not go beyond drafting a Virginia bill for greater proportionality between crimes and punishments.[17] Despite a suggestive preamble that promised "deduc[tion] from the purposes of society," the bill in fact is largely content to invoke the authority of common law—and even Anglo-Saxon—statutes and commentators. We learn, for instance, that "the laws of Æthelstan and Canute," a set of Anglo-Saxon dooms from the tenth and eleventh centuries, punished counterfeiters with cutting off the hand "that he the foul [crime] with wrought," and then displaying it "upon the mint-smithery."[18]

Jefferson, however, at least glimpsed the connection between government in general and punishment in particular. In the Declaration of Independence, he laid out the theory of legitimacy of the new American state in words that, duly secularized, still capture the core ideals of modern democratic government.

> We hold these truths to be self-evident, that all men are created equal, that they are endowed by their Creator with certain unalienable rights, that among

> these are life, liberty and the pursuit of happiness. That to secure these rights, governments are instituted among men, deriving their just powers from the consent of the governed.

Just a little later, in the preamble to his criminal law bill, Jefferson set himself the task of applying this general state theory to the problem of punishment, through which the state infringes the unalienable rights it exists to protect, in order to protect them.

> Whereas it frequently happens that wicked and dissolute men, resigning themselves to the dominion of inordinate passions, commit violations on the lives, liberties, and property of others, and the secure enjoyment of these having principally induced men to enter into society, government would be defective in its principal purpose, were it not to restrain such criminal acts by inflicting due punishments on those who perpetrate them; but it appears at the same time equally deducible from the purposes of society, that a member thereof, committing an inferior injury, does not wholly forfeit the protection of his fellow citizens, but after suffering a punishment in proportion to his offence, is entitled to their protection from all greater pain.[19]

Now what is the principle from which government drew its legitimacy? The consent of the governed. Why the consent of the governed? Because legitimate government is self-government, "of the people, by the people, for the people," in Lincoln's memorable phrase. The legitimacy of the state rests ultimately on the *autonomy* of its constituents, "the capacity of mankind for self-government," as Madison puts it in the Federalist Papers.[20]

As a type of state action, criminal law must derive its legitimacy from the same source as all other state action.[21] Punishment therefore can be legitimate only as *self-punishment*. Reconceiving the sharpest weapon of oppressive government as a manifestation of autonomy, rather than an instrument of heteronomy, is no small task. The notion of self-government in general was revolutionary enough, and putting it into practice has been notoriously difficult. But how could the criminal law, in the particular form of the notorious Bloody Code of late eighteenth-century Britain, be rendered consistent with autonomy, the one and only principle of political legitimacy?

This question never received an answer. American law never managed to come to terms with the obvious, and yet so counterintuitive, notion of self-punishment. The reason for this failure, or refusal, systematically to work out the ideal of autonomous punishment is this: offenders are not considered as constituents of the state, and punishment therefore is not a problem of government at all but a simple issue of public health.[22] In other words, punishment is a matter of police, rather than of law.

Police and Law

Criminal law, on this view, is an oxymoron. Take the Federalist Papers, for example, surely the most comprehensive, and influential, treatment of the principles of American government. The Federalists, it turns out, had a lot to say about a lot of things but very little about punishment. They were happy to leave criminal law to the states, more specifically to each state's power to regulate its "domestic police,"[23] that is, its "internal order, improvement, and prosperity."[24] When they did claim punitive power for the United States, it was only to "exact obedience,"[25] by punishing "disobedience to their resolutions"[26] and "the disorderly conduct of refractory or seditious individuals."[27] This power was necessary for the simple reason that "seditions and insurrections are, unhappily, maladies as inseparable from the body politic as tumors and eruptions from the natural body."[28] Federal punishment power therefore was needed to contain the "contagion" of insurgency, once it had erupted, from "communicat[ing] itself."[29]

The distinction between law and police was familiar to Jefferson, but has largely been forgotten. That's unfortunate because it brings out the distinguishing feature of law as a mode of governance—autonomy. Criminal law is law insofar as it is an instance of self-government, in this case of the offender. Otherwise it is a matter of heteronomy, of some people imposing their will on others. And by surrendering the ideal of autonomy, criminal police also surrenders the claim to a moral foundation, thereby extracting itself from the grasp of legitimacy scrutiny. Police isn't necessarily illegitimate; it is essentially alegitimate.

The distinction between law and police is worth reviving for purposes of critical analysis. For one thing, a theory of the law of crime and punishment needs not only a theory of crime and punishment but also of law. And the concept of police forces us to expand our focus from criminal law to law in general. Police, after all, is contrasted not only with punishment but also with law. By recovering the concept of police in its original form and scope, we see that the subordinate distinction between policing and punishing emerged only after the police concept had been contracted from the king's governance of his realm as the *pater patriae* to the mere prevention of harm. Where policing once pertained generally to the management of the commonwealth, it eventually came to be seen as a protocriminal law, which expanded penal sanctions from the infliction of personal harm to the threat of public inconvenience. So closely associated became penal police with criminal law that the distinction eventually disappeared.

Once exhumed, the origins of police turn out to differ dramatically from those of law, criminal or otherwise. For police presumes the hierarchical relationship between the members of the household—human or not, animate or not—and its head. The governor of police is the *pater familias* (*dominus* in Rome, *oikonomos* in Athens), the governed *his* household (*domus*, *oikos*).[30] By contrast, the governor of law is the moral person, who is the governed as well. The science of household management was *economics*; the science of state government, *politics*.[31] And *police* simply was the science of state government as household management—or *political economy*.[32]

The most influential American definition of police appeared in Blackstone's *Commentaries*. Blackstone derived the power to police from the king's status as "father" of his people,[33] and "*pater-familias* of the nation."[34]

> By the public police and oeconomy I mean the due regulation and domestic order of the kingdom: whereby the individuals of the state, like members of a well-governed family, are bound to conform their general behaviour to the rules of propriety, good neighbourhood, and good manners: and to be decent, industrious, and inoffensive in their respective stations.[35]

The Blackstonian concept of police dominated American police thought until the concept fell from general view in the late nineteenth century and was largely confined to various niches of American constitutional law, including the law of regulatory takings and commerce clause jurisprudence.[36] In the academic literature, traces of the distinction between police and law can be seen in First Amendment theory,[37] in Fuller's distinction between "managerial direction" and "law,"[38] in Hayek's vision of law as a "rule of just conduct,"[39] and in Herbert Packer's distinction between two models of the criminal process, "managerial" Crime Control and Due Process.[40]

The need to draw the distinction between police and law at the appropriate, fundamental, level of governance, however, disappeared with the concept of police itself. Once administrative *law* had come into its own as a *legal* discipline, the concept of police vanished. The purported legalization of the police state rendered the study of police irrelevant and transformed police science into an antiquarian pursuit. Police treatises became treatises (and casebooks) on administrative law. The last great police theorist, Ernst Freund, became the first great administrative law theorist. The last explicit attempt to distinguish law from police in general came in Freund's weighty police treatise, the culmination of the nineteenth-century tradition of police power treatises.[41]

Police and Punishment

Jefferson, who in 1779 set up a chair of Law and Police at the College of William and Mary,[42] went some way toward recognizing criminal law as a problem of *law*, rather than police. In the preamble to his criminal reform bill, he spoke of an offender as a "member" of "society" who need "not wholly forfeit the protection of his fellow citizens." But it's only the offender "committing an inferior injury" who remains within the realm of government and therefore of law; others, "whose existence is become inconsistent with the safety of their fellow citizens," are "exterminate[d]," even if only as "the last melancholy resource."[43] For the latter group, which includes traitors and murderers, punishment is not a matter of government but a matter of disposal. Literally *outlawed* beyond the community of the governed, these sources of danger must be disposed of, with or without their consent.

As imprisonment became the sanction of choice in the nineteenth century, objects of punishment—as inmates—were subjected to the discipline of their keeper—the warden. Prisons were quasi-familial institutions. They were run like families and laid out like military barracks. In the end, it mattered little which inferior position in the quasi-familial hierarchy the prisoner assumed, as child, military subordinate, "slave of the state,"[44] or all three.

The introduction of imprisonment as the paradigmatic punishment thus meant the transformation of all objects of punishment into objects of police.[45] To be punished meant to be policed. Modern imprisonment infantilized inmates by depriving them of all means of self-support. Isolated from the outside world, the inmate could not exist without the warden's assistance. Even if he had been a legal subject before, in prison he became an object of police.

The challenge facing any attempt to legitimate punishment in a modern democratic state is to render the punishment of a particular person consistent with the fundamental principle of legitimacy, autonomy. This challenge, once it is realized in its full scope, cannot be met by reclassifying persons as police objects. Denying the object of punishment the capacity for autonomy does not legitimate her punishment; it redefines her punishment as discipline and thus denies the need for legitimation in the first place.

The answer to the question of who is entitled to respect for her autonomy and thus to a legitimation of the infliction of punitive pain at the hands of the very state that exists to safeguard her autonomy is clear, and it has been clear at least since the Declaration of Independence, which declared in simple terms "that all men are created equal, that they are endowed by their Creator with certain unalienable rights, that among these are life, liberty and the pursuit of happiness."

The "unalienable" rights that the state both protects and infringes through punishment, in other words, are rights of "all men," that is, they are human rights. And the only way the state—or for that matter anyone else—may interfere with these rights is by the consent of those who possess them, unalienably. Or to put it more accurately, the state is categorically prohibited from interfering with the human rights of the men who "instituted" it "to secure these rights." At the same time, the state enjoys certain "just powers" to perform its function, if necessary through coercion. These coercive powers include the power to tax and the power to punish, both of which deprive men of the "lives, liberties, and property" they formed the state to protect. This deprivation doesn't amount to an interference with the governed's "unalienable" rights as a person if and only if she consents to it.

The experience of being deprived of "lives, liberties, and property" without their consent was very real to the Founding Fathers of the American republic. They knew very well what it was like to be treated as an object, but not as the subject, of government, as the governed, without being the governor. The famous preamble of the Declaration of Independence, after all, was just that, a preamble to a long list of grievances against "the present King of Great Britain." Among these were not only "imposing taxes on us without our consent" but also "depriving us in many cases, of the benefits of trial by jury," "transporting us beyond seas to be tried for pretended offenses," and even "declaring us out of his protection and waging war against us."

In other words, the British king treated Americans as objects of regulation, rather than as subjects of law. They had been declared outlaws, removed from the realm of law into that of war. They had no say in the making of coercive state measures. That's the problem with establishing taxes "without our consent." It wasn't that they objected to being taxed, that is, to being deprived of their property; they objected to being taxed *without their consent*.[46]

They had not only no say in the making of coercive state measures but no voice in their application either. Being transported to England meant being tried not by their peers but by Englishmen. But the whole point of the jury trial was to have the verdict rendered by representatives of the community of the accused. The jury verdict thus was an indirect self-judgment, a judgment if not by the accused himself then at least by his peers, that is, by those connected to him through a bond of mutual identification.[47] The jury wasn't just a voice of any community, but a voice of the community *of the accused*. This identification, however, was rendered impossible in a trial before a jury of nonpeers, hostile nonpeers to boot. In that case, the jury trial became a farce and rendered the application of penal norms more, rather than less, oppressive as the accused now faced not only the judge but also the jury.

At first sight, it might seem odd that Jefferson would group a complaint about taxation without consent, or the more familiar "taxation without representation," with a complaint about jury trials in England. The connection becomes clear, however, as soon as one realizes that taxation and punishment are but two ways in which the state deprives its constituents of the very goods—properties, Locke would say—it's supposed to protect. More fundamentally, both point up violations of the right to consent, one at the stage of making law, the other at the stage of applying it, that is, legislative and adjudicatory consent. In sum, state action—punishment or taxation—is legitimate only insofar as it is consistent with the principle of autonomy.

Substantive Criminal Law

In this, the final, section, let us briefly consider some central features of the norms of substantive criminal law in light of the principle of autonomy.

The concept of autonomy can be seen as underlying much of the criminal law's general part, which lays out the general principles of criminal liability.[48] Criminal liability attaches to persons capable of autonomy. Conversely, anyone without that capacity is not punishable—including the criminally insane and children. The capacity for autonomy is a necessary precondition for criminal liability, but it's not sufficient. To be punished, rather than merely punishable, a person must have actually exercised her capacity for autonomy in committing the crime. The voluntary act requirement ensures that punishment attaches only to actual manifestations of one's capacity for autonomy.[49]

To account for the act requirement, rather than the *voluntary* act requirement, we need to expand our focus from the offender's to the victim's autonomy. If it is correct that the state addresses the objects of its governance through law as persons, that is, as possessing a capacity for autonomy, then victims in the criminal law must be conceived of as persons as well. In fact, we might think of crime as a particular kind of interaction between two persons, both capable of autonomy. In this light, crime appears as a particular type of interference with one person's autonomy (the victim) by another (the offender); more specifically, it is one person's autonomous assault on the autonomy of another. The offender manifests her autonomy at the expense of the victim's. In her criminal act, she removes the victim's self from the position of control and replaces it with her own. In some cases, this act of interpersonal violation results in the permanent destruction of the victim's capacity for autonomy, through death or catastrophic brain injury. In others, it affects the victim's ability to exercise that capacity to a greater or lesser degree. Criminal law is the state's response to crime through punishment, designed to reaffirm the autonomy of the former without denying the autonomy of the latter.

It is the victim's right of autonomy that the offender has violated, or at least has done her best to violate.[50] The law's function is to protect that autonomy from serious interference. The *criminal* law helps the state discharge that function through deterrence and, if necessary, through punishment—that is, through the threat, imposition, and infliction of punishment, the various aspects of the criminal process that correspond to increasing levels of coercion. In this sense, one might say that the victim has a right to *have* the offender punished, provided that no other measures to vindicate her autonomy, such as through the law of compensation, are available.[51] Analogously, the offender can be said to have the right to *be* punished, insofar as treating her as an ahuman source of danger denies her the "dignity and respect" she "deserves," not as a victim or an offender but as a person.[52] In the criminal law, the state vindicates both rights, thereby doing its job of manifesting and protecting the autonomy of all of its constituents.

Now, if crime is one person's autonomous violation of the autonomy of another, such a violation will be impossible without an external act. The offender's act is the manifestation of her autonomy through the subjugation of the victim—the offender acts out her capacity for autonomy through heteronomy over the victim.[53] We need more than an act requirement; we need a voluntary act requirement, because otherwise this interference with the external world, however harmful to others it might be in a broad sense, is not a manifestation of the actor's autonomy.[54]

After *actus reus*, let's briefly consider *mens rea*, the other offense element of classical American criminal law. Without intent, the offender's act is not sufficiently directed at the denial—and even the destruction—of the victim's autonomy to qualify as a crime, that is, an *assault* on the victim as a person. It is for this reason, I think, that the criminal law has treated the punishment of negligent crimes with embarrassed silence—and has generally limited negligence liability to the infliction of serious harm (specifically death).[55] The victim of a negligent crime cannot be considered the *object* of the offender's act, against whom the crime was committed.[56] A person harmed as a result of a negligent crime is not victimized, or at least is victimized in a fundamentally different sense than is the victim of an intentional crime.

Negligent and intentional crimes share several features. Negligent crimes may end up severely compromising a person's autonomy, even to the point of destroying her autonomy altogether (as in the case of negligent homicide). They also are committed by a person, rather than a dog or a tree, and thereby satisfy another aspect of the definition of crime as the assault by one person on the autonomy of another.

But negligent crimes differ from intentional ones in that they do not represent an attempt by one person to subjugate, or objectify, another. They may interfere with a person's autonomy, but they do not do so for the greater glory of another. The victim of a negligent crime will suffer harm, even serious harm, to her ability to exercise her capacity for autonomy but not the indignity of having been treated as the means to another person's self-aggrandizement, taken in its strict sense, that is, as the expansion of the offender's self to engulf the victim as a mere appendage.

It is this personal assault on her personhood that entitles the crime victim to victims' rights, in particular the right to have the offender punished. The offender's punishment is nothing but the dramatic reaffirmation of the victim's autonomy after the offender's criminal attempt to deny that autonomy for the sake of her own. And a crucial aspect of that reaffirmation is putting the offender in her place, among the community of persons, alongside the victim. The victim's personhood therefore is reaffirmed by exposing the offender's attempt to deny it as unsuccessful and in fact futile. Punishment communicates to the offender, the victim, and the onlooker that the offender did not succeed, and could never have succeeded, in reducing the victim to a nonperson. The offender at best can *treat* the victim as a nonperson; she cannot transform her into one.

This process of autonomy affirmation does not, and cannot, take place in negligent crimes. Since negligent crimes are not crimes in this sense, their victims are not victims of crime. There are "objects" of negligent crimes, as there are "objects" of torts, only in the general, formal, sense of *object* as that person who suffers the harm described in the definition of the negligent crime or tort. Only in this, formal, sense can one define victim as "the person who is the object of a crime *or tort*,"[57] provided one keeps in mind the fundamental, substantive, distinction between victims of crime and of tort (or negligent "crime").

So much for the notion of an offense. Autonomy also figures prominently in the system of defenses. Justifications respect a particular act of self-government by the putative offender who considers the fundamental norms of her political community and applies them to a particular case, even in the face of previous attempts to codify these norms.[58] The law of justification treats her choice, made under the extraordinary circumstances of an emergency, as an act of direct immediate self-government that deserves legal recognition even when it conflicts with prior acts of indirect self-government taken by others (the legislators) on her behalf. (In this sense, justification defenses fulfill a function similar to jury nullification, condensed into one person's deliberation.)

Similarly, the defense of consent can be seen as insulating punishable conduct from criminal liability on the ground that it doesn't interfere with the autonomy of the consenting "victim."[59] By consenting, the apparent victim rebuts the presumption of victimhood. He indicates that another's act that facially satisfies the elements of a crime does no harm to his autonomy in fact. In the light of consent, an apparent act of heteronomy is revealed as an act of autonomy.

Consent is the main doctrinal category in the law of punishment that functions as a placeholder for considerations of the victim's personhood, that is, his capacity for autonomy. American criminal law has yet to fully appreciate the central significance of the consent defense. That defense stands as a constant reminder that criminal law is about persons first. Consent as a reflection of the criminal law's basis in personal autonomy is less a defense than a general limitation, less an exception than the rule. Consent deprives the criminal process of its legitimacy, of its reason for being. It finds its broadest recognition in the Model Penal Code. According to the Code, consent is a defense if nonconsent is an element of the offense charged or if it "precludes the infliction of the harm or evil sought to be prevented by the law defining the offense."[60] That harm, however, is always the interference with the victim's autonomy. That interference is absent in the presence of consent.

One therefore would expect consent to be a defense to, or nonconsent an implicit element of, every offense. It isn't, not even in the Model Code. The Code instead preserves the traditional, and traditionally ill-supported, exception for serious bodily harm.

Attempts to justify exceptions to a general consent defense tend to consist of general references to the unique nature of criminal law. Criminal law, so it is said, is not about individual victims but about the state (or the king).[61] Insofar as this view of the criminal law as police reflects a hierarchical political community, it is as we've seen, inconsistent with the ideal of equal personhood that underlies not only the political theory of American government in particular but also of Enlightenment moral and political theory in general. Moreover, it proves too much. If it is correct that the state is the victim of every crime, then consent should be a defense to none.

A failure to recognize consent as a defense in the law of punishment amounts to a violation of the prima facie victim's fundamental right to autonomy. It also violates the apparent *offender's* right to autonomy, assuming her facially criminal conduct manifested an agreement between her and the apparent victim (as opposed to merely carrying out the "victim's" orders, say).

Punishing the apparent offender therefore would do nothing to vindicate autonomy. On the contrary, it would deny the autonomy of offender and victim alike.

As to excuses, if crime is the autonomous violation of another person's autonomy, then the lack of the capacity for autonomy or the inability to exercise that capacity will bar criminal liability. This accounts for the incapacity excuses—insanity and infancy—as well as the inability excuses—duress, entrapment, intoxication, superior orders, provocation.

Autonomy shapes not only the general part of criminal law but also its special part, which deals with specific offenses, as opposed to general principles of liability. Here it's, once again, the victim's autonomy that matters. The scope of criminal law is defined by the state's authority to protect the autonomy, or personhood, of its constituents.[62] The German Penal Code, for example, makes the significance of autonomy explicit by classifying various crimes as crimes against autonomy.[63]

Autonomy, in other words, determines the nature of criminal harm—as well as the nature of criminal conduct. In this respect, it puts meat on the bones of Mill's "harm" principle, which recently has been rediscovered—by commentators and courts alike—as a stand-in for *criminal* harm.[64] Not all harm is criminal harm. Criminal harm is limited to autonomy harm. The criminal law protects different qualities and quantities of autonomy harm. One might, for instance, draw a qualitative distinction between harm to the capacity for autonomy and harm to the ability to exercise that capacity. Among harms to the capacity for autonomy, another line might be drawn between harm that amounts to a destruction of the capacity and harm that merely compromises it. Certain offenses permanently deprive the victim of her personhood. These include homicide and certain types of assault that eliminate the victim's capacity to govern herself, that is, to generate and to recognize norms as her own and to follow them in her conduct—assaults, in other words, that transform the victim into someone who, if charged with an offense, would be entitled to an insanity defense. The law further distinguishes homicide from these depersonalizing assaults, presumably on the ground that only the former definitively works a permanent destruction of personhood—no matter how reliable the predictions of medical science might be regarding the extent and the curability of a particular condition short of death.

Among harms to the ability to exercise one's capacity for autonomy, one might draw quantitative distinctions based on the centrality and permanence of the autonomy harm.[65] These distinctions, being merely quantitative, don't generate hard and fast rules. But we might conclude that, in general, physical health is more significant to the exercise of one's capacity for autonomy than psychological health, though psychological harm may of course also be debilitating. In the end, the distinction between physical and psychological harm may not be particularly useful. Regardless of their relative seriousness—understood as the degree of interference with the ability to exercise one's capacity for autonomy—it might still be useful to retain analytic distinctions among various aspects of autonomy that the criminal law, in its special part, sets out to protect and to manifest.

This focus on harm to autonomy draws into question a significant portion, and probably the bulk (no one can know for sure), of what goes under the name of modern criminal law. If autonomy is the legitimating principle of law, then the legitimacy of a particular exercise of law power turns on its proximity to autonomy. Most suspect are public welfare offenses, and police offenses generally speaking, which set out to extinguish threats—or police anything or anyone offensive—to, rather than actual violations of, well, public welfare and police rather than to particular groups or to individual persons, never mind their autonomy. The legitimacy of these offenses is suspect for two reasons: first, because they are not concerned with the protection or manifestation of personal autonomy but instead with some other interest, and second, because they are not concerned with autonomous violations of these interests but with offenses or threats to them, regardless of the personhood of the source of these offenses or threats. In other words, the legitimacy of police offenses is suspect because they treat neither victims nor offenders as persons capable of autonomy—they are both victimless and offenderless at the same time. In the final analysis, these offenses police threats to the authority of the state. They are pure disobedience offenses.

Possession offenses are suspect in this sense.[66] They punish the relation between an object and its possessor, often without regard to the possessor's awareness of the particular nature of the object, solely on the ground that this relation has been declared "unlawful" by the state. (That's why justification defenses, which assert the lawfulness of facially criminal conduct, are irrelevant in possession cases.[67]) They do not, in other words, punish a person for manifesting her autonomy—they are, in short, offenderless. There is likewise no connection to the autonomy of another person, the victim—they're victimless as well. The interference with another's autonomy requires an act of some sort—that's why we have the act requirement. Possession, however, isn't an act of any kind, autonomy limiting or affirming. Use at least has the potential of causing harm, or good. Possession, however, is twice removed from use; it is an inchoate, inchoate offense.

To see the remoteness of possession as a threat to some interest or right, one might distinguish between two types of possession offenses, *simple* possession and possession with intent, or *compound* possession. Simple possession itself can, but need not, require proof of actual or constructive awareness—that you knew or should have known that you possessed the object in question. If it doesn't, it's a strict liability offense. Possession with intent is by definition not a strict liability offense, since it requires proof of intent.

It may be helpful to view the varieties of possession along a continuum from dangerousness at the one end to its manifestation at the other. At the end of pure dangerousness is simple possession. Here we are farthest removed from the harm that the use of the object may cause. And in the strict liability variety of simple possession, the inference from the dangerousness of the item possessed to its possessor is most tenuous—since she by definition is not even aware of her possession. Next is compound possession, which still inflicts no harm since the possession itself is harmless, but at least we have the intent to use the item possessed in a way that may or may not be harmful. Moving further along the continuum we encounter the *preparation* to use the item possessed in some particular way. This preparation, as distinct from an attempt, is not criminalized.

Next comes the *attempt* to use the object possessed, which is a preparation that has almost, but not quite, borne fruit. And eventually, there is the use of the possessed item. In the case of drugs, that use may come in the form of a sale, as in the popular and often severely punished offense of possession with intent to distribute. Of course, the distribution itself is also entirely harmless. It's another kind of use, which may or may not follow the distribution, that renders drugs harmful: namely, their consumption. But the harmfulness of the use is not an element of a compound possession offense criminalizing possession with intent to distribute. There is no offense of possession with intent to consume.[68] Moreover, the consumption of drugs is not, or at least not without more, a harm to autonomy. On the contrary, it appears as an affirmation of the consumer's autonomy, at least with respect to substances not so addictive that their first consumption destroys the consumer's capacity for autonomy.[69] Drug possession offenses thus punish the relation between an object and its possessor, which might or might not transform itself into a particular use of that object by the possessor, which use (distribution) might or might not be transformed into another use (consumption) by some other person (the eventual consumer, who may or may not be the original recipient), which in turn appears as a prima facie affirmation of, rather than interference with, that person's autonomy. Gun possession offenses work much the same way, except that the connection between possession and use other than distribution is seen as less remote and that this eventual use is more likely to interfere with the autonomy of some person (and some person *other than* the user), where that use, moreover, is itself subject to criminal prohibition (unlike, say, the consumption of drugs).[70]

Possession offenses, in sum, are paradigmatic police offenses in that they enforce the authority of the state, in the name of extinguishing remote threats to the public police (in particular, its security) rather than punishing violations of the autonomy of particular persons. They treat their objects, possessors, not as persons who exercise their capacity for autonomy in one way or another (by not using the object possessed or by using it in a harmful, or harmless, way) but as hazards to the police and the state charged with maintaining it. Possessors, through their relation to an object, have revealed themselves as nuisances who, along with the object, require abatement. And so possessor and possessed alike are disposed of according to the nature and degree of their dangerousness. Some are cleansed of their dangerousness; others—those per se hazardous—are incapacitated. In a possession regime, everyone—except the state through its officials—is presumptively dangerous (that is, incapable of exercising one's capacity for autonomy in general or in a nonharmful way in particular). To escape punishment requires rebuttal of this presumption, through obtaining a discretionary "license" from the state or joining the state apparatus. In extreme cases, the possessor is considered so dangerous that possession in general is prohibited except as otherwise provided.[71]

In the end, possession offenses work very much like vagrancy offenses. Possession is criminal unless the possessor can give a good account of himself.[72] Both are discretionary police measures for the elimination of threats to the public police. Unlike the rather crude vagrancy offense, however, possession offenses supply the state with an efficient tool for the prolonged, and even the permanent, incapacitation of police hazards.[73]

Conclusion

The police power is a useful tool of critical analysis. On the one hand, it allows us to better appreciate the functioning of modern state government, by placing apparently disparate strategies and interventions within a systematic and historical context. On the other, it opens up opportunities for internal and external critique. To the extent that police government is subject to norms or at least guidelines, say, of efficiency or security or order or even welfare (i.e., *police* itself in its original, comprehensive, sense), its compliance with these norms can be assessed. Insofar as police government, as a mode and rationale of state governance, is also subject to the legitimacy norms generally recognized to apply to state action in, say, a liberal state or *Rechtsstaat* under the rule of law, then it can be subjected to the sort of legitimacy scrutiny outlined in this chapter.

SIX

Work and Authority in Policing

DAVID ALAN SKLANSKY

Etymology aside, what is the connection between the police power and the police? What links *police*, as an open-ended, antiliberal theory of state authority, with the uniformed police officers who are such familiar, if often controversial, fixtures of modern life?

At one level, of course, police officers are the police power incarnate. The infinitely varied ways police officers intervene coercively in the affairs of the people they "serve and protect," and the virtually limitless purposes of those interventions, offer a concrete, street-level version of what the police power provides in the abstract: an "expansive" and "amorphous" mandate, without clear limits, to act in furtherance of the public welfare.[1] Seen from this perspective, the American "criminal procedure revolution" of the 1960s was a direct attack on police as a "mode of patriarchal governance."[2] The Supreme Court sought to tame police officers, the most visible manifestations of the police power, by removing them from the realm of police and dragging them into the realm of law—the realm, that is to say, of the liberal ideal of limited government. The effort met only partial success, we might say, because the competing ideal of the well-regulated society—the ideal underlying the police power and providing police forces with their central mission—proved so stubbornly persistent.

This chapter will explore a different, less obvious connection between the police power and the police. My thesis is that the police mode of governance has frustrated efforts at American police reform over the past half century, including the criminal procedure revolution, not just by opposing those efforts from the outside but also by compromising them from within. The agenda of police reform has itself been shaped and limited by authoritarian assumptions about the nature of the police workplace: democracy in the broader society has been thought to require placing police officers under rigid, comprehensive rules, imposed from outside, or at least from the top. The contrary view—that rank-and-file police officers should participate collectively in the shaping of their work—has never gained significant traction. As a result, something like the police mode of governance has been replicated within the modern police-reform agenda.

In many ways, of course, police officers have always participated in the shaping of their work. Partners assigned to the same patrol car discuss how they should spend their time. Teams of officers plan undercover stings and neighborhood sweeps. Policing is heavily unionized, and police unions sometimes take strong positions on matters of departmental policy. Today they may be joined at the table by identity-based caucuses of police officers—groups, for example, of black or Latino or gay and lesbian officers. And even without pressure from below, wise sergeants, lieutenants, and captains—like wise supervisors in any occupation—find ways to enlist the rank and file in processes of cooperative problem solving.

But in law enforcement all of this occurs at the margins. It cuts against the grain. The dominant mind-set of police departments, police reformers, appellate judges, and criminal justice scholars—the dominant mind-set, in short, of nearly everyone who thinks about policing and its problems—is, and always has been, that policing is a place for top-down management. Good police officers are police officers who follow rules. Police unions, and police organizing more generally, are obstacles, not opportunities.[3] Democracy means the rule of law, and the rule of law means that policing is no place for exercises in workforce empowerment. If law enforcement has turned out, ironically, to be one of the last strongholds of trade unionism, it is also (and not accidentally) a lingering bastion of the Taylorist faith in scientific management. Police work is notoriously rule-bound, so much so that "all cops exist in a state of mild infraction."[4] The particular focus of police rule books is often the subject of criticism: too much attention to the proper kind of shoelaces, not enough attention to the grounds for an investigative stop. But except among police officers themselves, little sentiment can be found for giving line officers more of a say in how policing should be carried out.

Outside of policing, arguments for involving employees in workplace decision making have gained extraordinarily broad currency over the past several decades, in the public sector and private sector alike.[5] Many of those arguments, as it turns out, take on special strength when the employees in question are law enforcement officers. Nevertheless, even the fiercest foes of authoritarian workplaces tend to make an exception for law enforcement. As a result, policing has clung more stubbornly to authoritarian management practices than have other, traditionally hierarchical sectors of the American economy—manufacturing, for example, or even the military.[6] And workplace democracy has played little part in most discussions of democratic policing—far less than in discussions of the proper management of manufacturing facilities, the best way to carry out educational reform, or the optimal approach to military planning.

This chapter will explore why that is so. It will start by outlining the straightforward case for giving police officers a larger collective voice in the shaping of their work—a case that borrows heavily from arguments commonly made about other workplaces. It will then explore why those arguments are seldom heard in discussions of policing. Part of the explanation turns out to be an accident of history, but another part of the answer is more principled, having to do with a particular understanding of what the rule of law requires of the police. That understanding, I will argue, has paradoxical affinities with what might be called the police theory of state authority—not the working theory of police officers but the theory underlying the police power and traceable to the nineteenth-century, Continental understanding of police.

A few caveats are justified at the outset. *Law enforcement* and *policing* sometimes have different meanings. *Law enforcement* refers to efforts to enforce positive legal rules, whereas *policing* encompasses not only that activity but also the order-maintenance and community-caretaking functions commonly exercised by police officers. So, too, *workplace democracy* and *participatory management* often are distinguished from each other. *Workplace democracy* refers to unionism and other bottom-up efforts at employee empowerment; *participatory management* means efforts at cooperative problem solving implemented and controlled by management, often over strong objections from unions. Workplace democracy involves an actual *delegation* of power to workers, whereas participatory management typically involves only *consultation*. For the most part I will not be observing any of these distinctions. Generally, I will use *law enforcement* and *policing* interchangeably to refer to the activities of the police, and I will use both *workplace democracy* and *participatory management* to refer to efforts to allow employees, whether police officers or otherwise, to participate in the shaping of their work.

Something is lost when workplace democracy is defined so broadly: the reminder that things could be more radically restructured, that employees could be given collective authority instead of simply consulted. It is similar to what was lost when neighborhood policing, the largely unsuccessful movement in the late 1960s and early 1970s to hand over control of police departments to local residents, was replaced by community policing, the now ubiquitous set of arrangements through which police departments consult with groups outside law enforcement—with the police deciding when to consult, with whom, and about which subjects.[7] Defining democracy to encompass both delegation and consultation risks cheapening the term and obscuring the plainly important distinction between schemes that redistribute legal powers and those that seem to be just about talking. It risks obscuring, too, how systems of consultation—sometimes intentionally—can threaten to undercut more far-reaching efforts at workplace democracy, by mollifying employees and undercutting their solidarity.

I run these risks here, not because I think that underlying arrangements of power are unimportant or immutable, but because I think that certain formalized systems of consultation can be democratizing in their own right. That is to say, they can advance some, although obviously not all, of what we mean by *democracy*. They can allow people to participate collectively in the decisions that shape their lives; they can open up the channels of decision making to new perspectives and new concerns; they can advance John Dewey's project of "securing diffused and seminal intelligence."[8] This is the sense in which it makes sense to call community policing democratizing, even when—as almost always—it does little to limit the operational autonomy of the police. And in this sense even schemes of participatory management adopted unilaterally by employers and controlled by employers can, at least in some circumstances, appropriately be called democratizing.

Democracy, policing, and law enforcement are not the only terms I will define broadly. I also will take liberties with *Taylorism*. Strictly speaking, Taylorism called for simplifying manual tasks, by breaking them down and dividing them among employees, and then for controlling employees' every movement in order to eliminate inefficiency. Obviously, policing consists of more than manual labor, and no one has ever tried to break down and to routinize police work the way that Frederick Taylor broke down and routinized factory work.[9] More broadly, though, Taylorism has come to stand for a certain approach to managing work, an approach that shuns reliance on employees' intelligence and emphasizes the control of work through rigid rules promulgated from the top.[10] I will argue that we tend instinctively to take this approach to police work.

I will be contrasting Taylorism with workplace democracy, and this, too, is a simplification. A workplace can be completely undemocratic without having a touch of Taylorism. And some systems of participatory management are entirely compatible with the kind of detailed work rules Taylor favored—a point to which we return. Still, the crude dichotomy between workplace democracy, loosely defined, and Taylorism, loosely defined, will prove useful in identifying and challenging certain unstated preconceptions underlying almost all discussions of democratic policing.

I will be employing, too, the sharp distinction Markus Dubber has drawn between democracy and police as rival "modes of state governance." Dubber associates democracy with self-government, individual autonomy, and the rule of law; he associates police with autocratic "other-government, of the people by the state."[11] This way of seeing things downplays the possibility that the police power itself—that is to say, the theory that the state has broad authority, without any clear limits, to regulate in furtherance of the common welfare—might be employed democratically. It simplifies questions of state governance, that is to say, in much the same way that counterposing Taylorism and workplace democracy simplifies questions of industrial governance. Again, though, the simplification will prove useful in exploring the assumptions and limitations of modern American police reform, particularly because most discussions of democratic policing over the past half century have tended to assume a dichotomy very much like the one Dubber draws.

Police Departments as Workplaces

Top-down workplace regimentation of the kind famously advocated by Frederick Taylor still has fans, many of whom may never have heard of scientific management.[12] In the low-wage sector of the American economy, Taylorism continues to flourish, bolstered in many workplaces by new technologies of surveillance and monitoring.[13] But among management theorists and other students of employment, Taylor's ideas have long been out of fashion, and for good reasons. Fixed systems of rules that seek to control employees' every action are widely thought today to be bad for management, bad for employees, and bad for society. They are bad for management because they inevitably fail to address the full complexity of the tasks given to employees; because they make employees unmotivated and disloyal; and because they forfeit the knowledge and insights of the workforce—its "diffused and seminal intelligence."[14] They are bad for workers because they are stultifying and immiserating. And they are bad for society because they train workers in habits of alienation and passivity, rather than the habits of engagement, cooperation, and deliberation that help a democratic society flourish.

This multifaceted critique of Taylorism is conventional wisdom today among labor activists and management theorists alike. It has at least three sources: one in social theory, one in democratic theory, and one in management theory. The first source is the alienation indictment of industrial and postindustrial employment: the idea, as old as Taylorism itself, that the loss of meaningful work has helped to bring about the crippling sense of disconnection and disempowerment that pervades modern collective life.[15]

The second source is the notion that democracy consists not just in elections and representation but also, and more critically, in a broadly engaged citizenry. This way of thinking about democracy gained especially wide currency in the 1960s, when participatory democracy became the catchphrase of the New Left, but its roots are much older. It is the tradition of Rousseau, Tocqueville, and Dewey.[16] There is also a long tradition, revived in the late 1960s and early 1970s, of viewing workplaces as the ideal loci for experiments in participatory democracy: intimate enough for face-to-face conversations and important enough to make participation manifestly worthwhile.[17] The third source of disenchantment with Taylorism is the widespread enthusiasm among management theorists, beginning in the 1980s and 1990s, for workforces marked by teamwork and cooperation.[18] A large literature now advocates empowering workers, and treating them as team members instead of automatons, as a way to boost productivity and profits.

The agendas of meaningful work, industrial democracy, and cooperative management do not always coincide. Trade unions, the most familiar form of industrial democracy, can be impediments to management-controlled structures for employee participation in workplace decision making—in part because unions often suspect, sometimes with justification, that these structures are aimed chiefly at pacifying workers and undermining their solidarity.[19] Some tactics of cooperative management—quality circles, for example—have proven compatible with workplaces arguably as regimented as anything dreamed of by Frederick Taylor, even if the rules change more often, and even if employees participate in their revision.[20] For now, though, the important thing is that Taylor's agenda of improving workplace performance by minutely regulating job practices from the top down is now widely believed to be bad for management, bad for workers, and bad for society.

Each prong of the modern anti-Taylorist consensus has readily apparent implications for policing. Indeed the standard indictment of Taylorism takes on some special strength in the context of law enforcement. I will discuss that standard indictment, and its application to policing, by first considering the costs to management, then the costs to workers, and then the costs to society. Of course, the tripartite division is artificial: the interests of police managers overlap considerably both with the interests of rank-and-file police officers and with the interests of society. Still, separating out the costs to management, to officers, and to the public at large will be analytically useful.

Start with the view, now quite common, that authoritarian workplaces are bad for management. The standard arguments for this view are (a) that predetermined rules cannot possibly address the full complexity of any but the very simplest tasks, (b) that efforts to specify in advance the one best method to perform a particular job forfeit the diffused, hands-on knowledge that workers gain by actually doing the job, and (c) that rigid regulation of workers undercuts their loyalty and motivation. All three of these arguments apply at least in part to police officers, and the first and second apply with particular strength.

JOB COMPLEXITY

In the second half of the twentieth century we made a great discovery about policing: it is a very complicated job. This discovery was made in two stages. First, in the 1950s and 1960s, legal scholars and sociologists documented the extraordinary degree of discretion that police officers exercised in their work. To most of these scholars, the discretion exercised by police officers was alarming. It seemed lawless, arbitrary, and hence undemocratic.[21] The solution was to tame police discretion with rules—maybe rules promulgated by courts (the project taken up with enthusiasm by the Warren Court, and continued halfheartedly by the Burger Court), maybe rules promulgated by legislators or by the police themselves (the solutions urged by some academics), or maybe rules promulgated by civilian oversight boards (the program embraced by many community activists).[22] The second stage began in the 1970s, when skepticism began to mount that any set of rules could ever address, in anything like a comprehensive fashion, the endlessly changing circumstances encountered daily by the police.[23] Today this skepticism is conventional wisdom. Nowadays almost everyone who thinks seriously about the police recognizes that the job of a patrol officer is complex and demanding, in large part because it is so varied and unpredictable.[24]

It might be different if policing were mostly about applying the law—investigating crimes, arresting suspects based on probable cause, and so on. But we have known for decades that most activities of the police do not involve invoking the law.[25] If the police have a core function, it is not law enforcement narrowly defined but rather, in Egon Bittner's influential formulation, employing or threatening coercive force "in accordance with the dictates of an intuitive grasp of situational exigencies."[26] This is not the sort of thing that lends itself to rigid regulation.

Plenty of thoughtful people still believe we need stricter rules for the police, if not across the board, then at least with regard to particular parts of policing. But almost no one imagines that rules alone can give us better policing. The job of police officers is too varied and too complicated for that. It is surely more varied and more complicated than most factory work—jobs for which the managerial case against Taylorism has been made forcefully and cogently. If it is futile to try to prescribe in advance all the kinds of problems that an assembly line worker may confront and the solutions to each of those problems, it is even more futile to try to do the same thing for police officers.

CRAFT KNOWLEDGE

Some jobs are complicated but not by the kinds of things about which one can acquire and pass along knowledge. Mastery just comes with practice. Policing has often been thought to fall within this category. Maybe it is complicated, but it does not lend itself to the development of craft knowledge. The parts of policing that do not have to do with following rules have to do with instinct—with the gut rather than the head. Lots of people, including many cops, think this way about policing. Certainly the fictional police officers celebrated on television and in movies rely heavily on hunches and intuition.

And police departments, by and large, often seem to operate on some variant of this assumption. New officers spend time in an academy, and most sizable departments also provide opportunities for in-service training—advanced courses, for example, on developments in forensic science or in the law of search and seizure. But little effort is spent collecting and disseminating the lessons learned by officers on the job—neither the local lessons about who can or cannot be relied on in a particular neighborhood, the best routes to follow on patrol, and so forth, nor the global lessons about how to gain trust on the street, how to calm an agitated suspect, how to protect an informant, and so on.

It remains a "central fact of police work," as Egon Bittner pointed out years ago, that "every individual officer has important information that he does not share with anyone"—"substantive factual information about crime, people, social areas, conditions, etc., which are of use in getting the work of policing done." Writing in 1970, Bittner described a hierarchy of "systematic information denial," ameliorated by a "colossally complicated network of secret sharing": "Teams of partners do not talk about each other in the presence of nonteam members, line personnel do not talk about their peers in the presence of ranking officers and, of course, no members of the department talk about anything remotely connected with police work with any outsiders."[27] Police departments are less insular places today than they were in 1970, for reasons I will address later. But the pattern of "systematic information denial" remains, in large part because departments do little in any organized way to capitalize on the "diffused and seminal intelligence" of the rank and file.

It is not that police officers have nothing interesting and reflective to say about their jobs. It is a commonplace of scholarship about the police that individual officers are often far more thoughtful, reflective, and insightful than researchers expect them to be.[28] In places where rank-and-file officers have been asked to participate in policy making, the results have generally been impressive. In the early 1970s, for example, a team of researchers led by the criminologist Hans Toch asked a specially recruited group of Oakland police officers to find ways to reduce violence between officers and citizens. With the outside scholars serving largely as consultants, the officers set their own agenda, carried out their own research, and devised their own proposals. One of those proposals, a Peer Review Panel for counseling and assisting officers with a history of violent encounters, proved particularly effective. Toch and his collaborators came away impressed with the ability of rank-and-file officers to serve as "agents of change," not only in the day-to-day operation of the Peer Review Panel but also in coming up with the idea for the panel and in carrying out the research on which it was based.[29]

But such initiatives are rare. This is a loss, in the same way that it is a loss to the management of a manufacturing facility when insights from the shop floor are systematically ignored or a loss to educational reform when the views of teachers are disregarded. There may be reasons for top-down management of policing that do not apply to manufacturing. We will get to that question later. For now, though, the important point is that in policing, as elsewhere, failing to enlist rank-and-file employees in the ongoing reshaping of their job forfeits their diffused understanding and cognitive powers—"the vast amount of knowledge, insight, experience, and just plain street savvy that officers acquire," as well as their "constructive thinking, creativity, and resourcefulness."[30]

LOYALTY AND MOTIVATION

A major part of the case that management theorists advanced in the 1980s and 1990s for industrial "cooperativism" was that treating employees as tools or cogs undercuts their loyalty and motivation. Enlisting the minds and imaginations of employees was good for management not just because rules could not possibly cover all the various situations that employees confront, and not just because employees often acquired valuable knowledge and insights, but also because treating employees as team members would make them work harder and keep their jobs longer.[31]

This particular argument applies only in part to policing. Police officers tend to love their jobs and to keep them for a long time. The attrition rate for police departments has always been low—around 4 percent—even during periods when the police feel particularly embattled.[32] It is easy to lose sight of this fact, because police officers are grumblers; the occupation is marked by a kind of culture of complaint.[33] But one of the remarkable things about policing is how officers can hate the daily circumstances of their work and yet still love "the Job."[34] American police departments have many problems, but keeping officers loyal is not one of them.

Nor, in general, is getting officers to work hard. Many if not most cops are attracted to police work in part because of the excitement it promises and in part because of the opportunities it provides for service. They are attracted, in short, by the work, not just by the paycheck and the power.[35] Among their peers, cops gain respect by "good collars," by acts of physical courage, by being "completely gung-ho"[36]—not by cleverly avoiding work.[37] If anything, police tend to be *overly* enthusiastic about their work. Excessive zeal among the workforce is not a problem in most industries, but of course it has long been a major problem in policing. That is why so many of the rules imposed on police officers are aimed not at getting them to work hard but at reining in improper law enforcement tactics and why officers, especially young officers, tend to complain more bitterly about not being "allowed to do our jobs" than about the hours they have to work or the quotas they are expected to meet.[38]

Still, cynicism and shirking by police officers are hardly unknown. And it is striking how often officers themselves attribute the most notorious manifestations of these problems—the "drive-and-wave" approach to patrolling, for example—to one aspect or another of the top-down management of police departments: either to rules that prevent them from doing their jobs or to disciplinary codes that do not take sufficient account of the line officer's perspective.[39] Again, there may be good reasons—perhaps bound up with the rule of law—for denying rank-and-file officers a more significant voice in the formulation and application of the rules under which they work. We will address that possibility later. The point for now is simply that in policing, as elsewhere, there is reason to think that rigid top-down management undercuts employee motivation—even if police departments have largely managed to escape the problems of long-term loyalty that plague other employers.[40]

Law enforcement Taylorism may impose another, related cost on management: it may make it harder to recruit high-caliber officers in the first place. The educational credentials of police officers have improved dramatically over the past four decades. The vast majority of police officers in the early 1960s had never attended college; now most officers have at least two years of college education, and a sizable minority have graduate degrees.[41] Findings are inconclusive on the difference that higher education makes in police officers, but the bulk of the research suggests that, all things being equal, college-educated officers are more responsible, more imaginative, more understanding, more adaptable, better at building trust and confidence, and better at resolving conflicts.[42] For these reasons most police departments would like to hire more college-educated officers. One impediment to doing so, probably, is the lingering perception that policing is not a job that invites and rewards innovation.[43]

Some departments explicitly defend that view. New London, Connecticut, went to court several years ago to defend, successfully, its policy of refusing to hire applicants who scored too high on a test of "cognitive ability."[44] The publisher of the test recommends its use to screen out employees who will become bored by "unchallenging work"[45] with "rigid procedures"[46]—jobs "where creativity could be a detriment."[47] New London's deputy police chief told a reporter that the department had adopted the test because "police work is kind of mundane."[48] The president of the test-publishing company agreed: "You can't decide not to read someone their Miranda rights because you felt it would be more efficient, or you thought they knew them already."[49] All of this would make perfect sense to Frederick Taylor, who warned that "the man who is mentally alert and intelligent is for this very reason entirely unsuited" for monotonous work. An employee hired to handle pig iron, for example, should "be so stupid and so phlegmatic that he more nearly resembles in his mental make-up the ox than any other type."[50]

Few departments echo New London's in making this view of policing a matter of official policy. The vast majority of law enforcement executives today would endorse the position of police unionists that "the better the caliber of the police officer, the fewer problems you have in the community."[51] But by failing to encourage innovation and collective decision making among line officers, even progressive police departments may not only forfeit some of the advantage of their officers' intelligence but also send signals to potential recruits that law enforcement is not a field that welcomes thinkers. Those signals may make it hard to recruit the kinds of applicants most departments want.

ALIENATION

We have spent some time examining the attractions that participatory management in policing may hold for police departments and, by extension, for the communities they serve. But the earliest objections to scientific management centered not on its costs to employers but on the toll it took on employees. Those objections, still voiced today, are that rigidly rule-bound workplaces are stultifying, demeaning, and alienating. By "deskilling" workers and turning artisans into machines, Taylorism fosters a sense of powerlessness and disconnection. It fosters, that is to say, what many people see as modernity's defining social ills.

Although police officers rarely become so disenchanted as to quit, there are plenty of reports of police officers who grow to feel alienated and discouraged.[52] And a collective kind of alienation has been well documented in policing—better documented, probably, than alienation in any other occupation. A central theme of police ethnography since the 1950s has been the distinctive sense of estrangement that police officers feel from society. That estrangement—often accompanied by feelings of frustration, bitterness, and cynicism—has been blamed for a host of police pathologies: the "code of silence," the paranoia and insularity, the proclivity to violence, the intolerance and "authoritarianism."[53] This is not precisely the kind of alienation Taylorism is commonly blamed with fostering; it is "us against them" rather than "myself alone." And the estrangement of the police has itself typically been blamed not on the way their work is structured and managed but on their grinding, daily encounters with crime and disorder.[54]

Still, there may be connections between the collective estrangement experienced by the police and the sense of anxiety and personal isolation that many officers feel. Even if they are separate phenomena, they may well feed on and worsen each other. The widespread impression that police officers are especially prone to domestic violence and suicide has been hard to confirm statistically,[55] but there is no doubt that many officers suffer seriously from job-related stress, that their families often suffer along with them, and that a frustrated, alienated police officer is more likely to be a violent and abusive police officer. The stultification and immiseration of any group of employees should be a matter of social concern, but there are special reasons to be worried about unhappy police officers.

Are there reasons to think that unhappy police officers can be blamed in part on the rigid, top-down management of policing? Police officers regularly complain, and often bitterly, that their views are never consulted, that they are subject to arbitrary and irrational directives from above and without, and that the rules under which they operate are absurdly unrealistic—rules that could never have been promulgated by anyone familiar with the daily realities of law enforcement. Cops often seem to take a kind of subversive glee in the inanity of what they endure, and their shared sense of the thanklessness of their work can contribute in an odd way to esprit de corps. But police officers also tell researchers that they find the administrative and organizational aggravations of their work more stressful than the physical danger and psychological trauma.[56] It stands to reason that the ongoing experience of insult and voicelessness can take a toll, and that police officers—like any other group of employees—would feel more positive about their work if they participated in its management.

And, in fact, when police departments have experimented with participatory management, this has been the result. Wisconsin's Madison Police Department, which began experimenting with participatory decision making in the 1980s, found that it increased job satisfaction, made officers more open to reform, and improved the level of police service in the eyes of the public.[57] More recently, the police department in Broken Arrow, Oklahoma, has turned much of its policy making over to a twelve-member committee of management officials, union leaders, and rank-and-file officers, a move that appears to have contributed to greater productivity (as measured by arrest and clearance rates), a sharp drop in citizen complaints, and higher levels of job satisfaction.[58]

TEACHING DEMOCRACY

The costs that law enforcement Taylorism imposes on management and officers it also imposes on the public, because the public has an interest in the effective management of police forces and in the happiness and psychological well-being of individual police officers. And there is another potential cost to the public of rigid, top-down management of policing. It forfeits the opportunity to train police officers in the values and habits of democratic citizenship: values of openness, tolerance, and compromise; habits of engagement, cooperation, and deliberation.

There is long tradition of viewing the workplace as the ideal training ground for democratic citizenship. There are hints of the idea in the later work of John Stuart Mill and a sustained development of the notion in the early twentieth-century writings of G. D. H. Cole.[59] The idea went into something of a dormancy during the 1940s and 1950s, when mass participation in democratic governance came to be seen as not only unnecessary but positively pernicious.[60] But in the 1960s and 1970s the idea of participatory democracy regained favor, and with it the notion that rigid, autocratic workplaces stunted the political development of employees in ways that not only deprived them of full, satisfying lives but also weakened democracy in the broader society.[61]

That thesis has remained controversial. But even if democracy does not depend on fostering the political growth of *all* employees, there are special reasons to want *police officers* to internalize democratic values and habits. The police are often placed in positions where they can actively support or actively threaten democratic activities: they can protect political protesters, for example, or they can attack them; they can help create a climate of respect for individual privacy and autonomy, or they can make privacy insecure and nonconformity difficult; they can enforce norms of tolerance, or they can reinforce bias and prejudice; they can teach citizens that authority may safely be challenged, or they can teach the opposite.[62] Moreover, there are reasons to think that effective policing *in general*—at least the forms of effective policing most congenial to a free and open society—depends on some of the same values and skills often thought important for democratic citizenship more broadly.

This is the great lesson of William Ker Muir's classic study of Oakland police officers in the early 1970s. Muir's book remains unusual. Nearly every other police sociologist, before and after Muir, has sought to explain why the police, in general, are the way they are. Muir asked a different question, if anything, more pressing: what makes some police officers more effective and more trustworthy than others? His answer was that good police officers had democratic virtues: a comfort with moral ambiguity, an ability to see shades of gray, a broad capacity for tolerance and empathy, and perhaps most important, "an enjoyment of talk"—an affinity, that is to say, for conversation, argument, deliberation, advocacy, and compromise.[63]

Police officers developed these virtues, in part, by working in a department that itself embraced them. Among the heroes of Muir's book is Chief Charles Gain, a legendary reformer who ran Oakland's police force from 1967 to 1973. Gain ruled with a heavy hand and was never popular with the rank and file; in 1972 the Oakland Police Officers' Association voted no confidence in his administration.[64] Muir admired him nonetheless for infusing the department "with a sense of purpose from which his men derived dignity and moral meaning."[65] Much of that was accomplished, Muir thought, through a training style and a workplace climate that invited "participation, discussion, argument, and questioning."[66] What Muir liked about the Oakland Police Department, in short, was the way it operated as a school for democratic citizenry—or, more precisely, democratic leadership. Muir saw police officers as "streetcorner politicians," and they were most likely to grow in that role if they worked in departments that within themselves fostered "widespread political participation."[67]

Muir was not alone in thinking workplace democracy particularly important for police officers. The pioneering police ethnographer William Westley suggested in 1970 that the remedy for the alienated and repressive mentality of the police was, in large part, "participatory democracy." "Police organizations," he argued, "must be democratized by involving as many policemen as possible in decision-making on all aspects of the department's job."[68] Westley was echoing George Berkley, who had argued a year earlier in *The Democratic Policeman* that strong, democratic police unions and broad participation by officers in departmental decision making were critical for training the police in the "rules and values" of democracy. Berkley reasoned that a police force "cannot hope to function in a manner with a democratic society if its internal operations deviate from that society's norms and values." Only by "participating in the give-and-take of . . . deliberations" were police officers "likely to develop the respect for accommodation and conciliation along with the attitudes of patience and tolerance which are indispensable to the democratic process."[69]

The criminologist John Angell took an even stronger line in 1971, suggesting that the "basic hope for correcting the dysfunctional trends of American police organizations" was to bring law enforcement in line with the participatory, "humanistic-democratic values of the United States," especially as reflected in "the trend toward employee involvement in decision-making processes." That required, among other things, abolishing the chain of command.[70] Angell's program proved too radical even for reform-minded departments. But several police forces experimented in the 1970s with "team policing," a loosely defined idea that generally involved a designated group of officers working cooperatively and with shared operational independence to address the problems of a particular neighborhood.[71]

Team policing remained a "buzz phrase in police circles" well into the 1980s, but it soon lost its connotation of participatory management.[72] The Peer Review Panel in Oakland fell victim to budget cuts, and the gains the experiment had achieved evaporated.[73] By the end of the 1970s, moreover, arguments like Westley's, Berkley's, and Angell's had dropped out of sight. Except among police officers themselves, and often even there, enthusiasm largely vanished for bringing even the mildest forms of workplace democracy to American law enforcement.[74] With isolated exceptions, it has yet to reappear.

The Missing Strand in Democratic Policing

What happened? Why did the arguments for giving police officers a voice in the shaping of their work—arguments that attracted such thoughtful and well-informed supporters in the early 1970s—disappear by the decade's end? To be sure, a certain amount of disenchantment emerged by the 1980s about workplace democracy in general.[75] But shared decision making in the workplace soon found new fans among management theorists. And the case for participatory democracy had seemed in the early 1970s to apply with special urgency to law enforcement, because of the strong social interest in fostering democratic values and habits in the police. Why, then, did sentiment for workplace democracy in policing vanish so completely, and why has it never rematerialized? And why, for that matter, did the sentiment take until the 1960s to emerge in the first place? Why has internal democracy nearly always been the missing strand in discussions of democratic policing?

Some of the answer is bad timing. At the very point in the twentieth century when interest in workplace democracy reached its zenith—the late 1960s and early 1970s—American police departments seemed peculiarly inhospitable places for experiments in participatory management. Police forces at that time were almost uniformly white, male, and politically reactionary.[76] Grassroots activism among police officers was in fact on the rise, but it took discouraging forms: contempt for civilian authority, fierce opposition to outside oversight of any kind, organized brutality against student protesters, vigilante attacks on black militants, and active participation in far-right organizations.[77] As a result, the very scholars and community activists who might otherwise have been most sympathetic to calls for participatory management of law enforcement agencies instead concluded that democracy required tight, top-down control of the police.[78]

But even before the late 1960s, the spirit of Frederick Taylor hovered over the mid-twentieth-century pursuit of "police professionalism." The characteristic reforms of police professionalism were "bureaucratic—strong lines of administrative control and oversight, extensive rules and regulations, pre- and in-service training provided by police departments, elimination of discretion, and simplification of work tasks."[79] One might add to this list the heavy reliance on "integrity testing" and workplace spies for internal discipline.[80] None of this had much to do with viewing line police officers as "professionals" in the normal sense of that term; indeed it was incompatible even "with the recognition of the police as craftspersons."[81] Police professionalism sought to give individual officers less of a say in the shaping of their work, not more.

This aspect of police professionalism never encountered significant resistance, in part because police officers were poorly respected by the public; they seemed to need more direction, not more say in how they did their jobs. Throughout the first half of the twentieth century, police officers were widely viewed as slow-witted at best and venal at worst.[82] Improving this image was one of the express goals of police professionalism. (Chief William Parker of the Los Angeles Police Department, a famously fervent advocate for police professionalism, objected to his officers being called cops, because he thought the term had too many negative connotations.) But popular perceptions reinforced the ideology of progressive law enforcement administrators in steering police reform away from any experiments with participatory management.

The middle decades of the twentieth century were also the heyday of democratic pluralism, which downplayed the importance of widespread political participation and stressed the threats to democracy posed by the "authoritarian personality."[83] Democratic pluralism reinforced the tendency of mid-twentieth-century scholars and reformers to think that police officers should follow rules, not make them. Workplace democracy, like participatory democracy more generally, was off the pluralist agenda. And police officers, drawn from the working class and hardened by the nature of their work, seemed especially prone to the authoritarian personality feared by the pluralists—and especially important to bring under elite control, given their license and assignment to use coercive force.

James Q. Wilson, an enormously influential police scholar generally sympathetic to the interests of law enforcement, dismissed the resurgent, politically charged police unionism of the late 1960s as "criminal justice syndicalism."[84] Jerome Skolnick, an equally influential but much more liberal scholar than Wilson, nonetheless agreed with him on this point. Skolnick saw police activism as a threat to the rule of law, and he therefore concluded that police officers, like judges or soldiers, must forswear politics.[85]

Skolnick's thinking on this subject is particularly interesting, because he fully appreciated the tension between his approach and the ideal of participatory democracy scorned by the pluralists. Skolnick drew explicitly on a distinction the sociologist Reinhard Bendix had drawn in the late 1950s between "totalitarian" and "nontotalitarian" responses to the "strategies of independence" adopted by employees in a bureaucracy—responses, that is to say, to employees' "tacit evasion of rules and norms through application of individual judgment." In the coda to his magisterial study of managerial ideologies—the work to which the title of this chapter alludes—Bendix suggested that totalitarian regimes sought systematically to suppress independent judgment by employees, while nontotalitarian regimes sought to capitalize on it, addressing "managerial appeals . . . to the good faith of subordinates."[86] The "dilemma of the police in a democratic society," Skolnick suggested, "arises out of the conflict between the extent of initiative contemplated by nontotalitarian norms of work and restraints upon police demanded by the rule of law." Skolnick saw "forceful normative claims" on each side of this conflict,[87] particularly because he thought it entirely plausible that working in an authoritarian organization would make the police less sympathetic to democratic values and more attached to "social uniformity and routine and a somewhat rigid conception of order."[88] Ultimately, though, Skolnick took "the ideal of legality" to be the "highest stated commitment" of "democratic society." And that ideal required reining in police discretion with rules laid down by society; it did not tolerate "justice without trial."[89] That was a conclusion fully consistent with both the agenda of police professionalism and the tenets of democratic pluralism, and it was a conclusion rendered even more plausible by the nasty turn taken by police activism in the late 1960s and early 1970s.

American police reform in the 1950s, 1960s, and 1970s thus reflected, in critical respects, efforts to guard against the police state in its monstrous, twentieth-century form. There was a strong element of historical continuity here: the London Metropolitan Police, which served as the template for all modern Anglo-American police forces, had been consciously designed not to resemble the network of spies, informants, and intelligence monitors at the heart of the original, eighteenth-century police states.[90] Peel's police were made highly conspicuous by their uniforms; they spent their time conducting visible, preventive patrols, not infiltrating unseen or compiling secret dossiers; and they fought crime and disorder, not political opposition. The bobbies and their successors, that is to say, were "low police," not the feared "high police" perfected by Fouché on the other side of the channel.[91] Indeed, English reformers stripped the very term *police* of its broad, original meaning and reduced it to "a synonym for the constabulary."[92] Just as twentieth-century law enforcement in the United States was shaped by political ideals formed in conscious opposition to fascism and Stalinism, the London Metropolitan Police thus was earlier crafted against the "contrast-model" of Napoleonic France.[93]

Along with this continuity, though, there is a considerable bit of irony—and a different form of continuity. Nothing is to be gained by drawing strained parallels between modern American police forces and the Gestapo. But there is a sense in which American police reform in the twentieth century replicated, within police departments, some of the key ideas and practices that totalitarianism shared with earlier European police states: pervasive regulation of subject populations, extensive use of spies and informants (partly for their deterrent value), and an underlying ideology of control. The intellectual lineage of these practices can be traced back beyond Taylorism and across the Atlantic to Fouché and his predecessors.[94] They can be traced, in other words, to the original, Continental theory of police as mode of governance.

Police Departments and the Rule of Law

At the very point in the late 1960s and early 1970s when workplace democracy was most in vogue, police officers were monolithically white, male, and reactionary, and they were organizing themselves in ways that seemed to threaten democracy rather than support it. But the strong assumption that police departments must be controlled rigidly, from the top down, predates that historical moment, in ways we have explored. It has also proved lasting. In 1990, following years of community-policing reforms, the legal scholar Herman Goldstein complained that the "dominant form of policing" continued "to view police officers as automatons."[95] It still does today. Even the mildest versions of workplace democracy for police officers have stayed largely off the table. Encouraging patrol officers to be thoughtful and creative about their work is often said to be part of community policing and even more so of problem-solving policing.[96] In practice, though, this has rarely amounted to more than placing additional discretion in the hands of individual officers. There are few efforts to give officers a collective, deliberative voice in how policing is carried out or to enlist police unions or identity-based police organizations as partners in police reform. The "community" in *community policing* rarely includes police officers themselves.

Police departments today are very different places than in the late 1960s and early 1970s. Police unions are now firmly part of "the mainstream of American trade unionism," devoting the bulk of their attention to working conditions, job security, and the "bread-and-butter . . . issues that have been near and dear to the hearts of U.S. trade unionists for decades."[97] And police forces are no longer monolithically white, male, homophobic, and reactionary. Among the most important consequences of the new, more diverse demographics of American law enforcement is a dramatic decline in the solidarity and insularity of the police—hard to quantify, but widely remarked on by police officers and the scholars who study them. The informal, occupational norms of policing can still pose an obstacle to reform, but the notion of police departments as insular, homogeneous bastions of unchecked patriarchy, racism, and authoritarianism is out of date.[98] Police departments today are more socially complex, more open to debate and disagreement, and more reflective of the divisions in the communities they serve.[99] They are safer places, it might be thought, for experiments in workplace democracy.

But those experiments remain rare. Part of the reason is a certain understanding of the rule of law. Skolnick's influential account of democratic policing stressed the rule of law as the key to reconciling the "fundamentally authoritarian character" of the police "with the democratic society they were policing."[100] And he suggested that the rule of law required police to follow the directions laid down for them by the courts, elected officials, and the public at large; it was therefore inconsistent, in the context of policing, with "the extent of initiative" ordinarily "contemplated by nontotalitarian norms of work."[101] Skolnick never quite said that collective innovation by police officers should be discouraged, but his account left little room for it. Individual "strategies of independence" were inconsistent with "the principle of legality." So was police activism. Programs of participatory management controlled from above—say, some kind of law enforcement equivalent of quality circles—were not ruled out, but neither did Skolnick show any enthusiasm for them. The police-reform agenda suggested by his work was controlling the police from above and from outside.

And that is largely the police-reform agenda we have had since the 1960s. Police professionalism and community policing, despite their differences, both have been versions of this agenda. Democracy inside police departments, even in small doses, has seemed incompatible with the rule of law and therefore incompatible with democracy writ large. That assumed incompatibility has made rigid, top-down regulation of policing seem unambiguously democratic, as long as police chiefs remained accountable, at least in theory, to elected governmental officials. But it is also hard to square with any plausible understanding of the rule of law.

Like most scholars who invoke the rule of law, Skolnick was unapologetically vague about its details but seemed influenced by Lon Fuller's account.[102] Fuller identified eight elements in the rule of law: (a) rules of general application that are (b) publicized, (c) applied prospectively, (d) understandable, (e) noncontradictory, (f) capable of being followed, (g) stable, and (h) faithfully applied.[103] How many of these elements are truly separate is controversial.[104] More importantly, there is dispute about what the elements themselves mean and about how they should be weighted and combined. Depending on the answers to *those* questions, the "rule of law" can wind up meaning—as Richard Fallon demonstrated a decade ago—anything from originalism to formalism to fair process to substantive justice.[105]

As a result, it is not entirely clear what we mean when we talk about reconciling police with the rule of law. Four possibilities suggest themselves. First, the *rule of law* in policing could simply mean that the police do not themselves violate the law. Fuller himself seemed to think that "lawless conduct by the police" was the chief threat they posed to the rule of law.[106] Second, reconciling the police with the rule of law could mean ensuring that the police do not frustrate the application of the law to the people they police—by, for example, failing to arrest offenders. This view emphasizes the role of the police in securing the last of the eight elements Fuller identified in the rule of law, namely, "congruence between the rules as announced and their actual administration."[107] Third, the *rule of law* in policing could mean ensuring that all exercises of power by the police are governed by law, rather than simply being arbitrary exercises of discretion. This view seems consistent with Hayek's famous definition of the rule of law: "stripped of all technicalities this means that government in all its actions is bound by rules fixed and announced beforehand—rules which make it possible to foresee with fair certainty how the authority will use its coercive powers in given circumstances, and to plan one's individual affairs on the basis of this knowledge."[108] Fourth and finally, the *rule of law* in policing could mean that the police are subject to majoritarian control or judicial oversight—or some combination of those two checks. It may dilute the value of the term *rule of law* to employ it as a synonym for democracy or for the protection of civil rights,[109] but there is no doubt that the term is sometimes used in this way.

Fortunately, we do not need to decide for present purposes which of these formulations—or what admixture of two or more of them—best captures our intuitions regarding what it means to reconcile the police with the rule of law. None of these four versions of the rule of law in policing is actually inconsistent or even in strong tension with a resolve to greatly increase the voice of rank-and-file officers in the management of their departments.

This is perhaps most obvious with respect to the first formulation of the rule of law in policing, the formulation stressing the obligation of police officers not to break the law. *One* way for police officers to help shape the nature of their work is for them simply to ignore legal directives addressed to them. But this certainly is not the only way, nor is it a particularly powerful way. When we talk about workplace democracy in *any* field, what we typically have in mind is not employees ignoring the rules imposed on them but (a) employees collectively participating in the shaping of those rules, and (b) the rules leaving room for employees to be creative about how best to further the objectives of the organization. Both these possibilities seem worth exploring in the context of law enforcement. Rank-and-file officers could be involved in the formulation of the rules under which the police operate, and the rules could be designed to leave room for innovation by individual officers and teams of officers. Neither of these would involve *any* violation of the law by the police; they are alternative ideas about how the law governing the police should be hammered out in the first place and about what that law should look like.

The situation is slightly more complicated with respect to our second version of the rule of law in policing: the notion that police discretion should not be allowed to frustrate the neutral and consistent application of preannounced legal rules. This version of the rule of law is violated when the police decide on their own, for example, not to enforce a particular prohibition of which they disapprove (think of police during Prohibition refusing to pursue bootleggers), or to ignore violations of the law in a particular area (think of "the time-honored practice of ghetto confinement of deviance"[110]), or to refrain from arresting particular suspects, despite the existence of probable cause (think of the tacit condoning of lynching during Jim Crow). This version of the rule of law could also be violated, if less egregiously, by some of the innovations one might expect if police officers were given a larger say in the nature of their work: decisions by groups of officers, for example, to concentrate their efforts on certain areas or certain kinds of offenses, ignoring other areas or other offenses, or decisions by individual officers to look the other way in particular situations.

But this second formulation of the rule of law in policing is hopelessly unrealistic. Enforcement discretion in policing is unavoidable. Police departments *today* make decisions all the time about where to concentrate their resources; police officers *today* make decisions all the time about whether to look the other way. And very few of the legal rules imposed on officers *today* do anything to rein in enforcement discretion. Mandatory arrest rules for domestic violence suspects are an obvious exception. But these rules have been noteworthy and controversial in part because they are so unusual.[111] If the rule of law means that the police must arrest everyone who there is reason to believe has committed a crime, then the rule of law is pie in the sky, and we might as well stop talking about it. Police discretion, and a massive amount of it, is simply unavoidable.

This is a large part of the attraction of the third formulation of the rule of law in policing: the idea that all exercises of power by the police, including decisions not to invoke their power, should be governed by rules announced in advance. This version of the rule of law seems inconsistent, or at least in tension, with *some* of what I have been calling workplace democracy in policing. It seems in tension with the view that the rules under which the police operate should be structured to allow ample room for ad hoc decisions by individual officers—or, for the matter, by groups of officers—about how the mission of the police can best be advanced in particular situations.

But it is fully compatible with other forms of workplace democracy in policing—in particular, with those forms that involve rank-and-file police officers in the formulation of the rules under which they operate. Indeed, those forms of workplace democracy might *bolster* the third version of the rule of law in policing, in two different ways. First, police officers—like other employees—are more likely to comply with rules they think are legitimate, and they are more likely to think that rules are legitimate when they have a say in what the rules are. This role of legitimacy in securing compliance with workplace rules, and the role of procedural regularity in creating legitimacy, has long been a central part of the general argument for workplace democracy.[112]

It finds strong support in the recent research psychologist Tom Tyler has conducted on the reasons people obey the law. Law abidance, Tyler concludes, is tied to the perceived legitimacy of the legal system, and perceived legitimacy depends in significant part on opportunities for participation. Control over the results is not as important: "what people want is to feel that their input has been solicited and considered by decision makers."[113] Tyler's research has focused on the compliance of ordinary citizens with the criminal law, but perceived legitimacy seems, if anything, to be even more important in securing the compliance of police officers with the rules under which they are asked to operate. In choosing their jobs, after all, cops have bought into the legal system; they should be especially susceptible to the notion that everyone owes a duty of compliance to rules adopted and applied through fair procedures.

Second, wholly apart from how rank-and-file participation can make a police department's internal rules seem more legitimate, rules that cops themselves help to fashion may be more likely to be obeyed simply because they will be more sensible. William Simon, among others, has claimed precisely this kind of benefit for systems of workplace governance involving "rolling rule regimes"—sets of formal directives that are continually revised on the basis of the experience of the workers applying them. Simon argues that systems of this kind (typified by the Toyota Production System, much discussed by management theorists) combine "the normative explicitness associated with formal rules with the continuous adjustment to particularity associated with informal norms," charting a middle course between "the command-and-control model of Fordist bureaucracy" and the "traditional artisanal vision in which work is regulated by tacit norms that can be grasped only by prolonged socialization into guild and local workplace cultures."[114]

"Rolling rule regimes" may be particularly attractive forms of workplace democracy in policing for other reasons, as well. They may be the forms that have the best potential for developing the democratic skills and habits of officers and for giving officers a greater appreciation of democratic values. Collaborative, heuristic rulemaking could simultaneously give officers a collective voice in the shaping of their work, preserve their ability to respond flexibly to unforeseen circumstances, minimize arbitrary exercises of discretion, encourage patrol officers to think critically, explicitly, and systematically about how they go about their work, and cultivate in them an appreciation for the give-and-take of the democratic process.

Plainly, though, there are limits. A fair amount of ad hoc improvisation is inherent in policing, in part for reasons we have already discussed. So something further should be said, before we move on, about the tension between the third version of the rule of law in policing and the notion that the rules under which police operate should leave them room for creativity.

The fact that police discretion comes into conflict with a coherent and plausible conception of the rule of law does not mean that police discretion should be minimized. There are other things we care about, in addition to the rule of law—particularly this particular conception of the rule of law.[115] And compliance with this particular conception of the rule of law in policing will always be a matter of degree. Just as there is no way to eliminate enforcement discretion in policing, there is no way to bring all of that enforcement discretion under the control of rules. Rules simply cannot be drafted that will dictate, without ambiguity, the appropriate exercise of enforcement discretion in every imaginable situation. Nor can rules be drafted to specify, in advance, the proper application of all the other kinds of discretion exercised by the police when applying their coercive powers. Therefore it may make sense to expand, in certain contexts, even some kinds of workplace democracy that come into conflict with the third version of the rule of law in policing, the notion that all exercises of police authority should be governed by rules.

What about the fourth version of the rule of law in policing—the version that takes the rule of law to mean majoritarian control, or judicial oversight, or some combination of the two? The first thing to be said is that any kind of workplace democracy in policing could and should be subject to outside checks, both political and judicial. Giving police officers more of a say does not mean giving them a final say. None of the benefits of workplace democracy would be threatened by allowing for an electoral veto, a judicial veto, or both—so long as the veto power is not exercised excessively.

The caveat is significant, of course. At some point there *is* a tradeoff between giving police officers a greater voice and giving the public, or the courts, more control over policing. But tradeoffs between different elements of "democratic policing" are unavoidable, even without bringing workplace democracy for police officers into the mix. There is a familiar tradeoff, for example, between majoritarian control of policing and judicial control of policing. So the existence of tradeoff between workplace democracy for police officers and outside control of the police is not, by itself, sufficient reason to reject the notion that rank-and-file officers should play a greater role in shaping the nature of their work.

All the more so given how far we are from actually confronting that tradeoff. Few of the rules under which police currently operate were imposed by elected officials or adopted through other majoritarian processes. Judicial control of the police is more extensive. But even this is easy to overestimate. By far the largest source of constraints on the police is departmental management.

This is the great legacy of police professionalism: law enforcement agencies run their own shops, largely free from outside interference. Community policing has made departments less insular and more likely to consult with outsiders, but it has almost never meant a decrease in the operational autonomy of law enforcement. With minor exceptions, community-policing programs are adopted unilaterally by the police—and that means by police management.[116] Civilian oversight is now an accepted feature of law enforcement in most major American cities, but for the most part the oversight operates at the margins: reviewing selected disciplinary decisions, for example.[117] We could give police officers substantially more voice in shaping their work without diminishing outside control. What would have to yield is the ability of *management* to operate unilaterally. In this respect, at least, policing is not very different from other lines of work.

Conclusion

Despite the revolution over the past few decades in the ideology of American law enforcement—the much heralded shift from police professionalism to community policing as the reigning orthodoxy of managers and reformers alike—two basic assumptions have endured. The first is that the central task of police reform, and the central task in the ongoing legal regulation of the police, is reconciling law enforcement with the goals and principles of a democratic society. Police professionalism and community policing are in this sense different paths to the same destination: "democratic policing." The second enduring assumption is that democratic policing means making the police *answerable* to democracy, not bringing the benefits of democracy to police officers *themselves*. The democracy in democratic policing is external, not internal, to law enforcement. The thinking has been that external and internal democracy are two different things and that when it comes to police they are mutually incompatible.

Rigid, top-down management is not found only in policing. Police officers in fact enjoy a good deal more latitude in structuring their day-to-day routines than many other employees. But even the weak forms of workplace democracy encountered in other employment settings have few champions in policing, and even the strongest advocates of workforce empowerment in other sectors tend to make an exception for policing. And there are special reasons to care about participatory management in policing, including the importance of cultivating democratic values and habits in law enforcement officers.

No plausible account of democracy or the rule of law can explain the strong and persistent resistance to giving rank-and-file officers a greater collective voice in the shaping of their work. Nor can that resistance fairly be blamed, as it sometimes has been, on the influence of the military model in policing. Law enforcement has clung far more tenaciously than even the military to rigid, top-down methods of workplace governance.[118] If there is a conceptual paradigm to blame here, it is not the military model but something closer to home, at least etymologically: the premodern, antiliberal theory of police as a mode of state governance. That hardly proves that our current approaches to police reform are mistaken or incomplete, but it may provide, for anyone uncomfortable with giving the police power wide berth, reason to rethink some of our assumptions about how police departments should be run.

SEVEN

The Elusive Line Between Prevention and Detection of Crime in German Undercover Policing

JACQUELINE E. ROSS

Introduction

In all legal systems, the police must investigate past offenses while preventing future crimes. Most legal systems, however, do not regulate these functions separately. The German legal system is notable for formally distinguishing so-called repressive prerogatives of the police to enforce the criminal laws from preventive powers to promote public safety. These labels designate two distinct realms of police activity that are regulated by separate codes. Germany's Criminal Procedure Code governs how the police may investigate crimes that have already occurred. By contrast, separate police laws determine what the police may do to prevent future crimes and, more generally, to prevent future harm by eliminating threats to public safety. These preventive codes protect the public from a range of criminal and noncriminal disturbances. These range from parking violations, environmental hazards, and public protests (and the attendant risks of violence) to hostage takings and the planning of terrorist attacks. When the police act in their preventive capacity, their task is not to gather evidence or pursue criminal sanctions but to promote public order and safety in all realms of communal life. As Markus Dubber has shown, police power in this second, expansive sense has its origin in "the power of the state to govern the persons and things within its dominion as a householder would his household." In contrast with the enforcement of the criminal laws, he argues, the promotion of public welfare is governed by norms of risk management and efficiency rather than justice; inclines toward viewing persons as threats or as subjects to be governed rather than as autonomous agents and bearers of rights; and is less concerned with the *mens rea* and moral responsibility of offenders than with the collective interests of the community.[1] Though even the enforcement of the criminal laws serves some preventive purposes, the police codes permit the police to ward off more diffuse risks rather than concrete and immediate threats or incipient criminal activity by identified actors.[2] When serving this wider, caretaking function, the police also exercise a degree of discretion that the criminal procedure code denies them in enforcing the criminal laws.[3]

The distinction between prevention and repression remains an important constraint on the powers of the German police because it maps onto the division of labor between the states and the federal government. Preventive policing is regulated by the states; repressive powers are regulated by federal law (though, increasingly, the federal customs, border, and police authorities are being granted preventive powers once reserved to the states).[4] But the demarcation between preventive and repressive responsibilities plays another significant role as well: it reinforces the functional and institutional separation of policing from the work of Germany's domestic intelligence agencies. The principle of separation was introduced at the insistence of the Allies in 1949 as a means of avoiding dangerous concentrations of powers like those possessed by the Gestapo.[5] Coercive law enforcement powers, including arrest powers, were withheld from intelligence agencies, and the police were prohibited from gathering intelligence.

This chapter's empirical study will argue that proactive methods like undercover policing have to some extent eroded the distinction between preventive and repressive policing, along with the functional and institutional separation between the tasks of the police and those of intelligence agencies. Undercover policing in Germany has redirected investigative energies from a focus on past offenses defined by law to threats of future harm defined by the police, effectively turning many repressive investigations into preventive efforts at risk reduction. (In discussing the growth of preventive police powers generally, Pieroth, Schlink, and Kniesel note that the preventive realm has been gradually expanding for most types of police activity, in that the police have gradually acquired increased powers to monitor *potential* threats at ever-earlier gestational stages.[6]) The blurring of these functional divisions stands in tension with the principle of separation because the interplay of preventive and repressive operations means that undercover operations increasingly blend the pursuit of evidence with the collection of intelligence not tied to initiation of criminal proceedings against identified offenders for specified crimes. The German Constitution, of course, entrusts the pursuit of intelligence exclusively to the state and federal intelligence services, while the police function has long been thought to conflict with the use of covert tactics.[7]

My analysis of German undercover policing rests on eighty-nine field interviews that I conducted between 2002 and 2004 with state and federal police officials, undercover agents, training and supervisory officials, control officers, prosecutors, and judges in fifteen of the sixteen German states. I corrected for bias by cross-checking statements and perspectives. I compared claims made by sources against information provided by (a) colleagues in their own division or agency; (b) counterparts in other states; and (c) personnel in other parts of the legal system (checking variations in accounts by police officers, prosecutors, and judges). I also compared evidence from interviews with written sources, including ministry guidelines, training materials, prosecutors' memoranda, judicial opinions, scholarly criticism, and news stories.

In this chapter, I discuss the origin and purpose of Germany's distinction between preventive and repressive policing. After briefly outlining Germany's system for regulating undercover investigations and keeping them focused on their ostensible goal of gathering evidence (rather than collecting intelligence), I demonstrate how Germany's covert practices erode the system's fundamental distinctions between preventive and repressive policing and between the search for evidence and the (prohibited) pursuit of intelligence.

Preventive and Repressive Policing

Unlike Germany's, the American legal system does not differentiate preventive from repressive prerogatives. One reason for this may be that, in the United States, the public welfare model of policing has come to pervade and dominate the law enforcement function, affecting even the design and interpretation of substantive criminal law. Dubber argues that the expansion of strict liability and possession offenses manifests an emphasis on reducing risks and threats to public safety, reorienting criminal justice from the task of punishing intrinsically wrongful acts. Modern offense definitions thus dispense with many of the *actus reus* and *mens rea* requirements that the criminal law has traditionally treated as prerequisites of criminal responsibility.

In Germany the distinction between preventive and repressive policing matters because German law aims to regulate police powers comprehensively. American criminal procedure has little to say about police functions like traffic regulation, so long as these do not infringe Fourth or Fifth Amendment rights. But Germany's efforts to regulate all police powers commit its legal system to distinguishing among the different powers and functions of the police. This comprehensive aim has its historical origin in eighteenth- and nineteenth-century efforts to curb the powers of the state. With the advent of the Enlightenment, Germany's states gradually limited the absolute powers of its monarchs by separating the roles of the military and the police and limiting the ability of the military to quell domestic unrest and public disturbances.[8] Though the police were generally responsible for promoting the public welfare, a number of theorists argued that the functions of police should be limited to preventing threats to public safety.[9] Over the course of the nineteenth century, police powers came to be limited by the requirement of an explicit legal basis for all prerogatives of the police that affected liberty and property. In addition, courts imposed additional constraints through principles that required police conduct to be proportional, reasonable, rationally related to the means served, and minimally invasive. Statutes defining police powers had to clearly define and circumscribe the actions they authorized, and the predicates for police intervention.[10]

Against this normative backdrop, the distinction between preventive and repressive policing can be seen as an additional limitation on the powers of the police. The federal code of criminal procedure requires the police to confront criminal defendants as rights holders rather than subjects. When acting under the code, the police have to look back in time to past offenses, not forward to future threats, serve justice rather than public welfare, and punish harms to identified victims rather than disobedience to the state. When the police enforce the criminal code, the police must work closely with prosecutors; their investigative powers vary with the seriousness of the crime; and the police must seek advance judicial approval for a variety of investigative tactics such as searches, seizures, electronic surveillance, or even long-term visual surveillance. The police also enjoy less discretion when they act in their repressive capacity because Germany's version of the principle of legality requires the police to investigate (and prosecutors to charge) most serious criminal violations uncovered in repressive operations. And investigators know that the results of criminal investigations will be aired at trial, that defense counsel and courts will test the legality of investigative tactics and enforce the rights of criminal defendants, and that violations of investigative rules will be sanctioned by suppression of the evidence. When the police act preventively to protect the public, however, they enjoy a degree of discretion that the legal system denies them when they investigate crimes. Preventive investigations rarely require judicial approval or prosecutorial assistance, and they produce no evidence that may be scrutinized at trial. During preventive operations, collective interests take center stage because suspects have not yet acquired the protected status of criminal defendants.

By regulating preventive and repressive functions separately, Germany sharpens the institutional division between the search for intelligence and the pursuit of evidence for criminal prosecutions. Preventive policing bears some functional resemblance to the work of (domestic) intelligence agencies.

Both investigate future threats rather than past violations of the criminal laws. Both target groups and organizational structures rather than individual offenders. Both aim to influence, control, and when possible, disrupt the activities of their targets—not to bring them to justice. Both seek intelligence rather than evidence, preferring secrecy to a public airing of the information they acquire. Both are relatively unregulated by comparison to their counterparts who use investigative tactics to generate evidence for trial. Their respective activities do not clash with the trial rights of criminal defendants, because they will never directly confront their targets in court. Thus both operate with a significant degree of institutional autonomy, largely avoiding oversight by prosecutors and judges. By contrast, when the police act in their law enforcement capacity, they must pursue evidence, not intelligence. Their investigative powers will depend on the nature of the crimes they investigate. They must also work closely together with prosecutors; seek judicial warrants, in advance, for a wide range of investigative activities; and subject their tactics to subsequent scrutiny by defense counsel, trial judges, and the appellate bench. By differentiating the investigation of crime from the avoidance of threats, the German legal system sharpens the distinction between the (preventive) work of intelligence agencies and the crime-solving duties of the police (when they act as enforcers of the criminal code).

The distinction between preventive and repressive policing is designed to limit the power of criminal investigators. But modern methods of investigation have eroded the practical significance of the formal distinction between preventive and repressive policing. Covert agents target those who appear willing to commit crimes—whether or not they have (provably) offended in the past. Such investigations tend to conflate forward-looking risk reduction with backward-looking crime control because covert agents encourage targets to commit future crimes in order to catch them in the act. Undercover investigations also mix the pursuit of specific criminals with the surveillance of broader groups of potential offenders.

Because undercover operations yield insights about past crimes as well as future threats, the German legal system seeks to maintain the separation between preventive and repressive policing by subjecting such investigations to different regulatory regimes, depending on the purposes they serve. When the police use undercover operations to gather evidence for criminal prosecution, they must follow federal law, which requires them to work closely with prosecutors and to obtain judicial approval for the most intrusive undercover investigations, involving the long-term use of deep-cover agents.[11] To obtain authorization for such stings, the police must demonstrate some evidentiary basis for their suspicions. Such investigations are legitimated as necessary tactics for the fight against organized crime; they may be used to investigate only the most serious offenses. By contrast, when the police identify only diffuse threats or seek background information about places and milieus, the police laws of individual states permit investigators to conduct preventive undercover operations without resort to the federal warrant procedure. While some German states do prohibit preventive undercover investigations and others require a warrant, many states allow such investigations without limitations comparable to the requirements of federal law.

This dual system of regulation creates opportunities for the police to use their broad, preventive prerogatives in the service of (repressive) criminal investigations. Likewise, covert operations permit the police to pursue relatively ill-defined incipient threats in the guise of investigating criminal violations. Parallel regulation of preventive and repressive investigations allows the police to reinterpret and expand their law enforcement mandate, which normally permits them to exercise their repressive prerogatives only when they possess concrete evidence that a particular crime has occurred.

German Regulation of Undercover Policing

Germany's current system for regulating undercover operations arose, on the one hand, from concerns about privacy and, on the other hand, from efforts to increase the investigative powers of the police to combat organized crime. In 1983 Germany's constitutional high court held that the government's collection and processing of census data had to respect a newly recognized right of "informational self-determination," that is, a right of every citizen to know what information the government has collected about her and to control the use, storage, and transmission of the data.[12] The new legal construct was a hybrid of dignity and of privacy interests protected by the law of personality. Given their impact on the right of informational self-determination, covert practices needed to be codified.[13] In 1992 in the midst of mounting concern about organized crime, Germany's federal legislature enacted legislation that institutionalized long-term, deep-cover operations as an indispensable weapon against criminal networks.[14] The legislation also protected privacy by insisting that covert operations meet a variety of procedural requirements. The statute authorized deep-cover operations for the investigation only of serious crimes (such as drug and arms trafficking, counterfeiting, and the forgery of official documents) and offenses committed by career criminals or gangs. The police could resort to such tactics only when it had become too difficult to obtain evidence through other means. The police needed advance prosecutorial approval if the investigation had not yet focused on particular suspects and advance judicial approval—a warrant—for any undercover operation that targeted specific persons or that required entry into private homes.[15] (The statute did not require advance approval for shorter-term operations, involving what one might term *shallow-cover* agents.) The law also required the police to inform the owner of a residence that an undercover agent had entered the premises (though notification could wait until the investigation was over). While imposing new constraints, however, the 1992 statute also expanded covert policing by authorizing the creation of elaborate cover identities and intensive forms of long-term infiltration. This reform entrenched undercover policing in the organizational structure of the police. It necessitated the creation of specialized covert units staffed by trained undercover agents, control officers, and a logistical support staff, for whom undercover policing became a separate career path.

But the statute regulated only repressive undercover investigations, that is, those covert operations designed to produce evidence for criminal prosecutions. It did not apply to preventive undercover operations. Nor could it, since preventive policing remained the exclusive prerogative of the states and was subject to the police laws of the individual states. The reforms seemingly sharpened the demarcation between repressive and preventive undercover operations by requiring that preventive operations transform themselves into repressive (evidence-gathering) investigations, supervised by prosecutors or judges, or both, as soon as the preventive operation yielded concrete indications that a particular crime had been or was being committed. If the police continued to conduct covert operations in their preventive capacity after that point, without seeking prosecutorial or judicial approval, the evidence would be suppressed at trial. In this way, the law encouraged the police to transform preventive into repressive (crime-solving) stings as soon as there was sufficient evidence to initiate a formal criminal investigation. The warrant requirement thus functioned less as a threshold limiting the police from conducting crime-solving covert operations and more as a point beyond which they could no longer conduct such investigations purely in their preventive, community-caretaking capacity.

Concerns about privacy also led to the enactment of police laws governing preventive undercover investigations. These varied from state to state, as each state passed laws codifying the extent to which the police could gather private data in the course of protecting its citizens against threats. These reforms actually increased the preventive powers of the police. New state statutes for the first time established legal bases for visual surveillance, electronic surveillance, wiretapping, and the use of undercover agents. Commentators have criticized these prerogatives as infringements of the principle of separation, which denies intelligence services coercive prerogatives and prohibits the police from gathering intelligence about inchoate security threats. The Constitution entrusted the latter task to the state and federal *Verfassungsschutzaemter*, or agencies for the protection of the Constitution.[16] Preventive undercover operations threatened to blur the distinction between the prerogatives of the police and those of Germany's domestic intelligence agencies, since both preventive undercover investigations and intelligence-gathering operations targeted threats that had not yet ripened into criminal action. The preventive deployment of undercover agents could be defended as necessary means of protecting public safety—and thus as core functions of the police. But the legitimacy of repressive undercover investigations depended on the possibility of quarantining them from preventive operations, that is, on establishing their separate identity as sources of evidence for criminal prosecution. If the insights of preventively deployed infiltrators were allowed to gather evidence to supplement the prosecution's criminal case, the police could circumvent the statutory constraints on repressive undercover investigations; in effect, they would open themselves up to the charge not only of avoiding prosecutorial and judicial oversight but also of usurping the role of the intelligence agencies. By gathering evidence through preventive operations the police would expand the repressive, crime-solving mandate of the police to encompass the surveillance of inchoate threats that did not yet merit the formal initiation of a criminal investigation.

Thus the legitimacy of repressive undercover investigation depended on its use as a source of evidence rather than intelligence—and therefore on the possibility of neatly distinguishing repressive, evidence-gathering stings from preventive operations, which bore so uncomfortable a resemblance to the pursuit of intelligence.

As this study will show, this distinction proved difficult to maintain. For one thing, the police laws closely paralleled the criminal procedure laws. Preventive operations came to serve as auxiliaries to criminal investigations—as a way of reaching back investigatively to the stage preceding the evidentiary foundation for the initiation of a formal criminal investigation. What made this possible, in part, is that the covert powers of preventive investigations closely paralleled those in the criminal procedure realm (except that many states did not require judicial approval for undercover operations or even prosecutorial oversight). Nor could preventive operations be limited with any ease to the investigation of only certain, serious sorts of offenses—because the inchoate nature of the threats at which they were aimed made it to some extent uncertain what sorts of crimes the target might commit. As a result, preventive investigations have become important ways of supplementing evidence-gathering operations with background intelligence—even as logic of deep-cover repressive operations has increasingly reoriented even criminal investigations to the collection of intelligence and to the pursuit of crime-prevention and risk-management strategies far removed from their ostensible purpose of gathering evidence for criminal prosecution. I will examine first how preventive investigations have been expanded to increase the production of intelligence and next how repressive undercover investigations have reoriented themselves from search for evidence to the other crime-control functions, including the management of risk areas, or hot spots, and compilation of intelligence.

Undercover Policing as a Source of Intelligence, Not Just Evidence

INTELLIGENCE GATHERING BEFORE JUDICIAL AUTHORIZATION OF REPRESSIVE UNDERCOVER OPERATIONS

The greatest challenge to the legitimacy of the system emerges from the internal tension between the ostensible evidentiary goals of repressive investigations and their inherent potential for serving other purposes, including social control (through the neutralization of hot spots where drugs are sold); the perpetuation of infiltrators' cover; and especially, the gathering of intelligence. On the one hand, the 1992 statute tries to tame deep-cover investigations as evidence-gathering tactics, and on the other hand, it encourages undercover agents to gather information not geared toward presentation in court, diverting infiltrators to the pursuit of intelligence. Thus the logic of the reformed covert policing system drives the police, like intelligence agencies, to gather far more information than necessary to prove the elements of charged offenses.

This dynamic derives in part from the ways the reforms interacted with the German distinction between repressive and preventive police powers. Once the police have identified a target, the 1992 statute requires them to turn preventive undercover investigations into repressive stings (designed to arrest and charge the target).[17] But the police must create an infrastructure of surveillance before they can decide whom to target. Undercover investigations can secure evidence only if they have targeted the right suspects and identified their vulnerabilities and logistical needs (which an undercover agent can then offer to satisfy). These tasks require collecting intelligence through preventive undercover operations.[18] A German chief of a covert policing unit said, "We know, for example, that there's lots of extortion in the red light district. Motorcycle gangs compete to control security at nightclubs; they battle each other for turf. We send someone in to discover who's who. Our guy could be the bouncer. He tells us who the leaders are, and we build a repressive investigation around them."[19]

The statute thus made preventive, intelligence-gathering operations more important than ever, even as it sought to legitimate undercover operations in contradistinction to such investigations. Accordingly, evidence-gathering repressive stings have come to *supplement* rather than *replace* preventive undercover probes. As a supervisor of a German covert policing unit told me, "In one preventive operation, all we knew was that there were some businesses where something was wrong. We thought they might deal in arms but we had nothing specific. We sent the deep-cover agent in, and he could see how the organization worked. Then we could send in another deep-cover agent, short term, to gather evidence. But we left our guy in the organization, and now we could see, how does the organization adapt when one guy goes to jail?"[20] To guide repressive operations, preventive operations expanded their agenda from concrete dangers—the businessman seeking to burn down his warehouse, or the husband hiring a contract killer to murder his wife—to more diffuse threats and milieus in which "something illegal was going on." And the repressive phase in turn generates intelligence for new preventive operations.[21] Accordingly, said a German covert policing chief, "some of our undercover operations take place in the repressive realm, but most are preventive, in the pre-evidentiary realm. We use the deep-cover agent to find out who's connected to whom, doing what, where do they hang out, etc., and we feed that information to our investigative divisions in organized crime [who in turn design evidence-gathering operations]. That's the direction of the flow of information: from us [the covert unit] to organized crime; less often in the other direction."[22]

How the 1992 statute was implemented facilitated the expansion of preventive operations. Specialized covert policing units were skilled in devising intricate false documents and elaborate cover stories for deep-cover agents, who could be deployed preventively, to gather intelligence, as well as repressively, to collect evidence. The creation of the new units also multiplied the personnel available to staff preventive exploratory investigations. And the new covert policing units could supply preventive operations with informants, control officers, and logistical support.

The investment in deep-cover agents and the construction of convincing covers also created a need for preventive undercover operations. For preventive undercover operations not only help target and guide repressive operations but also build the cover stories of deep-cover agents. Undercover agents have to devote significant time to infiltrating the setting in which they must establish their cover. Creating one's cover story is effectively a kind of preventive undercover operation. The choice of the agent's cover is dictated by enforcement priorities. "We target particular ethnic minorities who are suspected of criminal activities. Then we recruit a German police officer who comes from that ethnic group to be a deep-cover agent."[23] He must then find a convincing footing in a social milieu that offers investigative opportunities and helps him bond with potential offenders. A supervisor of a German covert policing unit elaborates, "The cover has to be constructed in ways that make him interesting for potential targets, and we ask ourselves, What do the targets need? What services can he offer that will make him attractive?"[24] In the process of building his cover, the undercover agent investigates particular starting points for evidence-gathering probes. "For example, he may listen around and learn that there's a grouping that imports drugs in shipments of bananas. He learns their ports, their stopping places, the routes, the participants, and then he helps us figure out whether it's worth entering this business."[25] In one case, "the undercover agent built his cover as a porter on an overnight train, along a stretch that's known as a drug route. While building his cover, he was able to learn who the regulars were on the route."[26] In the process of accrediting himself, the deep-cover agent becomes a well-placed source of intelligence.

Ironically, statutory regulation of repressive, evidence-gathering stings made it possible for many preventive, intelligence-gathering operations to avoid regulation entirely, even under the state police laws that govern preventive undercover investigations. For these laws do not necessarily apply to cover-building operations. The supervisor of a German covert policing unit told me, "There's a fluid transition from the task of building one's cover story and the start of a preventive undercover investigation. That's what we call the 'early preventive realm.' It's a new requirement now that the prosecutor has to approve preventive investigations in our state. But that may not apply to those infiltrations that are necessary to build the agent's cover."[27] For this reason, a covert policing official worried, "In some cities, the deep-cover agents are always running into targets. They treat that as part of their work building their cover, but we [here in this state] would treat it as already subject to the laws governing preventive uses of undercover agents. . . . Staying in the cover-building realm too long is a problem if the investigation eventually leads to a full-blown repressive investigation and it turns out that the cover-building phase was used as a way around the preventive police laws."[28] But courts are unlikely to learn about undercover activity that preceded the prosecutor's application for judicial approval to conduct repressive operations. As one judge reported (and others confirmed), "Preventive undercover operations are never mentioned when the police seek approval for some evidence-gathering sting. These preventive operations should really be in the application, to provide factual support for the request; but in fact, they never are."[29] Accordingly, cover-building operations may generate intelligence without judicial or even prosecutorial scrutiny.

In sum, the more the police conduct covert operations in their repressive, crime-solving capacity, the more they will engage in less regulated preventive undercover activity. Statutory control of repressive operations after 1992 may have been counterbalanced by the discretion the police acquired to do advance work in their preventive capacity. The secrecy surrounding preventive work reduces the transparency and accountability that statutory regulation and judicial oversight envisaged for covert operations. Secrecy may also undermine the legal validity of warrant applications, if the police omit information about preventive activities that led them to their targets. More troubling, perhaps, the possibility of conducting undercover activity in advance of judicial and prosecutorial authorization suggests the difficulty of cleanly separating the pursuit of intelligence from the search for evidence, though this is one of the legitimating assumptions of statutory regulation. At best, evidentiary principles that make it difficult to use preventively gathered insights at trial can hope to quarantine information that was obtained in advance of judicial approval for evidence-gathering repressive operations. But this device may cordon off not only incriminating evidence but information that is favorable to the defendant (or reflects poorly on the police).

INTELLIGENCE GATHERING (AND RISK MANAGEMENT) AFTER JUDICIAL APPROVAL OF REPRESSIVE UNDERCOVER OPERATIONS

We have seen that a commitment to obtaining evidence through repressive undercover operations requires significant intelligence gathering preventively (before judicial authorization for infiltration is sought under the 1992 statute). Agents need to build cover stories and scout targets in advance. But intelligence gathering does not occur only in the preventive phase. It also occurs in the repressive stage (after judicial authorization of undercover operations). These (repressive) operations are supposed to obtain evidence against targets for criminal prosecution rather than gather intelligence. Yet they do gather intelligence. Indeed, the logic of deep-cover operations increasingly diverts them from gathering evidence to collecting intelligence. The following section explores these dynamics.

The 1992 reforms encouraged the police to obtain judicial approval as soon as they settle on particular suspects, thus transforming preventive into repressive operations at the earliest possible time. In principle, this directed the police to seek evidence rather than intelligence, since the object of repressive investigations is a criminal prosecution. By operating preventively, the police risk being barred from using the information they gather as evidence, particularly if courts conclude that they used their preventive powers under state law to circumvent the requirements of the federal statute.[30] To the extent the reforms aimed to discourage the police from extending the preventive phase to circumvent statutory constraints, they seem to have succeeded. Police and prosecutors prefer conducting undercover investigations in their repressive capacity because advance judicial approval ensures the admissibility of the evidence. If the police did stumble onto evidence during a preventive undercover operation, its usability in a criminal prosecution became doubtful.[31] A prosecutor explained, "If you use a deep-cover agent in a preventive investigation, you can't guarantee his anonymity at trial. So even if we could use his information as evidence, we wouldn't want to."[32] And when investigations were simultaneously preventive and repressive, the police sought advance approval from prosecutors. "When we infiltrate the motorcycle gangs suspected of carrying out a spate of burglaries, our investigation is both preventive and repressive. So we might as well get the prosecutor's approval in advance, to ensure the admissibility of the evidence."[33] Indeed, there was little incentive for them to circumvent the requirements of judicial approval under the 1992 statute, since many state police laws impose equivalent constraints. Several require the police to obtain advance judicial approval.[34] Some states require prosecutors to supervise preventive undercover investigations.[35] Many follow the federal code in limiting preventive undercover investigations to only the most serious crimes.[36] A prosecutor explained, "In our state, we have to show imminent danger to get authorization for preventive operations; but if there's imminent danger, then there's usually already some kind of crime. So you might as well proceed on the repressive track and get your approval."[37] Some police officials reported that the need to enter private apartments usually triggered a decision to seek judicial approval under the federal statute, even though police laws do not prohibit agents from visiting targets at home.

Nominally, preventive operations give the police greater autonomy. Most states do not require prosecutors to supervise investigations with no expected evidentiary payoff. But many preventive operations lead to prosecutions, and the police tend to involve prosecutors in the preventive phase whenever they expect an arrest.[38] The police have other reasons to involve prosecutors during the preventive stage of an investigation. "In theory, preventive operations give us more freedom from the prosecutor's eye," a police official reported.

"But if we want permission to monitor conversations electronically, we have to go to the prosecutor anyway, regardless of whether this is a preventive or repressive undercover operation."[39] Indeed, in many states telephone tapping is permissible only for repressive police investigations, though other forms of electronic eavesdropping are available preventively.[40] Accordingly, there are few incentives to circumvent the federal statute by unduly extending preventive investigations once a prosecution seems likely.

But encouraging the police to expedite passage from the preventive to the repressive phase does not necessarily succeed in shifting their interest from the collection of intelligence to the gathering of evidence. There are two reasons for this. First, obtaining statutory authorization for repressive operations sometimes allows the police to avoid constraints on gathering intelligence in the preventive phase. The federal authorities lack statutory authorization to conduct preventive undercover probes, and some states also disallow them.[41] When state law limits what the police can do preventively, the power to conduct repressive investigations shelters the search for intelligence, which the police could not otherwise have pursued through (preventive) undercover methods. According to a police official from one such jurisdiction, the police often conduct nominally repressive investigations in such ways that "we don't make buys. We simply gather information about foreign offender groups. . . . Once we spent three years on a foreign offender group, working with several undercover agents. We got to know them socially, made ourselves interesting to them by offering things they needed—partners in German businesses, contacts, transportation, access to airports. And in this way we got lots of information; that was the aim. We learned who organizes things, how do they cross borders, how do they distribute drugs, invest money, communicate with each other. And since we were just investigating anonymous targets, since we didn't really know who they were, all we needed was the prosecutor's go ahead. But somewhere down the road [this being a repressive investigation] there will have to be seizures and arrests."[42]

Authorities who could not preventively collect intelligence described other ways of doing so in the guise of gathering evidence. One division reported using shallow-cover agents to investigate drug dealing. When the agents purchased drugs undercover, they usually testified (or were prepared to do so). "But then we also send guys in to build up a network of contacts, learn where the stuff gets sold, and in what quantities. They might introduce a shallow-cover agent who's had fewer contacts with these guys, and he makes the buys. But [the first] guys move around in that community, visit bars, department stores, and people get to know them, and we start to know what the targets are up to. What we learn from these operations never comes before a court; it's just intelligence. It's background for our investigative divisions. . . . This way, mostly, we learn about the milieu, how the drugs are being sold, what the prices are."[43] That shallow-cover agents also purchased drugs undercover gave them a legitimate evidentiary reason for existing as an organizational unit. But at least part of their function was to gather intelligence in a nominally repressive capacity (lacking statutory authorization for doing so preventively). Questioned about shallow-cover agents who don't testify, a prosecutor from the same state asserted with apparent confidence, "I'm certain they don't exist."[44] But there was no reason for the prosecutor to know, since the police made no evidentiary use of their insights. "What we learn through these agents doesn't go into the file—because look, they've had way too many contacts with the target [to qualify as shallow-cover agents not requiring judicial approval]. We call these guys 'mutant' shallow-cover agents, because they're really deep-cover agents and require approval from the judge. But that's only if you want to use what they tell you as evidence."[45]

Where the police lack the authority to conduct preventive undercover investigations, even covert drug purchases—usually classic sources of evidence—can serve nonevidentiary functions. "We have a pool of shallow-cover agents in our unit," a covert policing official from one such jurisdiction says. "They don't enter apartments or carry false papers, and they have maybe two, three, or four meetings with the target. . . . They buy relatively small quantities; often they make the arrest themselves, usually in discos where we know drugs are being sold. Here the main aim is just to take drugs from the market on a targeted basis and to identify places where drugs are being sold."[46] A prosecutor from the same state described these shallow-cover operations as designed primarily "to target some hot spot for drug distribution and get the sellers to worry that they may be selling to the police. It's our way of reducing activity at these nodal points."[47] The purpose is as much to reduce the activity in certain hot spots (a preventive aim) and "to obtain intelligence about infrastructure and volume" as it is to gather evidence.[48] "The shallow-cover agent may testify openly, the case may go to court, but the operation always serves a mix of preventive and repressive purposes."[49]

There is a second reason why the police may emphasize the collection of intelligence over the pursuit of evidence when conducting repressive undercover operations. They need to protect the government's investment in deep-cover agents with elaborate false identities. Allowing the insights of undercover agents to be offered into evidence even indirectly, through the testimony of their control officers, jeopardizes the agents' cover. The handler's testimony may suggest to the defendant which of his acquaintances was really an undercover agent. The police expect deep-cover agents to remain undercover through successive prosecutions and, if possible, to continue using the same cover story. To avoid "burning" deep-cover agents or their long-term cover stories, the police found ways to use them as sources of intelligence rather than evidence.

Thus the police have powerful incentives to gather intelligence rather than evidence even when they investigate crimes in their repressive capacities. They employ a number of covert tactics that permit them to do so. The simplest is to keep information out of court. Accordingly, the police rarely record meetings between undercover agents and targets, forgoing the creation of evidence in favor of continuing access to intelligence.[50] A covert policing official complained, "Every cover is there to be burned. But many states put the cover above all else. They would try to protect the cover and avoid putting into the file many of the observations which the agent makes undercover. Those observations would never be used as evidence."[51]

The police also employ a series of nesting mechanisms to shield undercover operations from discovery. Since undercover purchases put agents' covers at risk, "most undercover buys are made by informants and shallow-cover agents."[52] By contrast, deep-cover agents are deployed primarily for long-term operations. But even when the police use shallow-cover operatives, the limits placed on what such agents may do and the imperatives of secrecy may sometimes keep what the officer learns out of court. When a shallow-cover agent becomes too deeply entangled with his targets, "we really have two options. Either let [him] function as a deep-cover agent, and seek judicial approval, which means that he won't testify, or replace him with a real deep-cover agent once you see that the investigation is going to take longer than you thought. But that's hard too. We might decide to use that operation just to gather information," instead of evidence.[53]

When the police do use long-term operatives, they tend to use deep- and shallow-cover agents in tandem, so they can keep the deep-cover agent out of the case.[54] "Instead of having the deep-cover agent make the buys himself, it's better to use shallow-cover agents and have the deep-cover agent continue in the background, gathering information about organizational structures, hierarchies, shipping routes, transportation, and the like."[55] "Ideally, the deep-cover agent works his way into the red light social scene and stays there. He leads the short-term guy, he can guide him, but he always stays out of the picture."[56] And just as shallow-cover agents can protect deep-cover agents from detection, informants who are newcomers may come to shield more-deeply embedded informants. "Often our informant is very close to the target. Then we introduce an informant from outside the milieu; he in turn introduces a [shallow-cover] agent, who makes the undercover buy."[57] In other investigations, "the informant will buy small samples and then introduce the shallow-cover agent for the main transaction."[58] Accordingly, a deeply embedded informant may hand off the target to a more distant informant, who may in turn pass the target along to the deep-cover agent. The deep-cover agent may introduce the target to a shallow-cover agent. This process screens three layers of intelligence from discovery—and possibly a fourth if only the shallow-cover agent's handler openly testifies. In this way, much of what undercover investigations yield will remain in the realm of intelligence, whether such operations are conducted preventively or repressively.

Another way of protecting the identity of undercover agents is to use infiltration as an invisible adjunct to other covert and open tactics. "The undercover agent is part of a larger mosaic, along with telephone tapping, visual surveillance of targets, financial investigations, etc."[59] "If we're doing a wiretap, he'll tell us 'letters' means false documents or counterfeit currency, and 'mozzarella' means cocaine."[60] He may "negotiate with the target and provoke incriminating chatter on the wire."[61] But "the aim of the undercover operation is always to get leads, not to get evidence. Where do the targets meet, where do they unload their goods; that leads you to surveillance and traffic stops and seizures."[62]

Undercover agents have other means of avoiding the limelight. They can use their supporting role to make conventional tactics more fruitful. "The undercover agent might learn that there's a fight about money; one of the targets has too much. The target may have secretly kept some of the loot from the others. We then use that knowledge to invite the guy who was shorted in for questioning and tell him that the other guy has been stealing from him. Now he might decide to take revenge by testifying about his accomplice, so that he can keep the business for himself."[63] This tactic also permits deep-cover agents to remain undetected. It outsources the task of influencing targets to uniformed personnel and ultimately makes targets themselves, rather than undercover agents, into witnesses. "The whole aim of the deep-cover operation is to use the agent as a bridge to other evidence. *He* should never be the evidence."[64]

Finally, informal charging discretion also helps police and prosecutors avoid using undercover agents' insights as evidence. "Often we don't even charge the offense that the undercover agent helped set up, once he leads us to other crimes that don't involve the agent himself. The offense that the undercover agent helped arrange will be small by comparison" and the undercover agent can safely be kept out of the case.[65] "If I charge the crime that the agent helped to set up, the whole case will be about entrapment. So why bother, if I can prove the other crimes?"[66]

Ironically, the statutory command to turn preventive into repressive operations at the earliest possible time makes it easier for the police to use

GRID A

Aspirations of the Post-1992 German System

	Evidence	Intelligence
Preventive Infiltration		
Repressive Infiltration	X	

GRID B

Actual Operation of the Post-1992 German System

	Evidence	Intelligence
Preventive Infiltration		X
Repressive Infiltration	X	X

repressive undercover investigations as sources of intelligence. The pressure to initiate repressive investigations as soon as suspicions crystallize around particular targets pushes repressive investigations back into ever earlier phases of the investigative process, where intelligence gathering becomes difficult to distinguish from the pursuit of evidence. Whether information becomes evidence or intelligence is then largely a matter of what use the police choose to make of it. By moving from the preventive to the repressive stage very early in the course of an undercover operation, the police gain more time to investigate. They can postpone the acquisition of evidence (e.g., through covert purchases and seizures) to the final stage of the investigation. In the meantime, they can interpose shallow-cover agents between deep cover agents and their targets, thereby protecting the confidentiality of deep-cover agents' identity. The police can also use wiretaps and other investigative tactics to pursue leads developed by deep-cover agents. The longer the repressive phase lasts, the more time the police have to insulate their deep-cover operatives from discovery.

Grids A and B show the four ways German regulation conceives of covert police operations. Undercover investigations can yield either evidence or intelligence. The police can perform such operations either preventively (to maintain order and prevent harm) or repressively (to solve crimes and catch criminals). The post-1992 German system sought to legitimate undercover policing by encouraging the police to conduct infiltration in their repressive capacity, on the assumption that this would turn undercover operations into producers of evidence, rather than intelligence.

As indicated in Grid A (second column, bottom row), the 1992 statute legitimated repressive undercover investigations as a technique for acquiring evidence for criminal prosecutions and required advance prosecutorial or judicial approval for those repressive investigations that involved deep-cover agents. It encouraged the police to turn preventive operations into repressive operations as soon as suspicion focused on particular individuals.[67] The post-1992 system did not envision covert police acquiring intelligence unless quickly transformed into evidence. But as Grid B illustrates, the system does not work as envisioned. In practice, German police and prosecutors have to build convincing cover stories and to gather advance intelligence. The statutory directive to move quickly from the preventive to the repressive phase did not simply transform the quest for intelligence into a search for evidence. Once duly authorized, repressive investigations came to shelter many intelligence-gathering tasks that the police could not perform in their preventive capacity. Moreover, reliance on long-term deep-cover tactics made it ever more important to differentiate intelligence from evidence and to shield intelligence from discovery. Though the reforms sought to legitimate undercover tactics as a source of evidence, they also institutionalized and entrenched deep-cover tactics in ways that made them more practical as sources of intelligence.

Conclusion

The 1992 reforms, then, created a tension. They legitimated deep-cover operations as sources of evidence for criminal prosecutions. Yet the internal logic of deep-cover investigations (the need to protect cover stories and personnel) pushes the insights of undercover agents back into the shadows, as intelligence and leads—but not as evidence. This may not be altogether a bad thing. Is it not preferable for the police to deemphasize the evidentiary significance of sting operations when the government can prove crimes that the target committed without prodding from undercover agents? American sting operations often yield prosecutions only for those offenses that undercover agents helped bring about. The German emphasis on proving crimes that targets commit independently of police influence may be salutary by ensuring that punishment reflects targets' autonomous decisions, not their latent inclinations. However, the secrecy surrounding the activities of deep-cover agents also creates problems for the legal system. Information that agents provide cannot be scrutinized by defense counsel and tested through the criminal process. Covert influences on seemingly independent crimes may never be known. The inside knowledge that agents can acquire may have only a limited payoff for criminal prosecutions if the need to protect agents' cover precludes revealing it in court.

That evidence-gathering stings often produce more intelligence than evidence may be particularly problematic for the legitimacy of such investigations when the undercover operatives are informants, not undercover agents. Informants are considerably less reliable, are often criminals themselves, and may have a host of motives for lying to the police or manipulating their targets. Intelligence that stems from informants is considerably more likely to be tainted by error, bias, or dishonesty. Yet the secrecy surrounding informants means that this intelligence may influence the investigation and the criminal process without being subject to scrutiny as evidence. Informants do not testify, though their handlers may. Ideally, from the perspective of police and prosecutors, even that would not be necessary. "My goal," a German prosecutor said, "is to get the informant out of the picture and find other evidence that's not tied to him."[68] "With multiple secret sources one can keep one out of the file."[69] Information that might wind up in court is often kept cloudy. "Questioning of informants is very limited, because we want to conceal its source. How the informant knows something is usually left very vague."[70] Frequently, how intelligence is acquired precludes its use as evidence. A chief of a covert policing unit said, "If information about a crime could lead to the identification of an undercover operative, we do not pursue that information, or we try to prove it through other means that won't disclose the source of the information. The confidentiality of the informant often conflicts with the aim of proving a crime. And we might decide not to pursue the investigation to protect the source."[71] Thus the imperatives of protecting informants (and their covers) limit their evidentiary value while obscuring their role in the investigation.

As the police and prosecutors filter an informant's information to obscure clues to his identity, they also jettison many of the indicators of that information's reliability. This is a cost of turning intelligence into evidence (ready to come into the public realm at trial). Thus, the internal logic of deep-cover operations shrouds the process of information acquisition with secrecy, defying the attempt to legitimate undercover tactics by decreeing that their insights should be brought out openly as evidence in criminal prosecutions. When turned into evidence, the insights of undercover agents and informants are stripped of context, including much background information obtained from layers of moles. These insights in their raw form remain unavailable to the criminal process and to those who must judge guilt or innocence.

The capacity of deep-cover investigations to encourage collection of intelligence alongside evidence reinforces concerns about the overlap between preventive and repressive operations and, more significantly, about the functional resemblance of the work of undercover police and domestic intelligence agencies. These dynamics erode the distinction between repressive and preventive policing, heightening tension between the pursuit of individualized justice and the reduction of threats to public safety. Efforts to use undercover investigations as sources of intelligence mean that the police look for information that goes well beyond what they need as evidence to secure a conviction at trial. Thus the criminal code no longer cabins the scope of criminal investigations, allowing the police to investigate inchoate threats rather than well-defined crimes, future conduct rather than past offenses, milieus and places rather than identified suspects. Most significantly, the tendency of undercover investigations to generate intelligence alongside (or instead of) evidence brings undercover operations into conflict with the principle of separation. This constitutional difficulty seemingly distinguishes Germany from the United States, which does not recognize the principle of separation. The FBI has always conducted counterintelligence investigations alongside its law enforcement operations. Since the September 11 attacks, the FBI has emphasized intelligence gathering and has acquired greater powers to investigate domestic political organizations.

But concerns about using covert investigations as sources of intelligence need not center only on the principle of separation. Using undercover investigations in this way also creates risks that police infiltrators will exert invisible influence either on crimes or, more broadly, on society. Infiltration fuels anxieties about excessive government surveillance and about agents provocateurs sowing mistrust, driving marginal groups underground, or manipulating incentive structures in ways that may never be known. To be sure, German concerns about the abuses of surveillance and infiltration arise at least partly out of the Nazi past. But the United States, too, has had experience with untrammeled uses of intelligence, including the erstwhile Red Squads and FBI surveillance and infiltration of social movements, particularly in its Hoover era.[72] After the September 11 attacks, Attorney General John Ashcroft expanded the use of undercover techniques in terrorism investigations by authorizing FBI agents to "attend public events . . . for the purpose of detecting or preventing terrorist activities, without the predication required to investigate leads or conduct a preliminary inquiry or full investigation."[73] Thus undercover agents may now visit churches or mosques without any allegation that congregants are involved in unlawful activity and thus without the prospect that the infiltrators' insights will produce evidence tested in court. Likewise, undercover police officers are once more infiltrating protests.[74] The expansion of surveillance as a source of intelligence is likely to pose problems of oversight and influence whenever the government's tactics remain insulated from challenge or exposure.

EIGHT

Vulnerability, Sovereignty, and Police Power in the ASBO

PETER RAMSAY

Introduction

The United Kingdom's Anti-Social Behaviour Order (ASBO) was enacted by parliament in the Crime and Disorder Act of 1998. It provides local authorities and police forces with a sweeping power to control behavior. Lindsay Farmer has pointed out that the ASBO is of particular interest because it

> would appear to be an excellent example of the traditional police power. . . . Yet it is clear that the development of the ASBO also suggests changes in the government and production of social order, and in analyzing this we can be more specific about both the content of the police power and the manner of its exercise.[1]

Here I want to take up Farmer's suggestion and explore the specific elements of continuity and change in the police power that are to be found in the ASBO. As a power of social control, the ASBO stands in a functional position adjacent to and overlapping with that occupied for more than a millennium by another legal power, latterly known as the bind over. But the ASBO's substantive terms and explicit rationale are quite different from that of the ancient power. This chapter explores these differences and considers their implications for the "new science of police."[2]

I begin by placing the argument in the context of Markus Dubber's historical analysis of the origins and development of the police power. Then I explain why the ASBO provides an example of the power of moral police. After that I compare and contrast the substantive legal terms of the ASBO with that of the bind over and seek to demonstrate how, in the contemporary period, the state's power of moral police has been pluralized. In the process, I will argue that the moral authority of the sovereign in the exercise of these powers has been explicitly marginalized. Finally, I consider how both British government policy toward antisocial behavior and judicial interpretation of the ASBO power seek to explain this particular shift in the substantive terms of the moral police. I will argue that the terms of the ASBO power, and of the official explanation of the need for it, manifest a distinct lack of confidence in the state's sovereign authority.

Police and Law

Dubber identifies *police* as one of the two "basic modes of state governance [that] can be traced throughout the history of Western political thought and practice."[3] The other mode is *law*, and Dubber relates them to each other in the following way:

> From the perspective of law, the state is the institutional manifestation of a political community of free and equal persons. The function of the law state is to manifest and protect the autonomy of its constituents in all of its aspects, private and public. From the perspective of police, the state is the institutional manifestation of a household. The police state, as *paterfamilias* seeks to maximize the welfare of his—or rather its—household.[4]

These contrasting functions imply different relations between the state and its citizens. The "law state" is one of self-government in which there is no formal distinction between government and governed or between the subjects and objects of government. In the law state the citizenry are sovereign and its principle is the autonomy of the individual.[5] Police, on the other hand, is a question of household management in which there is a sharp distinction between the subject of government and its objects. Under the "police state" the sovereign governs both persons and things (animate and inanimate) as the heteronomous objects of welfare, much as a patriarch would govern his household.[6] Indeed, Dubber demonstrates that patriarchy is the historical foundation of the state's power of police just as he argues that democracy is the ultimate foundation of the law state.[7] The two modes may not be clearly distinguished in the practice of government. As Dubber argues, much of what is conventionally described as American criminal law is better understood as police power.[8]

It is important to note at the outset that a single theoretical figure unites these two otherwise contrasting modes of governance—the figure of the sovereign. Under the governance of the democratic legal mode, autonomous individual subjects or citizens are ultimately sovereign in the political community of the state, since it is for the citizens to determine which of them shall make the laws and on what political basis. Under the governance of the patriarchal mode, the state as sovereign exercises the police power over those same individual citizens in the name of their collective welfare. Traditionally, in a state's external relations, and in international law, the distinction between the two modes disappears in the collective sovereignty that is exercised autonomously in relation to other sovereigns.[9]

Notwithstanding this ultimate unity, when viewed from the inside there is clearly a fundamental tension between these two modes of governance. From the basic distinction of police-heteronomy versus law-autonomy can be derived a whole matrix of contrasts between the realm of law and that of police. Dubber distinguishes the two along the lines of

> the different types of interference associated with police and law (prevention and remedy), the different objects of that interference (threats and persons), the different styles of government (informality and formality, flexibility and definiteness), the different types of scrutiny applied (effectiveness and justice), and—perhaps most important—the different relationships between the subject and the object of government that characterize police and law as modes of governance (hierarchy and equality).[10]

The aspect of the police power of particular concern in relation to the ASBO is that concerned with the police of *people* as threats to the public welfare. It is in this respect that the tension between these two modes of governance is at its most acute. For, as Dubber asks, "How can objects of police remain legal subjects. . . . How can an essentially heteronomous mode of governance comply with the basic legal principle of legal legitimacy, autonomy?"[11]

Dubber's account of the police power is of course not the only one.[12] But his attention to history makes his account particularly appropriate for assessing what a recent innovation like the ASBO represents, standing as it does in the place of a police power of such long standing as the bind over. Dubber argues that "it's impossible to understand the nature of the police power, and to appreciate the challenges it faces, particularly in a modern state, by taking an ahistorical view."[13] By thinking about the ASBO in terms of the concepts Dubber develops, it should be possible to identify what may be changing in the deployment of that power in the present and begin to think about the implications this has for the question of legitimacy that Dubber poses. To begin I will briefly describe the ASBO and explain why it can properly be understood as a police power.

The ASBO as Police Power

The ASBO is one of an expanding array of powers available to UK authorities in relation to antisocial behavior (or ASB in the official jargon).[14] In its substantive structure, the ASBO seems to be a distinctively British innovation, although the wider ASB powers and their context in the criminal justice system can be functionally compared with the so-called order maintenance policing of American cities.[15] The power of local authorities and local police chiefs to apply for, and of courts to grant, an ASBO is provided under section 1 of the Crime and Disorder Act (CDA) of 1998. Section 1(1) provides that

> an application for an order under this section may be made by a relevant authority if it appears to the authority that the following conditions are fulfilled with respect to any person aged 10 or over, namely—
> (a) that the person has acted . . . in an anti-social manner, that is to say, in a manner that caused or was likely to cause harassment, alarm or distress to one or more persons not of the same household as himself; and
> (b) that such an order is necessary to protect persons . . . from further anti-social acts by him.

There is a significant qualification to these grounds for granting an order in section 1(5), which provides that "for the purpose of determining whether the condition mentioned in subsection (1)(a) above is fulfilled, the court shall disregard any act of the defendant which he shows was reasonable in the circumstances."

Where "it is proved that the conditions mentioned in subsection (1) are fulfilled,"[16] then a magistrate has a discretion to make an order that may contain any "prohibitions . . . necessary for the purpose of protecting persons . . . from further anti-social acts by the defendant."[17] Typically these prohibitions will include exclusion zones, restrictions on associating with named individuals, communicating with other named individuals, using offensive language, wearing certain items of clothing, drinking alcohol, and so on.[18] The minimum period of an ASBO is two years; there is no maximum period.[19]

The ASBO is granted in civil proceedings, and while the standard of proof is formally the criminal standard of beyond reasonable doubt, hearsay evidence and the use of professional witnesses are permitted.[20] However, once an order has been granted, a defendant who breaches any of its terms is guilty of a criminal offense carrying a maximum of five years' imprisonment. This offense is one of strict liability unless the defendant can prove a reasonable excuse for the breach.[21]

An order is therefore a list of individualized criminal offenses that are tailored to the particular defendant *considered as a specific threat* to others' feelings of security or self-esteem. At their broadest, the grounds for imposing this particularized criminal liability are that

- the defendant has acted in a way "likely to cause harassment, alarm or distress,"
- the defendant does not have a good reason for having done so, and
- without obedience to an order the defendant is likely to do so again.

Unsurprisingly, legal critics have complained that these criteria are so vague and broad as to create a discretionary power in magistrates to criminalize on an occasional and individualized basis a very wide range of otherwise legal conduct.[22] My own synthesis of the combined effect of subsections 1(1)(a), 1(1)(b), and 1(5) suggests that, insofar as section 1 CDA 1998 can be regarded as containing a definition of the behavior that will render a person liable to an ASBO, it defines antisocial behavior as

> any manifestation of a disposition of indifference to the feelings of others which is contrary to public policy, and which, therefore, permits the exercise of the discretionary power to impose an ASBO.[23]

It is the attitude of disrespect that is the target of the ASBO. A person who manifests this attitude is liable to find himself or herself defending an ASBO application. In practice the working definition of antisocial behavior is left to Home Office guidance documents, which give police and local authorities nonexhaustive lists of the conduct appropriate for ASBO proceedings.[24] But what local authorities actually treat as ASB varies widely.[25] The vast discretion to criminalize otherwise lawful behavior that the scheme allows to police, local authorities, and magistrates caused leading academic criminal law specialists to describe the legislative scheme as an Undesirable Persons Act.[26] But we can here summarize the ASBO power by how it exhibits all the characteristics that Dubber attributes to the police power.

- The enormous breadth and vagueness of the definition of antisocial behavior, of the grounds for exercise of the power, indicates that the ASBO provides authorities with flexibility rather than citizens with a definite description of their potential liability.
- The purpose of the order is explicitly preventive. The terms of the order are not determined by punitive or deterrence criteria but by what is necessary in fact to prevent ASB by the defendant in the future.

- The grounds for granting the ASBO are concerned to ensure that the order is necessary but not that the defendant was at fault in the sense recognized by criminal lawyers that she intended to cause, or foresaw a risk of causing, harassment, alarm, or distress.[27] These grounds provide for an assessment of the defendant as a potential threat rather than a judgment of her actions as those of the autonomous person imagined in Dubber's account of law.[28]
- The emphasis in the ASBO process, especially in the relative informality and evidence rules of civil procedure, is effectiveness rather than justice to the defendant, at least in the conventional sense of criminal justice.
- The power to grant the ASBO is substantively a discretionary power under administrative law to vary the civil rights of individuals in pursuit of the aims of public policy.[29] There is no requirement for the authorities to prove a criminal offense or behavior that is in any way unlawful.[30] The relationship between the defendant of ASBO proceedings, on the one hand, and the applicant authority and the court, on the other, is therefore hierarchical.

Let's now compare the ASBO with the power to bind over a defendant to be of good behavior.

The Ancient Power to Bind Over

In *Public Wrongs*, volume 4 of his *Commentaries on the Laws of England*, William Blackstone devotes one chapter to "the means of preventing offences." We find that "this preventive justice consists in obliging those persons, whom there is probable ground to suspect of future misbehaviour, to stipulate with and to give full assurance to the public, that such offence as is apprehended shall not happen; by finding pledges or securities for keeping the peace or for their good behaviour."[31] The security given by the person "consists in being bound, with one or more sureties, in a recognisance to the king, entered on a record . . . whereby the parties acknowledge themselves to be indebted to the crown in the sum required"[32] until such time as the court required him to appear again, and if the person had been of good behavior in the intervening period, he was discharged of the debt.

The power to demand this security was at the discretion of a justice of the peace on his own initiative or the request of any person.[33] Where it concerned "recognisance, with sureties, for . . . good behaviour" then it was held "that a man may be bound to his good behaviour for causes of scandal, *contra bonos mores*, as well as *contra pacem*."[34] The purpose of exercising this power was "that the people be not troubled nor endamaged, nor the peace diminished, nor merchants and others, passing by the highways of the realm, be disturbed nor put in the peril which may happen by such offenders," and such offenders against whom this preventive power could be deployed included "all them that be not of good fame."[35] The definition of what it meant to be "not of good fame" was not so much broad as indeterminate. Blackstone offers a long list of examples, which include those who "haunt[] bawdy houses with women of bad fame . . . night-walkers; eaves-droppers; such as keep suspicious company or are reported to be pilferers or robbers; such as sleep in the day and wake on the night; common drunkards; whoremasters; the putative fathers of bastards; cheats; idle vagabonds," and concludes,

> and other persons, whose behaviour may reasonably bring them within the general words of the statute, as persons not of good fame: an expression, it must be owned, of so great a latitude, as leaves much to be determined by the discretion of the magistrate himself.[36]

Of Blackstone's list, Dubber comments that it

> displays the sort of impatience with principle and specificity that characterizes household governance. . . . The point of police is the suppression of threats to the public police. . . . In this light, the vagueness of a concept such as "nuisance" is not a problem, but an asset. Unconstrained by notice concerns, state officials . . . could mold it as they saw fit to deal with "annoyances" to the public at large.[37]

The power described by Blackstone in the eighteenth century dates back at least as far as the tenth century and was first given some statutory authority in the Justices of the Peace Act of 1361.[38] It has survived into the present, becoming known as the "bind over to keep the peace and/or be of good behaviour." The modern bind over was given a statutory procedure under the Magistrates Courts Act 1980 section 115, which permits a justice of the peace to require any person before a court to enter into a recognizance, with or without sureties, to keep the peace or be of good behavior. The bind over has been used extensively in magistrates' courts primarily as a means of preventive control against defendants who are acquitted of criminal charges or against whom charges are dropped, but also as a sentence on conviction for minor offenses.[39] The essence of the bind-over power is "an acknowledgement by the person bound over of his indebtedness to the sovereign in the sum of the recognisance,"[40] although a power to imprison anyone who refuses to make the recognizance as ordered for up to six months, or until they comply with the order, was added to the modern bind over.[41]

The bind over to keep the peace and the bind over to be of good behavior are two separate powers. Both have traditionally been deployed to catch actions on the edge of illegality that might escape criminal liability.[42] For a long time the grounds for the exercise of the two powers, and the definitions of what constituted conduct *contra pacem* and *contra bonos mores*, were equally vague. But in the 1980s, the Court of Appeal began the process of tightening up the definition of breach of the peace, describing it as

> an act done or threatened to be done which either actually harms a person, or in his presence his property, or is likely to cause such harm or which puts someone in fear of such harm being done.[43]

However, while the modern power to keep the peace began to juridify in this way, the meaning of actions *contra bonos mores* remained entirely within the magistrates' discretion. So in the High Court in 1988 Lord Justice Glidewell ruled that

> *contra bonos mores* means contrary to a good way of life. What is a good way of life is for the magistrates to decide . . . *contra bonos mores* is conduct which has the property of being wrong rather than right in the judgment of the vast majority of fellow citizens.[44]

The parallel with the ASBO is striking in that both are a measure of preventive justice based on prohibiting nuisances that are ill defined, allowing the maximum flexibility to the authorities and discretion to the courts. The ASBO occupies ground adjacent to and overlapping with the bind over since, as District Judge Paul Tain observes, "there are very few categories of bind-over behaviour which do not fit into the categories challenged by anti-social behaviour legislation."[45] As we shall see below, contemporary policy gives the rationale for the ASBO as the alleviation of the fear of crime that causes people to abandon public space just as Blackstone's recognizances with sureties were intended to ensure that people were not "troubled," the public peace not "diminished," users of public space not "put in peril."

The differences between the ASBO and the bind over are just as interesting as the similarities. In the first place, the ASBO provides a better-defined procedure than the bind over for which there were almost no formal rules of procedure or evidence.[46] Second, the ASBO requires a link between the scope of the order and the conduct complained of, since the grounds for granting an order include the requirement that it is "necessary" to protect people "from further anti-social acts" by the defendant.[47] While a modern bind over to keep the peace can be imposed only where the magistrate has some cause to believe that the conduct concerned would be repeated,[48] there is no such connection required in imposing a bind over to be of good behavior.[49] Third, there is a subtle difference between the definitions of the conduct to be controlled by the ASBO and by the bind over. And, arising from this third difference, a fourth is that, by comparison with the bind over, the ASBO can be deployed to control a broader scope of conduct and may penetrate deeper into the lives of those regulated by it. These last two differences need to be considered further because they raise key questions about the ASBO as a police power. The ASBO emerged and was enacted by parliament during the period when the bind over to be of good behavior was facing a particular threat from the European Convention on Human Rights. To understand the ASBO's substantive deepening and broadening of the moral police, it will help to compare the bind over and the ASBO in the context of the legal criticism and reform of the bind-over power that occurred during this period.

Pluralizing the Moral Police

The power described by Blackstone survived for more than a millennium, but in the late twentieth century it became increasingly controversial among lawyers in the United Kingdom. In 1994 the official advisory body on law reform, the Law Commission, published a report recommending the abolition of the bind over without replacement.[50] The ancient power was not without its supporters, however. Of the judges consulted by the Law Commission, all but two "rejected the assertion that there was anything unconstitutional in a court having power to restrict, by the imposition of custodial or financial sanctions, the repetition of conduct which, although it may not be criminal, is socially objectionable."[51] Moreover, the report admits that this was the view of the majority of organizations and individuals "who had experience of the way those powers operated in practice."[52] Nevertheless, the Law Commission recommended abolition.

The Law Commission had many procedural criticisms, but at the heart of its case for abolition was substantive vagueness. With respect to the bind over to be of good behavior, the commission's objection was that "the width and vagueness of the notion of being of good behaviour" rendered it "difficult, if not impossible, to define the limits of this power of control."[53] Such an order "fails to give sufficient indication to the person bound over of the conduct which he or she must avoid in order to be safe from coercive sanctions."[54] Keeping the peace was subject to a more restricted variant of the same criticism, given that its definition was generally clearer, but still contained potential vagueness in the idea of conduct causing another to apprehend harm to his person or property. These positions for and against the bind over, articulated in the commission report, encapsulate the perspectives of police and of law, respectively, as outlined by Dubber.

In a series of cases following the Law Commission report, the definition of conduct that breached the peace was further narrowed by the courts to mean conduct that causes a threat of imminent violence,[55] and a very restrictive approach to the use of the bind over to keep the peace against otherwise lawful behavior was endorsed.[56] As a consequence, when the bind over to keep the peace came to be challenged at the European Court of Human Rights (ECtHR), the Strasbourg court upheld the power on the ground that the concept of breach of the peace had by then been clarified by the English courts with the degree of precision required by the Convention.[57] With the breach of the peace power to a considerable extent juridified by these new requirements, it is the bind over to be of good behavior with which the vaguely defined ASBO power now warrants comparison. And the bind over to be of good behavior has not fared so well at Strasbourg.

In 2000 in *Hashman and Harrup v. UK*, the ECtHR took the Law Commission's view and ruled that the power to bind over on the ground that a person's actions were *contra bonos mores* violated article 10(2) of the European Convention on Human Rights.[58] In that case protesters against fox hunting had been bound over, and the court ruled that *contra bonos mores* was simply too vague to be regarded as an interference with the right to free expression that was truly "prescribed by law" as article 10(2) of the Convention requires. The legal basis of the power to bind over to be of good behavior is therefore now in doubt since, by virtue of section 6 of the Human Rights Act 1998, UK courts are required to act compatibly with the European Convention on Human Rights.[59] The problem for the ECtHR in *Hashman* was that a restriction on human rights must be sufficiently precise to be "foreseeable" on the part of persons subject to it for it to be prescribed by law. The court compared the definition of *contra bonos mores* with an Austrian provision, which impugned conduct "likely to cause annoyance" and which the Strasbourg court had upheld in the case of *Chorherr v. Austria*. The court had ruled that the Austrian power was prescribed by law within the meaning of the Convention because the behavior concerned was described "by reference to its effects"—namely, "annoyance."[60] By contrast, "conduct which is wrong rather than right in the judgement of the majority of fellow citizens . . . is conduct which is not described at all, but merely expressed to be 'wrong' in the opinion of a majority of citizens."[61] While this reasoning disapproves of the bind over to be of good behavior, it would seem to insulate the ASBO from any challenge on substantive grounds under the Convention, since the grounds for imposing an ASBO—though vague, subjective, and very broad—are nevertheless, like the power in *Chorherr*, defined by reference to the effect of conduct—namely, "harassment, alarm or distress."[62]

The *Hashman* court's reasoning is a pointed rejection of the idea that, when it comes to the power of police (though the court doesn't call the bind over that), the substantive definition of the moral welfare of the people can be left solely to the discretion of the sovereign householder in the shape of his justices of the peace. For Lord Justice Glidewell in *Hughes v. Holley* in the late 1980s (and the large majority of judges consulted by the Law Commission at around the same time), not only was behavior "contrary to the good way of life" sufficiently clearly defined as to raise no question as to the constitutionality of the bind-over power, but it was equally unproblematic that the Crown's loyal justices of the peace could be relied on to know such behavior when they saw it. Lord Glidewell asserts that whatever the historical origin of the power "it rests on the maxim or principle *salus populi suprema lex*" (the welfare of the people is the supreme law).[63] In rationalizing the bind-over power in these traditional terms, Lord Justice Glidewell simply assumes both the moral homogeneity of the people, as if they were indeed a single household, and the propriety of the wise discretion of the sovereign householder in protecting their welfare. This is the unquestioned and barely articulated source of the unbroken power that the Law Commission traces back to King Æthelstan and that Dubber identifies as patriarchal. For the ECtHR, however, the scope of this ancient power defined in these traditional terms is not foreseeable enough to be prescribed by law. But a similarly broad discretionary power becomes sufficiently foreseeable if it is defined in terms of its subjective effects on other citizens, as the ASBO power is. It is this pluralization of the grounds for the power's exercise that is the key substantive change, and it expresses a subtle shift in the moral content of the behavior that is controlled by the ASBO when compared with that controlled by the bind over.

Where the bind over required people not to do wrong, the ASBO requires them not to disrespect others by offending their sensibilities. The ASBO is concerned not with any moral quality that might be intrinsic to a defendant's conduct as such but only with the quality of the feelings that the conduct gives rise to in others. Feelings of "harassment, alarm or distress" are feelings associated with fear and anxiety. Preventing fear and anxiety is the ASBO's purpose.[64] Preventing the defendant from causing such feelings is not therefore a question of how good or bad her conduct is, except insofar as *good* means "reassuring" and *bad* means "not reassuring." The ASBO power endeavors to enforce reassuring behavior, and this shift in the content of the behavior controlled marks an important shift in the rationale of the state's power of police, one that seems to escape the legal problems encountered in recent years by the bind-over power. With the ASBO, the British state appears to have devolved to its many individual subjects a part of the distinctively sovereign moral authority to determine what behavior serves the moral welfare of the people. It has also reformulated what constitutes the moral welfare of the people in a more explicitly instrumental language, one that might even be thought of, paradoxically, as a literally demoralized language. The people's moral welfare appears as a matter of individuals' peace of mind and self-esteem, of whether others reassure them or undermine these feelings, rather than any shared substantive morality as such.

Of course the authorities still enjoy a very wide interpretive discretion, provided both by the ASBO's availability on the grounds that a person has behaved in a manner only "likely to cause harassment, alarm or distress" (which frees the police or local authority from having to prove any actual effects of behavior)[65] and by the discretion to ignore conduct that the defendant can show to be reasonable (which creates a very broad interpretive discretion toward any particular behavior). A de facto social norm may be officially constructed and imposed in this way;[66] the ASBO remains a police power with the ultimate determination of what is not reassuring remaining with the sovereign. But the discretion is to decide what will not reassure others, rather than to decide what is good. The grounds for the power's exercise are pluralized and contain no specific universally asserted substantive content, not even what would be "wrong rather than right in the judgment of the vast majority of fellow citizens." The ASBO's grounds require only that each individual must respect the actual sensibilities of others regardless of the content of those sensibilities (except where it is reasonable not to do so). The moral welfare of the people is *explicitly* presented as a question of what in fact makes them feel insecure, a matter for them to determine on an individual basis. The state's explicit role is only to support them in that, by enforcing the conditions of this pluralized moral welfare and tempering them with considerations of reasonableness.

The pluralization of the moral police in the ASBO marks a new basis for the exercise of police power, a basis that broadens and deepens the power's reach as well. The ASBO is a substantively broader power than the bind over in the sense that conduct that "causes harassment, alarm or distress" encompasses not merely what would meet the *contra bonos mores* definition of "wrong rather than right in the judgment of the vast majority of fellow citizens" but what in fact offends anyone, including people more sensitive to particular conduct than the majority. When a TV interviewer asked Home Office Minister Hazel Blears what antisocial behavior meant, she replied, "It means whatever the victim says it means."[67] The still broader statutory phrase "conduct likely to cause harassment, alarm or distress" has been interpreted by the courts in a similar way.[68]

These pluralized grounds for the exercise of the power of moral police necessarily "deepen" its penetration too. This is because the ASBO seeks to prevent the defendant from causing the particular form of harassment, alarm, or distress by setting out specific prohibitions breach of which will be a criminal offense. The ASBO is therefore more precise in its preventive intent. The purpose of the order is not so much to ensure good behavior in general but to give very explicit guidance to the defendant as to what she must avoid doing in the future if she is to avoid failing to reassure others. (And, theoretically at least, the ASBO carries greater deterrent power since failure to follow the court's precise instructions will render her liable to imprisonment up to a maximum of five years.) In this sense the ASBO goes deeper as a police power since it does not merely remind the subject of the sovereign's power over her to the extent of the debt but rather seeks to regulate the person subjected to it in detail.[69]

But these pluralized moral grounds for the ASBO's deployment, and their expansive consequences for the police power, pose further questions. This new power enforces a standard of civility that is potentially more exacting than the old one, and it regulates more closely the lives of those who fail to live up to that standard. The power is substantively structured and presented in a way that in certain respects displaces the wise discretion of the sovereign householder in favor of the subjective sensitivities of the household's members. A putatively shared moral code gives way to a still more demanding requirement of mutual reassurance. But why should this be? What is the rationale for this pluralized conception of moral police?

In being confronted with this question we are perhaps fortunate that, unlike the barely articulated source and rationale of the bind-over power, the ASBO, as a modern statutory power, comes accompanied by policy documents, ministerial speeches and statements explaining the official thinking behind it. In the next section I will look at these to see what the official argument for the power to impose an ASBO is and what this tells us about the ASBO as a police power.

Antisocial Behavior and Fear of Crime

In its origins the ASBO was a measure that emerged from the deliberations of housing managers on the problem of how to deal effectively with troublesome residents of social housing.[70] Not much deployed in the first few years after its 1998 enactment,[71] the ASBO was remotivated by the Home Office in New Labour's second term of office as part of a wider agenda that, following New Labour's reelection for a third term in 2005, became known as the Respect Agenda. In his first speech after winning the 2005 election, Prime Minister Tony Blair said that "a particular priority" was going to be "how we bring back a proper sense of respect in our schools, in our communities, in our towns and our villages."[72]

We have seen above that it is just this attitude of disrespect for others' feelings that is the target of the ASBO. Blair's language of respect is central to the 2003 Home Office white paper *Respect and Responsibility: Taking a Stand Against Anti-Social Behaviour*, which set out the policy underlying the broad range of antisocial behavior powers taken on by government. In *Respect and Responsibility*, ASB policy, in general, and the ASBO, in particular, are addressed to a specific mischief: "Anti-social behaviour gives rise to fear of crime."[73] Despite the fall in actual crime reported in victim surveys and recorded by the police,

> the fear of crime has not fallen to the same extent. And it is fear of crime—rather than actually being a victim—that can so often limit people's lives, making them feel afraid of going out or even afraid in their own homes.[74]

It is the fear of crime, and the consequent abandonment of public space, that "limit[s] people's lives," that for the Home Office makes ASB policy a question of rights: "Our job is . . . to shift the culture away from protecting the rights of the perpetrator toward protecting the rights of decent people."[75] In his "Ministerial Foreword," Home Secretary David Blunkett spelled out these rights of decent people:

> As a society, our rights as individuals are based on the sense of responsibility we have towards others and to our families and communities. This means respecting each other's property, respecting the streets and public places we share *and respecting our neighbours' right to live free from harassment and distress.* It is the foundation of civic society.[76]

The decent citizen's right to live free from harassment and distress, which the Home Office asserts as the basis of the ASBO power, has been judicially backed by the House of Lords. In the leading case of *McCann*, the House upheld the designation of the ASBO application proceedings as civil rather than criminal, allowing the use of hearsay evidence. Lord Steyn remarked, "My starting point is an initial scepticism of an outcome which would deprive communities of their fundamental rights."[77] Lord Steyn's upholding of the fundamental rights of the community occurs in the context of his observation that "the aim of the criminal law is not punishment for its own sake but to permit everyone to go about their daily lives *without fear of harm to person or property*."[78] The clear implication is that the duties imposed by the criminal law are entailed in the right of the community to be free of the fear of crime.

This official rationale explains the substantive pluralization of the police power that we noted above. If freedom from fear of crime is a "fundamental right," then deploying the criminal law in the form of the ASBO so as to enforce conduct that reassures others and preemptively to prohibit conduct that does not reassure would be one way of seeking to protect that right. The implications of this are interesting if we ask what sort of a citizen or subject it is who needs this right to be reassured.

In *McCann* Lord Hutton observed that, in respect of ASB, the community is "represented by weak and vulnerable people who claim they are victims of anti-social behaviour which violates their rights."[79] In a newspaper exchange with a critic of government criminal justice policy, the prime minister took up the vulnerability theme. He argued that antisocial behavior laws were intended to protect the "essential liberties" of "the vulnerable, the decent, the people who show respect and expect it back."[80] This language of vulnerability is very far from being unique to the discussion of antisocial behavior and is an increasingly prominent aspect of governmental technique in the United Kingdom.[81]

The understanding of the normal condition of citizenship as intrinsically vulnerable is, at least in part, a consequence of the political theories that have most influenced New Labour thinking, especially in their ASB and criminal justice policies. These theories set out from a conception of individual autonomy as essentially vulnerable to the hostility or indifference of others.[82] In Anthony Giddens's Third Way theory, "Freedom from the fear of crime is a major citizenship right."[83] This is because self-actualization, which is the end and meaning of individual autonomy for Giddens,[84] depends on the maintenance of the individual's "ontological security," their sense of a secure identity to be actualized, which, since it is relationally constituted, is always vulnerable to a breakdown in civility.[85] Responsibilities such as those that section 1 imposes on citizens are, for Giddens, therefore, the basis of the rights of citizenship.[86] Another significant influence on New Labour has been communitarianism. Communitarian writers are similarly doubtful that individuals can maintain their autonomy against a threatening intersubjective environment without the help of others,[87] and they favor a distribution of rights that is based on the fulfillment of duties of reassurance such as those found in the ASBO.[88] These theories of "vulnerable autonomy"[89] invoke a norm of universal human vulnerability, a condition that Michael Kottow aptly describes as "the dignified awareness of permanent menace to one's integrity."[90]

It is a measure of the influence of the discourse of vulnerability that one of the key arguments of the ASBO's critics is that the power is too readily used against some especially vulnerable people.[91] The criticism is factually well grounded insofar as the ASBO is routinely used against children and young teenagers, the homeless, the mentally ill, alcoholics, and street prostitutes. But despite this argument, the mainstream political consensus behind the use of the ASBO has, if anything, strengthened in recent years, with no major political party opposed to it. This emphasizes how the ASBO invokes an intrinsic vulnerability to which all are thought to be subject and that politically trumps the particular contingent vulnerability of the disadvantaged people against whom the ASBO is frequently deployed.[92]

Unlike the traditional justifications of the power of police in terms of the right of the householder-sovereign to ensure the welfare and security of the objects and persons who make up his household, the discretionary police power given to magistrates by section 1 CDA 1998 is explained as the means to protect the *rights* of persons who make up the sovereign's household, at least the rights of those defined as both "vulnerable" and "decent." This language of rights seems paradoxical since it implies that the police power in the ASBO exists to protect the freedoms of legal subjects from interference by others rather than protecting persons considered as heteronomous objects of the sovereign's care and concern. It can be argued that the rights of the "vulnerable" are merely a way of describing the duties of the sovereign under the maxim *salus populi suprema lex* from the point of view of their object. Since protection from threat has always been at the heart of the sovereign's police power, the vulnerability of the objects of police power was always implicit in that power. The ASBO, it might be said, infantilizes the citizenry it "protects" much as other police powers do. Without disputing that argument in its own terms,[93] it would be a mistake nevertheless to draw from it the conclusion that the "rights of vulnerable, decent people" invoked by official policy statements are merely patriarchal spin, and that the sovereign with his patriarchal duties remains implicit in the new police power in just the same way as he was in the old. Rather, further investigation of the basis of the belief in the vulnerability of decent citizens suggests that the ASBO is not so much an example of the long-enduring structure of patriarchal authority as it is an expression of its decline.

Vulnerability and Sovereignty

Official policy regards "decent" citizens as "vulnerable" because it views the law generally, and the criminal law in particular, as having failed in relation to antisocial behavior and fear of crime. Again this view is found in both government and judiciary. Tony Blair is explicit that the new ASB powers depart from legal norms in response to the failure of law to achieve security. In the newspaper exchange referred to above, he admitted that "we have disturbed the normal legal process with the anti-social behaviour laws," and in the same passage referred to earlier, he appears bullish as to why this was necessary:

> If the practical effect of the law is that people live in fear because the offender is unafraid of the legal process then, in the name of civil liberties, we are allowing the vulnerable, the decent, the people who show respect and expect it back, to have their essential liberties trampled on.[94]

The prime minister's argument here is not merely that particular laws are not up to the job but that "normal legal process" as such has failed. Despite many disagreements between the executive and higher judiciary at present, on this point Blair could be taking his cue from the House of Lords. For Lord Hope in *McCann*, "the apparent inability of the criminal law to restrain" the perpetrators of ASB was "unacceptable," while to expect victims to seek civil injunctions was "unrealistic."[95] For Lord Steyn "the criminal law by itself offered inadequate protection" to those who lived with the fear caused by persistent antisocial behavior. Moreover, Lord Steyn concludes his review of "the social problem" of ASB with the revealing observation that

> the criminal law offered insufficient protection to communities. Public confidence in the rule of law was undermined by a not unreasonable view in some communities that the law had failed them. This was the social problem which Section 1 was designed to address.[96]

We noted above that the mischief at which the ASBO is aimed is the fear of crime. But Lord Steyn points out that this mischief is a matter not merely of the direct effects of fear on those who endure it but also of the perception that as a result "the law had failed." This view of the aims of ASB policy is one shared by the Home Office. *Respect and Responsibility* argues that "nothing undermines public confidence more than the sense that no one is taking anti-social behaviour seriously." A tough approach to "enforcement" is therefore "critical" because without it civic renewal strategies "are meaningless and the community loses faith."[97] The object of the enforcement strategy is only secondarily to address the "perpetrator" and deal with her conduct. Its primary purpose is to restore the community's "faith" in government as such.

Both the executive and the House of Lords motivate the power of the police state on the basis of the inadequacy of the law state, and in particular the perception of its failure. The failure of the law state to enforce its norms is thought, unsurprisingly, to leave the decent citizen in a vulnerable position. Section 1 CDA 1998 draws the scope of this vulnerability very widely. The section contains no restrictions on the situations to which it applies. The ASBO power is one of general application to which all are potentially liable, however much discretion is exercised in practice. The requirement in section 1 that citizens reassure each other is of general application, and vulnerability to others is thereby constructed as a normal and representative characteristic of citizenship.

The ASBO's construction of the ordinary citizen as intrinsically vulnerable and in fear of crime and its pluralization of the moral police, which displaces the sovereign's explicit moral authority (when compared with the bind over to be of good behavior), together suggest that the ASBO is consistent with a high degree of uncertainty concerning the state's moral authority. Insofar as the ASBO power and its official rationale construct ordinary citizens as in a condition of "ontological vulnerability" or "dignified awareness of permanent menace to their integrity," so as to require preemptive prohibition of behavior that fails to reassure, this power can be understood only as a sovereign power in a very particular sense.

For the patriarch, threats and harms to his household arise on a contingent basis, and it is his duty and right to deal with them on that basis. Even if it follows from the existence of this patriarchal duty of police that, in this connection, the members of the household are necessarily vulnerable to threats, it would be perverse to understand the human members of a patriarch's household as essentially vulnerable *to each other*. To pose mutual vulnerability as characteristic of citizenship does not evoke an image of a well-ordered household, quite the reverse. If anything, it evokes the image of the subjects of Thomas Hobbes's state of nature.[98] More precisely, it evokes one aspect of that benighted state—its anomia. The postulated failure of law leads to a lack of expectation that known breaches of norms will be sanctioned.[99] It is to be expected that individuals in such an anomic environment will experience the feeling of vulnerability to those whose conduct fails to reassure them.

Considered in this light, it might be better to understand the ASBO power as referring to and defining the "state of exception." Giorgio Agamben imagines the state of exception as "a space without law (even though it is not a state of nature, but presents itself as the anomie that results from the suspension of law)."[100] Similarly the citizens imagined by section 1 exist in an anomic space where law has failed and normal legal process must, therefore, be "disturbed" with sweeping discretionary police powers that endeavor to achieve preemptive coercion of potential threats. In other words, if the ASBO is a power of the sovereign as patriarch then it is a power of that sovereignty in emergency mode, faced with what is *officially perceived* to be a crisis of order in the household. Moreover, it is a police power that operates in a way that Agamben regards as paradigmatic of contemporary government: the ASBO represents its emergency powers as the rule, the state of exception as the norm.[101]

This understanding of the ASBO power both confirms and qualifies David Garland's influential "limits of the sovereign state" thesis.[102] The ASBO's political premise that failure of law leaves citizens in the anomic state of exception is comparable with Garland's starting point that the criminal justice policy of the period before the ASBO was a response to the persistent normality of high crime rates. Garland argues that as a consequence of this experience of high crime rates "the threat of crime has become a routine part of modern consciousness,"[103] and this in turn threatens to expose the sovereign state's limitations as a form of social control.[104]

Now, we have seen above that the ASBO's terms and official rationale tend to confirm Garland's general proposition that policy development expresses the law's weakness and limitation.[105] But Garland, reviewing the experience of the 1980s and 1990s, sees the imposition of repressive police powers as a hysterical denial of the impotence of sovereign power. We have seen that, notwithstanding the harsh official rhetoric that often surrounds the ASBO, the underlying policy does not deny the failure of criminal law and criminal justice. On the contrary, *it is explicitly premised on that failure.* It would seem that Garland's argument that, in the earlier period, "the myth of the sovereign state" had shown "its resilience in the face of all contrary evidence"[106] can no longer be maintained, at least not in respect of the ASBO. If myth it was,[107] then it would be more accurate now to say that the myth "has been revealed";[108] and revealed above all to the governing elite. The ASBO is then an emergency police power deployed in the face of a perceived crisis of the sovereign authority. Moreover, the substantive terms of the ASBO represent the crisis conditions as the norm, and the official assertion of these emergency conditions appears to be part of a political strategy self-consciously aimed at restoring "public confidence" in the exercise of state power. The ASBO does not appear in this sense to be part of what might properly be called a "Hobbesian solution."[109]

From the point of view of the decisionistic theory of sovereignty this last point may seem strange,[110] since the very exercise of the ASBO power appears as the sovereign mode of governance par excellence. Thus Garland observes that, "like the decision to wage war, the decision to . . . extend police powers exemplifies the sovereign mode of state action."[111] In this sense, imposing ASBOs and punishing people for breach of them are the actions of a sovereign state. But to consider sovereignty *only* in its formal, decisionistic aspect is to consider only sovereign right and lose sight of the sovereign duty.[112] It is to overlook the specific normative issues, the way the state seeks to define right and wrong, the condition and character of the state's political legitimacy.[113] What we see with the extension of police power in the ASBO is the sovereignty in its formal aspect exercised with fanfares. But in its substantive moral claims, in its institutionalizing of the failure of legal norms and of the individual's essential vulnerability notwithstanding the criminal law, the ASBO expresses only doubt about the state's control and authority. A government that institutionalizes the understanding that citizens ordinarily exist in an anomic environment characteristic of emergency is a government exposing the fragility of its sovereign power in the very attempt to exercise it. As Otto Kirchheimer put it, "Emergency in permanence becomes the genuine symbol of the very absence of that system of coordination to which history traditionally affixes the attribute of sovereignty."[114]

Conclusion

To summarize, I have argued that the demise of the bind over to be of good behavior and the emergence of the ASBO indicate a broadening and deepening of the state's powers of moral police. This new power pluralizes the moral police so that the vulnerability of citizens displaces the sovereign's duties at the core of the police power's rationale. In this shift, the paternalistic mode of sovereign police power is displaced by an emergency power, the terms of which manifest perceived limits of sovereign authority.

Although the ASBO appears to give expression to official doubts about the state as sovereign, it does not give up on government by police as such but rather reformulates its basis. From an empirical perspective, the official perception of the limits, or even the crisis, of sovereign authority doubtless constitutes a politically motivated overstatement of the immediate concrete problems of social order.[115] Indeed this representation of crisis appears as one of the means by which, to use Farmer's words, "the government and production of social order" are being reorganized.[116] In the new order, the discretionary coercive powers of magistrates, local authority officials, and police officers are reinvigorated through the invocation of a sense of emergency. Nevertheless, we should not underestimate the significance of the resort to an institutionalized representation of emergency. We should rather expect the discourse of vulnerability to be productive of the social relations that it imagines. And what it imagines in the form of the ASBO is that the representative condition of UK citizens is one of mutual intersubjective vulnerability—which is another way of saying that the ASBO constructs the vulnerability of the UK's sovereign government itself.

Such an order of police throws the key problem identified by Dubber for a new police science into particularly sharp relief. How can the new police power be restrained by the principle of autonomy, the principle of self-government, if it exists to serve the autonomy of the vulnerable? Farmer proposes that we need to develop a "jurisprudence of security" through which the police power can be given its proper theoretical due, rather than being treated from the standpoint of the traditional jurisprudence of law as a residual executive power that is beyond control.[117] My argument here is that the other side of security is vulnerability; the investigation of security is also the investigation of vulnerability. The discourse of vulnerability will be an essential part of understanding how sovereign power is understood and exercised in the present.[118] The key question that human vulnerability raises for a jurisprudence of security is the extent to which the search for ontological security legitimates demands on the state for the deployment of preemptive coercion.[119] Where, if at all, does the right to security of vulnerable citizens place limits on the reach of such police powers?

NINE

Loitering in the City That Works

On Circulation, Activity, and Police in Governing Urban Space

RON LEVI

Il y a des villes parce qu'il y a la police.

—MICHEL FOUCAULT, *Leçon du 5 avril 1978*

Introduction

The Haussmannian reconstruction of Paris, conducted with great fervor throughout the second half of the nineteenth century, is identified as a critical moment in the geographic reworking of city governance.[1] The expansion of city streets, the promotion of public monuments and spaces, the centralizing of commerce, and the redesign of the flow of urban life were central to Haussmann's project. This Paris reconstruction is most often described as facilitating military control of the urban population, by making the city more "legible" to state authorities. And indeed, this administrative achievement was soon borne out: the successful and bloody repression of the Paris Communards made the link between urban design and sovereign control unmistakably apparent.[2]

Given its violent outcome, it is at times difficult to remember that this redesign of Paris was not exclusively meant to forcefully control the city's population. Quite to the contrary, it was steeped in the logic and language of police science, welfare, and good administration and represents a zenith of urban planning meant to ensure the salubrity of city residents. What perhaps distinguishes the Paris project is its emphasis on one component of the police project—namely, promoting the easy *circulation* of people and objects within the city.[3] Encouraging movement and mobility was the resurrection of an older Parisian ambition, when the revolutionary Commission des Artistes pioneered an urban regeneration plan to re-create the city from the street level itself.[4] This 1793 Plan des Artistes emphasized *movement* as the "central organizing principle for Paris" and is echoed by Haussmann's famous plan a century later.[5] Indeed, Haussmann was overtly contemptuous of the security focus of his day and spoke in terms of military security only when seeking support from other public officials.[6]

In his analysis of *French Modern*, Paul Rabinow suggests that the Paris redesign was significant because "state and society met at the street," so that urban space was integrally concerned with order, public health, and the population's welfare.[7] This was certainly the case: improving circulation was everywhere central to the Continental police project. Indeed, contemplating a well-regulated society in the nineteenth century could simply not ignore public mobility. Circulation, as a good, was underwritten through commercial, moral, aesthetic, and public health rationales and thereby understood to promote the availability of air, light, and water flow, as well as improve commerce and traffic.[8] Continental police texts extolled mobility and circulation as "indispensable elements of all advancing humanity"[9] and more generally as an inherently "valuable social resource."[10] It is not surprising, then, that drawing a link between mobility, salubrity, and urban design was equally the leitmotif of the Paris reconstruction.

This emphasis on circulation was by no means unique to Paris. In his compelling social history of the liberal city, Patrick Joyce demonstrates the emergence of free circulation in cities such as Manchester, where the 1893 municipal code "anathematises anything that prevents free circulation," whether it be people, goods, animals, traffic, or trash.[11] Within the history of police, however, Haussmann's Paris was certainly unique in giving the theme of circulation a reputational boost. This soon made its way across the Atlantic, to be instantiated in Burnham and Bennett's 1909 Plan of Chicago, where the U.S.-based City Beautiful movement equally took up the close link between circulation and urban salubrity.[12] This was not merely a practical response to the needs of a booming Chicagoan population. Adopting its Continental legacy in police science rather than merely its pragmatic benefits, urban circulation was here also seen as rooted in a deeply aesthetic vision of health, order, and peacefulness—whether its object was to relieve traffic congestion, modernize street systems, or enforce zoning and building regulations. As Hess concludes, "transportation improvements were generally by-products of civic leaders' desires to improve urban life, create cohesive communities . . . [and] raise civic pride,"[13] so that a hallmark of the City Beautiful movement lay in the very fact that it "combined urban landscape design with civic improvement."[14]

Yet if circulation through urban design was key to the turn-of-the-century imagination of Chicago and Paris, by the end of the twentieth century concerns over circulation in Chicago persisted, if with a different tone. Rather than seeking to widen the boulevards, rearrange the streets, or design urban parkways that might enhance the cityscape, Chicago City Council in 1992 was focused on the problems produced by the lack of mobility among urban youth, who were interfering with residential mobility and commerce. After an explosion of concern among city aldermen, the city council held public hearings in which it determined that the use of the city streets by law-abiding residents was being impeded by young men who were loitering on the public way.[15] Informing this conclusion was an underlying concern—voiced by Chicago politicians and taken up by academics and community organizers—that through such loitering gang members were intimidating other residents and gaining control over urban space without committing any overt criminal activity.[16] As Mayor Daley vividly described the problem, "It's the frustration of people saying, 'Hey. There's 30, 40 people on this corner. I live on this block. I can't even walk around the corner.'"[17]

As I discuss below, to understand this concern over loitering it is critical to highlight that in the early 1990s Chicago was in the midst of a dramatic increase in drug dealing, violence, and gang warfare. August 1991 was recorded as the deadliest month in Chicago history: the *New York Times* proclaimed that homicides were "surpassing the rate during the bloody years of the Al Capone era," and besieged by political opposition and media reports, Mayor Daley soon admitted that Chicago was "becoming like Colombia."[18] After holding public hearings with Chicago residents, the city's response was to enact a gang loitering ordinance, which made it an offense for apparent gang members to remain *in any one place with no apparent purpose* and to refuse to move along when instructed to do so by a police officer.[19] Enacted in the Chicago Municipal Code, the offense thereby focused attention on the visible lack of activity and circulation engaged in by young men. It is worth noting that, at least formally, this shifted legal attention away from an exclusive focus on drug dealing and violence: indeed, the ordinance would ostensibly not apply if individuals were visibly committing other crimes or actively harassing neighborhood residents, being instead restricted to when they were apparently doing *nothing at all*.[20]

Although this Chicago ordinance was found unconstitutional by the U.S. Supreme Court five years later, I suggest that its adjudication and legacy provide a unique conjuncture for reexamining the importance of mobility and circulation to the police project. There is a moral dimension to this production of circulation that is being negotiated, namely, the extent to which cities are not to be spaces of what Joyce identifies as "amoral circulation," or as "circulation untamed," so that public spaces (and individuals within them) are contemplated as needing social ordering.[21]

In this chapter, I focus on the Chicago ordinance and its adjudication in the case of *Chicago v. Morales*[22] and the tensions that were produced when reviving this nineteenth-century project during the late twentieth century. To be sure, there has already been significant legal attention given to the Chicago ordinance and its adjudication, focusing mainly on the constitutional questions raised and the likely efficacy of this measure to prevent crime.[23] The terms of the debate are as one would expect: either the ordinance is said to unduly interfere with civil liberties, or the ordinance is extolled as a benign method of responding to a pressing social problem. There has otherwise been little theorization or exploration of the ordinance.[24] And although the Chicago ordinance has been drawn into broader discussions of loitering laws,[25] there has indeed been little analysis of how it grapples with the question of urban circulation. This is not surprising: within criminological, legal, and sociolegal studies, studies of loitering and vagrancy have long been captured by debates over their constitutionality, their efficacy, or their role in controlling undesirable populations.[26]

Before moving on to the ordinance and its adjudication, the next section of this chapter begins by emphasizing the importance of circulation and movement to understanding the police project as a fundamentally *urban* governmentality. As Alan Hunt demonstrates, the police regulation of traffic is critical to the broader regulation of urban life.[27] This link between police, mobility, and the city has been drawn out in detail by Foucault's 1978 lectures on police, in which he argues that the *visible circulation* of people and goods is integral to the very possibility of the city—and that in turn, urban mobility is the linchpin of police itself.[28] At one level, this provides a conceptual backdrop for understanding the Chicago ordinance as not merely an anticrime measure or a tool of social control—though surely it is both these things—but also as part of an array of techniques for governing the urban itself. Having done so, Foucault's lectures then provide a key lens through which to examine the unnoticed tensions in the legal history of this ordinance.

Circulation, Splendor, and the Heart of Police

Michel Foucault's lectures on *Sécurité, Territoire, Population* provide a detailed historical analysis of the development of police governance in France.[29] This puts it in company with other recent historical work, which has sought to recover the legacy of police as an organizing dimension of the French state, stemming from the ancien regime to the present day.[30] What Foucault uniquely demonstrates in these lectures, however, is that French police did not merely extend to producing wealth and happiness for the population, along the social policy line that has generally informed U.S. police science.[31] Instead, Foucault emphasizes that police is most precisely a logic for governing *cities*—and because its goal is to produce a specifically urban salubrity, Foucault demonstrates that police requires the *circulation* and *activity* of the urban population.

Foucault begins his lecture of March 29, 1978—after being ironically delayed by a traffic jam—by introducing police as a form of government that explicitly seeks to improve the "splendor" of the state.[32] This terminology is itself important to understanding urban governance, since it simultaneously refers to the strengthening of the state's productive capacity (*l'utilité étatique*) and the ensuring of its internal order and security.[33] Everything is harnessed to produce this splendor, so that in the police tradition, even aesthetic elements, such as city design, are meant to enhance the order and security of the state.[34]

How, then, is this splendor—or in another vocabulary, this prosperity—produced?[35] To understand the workings of police, we must realize that splendor is not directly produced by the state's own capacities. To the contrary, it is achieved by harnessing men's activity, namely by ensuring that the urban population is rendered active and kept productive. Charged with achieving this splendor of the state, police administrators were to closely monitor and instruct youth to ensure their work and activity and above all to prevent their idleness[36]—and this can include a whole series of police administrators to ensure that young people identify and successfully pursue an occupation.[37] Indeed, ensuring that individuals are actively engaged in their stated occupation is, on Foucault's reading, at the "*very heart of police*," because it is thought to increase the resources, capacities, and internal order of the state itself.[38] It is important to note that in the postfeudal economy, the state's splendor does not depend on its citizens participating in a specific hierarchy of trades but instead on the very fact of activity itself: "the creation of public utility *through men's occupation, their activity, and their very doing*."[39]

If "the goal of police is the control and taking charge of men's activity,"[40] it is precisely for this reason that administrators work to enhance general well-being: ensuring, for instance, that the population is healthy, that it enjoys life's necessities, and is large enough to be productive.[41] It is here that one perceives the close and direct link between the goals of activity and of circulation: police must ensure that individuals are not idle and that they—as well as the commercial goods they produce—indeed circulate freely within and beyond the state.[42] Roads and navigation become critical to commercial and social interaction. What emerges is a governmental concern with *movement* in all its forms: idleness is to be prevented, commercial circulation promoted, vagabonds policed, workers' movement monitored, and so on.[43] It is not, then, that circulation is itself always encouraged but, most importantly, that it becomes a field unto itself: "it is this whole field of circulation that will become . . . the object of police."[44] The later legacy of this focus on movement is well known: by the late eighteenth century travelers and itinerants were increasingly policed, vagrancy increasingly criminalized, and documentation for mobility (such as passports) increasingly common.[45]

It is through its concern with activity and circulation, then, that police governmentality becomes closely tied to the urban itself—enhancing activity, circulation, and movement allows for the governance of densely populated territories and can meet the commercial demands of cities.[46] It is in this way that police, work, circulation, and commerce become a closely connected series. And the resulting police regulations—including the proper use of roads, public space, and the encouragement of activity—become the manner through which urbanization itself is conceived. City regulations thereby concern themselves with the everyday, with the mundane, and with details, seeking in particular to allow and to interdict flow and movement. "There are cities because there is police," Foucault concludes, so that "to police and to urbanize mean the same thing."[47]

Loitering in the "City That Works"

It is this field of mobility and circulation that became of central concern to Chicago in the early 1990s. The core problem was a spike in gang violence, thought to be brought on by the sale of crack cocaine. While other U.S. cities had been witnessing the emergence of crack since the early 1980s, Chicago's gangs had, perhaps ironically, worked together to avoid its sale in the city's core, so as to preserve established networks of drug dealing and protect profits. This strategy appears to have worked until 1991; and once introduced, the market for drugs in Chicago turned more violent than ever before.[48] The rate of violent crimes skyrocketed, the homicide rate hit its deadliest high ever, and some of the poorest neighborhoods "echoed with gunfire almost nightly."[49] Accounts of how precarious life had become for neighborhood residents proliferated in the Chicago media: as one resident poignantly stated, "People are in agony. People are being held hostage in their own neighborhoods," with another asking, "What do we have to do? Do we have to get on our knees to stop this?"[50] A poll on Chicago's West Side indicated that 96 percent of residents would not object to bringing in the National Guard to fight crime, with the ward's alderman adding that "when you live in crime and are grossly inhibited by crime activity, and people in front of your house are shooting, then you look at this thing differently than someone on the outside."[51] And in city hall, aldermanic voices reached "oratorical heights in crying out against the rising crime rate," with city and police officials agreeing that drastic steps needed to be taken.[52]

Deciding what to do about this violence was another matter. Concerned that Chicago would face "a long, violent summer," the police superintendent advocated increased funds for foot patrols and raised the possibility of an antiloitering ordinance to police gang members "that are out there intimidating people."[53] The state attorney, concerned over the constitutionality of a loitering ordinance, advocated tougher prosecutions and harsher penalties, including "more prisons and more prison beds."[54] And in the mayor's office, a third dimension was brewing: on the advice of an international management consulting firm, the city was developing a community policing program, to allay crime fears without spending additional funds and without alienating minority communities.[55] This became "the mayor's bible of police administration."[56]

With these options in the air, four Chicago aldermen submitted proposed ordinances to City Council, including a proposal—written in conjunction with a community group from a predominantly white area—for a gang congregation ordinance.[57] Alderman Wojcik, whose ward had a heavy concentration of senior citizens and new immigrants, explained that this was a struggle over the use of public space and the mobility of citizens within it:

> The problem here is gangs staking out turf. . . . They'll stake out a grocery store, for instance, and then put maybe two people on each corner and stand there, or sit with their legs out, or say things to people. After a while, the people in the community get scared and stay away, and the gang members have succeeded in making that their turf.[58]

In supporting the ordinance, Mayor Daley further emphasized this concern over space and circulation, by referring to community residents who felt "under siege" and who "can't even walk around the corner."[59]

This concern over urban mobility was also reported in the local press. Following a weekend drug raid, representatives of local community groups complained that "we are being overwhelmed. . . . You are hampered walking down the street because so many people are involved in loitering and standing around selling drugs in the wide open," and that "it's left residents unable to come out of their own homes—being almost besieged by gangbangers and drug dealers."[60] A coalition of neighborhood organizations later came to define the issue as the ability to live in the city itself, arguing that "although criminal gangs have long been part of the urban landscape, they have taken a dramatic new direction in recent years, away from small-scale and localized activities to highly organized takeovers of entire neighborhoods."[61]

Six months after this proposal was submitted to City Council, Chicago's Committee on Police and Fire[62] held a public meeting to discuss the ordinance and residents' concerns over crime. Held in May 1992, the two days of hearings were chaired by Alderman William Beavers, a 21-year police veteran, who worked on narcotics, gambling, prostitution, and gang crime.[63] These hearings were later described as an outpouring of the public's need for relief from gang loitering, with residents' testimonies continually marshaled in political forums and introduced in every trial case heard regarding the ordinance.[64] Yet more precisely, these hearings were designed to provide the city's Law Department with testimonial evidence to underwrite the loitering ordinance. As Alderman Beavers noted on the first day of the hearings,

> It's not against the law to stand on the corner. It's not against the law to stand on the corners anywhere in the City of Chicago. It's not against the law so the police cannot arrest them, and this is why we are here today to try to see can we get some support for this ordinance, and hopefully that we will, and maybe we will be able to alleviate some of the problems.[65]

While a closer study of the transcripts reveals a broader set of residents' concerns over their neighborhoods and city services,[66] residents did testify as to the problems of gang loitering as well. This includes a senior citizen worried about individuals "hanging on the corner," especially because there are "just gobs of them"; a business owner concerned about "corners loaded" with gangs; and a resident frustrated since "any person who has any type of business is not going to congregate in a group on a corner and hang out all day."[67] A store owner was similarly concerned because to "loiter at the entrance of a business" can "restrict passage to customers," and residents were concerned with the effects on their capacity to go outside and for neighborhood life more generally (as one resident noted, "on any given night 30 to 40 gangbangers hung out at the intersection" and "established the street as their own").[68] Overall, proper use of the city streets came to be seen as the core problem revealed by these testimonies:

> Many concerned citizens testified poignantly. . . . A mother of four, for instance, asserted that in her neighborhood, children no longer played hopscotch or jacks in the street: "I wish you could see the rust that has accumulated

> because they cannot ride [their] bikes." Eighty-eight-year-old Susan Mary Jackson spoke forcefully of the fear she [experienced] in public spaces: "We used to have a nice neighborhood. We don't have it anymore. . . . I am scared to go out in the daytime . . . you can't pass because they are standing. I am afraid to go to the store."[69]

It is in this context that loitering, apart from any overtly aggressive activity, was itself perceived as harmful to community order and to residents' ability to participate in civic life.[70]

Finally, it is important to note that the gang loitering ordinance was not passed in isolation but was echoed by other security strategies enacted during the same period. All of these had a similar flavor. This included a citywide ban on the retail sale of spray paint, a juvenile curfew ordinance, and a tightening of restrictions on outdoor pay phones, particularly in high-crime neighborhoods where they were thought to be monopolized by local drug dealers.[71] What links all of these is a focus on city design and the regulation of the public streets, including the channeling of flow and activity within them. These strategies all resonated with the mayor's broader agenda for the city: if in years past Chicago had come to be known for investment in large-scale infrastructure projects and as the "city that works," Mayor Daley now sought to rebuild the city piece by piece and to focus his attention on civic improvement and urban revitalization strategies.[72] With this as a key goal of his administration, it is not surprising that the field of mobility soon became a centerpiece of the city's security strategy.

The Gang Loitering Ordinance: Police and the Public Way

Relying on these public hearings, Chicago City Council approved the Gang Congregation Ordinance in June 1992, with a vote of 31–11.[73] Debate was highly acrimonious, with some aldermen comparing it to South African Pass Laws and to restrictions on Jews in Nazi Germany—and Chicago urban politics were very much in the air when Mayor Daley retorted that "the Police Department might not enforce the new law in the wards of those aldermen who voted against it."[74]

From a police science perspective, it is important to note that the ordinance was not designed merely to prevent future crimes. While it surely had a preventive dimension, the ordinance addressed a present harm that centered on the proper use of public space and ensuring the desired mobility of neighborhood residents. According to the city, visible public loitering "intimidates residents, who become afraid even to leave their homes," and this results in "a palpable detrimental effect on a family's sense of well being, on the willingness of parents to allow their children outside, and on the willingness of Chicago residents to remain in the City."[75] Following on this logic, the text of the ordinance began with nine whereas clauses, which link the city's increased rate of violence, homicides, and drug crimes to the presence of street gangs—and then go on to highlight that gang members gain and maintain their control by loitering on the public way. In this way, the preamble did not emphasize the need to address gang violence directly but rather to act on this problem through the logic of mobility and the governance of public space. The problem to be acted on was that "the burgeoning presence of street gang members in public places has intimidated many law abiding citizens," such that "aggressive action is necessary to preserve the city's streets and other public places so that the public may use such places without fear."[76]

Indeed, this preamble is particularly important for understanding the ordinance within the context of police science and the municipal regulation of mobility. In addressing a municipal offense, the ordinance does not, strictly speaking, deal with "criminal behavior."[77] This is a point often ignored by commentators, who focus instead on the Chicago ordinance as yet another instrument of the criminal law and ignore the unique origins and legacy of municipal governance.[78] But it is the preamble that indeed underwrote the municipality's jurisdiction to respond to this surge in violence, precisely by acting through the lens of mobility, the use of the streets, and the invocation of the public way. As Lawrence Rosenthal, deputy corporation counsel for the City of Chicago, stated before the Committee on Police and Fire, what is "important about this ordinance are the whereas clauses . . . [if] members of criminal street gangs use their access to the public way in order to engage in criminal activity . . . [that] is a fact conjoined with criminal activity and appropriately regulated by the municipality."[79] And quite tellingly, six of these nine clauses explicitly deploy the geographic terms *identifiable areas* and *public places*. Keeping this in mind—the ordinance as part of a tradition that regulates urban space and mobility rather than crime directly—will be of particular interest in considering the later adjudication of the ordinance before the U.S. Supreme Court.

Following the preamble, the ordinance made the following an offense:

> 8-4-015. (a) Whenever a police officer observes a person whom he reasonably believes to be a criminal street gang member loitering in any public place with one or more other persons, he shall order all such persons to disperse and remove themselves from the area. Any person who does not promptly obey such an order is in violation of this section.

While much of the section then turns to defining what is meant by a "criminal street gang,"[80] of particular importance for an analysis of mobility are the terms *loiter* and *public place*:

> (c) As used in this Section:
> (1) "Loiter" means to remain in any one place with no apparent purpose. . . .
> (5) "Public place" means the public way and any other location open to the public, whether publicly or privately owned.

At one level, these definitions remarkably expand the potential for policing. First, loitering is defined as "remaining in any one place with no apparent purpose," based on the perception of the police officer rather than on any objective measures of inactivity, and second, the requirement that the loitering be in a "public place" is undermined by including publicly or privately owned locations, thereby including the city streets, commercial enterprises, and municipally managed housing developments.

But beyond this, what is immediately apparent is the ordinance's emphasis on regulating movement, rather than on a strategy of criminalization. Once ordered to disperse, individuals must "remove themselves from the area," and it is indeed a refusal to do so that violates the section (it is worth noting that even if one of the individuals being policed is not a gang member, he or she must still disperse). This bears striking resemblance to the concerns sketched out by Foucault's lectures on police, by ensuring movement and preventing visible idleness—indeed, so long as movement is maintained, individuals can resume their (in)activity at another location, until ordered to disperse once more. In short, because there is no underlying activity criminalized (such as loitering while selling drugs) and no status targeted (such as being a "habitual loafer"[81]) the ordinance is focused solely on ensuring a seemingly continual movement.

This emphasis on movement is twinned with the regulation of public space. The struggle for municipal control over the public way—and ensuring that individuals could not take over the public way for their own purposes—continues a long police tradition of constituting and identifying the public itself.[82] This reached its heyday in nineteenth-century U.S. strategies to ensure the public welfare; "to remove and abate nuisances and encroachments on highways was a crucial instrument of sovereignty."[83] At its core, then, what was being addressed by the Chicago ordinance—namely, the apparent control and usurpation of the public way by private individuals, thereby removing it from enjoyment by the public itself—reflects the very essence of the police enterprise. As Novak concludes, it is precisely state regulation of public space that "reflected the *absolute* nature of public rights in the well-regulated society," so that any private claims over space would be trumped in favor of "public objectives" of movement, communication, circulation, and the like.[84]

In classic *salus populi* fashion, the Chicago ordinance explicitly sets aside the legal distinction between public and private and as a result provides a generous definition of what constitutes the public space to be protected. By defining public place to include privately owned locations, the ordinance applies not only on the public streets but also in parks, coffee shops, shopping malls, stores, movie theaters, public transit stops, municipally owned locations, and so on.[85] Defeating the distinction between public and private, in the name of preserving the public's right to circulate freely, demonstrates a broad police concern with governing public order that extends beyond the city streets.[86]

Finally, the goal of preventing private (individual or group) control over public space by preventing idleness was made further apparent by the practices and guidelines of the Chicago police in enforcing the ordinance. According to the Chicago Police Department's General Order 92-4,[87] only a specified group of officers could make arrests under the ordinance—but with no restriction on which police officers may order people to move along, suggesting that moving along and preventing idleness was in and of itself a key goal being pursued. In addition, the guidelines limited enforcement of the ordinance to specified urban spaces, rather than it being applicable to loitering wherever it occurred—although not disclosed to the general public, these enforcement areas were designated on the basis of a wide array of information, including crime patterns, citizen complaints, police observations, and the views of community members. The very heterogeneity of information being relied on—common knowledge, experience, trade knowledge, and statistical information—further reflects the European police tradition of seeking to improve the public welfare through administration.[88]

The upshot of these guidelines was a very active police program. Within three and a half years after its initial adoption, approximately forty-two thousand individuals were arrested, with yet another forty-three thousand orders to disperse.[89] As a crime prevention strategy, however, the ordinance appears to have enjoyed little success. Indeed, gang-related crimes increased in those areas of the city where the ordinance was most enforced, and crime declined where it was least enforced.[90] Yet in over eighty thousand instances, people were kept from appearing idle—and were kept moving along, even if briefly.

Adjudicating Police: Mobility and the City in the U.S. Supreme Court

In its adjudication in the Illinois courts following this massive number of arrests, thirteen different trial judges ruled on the constitutionality of the Chicago ordinance—with eleven finding the ordinance unconstitutional.[91] By 1993 fourteen defendants in *Chicago v. Youkhana*[92] successfully challenged the ordinance as being unconstitutional on its face, thereby leading to a reversal of dozens of convictions—and leading to a successful constitutional challenge before the U.S. Supreme Court in *Chicago v. Morales*[93] (1999), in which a majority of the Court found the Chicago ordinance unconstitutional.[94]

Doctrinally, the *Morales* decision treats a wide range of due process concerns.[95] For our purposes, the decision can be parsed as follows. The majority consists of six judges finding that the ordinance is void for vagueness, since it provides police with unlimited discretion in deciding whether to issue an order to disperse. In addition, a plurality of the Court found that the ordinance is void for vagueness because it provides inadequate notice to citizens regarding how they ought to conform their conduct to legal requirements, with this plurality also finding that the freedom to loiter is a constitutionally protected liberty. Finally, Justices Scalia, Thomas, and Rehnquist dissented from the majority decision, finding that loitering is not a constitutionally protected right and that the ordinance is not void for vagueness.

There has been no shortage of analysis of the *Morales* decision. The vast majority of these focus on the Court's concerns in *Morales* with the broad discretion granted to police officers, with some attention to the broader questions of vagueness and a potential liberty interest in loitering.[96] Yet what has received comparatively little attention is that, underlying the legal debates within the *Morales* decision, there is a broader question regarding the city itself, most notably the relationship of policing to the urban. If as Foucault suggests, "to police and to urbanize mean the same thing"[97]—and the hallmark of police is the emphasis on flow, mobility, and circulation—the Supreme Court decision in *Morales* represents a profound debate not only over the scope of constitutional rights but also over the role that police logics ought to play in shaping urban space.[98]

MOBILITY AND THE TARGETED CITY

The majority decision begins by arguing that the ordinance does not provide minimal guidelines to govern law enforcement because officers are to rely on people's "apparent purpose," without having to inquire into what their purpose may be.[99] As a result, the ordinance confers "absolute discretion to police officers" to issue an order to disperse, and runs afoul of the Constitution because it "entrusts lawmaking to the moment-to-moment judgment of the policeman on his beat."[100] While some of this is limited by the Chicago police General Order, the majority dismisses these administrative limits, since they could not constitute a defense for someone arrested under the ordinance.[101]

Yet although the majority decision argues that the ordinance is unconstitutional because it fails to provide "minimal guidelines to govern law enforcement"[102] and although law review commentary has focused on this point, unbridled police discretion is not the only concern motivating the majority. Rather, Justice Stevens's written opinion is often concerned with how the City of Chicago has implicitly imagined the polity through the ordinance—and the degree to which the police emphasis on *mobility* is closely connected with the *urban imaginary*. Indeed, while framed in the language of police discretion, Justice Stevens's majority opinion appears most concerned with when mobility is enforced broadly, to everyone across the city—but would appear to have no trouble with the discretion the ordinance contemplates, so long as it would focus on particular groups, in particular spaces, at particular times. This lies in contrast to the constitutional decisions of the U.S. Supreme Court in the 1960s where police discretion (including in vagrancy cases) was being limited particularly when specific groups were being targeted.[103]

The majority's concerns come through in its response to the city's argument that police discretion was sufficiently contained, since an officer could issue an order to disperse only when he or she reasonably believed someone in the group to be a criminal street gang member:

> It is true, as the city argues, that the requirement that the officer reasonably believe that a group of loiterers contains a gang member does place a limit on the authority to order dispersal. That limitation would no doubt be sufficient if the ordinance only applied to loitering that had an apparently harmful purpose or effect, or possibly if it only applied to loitering by persons reasonably believed to be criminal gang members. But this ordinance . . . applies to everyone in the city who may remain in one place with one suspected gang member as long as their purpose is not apparent.[104]

There are, then, two possibilities expressed for when this ordinance might be constitutional: either the ordinance would apply only to individuals loitering with "an apparently harmful purpose or effect," or it would apply only to those loiterers who are "reasonably believed to be gang members."

Neither of these limitations would in fact minimize the discretion of police officers; but what I want to stress here is that both resist the promotion of mobility and activity as a general urban matter and resist treating idleness as a generic problem to be policed. The first suggestion—that the ordinance be limited to loitering with an apparently harmful purpose or effect—does little to cabin police discretion, especially given the problems that would arise over how an "apparently harmful" standard might be interpreted. Yet what the majority *is* here doing is implicitly rejecting the city's premise that idleness is a problem to be addressed in and of itself.[105] More centrally, the majority suggests that the current ordinance *might* be constitutional if it were simply limited to loitering by those reasonably believed to be gang members. Yet this would surely fail to cabin police discretion, since it would continue to reach "a substantial amount of innocent conduct" and vest police officers with the same scope of discretion—though limited to a narrower set of people.[106] Taken together, however, it would seem that the Court's concern might be less with the scope of police discretion than with whether idleness (and its effects on other residents) is a legitimate problem to be addressed by the city, expressing at another point its concern that "friends, relatives, teachers, counselors, or even total strangers might unwittingly engage in forbidden loitering if they happen to engage in idle conversation with a gang member."[107]

How can we understand the concern with policing idleness here—perhaps acceptable if limited to those believed to be gang members but not acceptable if it reaches beyond that group? A clue might be found in the language that the majority intersperses throughout its opinion:

> *In any public place in the city of Chicago*, persons who stand or sit in the company of a gang member may be ordered to disperse. . . .
>
> It matters not whether the reason that a gang member and his father, for example, might loiter near Wrigley Field is to rob an unsuspecting fan or *just to get a glimpse of Sammy Sosa leaving the ballpark*. . . .
>
> *It applies to everyone in the city* who may remain in one place with one suspected gang member. . . .
>
> That the police have adopted internal rules limiting their enforcement to certain designated areas of the city would not provide a defense to *a loiterer who might be arrested elsewhere*. Nor could a person who knowingly loitered with a well-known gang member *anywhere in the city* safely assume that they would not be ordered to disperse.[108]

While the majority nowhere indicates that limiting the ordinance geographically might preserve its constitutionality, its citywide applicability seems a foremost concern. While articulating this as a concern with policing individuals who are not gang members, its language suggests that a concern with spaces, rather than individuals, is motivating its decision. Justice Stevens—himself from Chicago—seems to have written the majority judgment through a lens skeptical of enforcing mobility as a general urban matter, rather than limiting this goal to crime-ridden neighborhoods (or hot spots). This is further reflected in the majority's analysis of the police department's General Order. Although the general order purports to limit police discretion in a wide range of areas relating to the ordinance's enforcement, the majority focuses exclusively on the geographic limitations it imposes and interrogates whether these sufficiently limit police discretion.[109] This is further evidence of the majority's concern over the ordinance's citywide applicability.

Perhaps one way of understanding this concern is that the targeting of specific neighborhoods is part and parcel of new directions in city governance: as Valverde states, "There seems to be a sense that the city or the nation as a whole cannot or should not be policed: instead, there should be a rational selection of high risk spaces."[110] There is a neoliberal quality to this analytic move that fractures the social through geography[111] and that is particularly surprising given that applicability across the city is generally conceived of as the sine qua non of municipal ordinances.[112] In the majority opinion, the policing of idleness—which at a different time was regarded as a *unifying* principle for building cities, as exemplified in Haussmann's Paris—is circumscribed and targeted geographically, perhaps rearticulating the acceptable policing of mobility within the context of neoliberal approaches to urban life.[113]

FAIR NOTICE AND THE FREEDOM TO LOITER

Beyond the majority opinion, a plurality of the court determined that the ordinance is unconstitutional because loitering is a constitutionally protected liberty and the ordinance provides citizens with inadequate notice regarding how they ought to conform their conduct to legal requirements.

While providing little analysis of this point, the plurality locates a "freedom to loiter for innocent purposes" largely by assimilating loitering to the freedom of locomotion and travel within the United States.[114] Having done so, it determines that the ordinance is unconstitutionally vague, since it infringes on this freedom without giving people fair notice as to how to conform their conduct to the law. With loitering defined as "to remain in any one place with no apparent purpose," it becomes impossible to know whether any "purpose" one might have is "apparent" to an officer.[115] Importantly, the plurality then rejects the argument that the police order to disperse (which, if complied with, incurs no sanction) provides the required notice: "because an officer may issue an order only after prohibited conduct has already occurred, it cannot provide the kind of advance notice that will protect the putative loiterer from being ordered to disperse."[116] And indeed, because an officer's notice to disperse may itself be vague (what distance, for instance, would a loiterer have to go in order to comply?), the plurality finds that this only compounds the vagueness of the ordinance itself.[117]

The plurality's assimilation of a freedom to loiter with the freedoms of traveling and movement obviously resonates with the majority's concerns over the generalized regulation of idleness. Its discussion of fair notice, however, bears additional reflection. As presented by the plurality, individuals must receive not only notice before facing possible sanction but sufficient notice so as to avoid police interaction altogether. This is an extension of what fair notice would usually require and highlights a tension in applying the police power in a modern context of urban citizenship.

The question of notice, of course, has a long history within the police context. As Novak demonstrates in the context of private property, the police power often dispenses with notice requirements altogether (such as in the context of fire regulations).[118] It is not surprising then that during oral arguments, counsel for the city sought to analogize to the regulation of traffic, suggesting that "when a police officer refuses to let cars go down a street, we know of no principle of constitutional law that says the police officer must explain why that street has been closed."[119] Thus, although the plurality treats the question of notice as uniquely one of civil liberties, as the city's lawyer implicitly points out it is instead deeply connected to whether one views the policing of idleness from the lens of the criminal law or instead as part of the police regulation of flow, mobility, and traffic.[120]

In contrast to this police legacy, ensuring adequate notice has long been a constitutive element of procedural due process. In this way, the plurality opinion merely draws out an existing tension between law and police as modalities of rule[121]—or as Dubber asks, "How can objects of police remain legal subjects?"[122] As with constitutional decisions of years past, underlying questions regarding the scope of the police power are ignored, in favor of analyses that seek merely to ensure procedural due process.[123] Yet it is the plurality's staunch views on what constitutes fair notice that vividly demonstrate the different urban subject than that contemplated by police science. By requiring that individuals be able to manage their conduct so as to avoid an order to disperse (even if no sanction is attached), the plurality here seems to be working with an image of *Homo prudens* who must be provided with the capacity to successfully *plan* their activities.[124] As we will see next, it is the very opposite view—one that focuses on the loitering ordinance as the urban regulation of circulation and mobility—that animates the decisions of the dissenting judges.

MOBILITY, POLICE, AND CITIZENSHIP

It is the dissenting judges—Justices Scalia and Thomas and Chief Justice Rehnquist, the most conservative members of the Court—who most explicitly take up the police legacy of the Chicago ordinance. In so doing, the dissenting judgments shift the debate away from individual police encounters with citizens, instead focusing on the regulatory aspects of social life that have been prevalent throughout U.S. history. Perhaps surprisingly, however, the dissenting judges view this police power as inherently democratic and indeed as constitutive of democratic polities.

In contrast to the majority decision, Justice Scalia's judgment presents a more unified view of the polity. He begins by relying on some of the most mundane forms of municipal regulation—and in particular, traffic laws and regulation of the public streets—and elevates these classic police concerns with mobility as themselves evidence of a social contract that unites Chicago citizens:

> The citizens of Chicago were once *free to drive about the city* at whatever speed they wished. At some point Chicagoans (or perhaps Illinoisans) decided this would not do, and imposed prophylactic speed limits designed to assure safe operation by the average (or perhaps even subaverage) driver with the average (or perhaps even subaverage) vehicle. This infringed upon the "freedom" of all citizens, but was not unconstitutional.
>
> Similarly, the citizens of Chicago were once *free to stand around and gawk at the scene of an accident.* At some point Chicagoans discovered that this obstructed traffic and caused more accidents. They did not make the practice unlawful, but they did authorize police officers to order the crowd to disperse. . . . Again, this prophylactic measure infringed upon the "freedom" of all citizens, but was not unconstitutional.
>
> Until the ordinance that is before us today was adopted, the citizens of Chicago were *free to stand about in public places* with no apparent purpose—to engage, that is, in conduct that appeared to be loitering. . . . Once again, Chicagoans decided that to eliminate the problem it was worth restricting some of the freedom that they once enjoyed. . . . The minor limitation upon the free state of nature that this prophylactic arrangement imposed upon all Chicagoans seemed to them (and it seems to me) a small price to pay for *liberation of their streets.*[125]

Although likely overstating the historical freedoms of Chicago residents, what is important to note here is that Justice Scalia elevates the police governance of urban life—and in particular, concern over the streets and mobility—to a democratic uniting of the "citizens of Chicago." Though they would both surely resist the comparison, there is perhaps a bit of Foucault here—there are polities, one might conclude, because there is police. And indeed, this conflating of police governance with a united, democratic polity is what Justice Scalia relies on to criticize the majority's view that the ordinance might be constitutional if applied solely to apparent gang members, concluding that "surely gang members cannot be decreed to be outlaws, subject to the merest whim of the police as the rest of us are not."[126]

If Justice Scalia begins with traffic laws, his view of the close connection between mobility, police, and urban citizenship continues throughout the text of his decision. When responding to the plurality's view that an officer's dispersal order would itself be vague, Justice Scalia responds that "no modern urban society—and probably none since London got big enough to have sewers—could function under such a rule."[127] Though neglecting the early Parisian adoption of sewers, the unified polity that Justice Scalia presents is linked together through mundane police regulation—through mention of sewers, speed limits, and the flow of highway traffic—rather than through any transcendent moral relationship. Indeed the heterogeneous list that Justice Scalia produces, in which sewage, traffic, and individuals are seemingly interchangeable objects for ensuring *flow* and *motion*, mirrors Patrick Joyce's analysis of how the regulation of these same material objects produced the liberalism of English cities in the nineteenth century.[128]

In this way, for Justice Scalia the loiterer appears as simply one other aspect of traffic to be controlled. Having "no apparent purpose," in his view, relates to someone who *remains* in any one place and has no apparent reason to *move from there*, so that in his view the lack of movement is what is being policed, rather than those who are mobile (even if aimless).[129] He caustically concludes that this is visible on its face:

> The Ordinance does not apply to "standing," but to "remaining"—a term which in this context obviously means "[to] endure or persist. . . ."
> . . . Chicago police officers enforcing the Ordinance are not looking for people with no apparent purpose (who are regrettably in oversupply); they are looking for people "who remain in any one place with no apparent purpose"—that is, who remain there without any apparent reason *for remaining there*. That is not difficult to perceive.[130]

Indeed, Justice Scalia concludes that the point of regulating loiterers here has little to do with seeking criminal acts or intentions—and that as with other regulated aspects of life, such as riding a motorcycle, harmless conduct can be regulated precisely because of the risk it poses.[131]

Justice Scalia's link between the streets, mobility, and the democratic intentions of the "citizens of Chicago" is echoed in Justice Thomas's opinion, in which both Justice Scalia and Chief Justice Rehnquist join. Justice Thomas's opinion equally turns to broader notions of police, citing among others Ernst Freund's (1904) classic text on the preventive dimension of the police power and Tiedeman's (1886) analysis of the limits of the police power.[132] Yet rather than focusing on the more regulatory dimensions of police, read closely Justice Thomas turns his constitutional analysis on demonstrating that ensuring mobility is also core to the police goals of police and security.

Justice Thomas equally begins by invoking the "citizens of Chicago," who in enacting the ordinance "sensibly decided to return to basics"[133]—and refutes a possible constitutional freedom to loiter by noting the long history of municipal and state acts to regulate the idle and disorderly.[134] He then places the ordinance within the history of police, indicating that achieving *security* has long been a police goal that runs far beyond crime and is instead related to "the power to maintain the public peace"[135] and quoting Freund for the proposition that this police power "needs no special legal authority" and that police and the criminal law are separate modalities for achieving security.[136] *Dispersal*, for Justice Thomas, is a central aspect of this power to ensure public peace and security, quoting, for instance, a nineteenth-century New York police manual that emphasizes the duty to "disperse unlawful or dangerous assemblages, and assemblages that obstruct the free passage of public streets, sidewalks, parks and places."[137] For Justice Thomas, loiterers and vagrants simply fall within this general police power—which sits apart from the criminal law entirely and lands instead within the "peace-keeping" role of police.[138]

If the field of mobility is, for Justice Thomas, core to the peacekeeping function of police, he also appears to take a Haussmannian view of mobility as critical to urban citizenship. Justice Thomas concludes his decision with the following passage:

> The people who will have to live with the consequences of today's opinion do not live in our neighborhoods. . . . They are good, decent people who must struggle to overcome their desperate situation, against all odds, in order to raise their families, earn a living, *and remain good citizens*. As one resident described, "There is only about maybe one or two percent of the people in

> the city causing these problems maybe, but it's keeping 98 percent of us in our houses and off the streets and afraid to shop." . . . The Court today has denied our most vulnerable citizens the very thing that Justice Stevens elevates above all else—the "freedom of movement."[139]

If Justice Thomas adopts a view of security here, it is linked with the ability to circulate, to work and to shop, and to participate in the public dimensions of city life. In addition to echoing the medieval principle that "city air makes one free,"[140] mobility, police, and urban citizenship are here wrapped all together; and indeed, Justice Thomas returns us to a theory of mobility that represents it as a sine qua non of salubrity and good citizenship.

Conclusion

Let us return, then, to the questions motivating this chapter. By chronicling the rise and fall of the Chicago ordinance as not solely an account of crime control but instead as a moment in the governance of urban mobility, we at one level see the persistence of police logics within contemporary political and legal struggles. This is no small point. As Dubber discusses in his analysis of vagrancy and the police power, police often focuses on the elimination of threats—and precisely in so doing, has often managed to stay beyond the reach of legal regulation.[141]

Yet the focus on mobility with which we began also provides a separate source of insight. The historical emphasis placed on ensuring *activity* and *circulation*, a principle that informed the design of cities such as Chicago and Paris and was identified as the heart of police by Foucault, reminds us that urban crime-control initiatives are closely linked with an imagination of the city itself. The production of urban splendor, as Foucault recounts, surely relied on an aesthetic rationale regarding movement and activity but also conceived of such activity as inherently productive for the state and its residents. Patrick Joyce builds on this set of insights to demonstrate how, through the field of circulation, city design and urban ordering produced pedestrians who would productively "move in the city" and for whom walking in public was "civilizing" for pedestrians and onlookers alike.[142]

Although enacted over two centuries later, I suggest that the 1992 Chicago ordinance carried much of the same rationale and flavor. Stemming from some of the most violent months in recent U.S. urban history, the ordinance was designed to police the (apparent) doing of "nothing," not only to prevent the doing of "something" but to address concerns over the limited circulation of law-abiding residents pursuing recreational, familial, and commercial activity. As a result, although underwritten through residents' fear of violence, the ordinance was explicitly articulated to instead resonate with regulating streets, mobility, and circulation—a point that, when enacted, fit with the local political winds by emphasizing urban development but was also perceived as potentially insulating it from legal challenge.[143] There was perhaps a cynicism to this extensive policing of spatial immobility, precisely in a city where economic immobility and the punitive effects of criminal justice policies are themselves spatially concentrated.[144]

While extensively used over a brief three-and-a-half-year period, the Supreme Court found the ordinance unconstitutional in 1999. Depending on one's side of the normative fence, this was perceived either as a triumph of civil liberties or as an anachronistic defeat of innovative policing that could respond to increasingly dangerous cities.[145] Yet in contrast to most research on the ordinance to date, the point of this chapter is neither to defend nor denounce its use but instead to draw out the governmental rationalities and techniques that animate it—and to thereby develop an analysis that highlights the often overlooked relationship between loitering laws and the contemporary production of state splendor. Read from this lens, the different judgments of the Court equally suggest that the constitutionality of the ordinance was not solely one of defining the limits of civil liberties but was wrapped up with ideas about urban citizenship, city life, and the importance of mobility within those logics. If the contest continues to be over whether police regulation can be set apart from the demands of the criminal law, it is a contest that cannot easily be divorced from how we contemplate urban life itself—and indeed, how we contemplate the subjects of law and of police.[146]

Following the Supreme Court decision, Chicago City Council introduced a revised ordinance in February 2000.[147] The ordinance is now limited to those circumstances where there is a reasonably believed harmful purpose or effect; police officers are directed on how to order individuals to disperse and how far they must go; and it is limited in operation to specified enforcement areas, rather than applying to the city at large. The importance of moving along, however, takes even greater pride of place in this new ordinance: in an effort to meet constitutional due process demands, the ordinance now specifies that individuals are to "remove themselves from within sight and hearing of the place" for three hours.[148] The logic of police—and with it, what Foucault calls the field of circulation that is at its core—continues apace.

Reference Matter

Notes

INTRODUCTION

1. 545 U.S. 469 (2005).

2. See inter alia Bernard W. Bell, "Legislatively Revising *Kelo v. City of New London*: Eminent Domain, Federalism, and Congressional Powers," *Journal of Legislation* 32 (2006): 165. On the political context of this case, and on the more general campaign to undermine New Deal jurisprudence and increase private property rights, see the useful overview by Jeffrey Rosen, "The Unregulated Offensive," *New York Times Magazine*, April 17, 2005.

3. Transcript, Oral Argument in *Kelo v. City of New London*, no. 04-108 (U.S. Sup. Ct., Feb. 22, 2005), http://www.oyez.org/cases/2000-2009/2004/2004_04_108/argument/ (accessed Mar. 15, 2007).

4. Brief of Jane Jacobs as *Amicus Curiae* in Support of Petitioners (Dec. 3, 2004), p. 3.

5. See *Commonwealth v. Alger*, 61 Mass. 53, 84–85 (1851).

6. See Robert Brauneis, "'The Foundation of Our "Regulatory Takings" Jurisprudence': The Myth and Meaning of Justice Holmes's Opinion in *Pennsylvania Coal Co. v. Mahon*," 106 Yale L.J. 613 (1996).

7. 545 U.S. at 494, 519 (O'Connor, J., dissenting).

8. 198 U.S. 45 (1905). For more on *Lochner* as a police power case, see Chapter 2; see also Markus D. Dubber, *The Police Power: Patriarchy and the Foundations of American Government* (New York: Columbia Univ. Press, 2005), ch. 9.

9. Walton H. Hamilton & Carlton C. Rodee, "Police Power," in *Encyclopedia of the Social Sciences*, vol. 12, 190 (1933).

10. Useful overviews of the issues surrounding downtown redevelopment efforts include Bernard J. Frieden & Lynne B. Sagalyn, eds., *Downtown, Inc: How America Rebuilds Cities* (Cambridge, Mass.: MIT Press, 1989), and Alison Isenberg, *Downtown America: A History of the Place and the People Who Made It* (Chicago: Univ. of Chicago Press, 2004).

11. See William J. Novak, *The People's Welfare: Law and Regulation in Nineteenth-Century America* (Chapel Hill: Univ. of North Carolina Press, 1996).

12. Markus D. Dubber and Mariana Valverde, eds., *The New Police Science: The Police Power in Domestic and International Governance* (Stanford, Calif.: Stanford Univ. Press, 2006).

13. See Chapter 2.

14. Levi and Hagan, in *The New Police Science* (supra note 12); Dean, *The New Police Science.*

15. See, generally, Dubber, *Police Power.*

16. See Chapter 2.

17. Mariana Valverde, *Law's Dream of a Common Knowledge* (Princeton, N.J.: Princeton Univ. Press, 2003), ch. 6.

18. *Maynard v. Hill*, 125 U.S. 190 (1888).

19. See *Loving v. Virginia*, 388 U.S. 1 (1967).

20. Dubber, *Police Power*, 44, 82, 94, 195, 198.

21. See Mariana Valverde, "'Peace, Order, and Good Government': Policelike Powers in Postcolonial Perspective," in *The New Police Science*, p. 73, and Chapter 2.

22. See Dubber, *Police Power*, 87, 145, 181 (discussing *United States v. Lopez*, 514 U.S. 549 [1995]).

23. William Blackstone, *Commentaries on the Laws of England* (Oxford: Clarendon, 1769), 4:162.

24. See *Commonwealth v. Keller*, 35 D. & C.2d 615 (Pa. Ct. Com. Pleas 1964) (common law misdemeanor).

25. Valverde, *Law's Dream of a Common Knowledge*, chap. 6.

26. Markus D. Dubber, "Policing Possession: The War on Crime and the End of Criminal Law," *Journal of Criminal Law & Criminology* 19 (2002): 829.

27. See Mark Neocleous, "Theoretical Foundations of the 'New Police Science,'" in *The New Police Science*, p. 17.

28. Christopher L. Tomlins, *Law, Labor and Ideology in the Early American Republic* (Cambridge and New York: Cambridge Univ. Press, 1993).

29. See Robert J. Steinfeld, "Property and Suffrage in the Early American Republic," *Stan. L. Rev.* 41 (1989): 335; Markus D. Dubber, "'An Extraordinarily Beautiful Document': Jefferson's *Bill for Proportioning Crimes and Punishments* and the Challenge of Republican Punishment," in *Modern Histories of Crime and Punishment*, Markus D. Dubber & Lindsay Farmer, eds. (Stanford, Calif.: Stanford Univ. Press, 2007), p. 115.

30. See Dubber, *Police Power*, pp. 85–87, 145.

31. See *United States v. Lopez*; Dubber, *Police Power*, pp. 191–92.

32. See Dubber, *Police Power*, pp. 95–118.

33. See *Heath v. Alabama*, 474 U.S. 82 (1985) (dual sovereignty exception to double jeopardy protection).

34. See Peter Scharf & Joseph Hickey, "Thomas Mott Osborne and the Limits of Democratic Prison Reform," *Prison Journal* 57 (1977): 3. For a comparative perspective, see James Q. Whitman, *Harsh Justice: Criminal Punishment and the Widening Divide Between America and Europe* (New York: Oxford Univ. Press, 2003); Liora Lazarus, *Contrasting Prisoners' Rights: A Comparative Examination of Germany and England* (Oxford: Oxford Univ. Press, 2004).

35. Blackstone, *Commentaries*, p. 162.

36. Dubber, "Policing Possession."

CHAPTER ONE

1. Cf. Paul Veyne, "Foucault Revolutionizes History," in *Foucault and His Interlocutors*, A. Davidson, ed. (Chicago: Univ. of Chicago Press, 1997).

2. Michel Foucault, *Sécurité, Territoire, Population: Cour au College de France*, 1975–1976 (Paris: Gallimard, 2005).

3. Ibid., p. 120.

4. Ibid., p. 121.

5. The emphasis on how governing practices construct the very subject that is supposed to exist prior to being governed is a debt Foucault owes to Nietzsche; on Nietzsche and legal subjectivity, see *Nietzsche and Legal Theory: Half-written Law*, Peter Goodrich & Mariana Valverde, eds. (New York: Routledge, 2005).

6. Veyne, supra note 1, p. 181.

7. Foucault, supra note 2, p. 124.

8. Colin Gordon, "Governmental Rationality: An Introduction," in *The Foucault Effect: Essays on Governmentality*, Graham Burchell, Colin Gordon, & Peter Miller, eds. (Chicago: Chicago Univ. Press, 1991), p. 2.

9. Nikolas Rose & Peter Miller, "Political Power Beyond the State: Problematics of Government," *British Journal of Sociology* 43 (1992): 173–205.

10. Michel Foucault, *Discipline and Punishment: The Birth of the Prison* (New York: Vintage, 1979).

11. Michel Foucault, *The History of Sexuality, vol. 1: An Introduction* (New York: Vintage, 1980).

12. See *The Foucault Effect: Essays on Governmentality*, Graham Burchell, Colin Gordon, & Peter Miller, eds. (Chicago: Chicago Univ. Press, 1991).

13. See, for example, *Foucault and Political Reason*, Andrew Barry, Thomas Osborne, & Nikolas Rose, eds. (London: UCL Press, 1996); Mitchell Dean, *Governmentality* (London: Sage, 1999); Nikolas Rose, *Powers of Freedom: Reframing Political Thought* (Cambridge: Cambridge Univ. Press, 1999).

14. For an extended commentary on this set of lectures, see Mariana Valverde, "Review Essay: Michel Foucault's *Society Must Be Defended*," *Law, Culture and Humanities* 1 (2005): 113–33.

15. These have been reprinted in a number of volumes; see, for example, *Michel Foucault: Politics, Philosophy, Culture: Interviews and Other Writings, 1977–1984*, Lawrence Kritzmann, ed. (New York: Routledge, 1988).

16. Paolo Napoli, *Naissance de la Police Moderne* (Paris: La Decouverte, 2004).

17. Foucault, supra note 2, p. 126; Kritzmann, ed., supra note 15, p. 61.

18. Kritzmann, ed., supra note 15, p. 60.

19. Foucault, supra note 2, pp. 157–58, 177.

20. Ibid., p. 187.

21. Ibid.

22. Kritzmann, ed., supra note 15, p. 71.

23. Foucault, supra note 2, pp. 46–47.

24. Ibid., p. 19.

25. Ibid., p. 251.

26. On policy and politics, see *The New Police Science: The Police Power in Domestic and International Governance*, Markus D. Dubber & Mariana Valverde, eds. (Stanford, Calif.: Stanford Univ. Press, 2006), especially chapters by Pasquale Pasquino, Markus D. Dubber, & Chris Tomlins. See also Wendy Brown, "Genealogical Politics," in *The Later Foucault*, Jeremy Moss, ed. (London: Sage, 1998).

27. Isolated comments about Stalinist practices in Foucault's published work mainly highlight biopolitical campaigns, such as psychiatrizing dissidents in the name of the health of socialism. How communist sovereignty differs from or is similar to liberal sovereignty is not a question addressed by Foucault.

28. See, for example, William Novak, *The People's Welfare* (Chapel Hill: Univ. of North Carolina Press, 1996).

29. Foucault, supra note 2, p. 344.

30. Mariana Valverde, "Police Science, British Style: Pub Licensing and Urban Disorder," *Economy and Society* 32, no. 2 (2003): 234–52; Markus D. Dubber, *The Police Power: Patriarchy and the Foundations of American Government* (New York: Columbia Univ. Press, 2005).

31. Cf. *The New Police Science: The Police Power in Domestic and International Governance*, Markus D. Dubber & Mariana Valverde, eds. (Stanford, Calif.: Stanford Univ. Press, 2006).

32. Foucault, supra note 2, p. 334.

33. Nevertheless, Foucault read the major works of Patrick Colquhoun and called him "the creator of the police in England." See Michel Foucault, "Truth and Juridical Forms," in *The Essential Works of Michel Foucault*, Paul Rabinow & James Faubion, eds. (New York: The New Press, 2000), 3:69.

34. Foucault, supra note 2, p. 347. For Foucault, *coup d'etat* is not the overthrow of government but rather the government's own suspension of law, what Schmitt and other theorists would call "the state of exception." See ibid., p. 267.

35. Dubber, supra note 30.

36. Jacques Donzelot's groundbreaking work *The Policing of Families* (Baltimore, Md.: Johns Hopkins Univ. Press, 1979) mapped this terrain to some extent (and it is worth noting in the present context that its original title was *La Police des Familles*, in a direct reference to the police tradition researched by Foucault when Donzelot was working with him). But this work tends to treat families as conduits for sovereign and police rationalities, without much attention to intrafamily dynamics, either patriarchal or pastoral.

37. Foucault, supra note 2, p. 355.

38. Valverde, supra note 30.

39. Foucault, supra note 2, pp. 294–300.

40. Ibid., p. 322.

41. Ibid.

42. Nikolas Rose, Pat O'Malley, & Mariana Valverde, "Governmentality," *Annual Review of Law and Social Science*, December 2006, 30:83–104.

43. Foucault, supra note 2, p. 67.

44. Ibid., p. 113.

45. Ibid., pp. 7, 9, 21.

46. Graham Burchell, "Peculiar Interests: Civil Society and Governing 'the System of Natural Liberty,'" in *The Foucault Effect: Essays on Governmentality*, Graham Burchell, Colon Gordon, & Peter Miller, eds. (Chicago: Univ. of Chicago Press, 1991).

47. Cf. Pat O'Malley, Lorna Weir, & Clifford Shearing, "Governmentality, Criticism, Politics," *Economy and Society* 26, no. 4 (1997): 501–7.

48. Foucault, supra note 2, pp. 8, 31–49.

49. Ibid., p. 19.

50. Ibid., p. 46.

CHAPTER TWO

1. Christopher L. Tomlins, *The State and the Unions: Labor Relations, Law, and the Organized Labor Movement in the United States, 1880–1960* (Cambridge and New York: Cambridge Univ. Press, 1985).

2. Peter B. Evans, Dietrich Rueschemeyer, & Theda Skocpol, eds., *Bringing the State Back In* (Cambridge and New York: Cambridge Univ. Press, 1985).

3. Thomas Bender, "Historians, the Nation and the Plenitude of Narratives," in *Rethinking American History in a Global Age*, Thomas Bender, ed. (Berkeley: Univ. of California Press, 2002), p. 6.

4. On the origins of the "myth of American statelessness" in U.S. scholarship, see William J. Novak, *The People's Welfare: Law and Regulation in Nineteenth-Century America* (Chapel Hill: Univ. of North Carolina Press, 1996), p. 3.

5. See, e.g., Stephen Skowronek, *Building a New American State: The Expansion of National Administrative Capacities, 1877–1920* (Cambridge and New York: Cambridge Univ. Press, 1982), pp. 19, 23, criticized in Richard R. John, "Affairs of Office: The Executive Departments, the Election of 1828, and the Making of the Democratic Party," in *The Democratic Experiment: New Directions in American Political History*, Meg Jacobs, William J. Novak, & Julian E. Zelizer, eds. (Princeton, N.J.: Princeton Univ. Press, 2003), pp. 50–84, at 53–54.

6. See, generally, Meg Jacobs & Julian E. Zelizer, "The Democratic Experiment: New Directions in American Political History," in *The Democratic Experiment*, supra note 5, pp. 1–20.

7. Ibid. See also Tomlins, supra note 1; Christopher L. Tomlins, "The Heavy Burden of the State: Revisiting the History of Labor Law in the Interwar Period," *Seattle University Law Review*, 23(3) (Winter, 2000): 605–29.

8. Christopher L. Tomlins, *Law, Labor and Ideology in the Early American Republic* (Cambridge and New York: Cambridge Univ. Press, 1993); Novak, supra note 4; Markus D. Dubber, *The Police Power: Patriarchy and the Foundations of American Government* (New York: Columbia Univ. Press, 2005).

9. Tomlins, supra note 8, pp. 55–59; Dubber, supra note 8, p. xi.

10. By *governmentality*, I mean, prompted by Colin Gordon's exposition of Foucault, "government as an activity or practice, and . . . arts of government as ways of knowing what that activity consisted in, and how it might be carried on." Colin Gordon, "Governmental Rationality: An Introduction," in *The Foucault Effect: Studies in Governmentality*, Graham Burchell, Colin Gordon, & Peter Miller, eds. (Chicago: Univ. of Chicago Press, 1991), p. 3.

11. On which see also Mariana Valverde's highly instructive revisionist account of Foucault's 1976–1978 Lectures at the College de France, "Police, Sovereignty and Law: Foucaultian Reflections," Chapter 1, particularly at p. 26 ("police is the direct governmentality of the sovereign as sovereign").

12. For a recent, although not altogether satisfying, attempt from which I have learned, see T. Alexander Aleinikoff, *Semblances of Sovereignty: The Constitution, the State and American Citizenship* (Cambridge, Mass.: Harvard Univ. Press, 2002). For a much more extensive, even exhaustive, treatment, which nevertheless preserves the traditional distinction between domestic and external manifestations of sovereignty that this chapter attempts to erode, see Sarah H. Cleveland, "Powers Inherent in Sovereignty: Indians, Aliens, Territories, and the Nineteenth Century Origins of Plenary Powers over Foreign Affairs," *Texas Law Review* 81 (2002): 1–284.

13. Akhil Reed Amar, *America's Constitution: A Biography* (New York: Random House, 2005), p. 243.

14. Ibid., p. 5.

15. See J. Willard Hurst, *Law and the Conditions of Freedom in the Nineteenth-Century United States* (Madison: Univ. of Wisconsin Press, 1956), pp. 3–6; Forrest McDonald, *Novus Ordo Seclorum: The Intellectual Origins of the Constitution* (Lawrence: Univ. Press of Kansas, 1985), pp. 262, 276. "MDCCLXXVI" (1776) and "Novus Ordo Seclorum" ("a new order of the ages") appear on the Great Seal of the United States, signifying the beginning of the new (American) era.

16. See, generally, Christopher Tomlins, "Framing the Fragments. Police: Genealogies, Discourses, Locales, Principles," in *The New Police Science: The Police Power in Domestic and International Governance*, Markus D. Dubber & Mariana Valverde, eds. (Stanford, Calif.: Stanford Univ. Press, 2006).

17. Tomlins, supra note 8, pp. 35–59.

18. Amar, supra note 13, pp. 5, 8–13, 29. On popular sovereignty, see also Larry D. Kramer, *The People Themselves: Popular Constitutionalism and Judicial Review* (New York: Oxford Univ. Press, 2004).

19. We shall see that this is precisely what occurred over the following century.

20. William Blackstone, *Commentaries on the Laws of England* (Chicago: Univ. of Chicago Press, 1979), 4:162.

21. British North America Act (1867), patriated in 1982 under the new title The Constitution Act (1867), at http://www.solon.org/Constitutions/Canada/English/ca_1867.html (accessed January 27, 2006), §91.

22. Mariana Valverde, "'Peace, Order, and Good Government': Policelike Powers in Postcolonial Perspective," in Dubber & Valverde, supra note 16. Such powers stretch

to include whatever "the state perceives as a necessary power for survival." Nasser Hussain, *The Jurisprudence of Emergency: Colonialism and the Rule of Law* (Ann Arbor: Univ. of Michigan Press, 2003), pp. 1–2.

23. POGG powers turn up in various incarnations virtually wherever the British have been. On Australia, see the *Commonwealth of Australia Act* (63 & 64 Vic. C. 12, 1900), at 1.V.51 ("peace, order and good government"); the *New South Wales Act* (1823), 37 ("peace, welfare and good government"), also in the *New South Wales Constitution Act* (1842), 19, the *Australian Constitutions Act* (1850), 9, and the preamble to the Constitution Act (Tasmania) (1855), all at http://www.foundingdocs.gov.au/default.asp (accessed July 15, 2005). On New Zealand, see the preamble to the *Treaty of Waitangi* (1840), the founding document of nonindigenous government in Aotearoa, stating, "Her Majesty, Victoria . . . regarding with Her Royal Favour the Native Chiefs and Tribes of New Zealand, and anxious to protect their just Rights and Property, and to secure to them the enjoyment of Peace and Good Order . . . therefore being desirous to establish a settled form of Civil Government . . . ," at http://www.treatyofwaitangi.govt.nz/treaty/index.php (accessed July 15, 2005). On India, see the *Indian Councils Act* (1861), ¶¶23, 42, 44, and 48 ("peace and good government"), also in the *Government of India Act* (1919), ¶10, at http://projectsouthasia.sdstate.edu/Docs/history/primarydocs/Political_History/ (accessed July 15, 2005); also the Indian Constitution of 1947, §240 ("peace progress and good government"), at http://indiacode.nic.in/coiweb/welcome.html (accessed January 27, 2006). On the British Mandate in Palestine, see *The Palestine Order in Council, 1922*, clause 18 ("peace, order and good government"), at http://domino.un.org/UNISPAL.NSF/0/c7aae196f41aa055052565f50054e656?OpenDocument (accessed February 28, 2006).

24. First Charter of Virginia (1606). See also, for example, the charters of New England ("well ordering and good Government"), Maryland and Pennsylvania ("good and happy government"), Rhode Island ("peaceable and orderly Government"), and Delaware ("Well-being and good Government"), all in Francis Newton Thorpe, *The Federal and State Constitutions, Colonial Charters, and other Organic Laws of the States, Territories, and Colonies Now or Heretofore Forming the United States of America* (Washington: Government Printing Office, 1909), pp. 558, 1669, 1839, 3035, 3217, 3784. Unsurprisingly, POGG discourse also turns up quite routinely in the formal jurisdictional declarations that enable continuity in governance in the British mainland colonies. Thus, for example, George II's commission appointing Sir William Anne van Keppel, second Earl of Albemarle, governor of Virginia in 1737, grants "power and authority to the said William Earl of Albemarle with the consent of the Council and Assembly, or the major part of them respectively, to make, constitute and ordain Statutes and Ordinances for the public peace, welfare and good government of the said colony, and the people and inhabitants thereof." The actions of the council and assembly make it quite clear that the Crown's language was taken very seriously. See William Waller Hening, *The Statutes At Large: Being a Collection of all the Laws of Virginia, from the First Session of the Legislature, in the Year 1619*, vol. 5 (Richmond, Va.: Franklin Press, 1819), editor's note at pp. 432–33 (see also 435, 436, and generally, 432–36, http://www.vagenweb.org/hening/vol05-25.htm, accessed January 5, 2008).

25. See Tomlins, supra note 16.

26. 61 Mass. 53, at 85. Shaw's definition came almost verbatim from the Massachusetts constitution (1780). See part 2 ("The Frame of Government"), chap. 1, §1, article 4, granting the General Court "full power and authority . . . to make, ordain, and establish all manner of wholesome and reasonable orders, laws, statutes, and ordinances, directions and instructions, either with penalties or without, so as the same be not repugnant or contrary to this constitution, as they shall judge to be for the good and welfare of this commonwealth, and for the government and ordering thereof, and of the subjects of the same." Shaw's definition omitted the words "and for the government and ordering thereof," suggesting he took "government and ordering" to mean the same thing as "the good and welfare" of the commonwealth and its "subjects."

27. 61 Mass. 53, 65–83, 82, 83, 85. Shaw refers to the Charter of New England (1620) along with the Massachusetts Bay Company Charter (1629) as that "under which the colony was formed and settled." The short extract I have quoted is not mentioned in *Alger.* See Thorpe, *Federal and State Constitutions*, p. 1833. As Novak, supra note 4, pp. 20–21, argues, *Alger* was an easy case. Police was long since established as "a settled principle, growing out of the nature of well ordered civil society." Though its jurisdictional frontiers could not be marked, the fitness of its exercise by "well-ordered governments" was "so obvious, that all well-regulated minds will regard it as reasonable" (84–85). *Alger*'s importance lies not in any "invention" of the police power but its normalization in high constitutional discourse.

28. Massachusetts constitution, part 1 ("A Declaration of the Rights of the Inhabitants") articles 4 and 5. See also the constitution of Virginia (June 1776): Bill of Rights, §§2–3, http://www.yale.edu/lawweb/avalon/states/va05.htm (accessed January 27, 2006): "all power is vested in, and consequently derived from, the people; that magistrates are their trustees and servants, and at all times amenable to them"; and "government is, or ought to be, instituted for the common benefit, protection, and security of the people, nation, or community; of all the various modes and forms of government, that is best which is capable of producing the greatest degree of happiness and safety."

29. Willi-Paul Adams, *The First American Constitutions: Republican Ideology and the Making of the State Constitutions in the Revolutionary Era* (Lanham, Md.: Rowman & Littlefield, 2001), pp. 136, 286–87. The March 1776 Constitution of South Carolina had already declared that "some mode should be established by common consent, and for the good of the people, the origin and end of all governments, for regulating the internal polity of this colony." http://www.yale.edu/lawweb/avalon/states/sc01.htm (accessed January 27, 2006).

30. All at http://www.yale.edu/lawweb/avalon/18th.htm (accessed January 27, 2006).

31. See 61 Mass. 53, 78.

32. Novak, supra note 4, p. 1.

33. Blackstone, supra note 20, p. 162. Markus Dubber tends to collapse distinctions between police and criminal law. See Dubber, supra note 8, pp. 124–38.

34. *Thorpe v. Rutland and Burlington Railroad Company*, 27 Vt. 140 (1854). *Alger* and *Thorpe*, in tandem, were taken to supply sufficient constitutional discussion of the police power in the nineteenth-century United States that their key points were picked up by the U.S. Supreme Court and cited without further gloss or elaboration. See also two key lead-ins to the decisions: *Commonwealth v. Tewkesbury*, 11 Metc. 55 (1846), and *Spalding v. Preston*, 21 Vt. 9 (1848).

35. 27 Vt. 140, 149. Note that Redfield invokes state constitutions not as the point of origin of specific powers of governance, but as specifications of restraint on governance powers otherwise unlimited.

36. Ibid., pp. 147, 149 (emphasis added).

37. Ibid., p. 150; 61 Mass. 53, 84–85, and generally, 90–98.

38. 27 Vt. 140, 150, 156 (footnote).

39. J. I. Clark Hare, *American Constitutional Law* (Boston: Little, Brown, 1889), 2:766–67 (emphasis added).

40. Ernst Freund, *The Police Power: Public Policy and Constitutional Rights* (Chicago: Callaghan, 1904), pp. iii, 2.

41. Gordon, supra note 10, pp. 8–9. See, generally, Christopher Tomlins, "To Improve the State and Condition of Man: The Power to Police and the History of American Governance," *Buffalo Law Review* 53 (2006): 1215–71; Tomlins, supra note 16.

42. Freund, supra note 40, p. 63.

43. Ibid., pp. 62–65.

44. The concept of plenary power as a synonym for exclusive jurisdiction appears early in commerce clause jurisprudence. See, e.g., *Gibbons v. Ogden*, 22 U.S. 1, 197 (1824). The doctrine of plenary powers, meaning absolute and unchecked sovereign authority, was first articulated in *United States v. William Rogers*, 45 U.S. 567 (1846).

45. 130 U.S. 581, 606. And see, in general, ibid., pp. 603–11.

46. *Fong Yue Ting v. United States*, 149 U.S. 698, 712, 731 (1898).

47. Thus, in *Nishimura Ekiu v. United States*, the Court found, "It is an accepted maxim of international law, that every sovereign nation has the power, as inherent in sovereignty, and essential to self-preservation, to forbid the entrance of foreigners within its dominions, or to admit them only in such cases and upon such conditions as it may see fit to prescribe." 142 U.S. 651, 659 (1891).

48. 149 U.S. 698, 704–732. This point had been broached in qualified fashion by Justice Field in *Chae Chan Ping*. "The powers to declare war, make treaties, suppress insurrection, repel invasion, regulate foreign commerce, secure republican governments to the States, and admit subjects of other nations to citizenship, are all sovereign powers, restricted in their exercise only by the Constitution itself and considerations of public policy and justice which control, more or less, the conduct of all civilized nations." 130 U.S. 581, 604. However, in *Fong Yue Ting*, Field placed himself in the minority (with Justices Fuller and Brewer), vociferously objecting to the majority's assertion that as a sovereign nation the United States exercised certain powers "inherent in sovereignty" derived from international law.

49. See *Johnson v. M'Intosh*, 21 U.S. 543 (1823); *Cherokee Nation v. Georgia*, 30 U.S. 1 (1830); *Worcester v. Georgia*, 31 U.S. 515 (1832); *U.S. v. Rogers*, 45 U.S. 567 (1846).

50. *The Schooner Exchange v. M'Faddon*, 11 U.S. 116, 136, 146 (1812).

51. Ibid., pp. 135–47.

52. 21 U.S. 543, 590. This point was reinforced in *Cherokee Nation v. Georgia*.

53. Ibid., pp. 588, 591, and generally, 587–91. See also *Sere & Laralde v. Pitot and Others*, 10 U.S. 332, 336–37 (1810): "The power of governing and of legislating for a territory is the inevitable consequence of the right to acquire and to hold territory. Could this position be contested, the Constitution of the United States declares that 'Congress shall have power to dispose of and make all needful rules and regulations respecting the territory or other property belonging to the United States.'"

54. 45 U.S. 567, 572.

55. 118 U.S. 375, 379, 383. For the immediate background to *Kagama*, see *Ex Parte Crow Dog*, 109 U.S. 556, 565 (1883). In a proviso attached to the Indian Appropriation Act of 1871 and thereafter permanently adopted, Congress had declared that, though it would continue to honor the provisions of treaties made before that time, thereafter "no Indian nation or tribe within the territory of the United States, shall be acknowledged or recognized as an independent nation, tribe, or power with whom the United States may contract by treaty." As the Court explained in *Kagama*, at 381–82, both past and current practice were simply alternative modes of governance of the tribes determined by the United States according to criteria of policy and convenience. The United States had followed the "policy" of the European governments that had preceded it in acknowledging the Indians' "possessory" rights to "the soil over which they roamed." But as sovereign successor to those European governments, the United States, as they had, "asserted an ultimate title in the land itself." Accordingly, Indian tribes were "forbidden to sell or transfer it to other nations or peoples without the consent of this paramount authority." Hence "when a tribe wished to dispose of its land, or any part of it, or the State or the United States wished to purchase it, a treaty with the tribe was the only mode in which this could be done." Nor could a tribe treat with whomever it deemed fit, "private persons, or . . . other nations," but only with the United States, for the United States had never recognized tribes as possessed of "full attributes of sovereignty" but only as "wards," or "pupils," or dependencies. Having chosen for a century to govern the tribes by treaty, the United States had now instituted a new policy, just as a sovereign might do in its relations with subjects or dependents. "After an experience of a hundred years of the treaty-making system of government, Congress has determined upon a new departure—to govern them by acts of Congress."

56. 187 U.S. 553, 565 (1903).

57. *Chae Chan Ping v. United States*, 1889 U.S. Lexis 1778 (1889), Supplementary Brief for Plaintiff (filed by James Coolidge Carter), §III, ¶1.

58. 130 U.S. 581, 603, 609. "The exclusion of paupers, criminals and persons afflicted with incurable diseases, for which statutes have been passed, is only an application of the same power to particular classes of persons, whose presence is deemed injurious or a source of danger to the country. As applied to them, there has never been any question as

to the power to exclude them. The power is constantly exercised; its existence is involved in the right of self-preservation." Ibid., p. 608.

59. 142 U.S. 651, 659.

60. 149 U.S. 698, 707 (emphasis added). See also p. 711, where the Court states that the right to exclude or to expel was "an inherent and inalienable right of every sovereign and independent nation, essential to its safety, its independence and its welfare." *United States v. Hing Quong Chow*, 53 F. Cas. 233 (E.D. La. 1892) names the congressional legislation under inspection in *Fong Yue Ting* as a police measure. And see Dubber, supra note 8, pp. 141–43.

61. Ibid., p. 737. Fish had originally been cited by Field in *Chae Chan Ping*. In *Fong*, however, Field joined Brewer (and Chief Justice Fuller) in decrying the majority's slighting of the Constitution.

62. The precise cohort of cases constituting the Insular Cases is a matter of debate. The cases directly or indirectly touched on here are *Neely v. Henkel*, 180 U.S. 109 (1901); *De Lima v. Bidwell*, 182 U.S. 1 (1901); *Dooley v. United States*, 182 U.S. 222 (1901); *Armstrong v. United States*, 182 U.S. 243 (1901); *Downes v. Bidwell*, 182 U.S. 244 (1901); *Dooley v. United States*, 183 U.S. 151 (1901); *Fourteen Diamond Rings, Emil J. Pepke, Claimant v. United States*, 183 U.S. 176 (1901); *Hawaii v. Mankichi*, 190 U.S. 197 (1903); *Kepner v. United States*, 195 U.S. 100 (1904); *Dorr v. United States*, 195 U.S. 138 (1904); *Rassmussen v. United States*, 197 U.S. 516 (1905); *Balzac v. People of Porto Rico*, 258 U.S. 298 (1922).

63. 182 U.S. 1, 196.

64. What infuriated the minority was the majority's implication that the United States as nation-state could not dispose of colonial acquisitions like any other great power; that once ceded, territory ceased to be "foreign" and was automatically brought within the realm of the Constitution. "It takes this great country out of the world and shuts it up within itself. It binds and cripples the power to make war and peace." Ibid., p. 218. To the minority, the Constitution was "a charter of great and vital authorities" but limited in scope; yet whose limitations "serve and assist government, not destroy it" by enabling the United States to have "'an equal station among the Powers of the earth,' and to do all 'Acts and Things which Independent States may of right do.'" Ibid., p. 220.

65. The Court was divided into two blocs: Gray, McKenna, Shiras, and White took the "sovereignty" position; Brewer, Fuller, Harlan, and Peckham took the "Constitution" position. Brown also took the sovereignty position but was the swing vote, by dint of which he wrote the lead opinions in both *De Lima* and *Downes*. Substantively, *De Lima* turned on circumstances in effect after the Treaty of Paris but before the enactment of the Foraker Act. Brown's lead opinion in that case evaded the much wider argument going on around him by defining the issue narrowly as a default question, namely, "whether territory acquired by the United States by cession from a foreign power remains a 'foreign country' within the meaning of the tariff laws." Ibid., p. 174. He postponed the wider argument to *Downes*, which addressed the effects and constitutionality of the Foraker Act. When the wider argument was fully joined in *Downes*, Brown's lead opinion gave enthusiastic voice to the sovereignty position. But though a majority of sorts coalesced around Brown's opinion in *Downes*, it clearly considered

Brown's statement of the sovereignty position inadequate. Thus, White and Gray concurred in Brown's opinion, but White also wrote a separate concurring opinion joined by Shiras and McKenna. Gray also wrote a separate concurring opinion. The minority showed more solidarity. Fuller wrote a dissent in which he was joined by Harlan, Brewer, and Peckham. But Harlan also added his own separate dissent.

66. 182 U.S. 244, 279 (Brown). "The power to acquire territory by treaty implies not only the power to govern such territory, but to prescribe upon what terms the United States will receive its inhabitants, and what their status shall be in what Chief Justice Marshall termed the 'American Empire.'"

67. Noting "grave apprehensions" that "an unrestrained possession of power on the part of Congress may lead to unjust and oppressive legislation," Brown assured his audience that "there are certain principles of natural justice inherent in the Anglo-Saxon character which need no expression in constitutions or statutes to give them effect." Ibid., p. 280.

68. "The Constitution was intended to establish a permanent form of government for the States which should elect to take advantage of its conditions." As to territories subsequently acquired, "our power . . . is the same power which other nations have been accustomed to exercise with respect to territories acquired by them. If, in limiting the power which Congress was to exercise within the United States, it was also intended to limit it with regard to such territories as the people of the United States should thereafter acquire, such limitations should have been expressed." It would be disastrous now to adopt a construction of the Constitution that would impose such limitations. "A false step at this time might be fatal to the development of what Chief Justice Marshall called the American Empire." Ibid., pp. 284, 285, 286.

69. Ibid., p. 306.

70. Ibid., pp. 359, 369.

71. Ibid., pp. 379–80, 384.

72. *Dooley v. United States*, 182 U.S. 222 (1901); *Armstrong v. United States*, 182 U.S. 243 (1901); *Fourteen Diamond Rings, Emil J. Pepke, Claimant v. United States*, 183 U.S. 176 (1901).

73. *Dooley v. United States*, 183 U.S. 151 (1901); *Hawaii v. Mankichi*, 190 U.S. 197 (1903); *Dorr v. United States*, 195 U.S. 138 (1904).

74. Thus see Day's opinion for the Court in *Dorr* (1904), which cemented *Downes* as the decisive Insular Case. 195 U.S. 138, 149.

75. Ron Levi & John Hagan, "International Police," abstract, paper presented at "The New Police Science: Police Powers in Comparative Perspective," Baldy Center for Law and Social Policy, SUNY-Buffalo (June 2004), published in revised form in Dubber & Valverde, supra note 16, pp. 207–47. See particularly 207–22.

76. Ibid., p. 214 (emphasis in original).

77. 22 U.S. 1, 196. The Court continued, "If, as has always been understood, the sovereignty of Congress, though limited to specified objects, is plenary as to those objects, the power over commerce with foreign nations, and among the several States, is vested in Congress as absolutely as it would be in a single government, having in its constitution

the same restrictions on the exercise of the power as are found in the constitution of the United States." Ibid., p. 197.

78. Ibid., pp. 204, 208.

79. 36 U.S. 102, 139. *Miln* was the Supreme Court's first attempt to summarize what it knew of the extent of state police powers. Describing police as "diversified and multifarious," the Court first attempted a covering statement: police embraced every law "which concerned the welfare of the whole people of a state, or any individual within it; whether it related to their rights, or their duties; whether it respected them as men, or as citizens of the state; whether in their public or private relations; whether it related to the rights of persons, or of property, of the whole people of a state, or of any individual within it; and whose operation was within the territorial limits of the state, and upon the persons and things within its jurisdiction." As illustration the Court produced a disjointed and indiscriminate list of state capacities that emphasized discretion over definition: the right to punish; the right "to guard, by anticipation, against the commission of an offence," that is, to prevent; the right to protect, including precautionary measures against disease, but also against "the moral pestilence of paupers, vagabonds, and possibly convicts." State police powers might thus be expressed in "inspection laws, quarantine laws, health laws of every description, as well as laws for regulating the internal commerce of a state." Ibid., pp. 139–43.

80. The Taney Court adopted this position in *Cooley v. Board of Wardens*, 53 U.S. 299, 319 (1852), with some slight qualification: "Whatever subjects of this power are in their nature national, or admit of one uniform system or plan of regulation, may justly be said to be of such a nature as to require exclusive legislation by Congress."

81. The broadest Taney Court statement came in *Thurlow v. Massachusetts* (*License Cases*), 46 U.S. 504, 583 (1847): What are the police powers of a State? They are nothing more or less than the powers of government inherent in every sovereignty to the extent of its dominions . . . that is to say, the power of sovereignty, the power to govern men and things within the limits of its dominion."

82. *Slaughter-House Cases*, 83 U.S. 36 (1873); *Henderson v. Mayor of the City of New York*, 92 U.S. 259 (1876); *Munn v. Illinois*, 94 U.S. 113 (1877); *Railroad Company v. Husen*, 95 U.S. 465 (1878). See also *Chicago, Burlington and Quincy Railroad Company v. Iowa*, 94 U.S. 155 (1877); *Peik v. Chicago and North-Western Railway Company*, 94 U.S. 164 (1877); *Hall v. DeCuir*, 95 U.S. 485 (1878).

83. *Wabash, St. Louis and Pacific Railway Company v. Illinois*, 118 U.S. 557, 567 (1886).

84. 134 U.S. 418, 456–58. The crucial difference between the commerce cases and the Fourteenth Amendment cases is that the commerce cases charted a frontier between jurisdictions (federal and state), whereas the Fourteenth Amendment cases dealt with what states might actually do within their otherwise uncontested spheres of sovereign jurisdiction. See, for example, *Crowley v. Christensen*, 137 U.S. 86 (1890).

85. 165 U.S. 578, 590, 591.

86. 169 U.S. 366, 392 (emphasis added). As usual, the majority made little attempt to *define* the state's police powers beyond quoting from *Alger* and adding the typical quasi-random list of examples: quarantine laws, insane asylums, public hospitals, institutions

for the care and education of the blind, measures for the exclusion of infected cattle, rags and decayed fruit, working hours for women and children. Ibid., p. 395.

87. 197 U.S. 11, 26, 29–30. The majority opinion was written by Harlan, but this passage is noticeably Holmesian.

88. 198 U.S. 45, 53, 54, 56.

89. Ibid., pp. 57, 62.

90. Ibid., pp. 60–61. Here Peckham aims directly at Harlan, who wrote the majority opinion in *Jacobson*, but also at Holmes, for whom the health of the state was sacrosanct.

91. On convergence, see Valverde, supra note 22; Levi & Hagan, supra note 75; Tomlins, supra note 16.

92. 198 U.S. 45, 65, 67, 68 (emphasis added).

93. Ibid., pp. 75, 76.

94. Holmes's opinion in *Buck*, 274 U.S. 200, 208, pointedly recalled *Jacobson*: "We have seen more than once that the public welfare may call upon the best citizens for their lives. It would be strange if it could not call upon those who already sap the strength of the State for these lesser sacrifices, often not felt to be such by those concerned, in order to prevent our being swamped with incompetence. It is better for all the world, if instead of waiting to execute degenerate offspring for crime, or to let them starve for their imbecility, society can prevent those who are manifestly unfit from continuing their kind. The principle that sustains compulsory vaccination is broad enough to cover cutting the Fallopian tubes." Holmes's enthusiasm in *Jacobson* and *Buck* for what, following Foucault, we might term "biopolice" (and on this see also his dissenting opinion in *Adkins v. Children's Hospital* (1923), infra note 99, helps underscore how *Lochner* stands at a moment of mutation in "mandarin" police discourse beyond the sovereign distribution of population of the nineteenth century to the detailed intrusions upon bodies of the twentieth.

95. Dubber, supra note 8, p. 195. See, generally, ibid., pp. 190–202.

96. 208 U.S. 412.

97. 211 U.S. 539. *McLean* upheld an Arkansas statute establishing standards for payment of wages in the state's coal mines. The police power of the state was subject to judicial review, and might not be exercised in an arbitrary or oppressive manner, but no grounds for annulment of a police law existed "unless the act in question is unmistakably and palpably in excess of legislative power." Presuming the law in controversy to have "a reasonable relation to the protection of the public health, safety or welfare it is not to be set aside because the judiciary may be of opinion that the act will fail of its purpose, or because it is thought to be . . . unwise." Hence, "if there existed a condition of affairs concerning which the legislature of the State . . . might pass the law, it must be sustained; if such action was arbitrary interference with the right to contract or carry on business, and having no just relation to the protection of the public within the scope of legislative power, the act must fail." Ibid., pp. 547–48. *McLean*, of course, was light-years from *Lochner*'s "proper, reasonable and fair" standard and begged all the questions it raised. *Lochner* was not mentioned in the judgment, but the majority opinion (written by Justice

Day) embraced the language of Harlan's *Lochner* dissent in adopting "unmistakably and palpably in excess of legislative power" as its standard for review in place of "proper, reasonable and fair," and drove the point home by citing *Jacobson* with approval. Peckham of course dissented. And one commentator concluded that in finding the statute a valid exercise of the police power, the Court "seems to have extended that doctrine to a much greater length than it has in some of its later decisions." Note and Comment (J. F. K.), "The Police Power and Liberty of Contract," *Michigan Law Review* 7 (1909): 507.

98. 208 U.S. 412; 243 U.S. 426. See also *Stettler v. O'Hara* and *Simpson v. O'Hara*, 243 U.S. 269 (1917). Dissenting in *Adkins v. Children's Hospital*, Chief Justice Taft argued that *Bunting* had overruled *Lochner* "sub silentio." 261 U.S. 525, 564 (1923).

99. 261 U.S. 525. The law in question applied to the District of Columbia; the amendment in play was the Fifth; the legislature under examination was Congress; the implications, therefore, were weighty. Said Holmes—recalling *Jacobson*, previewing *Buck*—"the power of Congress seems absolutely free from doubt. The end, to remove conditions leading to ill health, immorality and the deterioration of the race, no one would deny to be within the scope of constitutional legislation. The means are means that have the approval of Congress, of many States, and of those governments from which we have learned our greatest lessons." The only objection offered lurked "within the vague contours of the Fifth Amendment, prohibiting the depriving any person of liberty or property without due process of law," to which Holmes replied, "pretty much all law consists in forbidding men to do some things that they want to do, and contract is no more exempt from law than other acts." Ibid., pp. 567–68.

100. See *Meyer v. Nebraska*, 262 U.S. 390 (1923) and *Bartels v. Iowa*, 262 U.S. 404 (1923), with numerous companion cases from Iowa, Ohio, and Nebraska, reversing criminal convictions obtained under state police laws prohibiting the teaching of school children in languages other than English (Holmes dissenting).

101. Upholding Washington State's minimum wage statute in *West Coast Hotel*, the Supreme Court unleashed all the classic tropes of police: prevention, discretion, and even peace, order, and good government. "The legislature has necessarily a wide field of discretion in order that there may be suitable protection of health and safety, and that peace and good order may be promoted." 300 U.S. 379, 391, 393 (emphasis added).

102. For a comprehensive summary, see Jack M. Balkin, "'Wrong the Day It Was Decided': Lochner and Constitutional Historicism," *Boston University Law Review* 85 (2005): 677–726.

103. Roscoe Pound, "Liberty of Contract," *Yale Law Journal* 18 (1909): 454, 457–58, 464. What this meant in practice is illustrated by the approach Pound advocated in the realm of criminal and municipal justice. Rather than scrutinize state authority to discipline and punish, Pound desired its refinement and extension to "secur[e] social interests regarded directly as such." What were those social interests? "The general security, the security of social institutions, the general morals, the conservation of social resources, the general progress" and, trailing last, "the individual life." Preemptive interventions "to prevent disobedience" would be the new order of things—social control, "preventive justice." Roscoe Pound, "Introduction," to Francis Bowes Sayre, *A Selection of Cases on*

Criminal Law (Rochester, N.Y.: Lawyers Co-operative Publishing, 1927), pp. xxx, xxxii, xxxv, xxxvi. See Michael Willrich, *City of Courts: Socializing Justice in Progressive Era Chicago* (Cambridge and New York: Cambridge Univ. Press, 2003), pp. 98, and generally, xxxi–xxxii, 96–115.

104. To repeat, under certain political circumstances—a state fully under democratic control—police can be precisely the instantiation of the will of popular democracy that one might desire. But the "state sovereignty" discourse summarized here climaxed over precisely the same period (the late nineteenth and early twentieth centuries) that American politics was undergoing its own structural transformation, from participatory to administrative politics, rendering meaningful scrutiny of a Progressive state obsessed with ideologies of expertise embodying the therapeutic manipulation of populations at the same time both vital and unlikely. For the transformation of American politics, see Mark Kornbluh, *Why America Stopped Voting: The Decline of Participatory Democracy and the Emergence of Modern American Politics* (New York: New York Univ. Press, 2000).

105. Kornbluh, supra note 104, pp. 159–60, concludes, "The development of the administrative state substantially insulated government from public involvement. Mass participation in electoral politics fell off precipitously and unevenly, creating an electorate that no longer accurately represented the American public. Not only did Americans stop voting, but also elections lost much of their meaning, for the arena of political decision making had shifted to one in which organized interests and their financial resources counted, rather than ballots. Although the transformation of American politics at the turn of the century created a government capable of responding to the demands of a modern society, the nature of this transformation raised serious questions about the quality of twentieth-century American democracy."

106. Levi & Hagan, supra note 75.

107. Blackstone, supra note 20 (emphasis added).

108. Richard Tuck, *The Rights of War and Peace: Political Thought and the International Order from Grotius to Kant* (Oxford: Oxford Univ. Press, 1999).

109. The Roosevelt Corollary makes that abundantly clear for its moment, just as Michael Ignatieff's Blairite neoliberal, neoimperial theory of internationalized POGG makes it as clear for ours. On this, see Levi & Hagan, supra note 75; Valverde, supra note 22; Tomlins, supra note 16.

CHAPTER THREE

1. For further development of some of these themes, see William J. Novak, "The Legal Origins of the Modern American State," in *Looking Back at Law's Century*, Austin Sarat, Bryant Garth, & Robert A. Kagan, eds. (Ithaca, N.Y.: Cornell Univ. Press, 2002), pp. 249–83; and William J. Novak, "The Legal Transformation of Citizenship in Nineteenth-Century America," in *The Democratic Experiment: New Directions in American Political History*, Meg Jacobs, William J. Novak, & Julian Zelizer, eds. (Princeton, N.J.: Princeton Univ. Press, 2003), pp. 85–119.

2. For the best theoretical discussions of the significance of modern conceptions of police, see *The New Police Science: The Police Power in Domestic and International Governance*, Markus D. Dubber & Mariana Valverde, eds. (Stanford, Calif.: Stanford Univ. Press, 2006); and Markus D. Dubber, *The Police Power: Patriarchy and the Foundations of American Government* (New York: Columbia Univ. Press, 2005). See also Michel Foucault, *Security, Territory, Population: Lectures at the College de France* (New York: Palgrave Macmillan, 2007); Graham Burchell, Colin Gordon, & Peter Miller, eds., *The Foucault Effect: Studies in Governmentality* (Chicago: Univ. of Chicago Press, 1991); David Garland, *The Culture of Control: Crime and Social Order in Contemporary Society* (Chicago: Univ. of Chicago Press, 2001); Nikolas Rose, *Powers of Freedom: Reframing Political Thought* (New York: Cambridge Univ. Press, 1999); and Mitchell M. Dean, *Governmentality: Power and Rule in Modern Society* (London: Sage, 1999).

3. Mariana Valverde, Chapter 1; Michel Foucault, "*Omnes et Singulatim*: Towards a Criticism of Political Reason," in Sterling M. McMurrin, ed. The Tanner Lectures on Human Values, vol. 2 (Salt Lake City: Univ. of Utah Press, 1981), pp. 225–54. Also see Marc Raeff, *The Well-Ordered Police State: Social and Institutional Change through Law in the Germanies and Russia, 1600–1800* (New Haven, Conn.: Yale Univ. Press, 1983).

4. Christopher Tomlins, Chapter 2. Also see W. G. Hastings, "The Development of Law as Illustrated by the Decisions Relating to the Police Power of the State," *Proceedings of the American Philosophical Society* 39 (1900): 359–554; William J. Novak, *The People's Welfare: Law and Regulation in Nineteenth-Century America* (Chapel Hill: Univ. of North Carolina Press, 1986).

5. Markus D. Dubber, Chapter 5; William Packer Prentice, *Police Powers Arising under the Law of Overruling Necessity* (Albany, N.Y.: Banks & Brothers, 1894).

6. Giorgio Agamben, *State of Exception* (Chicago: Chicago Univ. Press, 2005).

7. One of the most effective challenges to this classical liberal legal framework was the work of early American sociological jurisprudence and legal realism. See, for example, Roscoe Pound, "The Scope and Purpose of Sociological Jurisprudence," *Harvard Law Review* 24 (1911): 591–619; 25 (1912): 140–68, 489–516; Morris R. Cohen, "Property and Sovereignty," *Cornell Law Quarterly* 13 (1927): 8–30; and Robert Lee Hale, "Coercion and Distribution in a Supposedly Non-Coercive State," *Political Science Quarterly* 38 (1923): 470–94.

8. William J. Novak, "The American Law of Association: The Legal-Political Construction of Civil Society," *Studies in American Political Development* 15 (2001): 163–88.

9. *Brown v. Maryland*, 12 Wheat. 419 (U.S., 1827); *Commonwealth v. Alger*, 7 Cush. 53 (Mass., 1851); Leonard W. Levy, *The Law of the Commonwealth and Chief Justice Shaw* (Cambridge, Mass.: Harvard Univ. Press, 1957).

10. Ernst Freund, *The Police Power: Public Policy and Constitutional Rights* (Chicago: Univ. of Chicago Press, 1904).

11. Sidney George Fisher, *The Trial of the Constitution* (Philadelphia, Pa.: Lippincott, 1862); John Alexander Jameson, *The Constitutional Convention* (New York: Scribner, 1867); Orestes A. Brownson, *The American Republic: Its Constitution, Tendencies, and Destiny* (New York: P. O'Shae, 1865); John C. Hurd, *The Theory of Our National Existence*,

As Shown by the Action of the Government of the United States Since 1861 (Boston, Mass.: Little, Brown, 1881); Elisha Mulford, *The Nation: The Foundations of Civil Order and Political Life in the United States* (New York: Hurd & Houghton, 1870). Of course, such nationalistic and statist lessons were not solely the product theory. They were also embodied—made manifest—in the unprecedented national state-building practices of the wartime presidency of Abraham Lincoln and the radical reconstruction efforts of the postwar Congress.

12. Fisher, supra note 11, p. 199. Also see Harold M. Hyman, *A More Perfect Union: The Impact of the Civil War and Reconstruction on the Constitution* (New York: Knopf, 1973); Richard Franklin Bensel, *Yankee Leviathan: The Origins of Central State Authority in America, 1859–1877* (New York: Cambridge Univ. Press, 1990); Daniel T. Rodgers, *Contested Truths: Keywords in American Politics since Independence* (New York: Basic Books, 1987), chap. 5.

13. John Austin, *The Province of Jurisprudence Determined* (London: J. Murray, 1832); Johann Kaspar Bluntschli, *The Theory of the State*, D. G. Ritchie, P. E. Matheson, & R. Lodge, trans. (Kitchener: Botoche Books, 2000). For more general discussions of the important international influences on American political and social thought in this period see Daniel T. Rodgers, *Atlantic Crossings: Social Politics in a Progressive Age* (Cambridge, Mass.: Harvard Univ. Press, 1998); and James T. Kloppenberg, *Uncertain Victory: Social Democracy and Progressivism in European and American Thought, 1870–1920* (New York: Oxford Univ. Press, 1986).

14. Vernon Louis Parrington, *Main Currents in American Thought*, vol. 3, *The Beginnings of Critical Realism in America: 1860–1920* (New York: Harcourt, Brace & World, 1930), pp. 117, 125. Unfortunately, this crucial section of Parrington's tract remained unfinished. He only began his discussion of John W. Burgess and sovereignty, and he had planned to add another entire section titled "The New Ally: The Courts; the Police Power and the Fourteenth Amendment; the Injunction."

15. Theodore D. Woolsey, *Political Science; or, The State Theoretically and Practically Considered*, 2 vols. (New York: Scribner, Armstrong, 1878); John W. Burgess, *Political Science and Comparative Constitutional Law*, 2 vols. (Boston, Mass.: Ginn, 1890); Woodrow Wilson, *The State: Elements of Historical and Practical Politics*, rev. ed. (Boston, Mass.: D. C. Heath, 1904 [1890]); Westel Woodbury Willoughby, *An Examination of the Nature of the State: A Study in Political Philosophy* (New York: Macmillan, 1896).

16. G. W. F. Hegel, *Elements of the Philosophy of Right*, Allen W. Wood, ed. (Cambridge: Cambridge Univ. Press, 1991), p. 279; Bluntschli, supra note 13, pp. 7, 69. Twenty-five years later, Willoughby still began his treatise on *Public Law* with the discussion of Bluntschli: "The idea (Idee) of the State presents a picture, in the splendor of imaginary perfection, of the State as not yet realized, but to be striven for." Willoughby, supra note 15, p. 14; Westel Woodbury Willoughby, *The Fundamental Concepts of Public Law* (New York: Macmillan, 1924), p. 17.

17. Willoughby, *Public Law*, supra note 16, pp. 10, 31.

18. Morris Cohen, "Communal Ghosts and Other Perils in Social Philosophy," *Journal of Philosophy* 16 (1919): 673–90. As David Runciman notes concerning the Brit-

ish "personality of the state" debate, "Many of the arguments with which this book has been concerned belong to a past age." *Pluralism and the Personality of the State* (Cambridge: Cambridge Univ. Press, 1997). Ernest Barker reflected some of the exhaustion of the legal personality debate and the transition to more constructive sociological forms of inquiry into the nature of groups (like trade unions) and the state when he argued in 1951: "The real question, in any discussion of the relation of trade unions to the State, is not the question of whether they are persons, of whatever sort or character. . . . The 'being' of the group (person or not-person? and, if a person, which sort of person, the moral or the legal?) is irrelevant to that question: the one thing relevant is what the group does, what its activity is, and whether that activity can, and should, be regulated by law." *Principles of Social and Political Theory* (Oxford: Clarendon, 1951), p. 75.

19. For a sampling of the American reception of legal positivism, see John Chipman Gray, *The Nature and Sources of the Law* (New York: Columbia Univ. Press, 1909); Henry T. Terry, *Some Leading Principles of Anglo-American Law: Expounded with a View to Its Arrangement and Codification* (Philadelphia, Pa.: T. & J. W. Johnson, 1884); and the collection of essays in *The Rational Basis of Legal Institutions*, John H. Wigmore & Albert Kocourek, eds. (New York: Macmillan, 1923).

20. Gray, supra note 19, p. 63.

21. Hurd, supra note 11, p. iii.

22. Burgess, supra note 15, 1:74.

23. Willoughby, supra note 15; Westel Woodbury Willoughby, *The American Constitutional System: An Introduction to the Study of the American State* (New York: Century, 1904); Westel Woodbury Willoughby, *The Constitutional Law of the United States*, 2 vols. (New York: Baker, Voorhis, 1910); Willoughby, *Public Law*, supra note 16. Also see *Essays in Political Science in Honor of Westel Woodbury Willoughby*, John Mabry Mathews & James Hart, eds. (Baltimore, Md.: Johns Hopkins Univ. Press, 1937).

24. Willoughby, supra note 15, p. 180.

25. Willoughby, *The American Constitutional System*, supra note 23, p. 33.

26. Rudolf von Jhering, *Law as a Means to an End*, Isaac Husik, trans. (Boston, Mass.: Boston Book, 1913); Jhering, *The Struggle for Law*, John J. Lalor, trans. (Chicago: Callaghan, 1879).

27. Elihu Root, "Address to the American Law Institute," *American Law Institute Proceedings* 1 (1923): 49.

28. Charles E. Merriam, "Government and Society," in *Recent Social Trends in the United States: Report of the President's Research Committee on Social Trends*, vol. 1, Wesley Clair Mitchell & United States, President's Research Committee on Social Trends, eds., pp. 1489–1541 (New York: McGraw-Hill, 1933), p. 1515; R. F. Fuchs, "Quantity of Regulatory Legislation," *St. Louis Law Review* 16 (1930): 51–55, 52.

29. John Maurice Clark, *Social Control of Business* (Chicago: Univ. of Chicago Press, 1926), p. 4.

30. James W. Garner, *Introduction to Political Science: A Treatise on the Origin, Nature, Functions, and Organization of the State* (New York: American Book Co., 1910), pp. 318–20. Garner contributed the opening biographical assessment to Westel Woodbury

Willoughby's Festschrift. *Essays in Political Science: In Honor of Westel Woodbury Willoughby*, John Mabry Mathews & James Hart, eds. (Baltimore, Md.: Johns Hopkins Univ. Press, 1937).

31. See, generally, William J. Novak, *The People's Welfare: Law and Regulation in Nineteenth-Century America* (Chapel Hill: North Carolina Univ. Press, 1996).

32. Freund, supra note 10; Ernst Freund, *Standards of American Legislation* (Chicago: Univ. of Chicago Press, 1917); Ernst Freund, *Administrative Powers over Persons and Property: A Comparative Survey* (Chicago: Univ. of Chicago Press, 1928); Ernst Freund, *Legislative Regulation: A Study of the Ways and Means of Written Law* (New York: The Commonwealth Fund, 1932). In addition to his legal writings, Freund was active in progressive Illinois and Chicago politics, drafting a charter for the city of Chicago, participating in the National Conference of Commissioners on Uniform State Laws, and working on such reform issues as child welfare and immigration. Jane Addams memorialized Freund as "The Friend and Guide of Social Workers," *University Record* 19 (1933): 43–44. For a serviceable introduction to Freund's career and writing, see Oscar Kraines, *The World and Ideas of Ernst Freund: The Search for General Principles of Legislation and Administrative Law* (Tuscaloosa: Univ. of Alabama Press, 1974). Freund died suddenly in the fall of 1932 only weeks before the election of Franklin Delano Roosevelt—thus failing to witness the final federal institutionalization of many of the legislative, administrative, and regulatory issues he worked toward his whole life.

33. Freund's commitment to the legislature over and against the executive power reflected a faith in American democratic processes that needed to be reformed and modernized but not displaced. Freund, *Legislative Regulation*, supra note 32, pp. 20–21.

34. Francis A. Allen, "Ernst Freund and the New Age of Legislation," in Freund, *Standards of American Legislation*, 1965 ed., pp. vii–xlvi (Chicago: Univ. of Chicago Press, 1965); Ernst Freund, "The Problem of Intelligent Legislation," *Proceedings of the American Political Science Association* 4 (1907): 69–79, 70.

35. Freund, *Legislative Regulation*, supra note 32, p. 12; Ernst Freund, *Jurisprudence and Legislation* (St. Louis, Mo.: Congress of Arts and Science, Universal Exposition, 1904), p. 11.

36. Freund, *Police Power*, supra note 10; Hastings, supra note 4; Alfred Orendorff, "Public Policy and the Police Power of the State," *Chicago Legal News* 14 (1882): 256–57; B. J. Ramage, "Social Progress and the Police Power of a State," *American Law Review* 36 (1902): 681–99; J. M. Blayney Jr., "The Term 'Police Power,'" *Central Law Journal* 59 (1904): 486–92; Walter Wheeler Cook, "What Is the Police Power?" *Columbia Law Review* 7 (1907): 322–36; George Wickersham, "The Police Power, the Product of the Rule of Reason," *Harvard Law Review* 27 (1914): 297–316; Thomas Reed Powell, *The Supreme Court and State Police Power, 1922–1930* (Charlottesville, Va.: Michie, 1932).

37. Freund, *Police Power*, supra note 10, pp. 5–6 (emphasis in original).

38. Ibid., p. iii; Lewis Hockheimer, "Police Power," *Central Law Journal* 44 (1897): 158–62, 158.

39. *Bacon v. Walker*, 204 U.S. 311, 317–18 (1907); *Chicago, Burlington & Quincy Railway Company v. Drainage Commissioners*, 200 U.S. 561 (1906). McKenna noted that in *Chicago,*

Burlington, & Quincy "we rejected the view that the police power cannot be exercised for the general well-being of the community. That power, we said, embraces regulations designed to promote the public convenience or the general prosperity, as well as regulations designed to promote the public health, the public morals or the public safety." For statements to similar effect concerning the police power and general welfare, also see *Barbier v. Connolly*, 113 U.S. 27 (1885); and *Manigault v. Springs*, 199 U.S. 473 (1905). Also see the general discussion in Scott M. Reznick, "Empiricism and the Principle of Conditions in the Evolution of the Police Power: A Model for Definitional Scrutiny," *Washington University Law Quarterly* 1978 (1978): 1–92, 31–32.

40. Harrison H. Brace, "To What Extent May Government in the Exercise of Its Police Power, Take, Destroy or Damage Private Property Without Giving Compensation Therefor?" *Chicago Legal News* 18 (1886): 339–41, 341; B. J. Ramage, supra note 36, p. 698.

41. Samuel P. Hays, "The Social Analysis of American Political History, 1880–1920," *Political Science Quarterly* 80 (1965): 373–94, 391. For a similar interpretation, see Robert Wiebe, *The Search for Order, 1877–1920* (New York: Hill & Wang, 1967).

42. Leonard D. White, "Public Administration" in *Recent Social Trends in the United States*, 1391–1429 (New York: McGraw-Hill, 1933), p. 1394.

43. *United States v. Dewitt*, 76 U.S. 41 (1870). *Dewitt* concerned a federal statute of 1867 regulating the sale of naphtha and other dangerous illuminating oils. Chase cited *The License Cases*, 5 Howard, 504 (U.S., 1847); *The Passenger Cases*, 7 How. 283 (U.S., 1849); and *The License Tax Cases*, 5 Wallace, 470 (U.S., 1866) to establish the "obvious" and "fully explained" antebellum consensus about federal regulations of internal state police. *Barron v. Baltimore*, 32 U.S. 243, 250–51 (1833).

44. Charles Evans Hughes, "New Phases of National Development," *American Bar Association Journal* 4 (1918): 92–110, 93–94.

45. Ernst Freund, "The New German Constitution," *Political Science Quarterly* 35 (1920): 177–203, 181; Walter Thompson, *Federal Centralization: A Study and Criticism of the Expanding Scope of Congressional Legislation* (New York: Harcourt, Brace, 1923), p. 10.

46. Robert Eugene Cushman, *Studies in the Police Power of the National Government* (Minneapolis: Minnesota Law Review, 1919–1920), p. 291; James A. Lyons, "Development of a National Police Power," *Tennessee Law Review* 14 (1935): 11–20.

47. Austin F. MacDonald, *Federal Aid: A Study of the American Subsidy System* (New York: Thomas Y. Crowell, 1928); Harry N. Scheiber, "Federalism and the American Economic Order, 1789–1910," *Law and Society Review* 10 (1975): 57–118.

48. Walter Thompson, supra note 45. For an example of some predictable critiques of this extension of national police power, see H. M. Cox, "Passing of State Autonomy," *Central Law Journal* 67 (1908); William Jennings Bryan, "Is There a Twilight Zone Between the Nation and the State?" *Central Law Journal* 67 (1908); Philander C. Knox, "The Development of the Federal Power to Regulate Commerce," *Yale Law Journal* 17 (1908): 139–150. For an excellent study of the nationalizing force of the spending power, see Michele Landis Dauber, "The Sympathetic State," *Law and History Review* 23 (2005): 387–442.

49. *Final Report of the Attorney General's Committee on Administrative Procedure* (Sen. Doc. No. 8, 77th Cong., 1941), p. 8.

50. Leonard D. White, *The Federalists: A Study in Administrative History* (New York: Macmillan, 1948); White, *The Jeffersonians: A Study in Administrative History, 1801–1829* (New York: Macmillan, 1951); White, *The Jacksonians: A Study in Administrative History, 1829–1861* (New York: Macmillan, 1954). For an overview of White's historical contribution see Richard R. John, "Leonard D. White and the Invention of American Administrative History," *Reviews in American History* 24 (1996): 344–360. For a more detailed investigation of the antebellum administrative powers of the U.S. Postal Service, also see John's excellent monograph, *Spreading the News: The American Postal System from Franklin to Morse* (Cambridge, Mass.: Harvard Univ. Press, 1995). For the best new reinterpretation of the vast powers of early American federal administration, see Jerry Louis Mashaw, "Recovering American Administrative Law: Federalist Foundations, 1787–1801," *Yale Law Journal* 115 (2006): 1256–1344.

51. For an excellent overview see Dwight Waldo, *The Administrative State: A Study of the Political Theory of American Public Administration* (New York: Ronald Press, 1948); and Leonard D. White, *Introduction to the Study of Public Administration* (New York: Macmillan, 1933). The best discussion of the independent regulatory commissions was produced by one of the great commentators on national police power Robert E. Cushman, *The Independent Regulatory Commissions* (New York: Oxford Univ. Press, 1941).

52. Max Weber, *Economy and Society: An Outline of Interpretive Sociology*, Guenther Roth & Claus Wittich, eds., 2 vols. (Berkeley: Univ. of California Press, 1978), 1:217–20. See also Max Weber, *The Theory of Social and Economic Organization* (New York: Oxford Univ. Press, 1947), pp. 154–56. For an excellent presentation see Reinhard Bendix's discussion of Weber's view of "The Modern State and Its Legitimacy," in *Max Weber: An Intellectual Portrait* (Garden City, N.Y.: Anchor Books, 1962), pp. 417–23.

53. Theodore J. Lowi, *The End of Liberalism: The Second Republic of the United States*, 2d ed. (New York: Norton, 1979), p. 21.

54. Woodrow Wilson, "The Study of Administration," *Political Science Quarterly* 2 (1887): 197–222, 209, 212; Woodrow Wilson, "The New Meaning of Government," *Woman's Home Companion* 39 (1912), reprinted in *Public Administration Review* 44 (1984): 193–95.

55. White, *Study of Public Administration*, supra note 51, p. 2.

56. Wilson, "New Meaning of Government," supra note 54, p. 194.

57. See, for example, Stephen Skowronek, *Building a New American State: The Expansion of National Administrative Capacities, 1877–1920* (New York: Cambridge Univ. Press, 1982); Daniel P. Carpenter, *The Forging of Bureaucratic Autonomy: Reputations, Networks, and Policy Innovation in Executive Agencies, 1862–1928* (Princeton, N.J.: Princeton Univ. Press, 2001); Scott C. James, *Presidents, Parties, and the State: A Party System Perspective on Democratic Regulatory Choice, 1884–1936* (New York: Cambridge Univ. Press, 2000); John A. Rohr, *To Run a Constitution: The Legitimacy of the Administrative State* (Lawrence: Univ. Press of Kansas, 1986); Brian J. Cook, *Bureaucracy and Self-Government: Reconsidering the Role of Public Administration in American Politics* (Baltimore, Md.: Johns Hopkins Univ.

Press, 1996); Richard J. Stillman II, *Creating the American State: The Moral Reformers and the Modern Administrative World They Made* (Tuscaloosa: Univ. of Alabama Press, 1998).

58. The recent work of Karen Orren has been particularly important in understanding the importance of this transformation in conceptions of *office*. See Karen Orren, "The Work of Government: Recovering the Discourse of Office in *Marbury v. Madison*," unpublished MS; and Karen Orren, "Officers' Rights: Toward a Unified Field Theory of American Constitutional Development," unpublished MS.

59. Indeed, a host of nineteenth-century international legal and political commentators located in the common law and particularly the justices of the peace present a compelling self-government alternative to Napoleonic state centralization. See, for example, the discussion of the jurisprudence of Rudolf von Gneist among others in Munroe Smith, *A General View of European Legal History and Other Papers* (New York: Columbia Univ. Press, 1927), p. 216ff.

60. For the classic statement of the same theme with respect to the administration of the private business corporation, see Adolf A. Berle & Gardiner C. Means, *The Modern Corporation and Private Property* (New York: Macmillan, 1932).

61. Woodrow Wilson, "The Study of Administration," *Political Science Quarterly* 2 (1887): 197–222, 213; Woodrow Wilson, *Constitutional Government in the United States* (New York: Columbia Univ. Press, 1908), p. 197. Also see the insightful study of administrative law by Waldo, supra note 51, pp. 104–55.

62. Weber, *Economy and Society*, supra note 52, 2:959, 973 (emphasis in original).

63. Frank J. Goodnow, *Selected Cases on American Administrative Law with Particular Reference to the Law of Officers* (Chicago: Callaghan, 1906); *Selected Cases on Government and Administration* (Chicago: Callaghan, 1906); *Comparative Administrative Law* (New York: Putnam, 1893); *Principles of the Administrative Law of the United States* (New York: Putnam, 1905); *Politics and Administration* (New York: Macmillan, 1900); *Social Reform and the Constitution* (New York: Macmillan, 1911); *Principles of Constitutional Government* (New York: Harper, 1916); *Municipal Home Rule: A Study in Administration* (New York: Macmillan, 1985); *City Government in the United States* (New York: Century, 1906); *Municipal Government* (New York: Century, 1919). See also *Essays on the Law and Practice of Governmental Administration: A Volume in Honor of Frank Johnson Goodnow*, Charles G. Haines & Marshall E. Dimock, eds. (Baltimore, Md.: Johns Hopkins Univ. Press, 1935), p. v.

64. Goodnow, *Social Reform*, supra note 63, pp. 1, 308.

65. Theodore Roosevelt, "The Right of the People to Rule," March 20, 1912, Carnegie Hall, New York; Goodnow, *Principles of Constitutional Government*, supra note 63, p. 11.

66. Goodnow, *Social Reform*, supra note 63, pp. 11, 221.

67. Wilson, "Study of Administration," supra note 54, p. 213.

68. Goodnow, *Politics and Administration*, supra note 63, pp. 22, 85–86. Only with regard to the executive function did Goodnow concede a great role for the function of politics.

69. Goodnow, *Social Reform*, supra note 63, pp. 18–32, 32.

70. Felix Frankfurter, "Foreword: Courts and Administrative Law," *Harvard Law Review* 49 (1936): 426–28, 427; Felix Frankfurter, *The Public and Its Government* (New Haven, Conn.: Yale Univ. Press, 1930).

71. James M. Landis, *The Administrative Process* (New Haven, Conn.: Yale Univ. Press, 1938), p. 5.

72. Charles A. Beard & William Beard, *The American Leviathan: The Republic in the Machine Age* (New York: Macmillan, 1930).

73. Ibid., p. vii.

CHAPTER FOUR

1. Markus D. Dubber, "'An Extraordinarily Beautiful Document': Jefferson's *Bill for Proportioning Crimes and Punishments* and the Challenge of Republican Punishment," in *Modern Histories of Crime and Punishment*, Markus D. Dubber & Lindsay Farmer, eds. (Stanford, Calif.: Stanford Univ. Press, 2007), pp. 115, 117.

2. Markus D. Dubber, *The Police Power: Patriarchy and the Foundations of American Government* (New York: Columbia Univ. Press, 2005), p. 83.

3. For recent versions of the necessity argument, see Jane Mansbridge, "Using Power/Fighting Power: The Polity," in *Democracy and Difference: Contesting the Boundaries of the Political*, Seyla Benhabib, ed. (Princeton, N.J.: Princeton Univ. Press, 1996), pp. 46, 59–60; Cass R. Sunstein & Richard H. Thaler, "Libertarian Paternalism Is Not an Oxymoron," *University of Chicago Law Review* 70 (2003): 1, 4–5, 16–20, 26; John Rawls, *Political Liberalism*, expanded ed. (New York: Columbia Univ. Press, 2005), pp. 139–40; Amy Gutmann & Dennis Thompson, *Why Deliberative Democracy?* (Princeton, N.J.: Princeton Univ. Press, 2004), p. 45; Emily Hauptmann, "Deliberation = Legitimacy = Democracy," *Political Theory* 27 (1999): 866.

4. Dubber, *Police Power*, p. 58.

5. Ibid., pp. 96, 115. Note that Christopher Tomlins in Chapter 2 suggests that the idea of state sovereignty implies the power to police.

6. See Mark E. Kann, *Punishment, Prisons, and Patriarchy: Liberty and Power in the Early American Republic* (New York: New York Univ. Press, 2005), part 2.

7. Benjamin Rush, "An Enquiry into the Effects of Public Punishments upon Criminals, Read in the Society for Promoting Political Enquiries, Convened at the House of Benjamin Franklin, Esq. in Philadelphia, March 9th, 1787," in Benjamin Rush, *Essays, Literary, Moral and Philosophical* (Schenectady, N.Y.: Union College Press, 1988), p. 87 (originally published in 1798); Edward Livingston, *A System of Penal Law for the State of Louisiana* (Union, N.J.: Lawbook Exchange, 1999), p. 145 (originally published in 1833); Patrick Colquhoun to Thomas Eddy, February 16, 1803, Samuel L. Knapp, *The Life of Thomas Eddy* (New York: Arno Press, 1976), p. 194 (originally published in 1834).

8. Jacques Pierre Brissot De Warville, *On America: New Travels in the United States of America Performed in 1788*, 2 vols. (New York: Augustus M. Kelley, 1970), 1:371–73 (originally published in 1792).

9. William Stuart, *Sketches of the Life of William Stuart: The First and Most Celebrated Counterfeiter of Connecticut* (Bridgeport, Conn.: W. Stuart, 1854), pp. 221–22.

10. Stephen Burroughs, *Memoirs of the Notorious Stephen Burroughs* (New York: Cornish Lamport, 1852), p. 99.

11. Ibid., p. 108.

12. John Reynolds, *Recollections of Windsor Prison; Containing Sketches of Its History and Discipline* (Boston, Mass.: A. Wright, 1834), p. 207.

13. W. A. Coffey, *Inside Out; or, An Interior View of the New-York State Prison* (New York: J. Costigan, 1823), p. 98.

14. Louis Reneau quoted in Edward L. Ayers, *Vengeance and Justice: Crime and Punishment in the 19th-Century American South* (New York: Oxford Univ. Press, 1984), pp. 46–47; Reynolds, *Recollections of Windsor Prison*, p. 136.

15. Thomas Eddy to George Tibbits, Stephen Allen, and Samuel M. Hopkins, Esquires, Commissioners appointed by the Legislature to examine and report on certain questions relating to the State Prisons, January 7, 1825; Knapp, *The Life of Thomas Eddy*, pp. 84–85; John H. Griscom, ed., *Memoir of John Griscom, LL.D.* (New York: Robert Carter, 1859), pp. 164–65; Hugh Maxwell quoted in ibid., p. 181; John R. Sutton, *Stubborn Children: Controlling Delinquency in the United States, 1640–1981* (Berkeley: Univ. of California Press, 1988), p. 76.

16. "An Act to Incorporate the Society for the Reformation of Juvenile Delinquents in the City of New-York. Passed March 29, 1824," Society for the Reformation of Juvenile Delinquents in the City of New York, *Documents Relative to the House of Refuge, Instituted by the Society for the Reformation of Juvenile Delinquents in the City of New-York, in 1824* (New York: Mahlon Day, 1832), p. 304; Society for the Prevention of Pauperism, *Report of a Committee Appointed by the Society for the Prevention of Pauperism in the City of New York on the Expediency of Erecting an Institution for the Reformation of Juvenile Delinquents* (New York: Mahlon Day, 1823), pp. 24–27; see also Griscom, *Memoir*, p. 183.

17. Society for the Reformation of Juvenile Delinquents in the City of New York, "First Annual Report, &c.," *Documents Relative to the House of Refuge*, pp. 17, 57; "Second Annual Report, &c.," Ibid., pp. 89, 93–95; "Fourth Annual Report, &c.," Ibid., p. 175; "Fifth Annual Report, &c.," Ibid., p. 187; "Sixth Annual Report, &c.," Ibid., p. 240; *Reports of the Prison Discipline Society of Boston*, 6 vols. (Montclair, N.J.: Patterson Smith, 1972), 1:245 (originally published in 1855).

18. Markus D. Dubber, "The New Police Science and the Police Power Model of the Criminal Process," in *The New Police Science: The Police Power in Domestic and International Governance*, Markus D. Dubber & Mariana Valverde, eds. (Stanford: Stanford Univ. Press, 2006), p. 107; Dubber, *Police Power*, pp. 73, 101, 143.

19. Thomas Eddy, *An Account of the State Prison or Penitentiary House in the City of New York* (New York: Isaac Collins & Son, 1801), pp. 62–63.

20. *Reports of the Prison Discipline Society of Boston*, 1:228, 257, 261, 339.

21. Benjamin Rush, *Medical Inquiries and Observations upon the Diseases of the Mind* (New York: Hafner, 1962), pp. 267–68 (originally published in 1812).

22. Livingston, *A System of Penal Law*, pp. 318–20, 559.

23. Ibid., p. 322.

24. Franklin Bache quoted in William Crawford, *Report on the Penitentiaries of the United States* (Montclair, N.J.: Patterson Smith, 1969), appendix, p. 3 (originally published in 1835); James Mease, *Observations on the Penitentiary System and Penal Code of Pennsylvania with Suggestions for Their Improvement* (Philadelphia, Pa.: Clark & Raser, 1828), p. 18; Charles Bulfinch, *Bulfinch on Penitentiaries: Report of Charles Bulfinch on the Subject of Penitentiaries* (Washington: Gales & Seaton, 1827), p. 8.

25. William Bradford, *An Enquiry How Far the Punishment of Death Is Necessary in Pennsylvania*, *Reform of Criminal Law in Pennsylvania: Selected Inquiries, 1787–1819* (New York: Arno Press, 1972), p. 20 (originally published in 1793); Eddy, *An Account*, p. 9.

26. Stephen Allen, *Observations on Penitentiary Discipline addressed to William Roscoe, Esq.* (New York: Totten, 1827), pp. 6–7; Gershom Powers, *A Brief Account of the Construction, Management, and Discipline &c. &c. of the New York State Prison at Auburn* (Auburn, N.Y.: U. F. Doubleday, 1826), p. 54.

27. Moses C. Welch, *The Gospel to Be Preached to All Men* [1805], in Daniel A. Cohen, *Pillars of Salt, Monuments of Grace: New England Crime Literature and the Origins of American Popular Culture, 1674–1860* (New York: Oxford Univ. Press, 1993), pp. 111–12.

28. Reynolds, *Recollections*, pp. 41–42.

29. Sean McConville, "Local Justice: The Jail," in *The Oxford History of the Prison: The Practice of Punishment in Western Society*, Norval Morris & David J. Rothman, eds. (New York: Oxford Univ. Press, 1998), p. 276.

30. "Mr. Dickens' Report of His Visit to the Eastern Penitentiary [1842]," in Negley K. Teeters, *They Were in Prison: A History of the Pennsylvania Prison Society (Formerly The Philadelphia Society for Alleviating the Miseries of Public Prisons), 1787–1937* (Chicago: Winston, 1937), pp. 219–21, 227–29; Eddy to Tibbits, Allen, and Hopkins, January 7, 1825, in Knapp, *The Life of Thomas Eddy*, p. 89.

31. Elam Lynds quoted in Gustave de Beaumont & Alexis de Tocqueville, *On the Penitentiary System in the United States and Its Application in France*, Francis Lieber, trans. (Carbondale: Southern Illinois Univ. Press, 1964), p. 163 (originally published in 1833); Levi Burr quoted in Scott Christianson, *With Liberty for Some: 500 Years of Imprisonment in America* (Boston, Mass.: Northeastern Univ. Press, 1998), p. 125; Crawford, *Report on the Penitentiaries*, pp. 19, 22.

32. Caleb Lownes, *An Account of the Alteration and Present State of the Penal Laws of Pennsylvania* [1793], in Bradford, *An Enquiry How Far the Punishment of Death Is Necessary in Pennsylvania*, pp. 83–86; William Roscoe, *Observations on Penal Jurisprudence and the Reformation of Criminals* [1819], in *Reform of Criminal Law in Pennsylvania*, p. 108.

33. Crawford, *Report on the Penitentiaries*, appendix, pp. 68, 96, 133; Stuart, *Sketches*, pp. 203–4.

34. Mease, *Observations*, pp. 56–57; Francis Lieber, "Translator's Preface," in Beaumont & Tocqueville, *On the Penitentiary System*, p. 16.

35. Eddy, *An Account*, pp. 35–36.

36. Livingston, *A System of Penal Law*, pp. 44, 340, 709, 727.

37. *Reports of the Prison Discipline Society of Boston*, 1:289–90, 295–97.

38. The relative palatability of police power in the early American republic (and elsewhere) invites one to question whether this virtually unlimited, undefinable power was inherently "illiberal" or, to the contrary, a necessary and essential element in any modern liberal state (as one might infer from William Novak's Chapter 3 in this volume).

39. Reynolds, *Recollections*, pp. 6, 8, 14, 22–23, 25.

40. Stuart, *Sketches*, pp. 197, 218; Ann Carson, *The Memoirs of the Celebrated and Beautiful Mrs. Ann Carson*, Two Volumes in One (New York: Arno Press, 1980), 2:69, 71 (originally published in 1838).

41. Coffey, *Inside Out*, pp. 22, 44–46, 56, 78–79.

42. Paul W. Keve, *The History of Corrections in Virginia* (Charlottesville: Univ. Press of Virginia, 1986), p. 34.

43. Samuel M. Hopkins quoted in Orlando F. Lewis, *The Development of American Prisons and Prison Customs, 1776–1845* (Montclair, N.J.: Patterson Smith, 1967), pp. 114–15 (originally published in 1922).

44. Markus D. Dubber, "'An Extraordinarily Beautiful Document': Jefferson's *Bill for Proportioning Crimes and Punishments* and the Challenge of Republican Punishment" (http://papers.ssrn.com/sol3/cf_dev/AbsByAuth.cfm?per_id=75272, accessed January 6, 2006), p. 11.

45. Dubber, "The New Police Science," p. 6.

46. *Reports of the Prison Discipline Society of Boston*, 1:20.

47. Beaumont & Tocqueville, *On the Penitentiary System*, pp. 77, 79.

48. Robert J. Turnbull of South Carolina, *A Visit to the Philadelphia Prison* (Philadelphia, Pa.: James Phillips & Son, 1797), pp. 25, 32, 46.

49. Powers, *A Brief Account*, p. 61; "The Life and Dying Confession of Richard Barrick, High-Way Robber," in Daniel E. Williams, *Pillars of Salt: An Anthology of Early American Criminal Narratives* (Madison, Wisc.: Madison House, 1993), p. 246; Reynolds, *Recollections*, p. 25.

50. Reynolds, *Recollections*, p. 55; Mease, *Observations*, p. 12; Livingston, *A System of Penal Law*, p. 691; "A View of the New-York State Prison. By a Member of the Institution [1817]," in Roscoe, *Observations*, appendix, p. 35; Roscoe, *Observations*, p. 12.

51. Gershom Powers, *Letter of Gershom Powers, Esq. in Answer to a Letter of the Hon. Edward Livingston in Relation to the Auburn State Prison* (Albany: Croswell & Van Benthuysen, 1829), p. 22.

52. Society for the Reformation of Juvenile Delinquents in the City of New York, "Third Annual Report, &c.," in *Documents Relative to the House of Refuge*, pp. 126, 138, 141; Livingston, *A System of Penal Law*, p. 344; Griscom, *Memoir*, pp. 173, 180, 191.

53. Sutton, *Stubborn Children*, pp. 11, 45, 75–76, 78, 240; Steven Schlossman, "Delinquent Children: The Juvenile Reform School," in *The Oxford History of the Prison: The Practice of Punishment in Western Society*, Norval Morris & David J. Rothman, eds. (New York: Oxford Univ. Press, 1997), p. 328.

54. Rush, "An Enquiry into the Effects of Public Punishments upon Criminals," pp. 88–89; Benjamin Rush, *The Autobiography of Benjamin Rush*, ed. George W. Corner (Princeton, N.J.: Princeton Univ. Press, 1948), pp. 354–55.

55. Burroughs, *Memoirs*, pp. 130–31.

56. Although this argument anticipates Peter Ramsay's analysis of the Anti-Social Behavior Order (Chapter 8 in this volume), it differs in two ways. First, this argument augments the patriarchal justification of police power rather than serves as an alternative to it. Second, it suggests that police power can be used to enhance the autonomy and liberty not only of the law-abiding citizenry but also of the convicts themselves.

57. Thomas Jefferson, "Answers and Observations for Démeunier's Article on the United States in the *Encyclopédie Methodique*, 1786," in Thomas Jefferson, *Writings*, ed. Merrill D. Peterson (New York: Library of America, 1984), pp. 579–80.

58. Rush, *Medical Inquiries*, pp. 32–33, 174, 183, 191, 238–39, 335, 347, 350–55; Rush, "Of the Mode of Education Proper in a Republic," in *Essays, Literary, Moral and Philosophical*, p. 9; Rush, "An Enquiry into the Influence of Physical Causes upon the Moral Faculty," in Benjamin Rush, *Two Essays on the Mind* (New York: Brunner/Mazel, 1972), pp. 18, 24; Rush to Thomas Jefferson, June 28, 1811, in Benjamin Rush, *Letters of Benjamin Rush*, ed. L. H. Butterfield, 2 vols. (Princeton, N.J.: Princeton Univ. Press, 1951), 2:1087–88; Rush to Jeremy Belknap, May 6, 1788, in ibid., 1:460; Rush, *The Autobiography*, p. 185.

59. Michael Ignatieff, *A Just Measure of Pain: The Penitentiary in the Industrial Revolution, 1750–1850* (London: Penguin, 1978), p. 167.

60. Bradford, *An Enquiry How Far the Punishment of Death Is Necessary in Pennsylvania*, p. 86.

CHAPTER FIVE

1. See Markus D. Dubber, *The Police Power: Patriarchy and the Foundations of American Government* (New York: Columbia Univ. Press, 2005).

2. See Markus D. Dubber, "The Criminal Trial and the Legitimation of Punishment," in *The Trial on Trial*, R. A. Duff et al., eds. (Oxford: Hart, 2004), p. 85; Markus D. Dubber, "Toward a Constitutional Law of Crime and Punishment," *Hastings Law Journal* 55 (2004): 509.

3. See, e.g., John Rawls, *A Theory of Justice* (Cambridge, Mass.: Belknap Press of Harvard Univ. Press, 1971) (ideal political theory of well-ordered society); Jürgen Habermas, *Between Facts and Norms: Contributions to a Discourse Theory of Law and Democracy*, William Rehg trans. (Cambridge, Mass.: MIT Press, 1996), p. xxxix (criminal law not covered). But see Sharon Dolovich, "Legitimate Punishment in Liberal Democracy," *Buffalo Criminal Law Review* 7 (2004): 307.

4. See Markus D. Dubber, "Penal Panopticon: The Idea of a Modern Model Penal Code," *Buffalo Criminal Law Review* 4 (2000): 53, 55; see also Claire Finkelstein, "Positivism and the Notion of an Offense," *California Law Review* 88 (2000): 335, pt. 3.

5. See N.Y. Penal Law §120.15 (menacing: "intentionally plac[ing] or attempt[ing] to place another person in fear of death, imminent serious physical injury or physical injury").

6. See ibid. §250.05 (eavesdropping: "wiretapping, mechanical overhearing of a conversation, or intercepting or accessing of an electronic communication").

7. See ibid. arts. 100, 105.

8. See ibid. §140.05 (trespass: "knowingly enter[ing] or remain[ing] unlawfully in or upon premises").

9. See ibid. art. 120.

10. See ibid. arts. 220–21 (drugs), 265 (weapons).

11. See N.H. Crim. Code §644:11 (defamation: "purposely communicat[ing] to any person, orally or in writing, any information which he knows to be false and knows will tend to expose any other living person to public hatred, contempt or ridicule").

12. See ibid. §633:3 (false imprisonment: "knowingly confin[ing] another unlawfully . . . so as to interfere substantially with his physical movement").

13. See N.Y. Penal Law §125.25 (murder in the second degree: "with intent to cause the death of another person, . . . causing the death of such person").

14. Karl Marx, "German Ideology," in *Marx's Concept of Man*, Erich Fromm ed., (New York: Frederick Ungar, 1966), pp. 197, 206.

15. Markus D. Dubber, *The Sense of Justice: Empathy in Law and Punishment* (New York: New York Univ. Press, 2006).

16. Namely, the bundle of capacities that constitute personhood. See ibid.

17. See, generally, Markus D. Dubber, "'An Extraordinarily Beautiful Document': Jefferson's *Bill for Proportioning Crimes and Punishments* and the Challenge of Republican Punishment," in *Modern Histories of Crime and Punishment*, Markus D. Dubber & Lindsay Farmer, eds. (Stanford: Stanford Univ. Press, 2007), p. 115.

18. Æthelstan was king of England from 924 to 939, Canute from 1016 to 1035. The full text of the provision reads, in a more modern translation: "Of moneyers. 15. Thirdly: that there be one money over all the king's dominion, and that no man mint except within port. And if the moneyer be guilty, let the hand be struck off that wrought the offense, and, be set up on the money-smithy but if it be an accusation, and he is willing to clear himself; then let him go to the hot-iron, and clear the hand therewith with which he is charged that fraud to have wrought. And if at the ordeal he should be guilty, let the like be done as here before ordained."

19. Thomas Jefferson, *A Bill for Proportioning Crimes and Punishments* §1 (1778).

20. No. 39.

21. On the continent, political thinkers as diverse as Beccaria and Hegel recognized the general need to derive the legitimacy of punishment from the consent of the punished. See, e.g., G. W. F. Hegel, *Grundlinien der Philosophie des Rechts* Z 100 (1821) (discussing Beccaria). Beccaria's work on punishment exerted considerable influence on Americans at the time, including Jefferson. See, e.g., Thomas Jefferson, *A Bill for Proportioning Crimes and Punishments* §§iv, xii, xiii, xiv (1778); Thomas Jefferson, *Autobiography* (1821); James Wilson, "Executive Department, Lectures on Law," in 2 *The Works of James Wilson*, Robert Green McCloskey, ed. (Cambridge, Mass.: Belknap Press of Harvard Univ. Press, 1967 [1791]), pp. 442–44; Benjamin Rush, *An Enquiry into the Effects of Public Punishments Upon Criminals and Upon Society* (Philadelphia, Pa.: Joseph James, 1787); see, generally, Bernard Baylin, *The Ideological Origins of the American Revolution: Enlarged Edition* (Cambridge, Mass.: Belknap Press of Harvard Univ. Press, 1992 [1967]),

p. 27; see also William Blackstone, *Commentaries on the Laws of England* (Chicago: Univ. of Chicago Press, 1769), 4:3.

22. See, e.g., Richard A. Posner & Tomas J. Philipson, "The Economic Epidemiology of Crime," *Journal of Law and Economics* 39 (1996): 405. That's not to say that crime can't be studied profitably as a matter of public health, just that treating it as such doesn't help us legitimate punishment, the state's response to crime through criminal law. In terms of the distinction between police and law, discussed below, economic analysis in particular can help us understand the reality of American punishment as a—badly run—police system, rather than as a system of law, or a "criminal justice system."

23. No. 17 (Hamilton).

24. No. 45 (Madison).

25. No. 21 (Hamilton).

26. Ibid.

27. No. 16 (Hamilton).

28. No. 28 (Hamilton).

29. Ibid.

30. Aristotle, *Politics*, Ernest Barker, trans. (rev. ed.) (Oxford: Oxford Univ. Press, 1988), bk. 1; David Herlihy, *Medieval Households* (Cambridge, Mass.: Harvard Univ. Press, 1985), pp. 2–3; Jean Jacques Rousseau, *A Discourse on Political Economy*, Roger D. Masters, ed., Judith R. Masters, trans. (New York: St. Martin's, 1978 [1755]).

31. Aristotle, *Politics*, bk. 1.

32. Adam Smith differentiated between *justice* and *police*, the two fundamental aspects of *jurisprudence*—or "juris prudence," according to the student notes of his Edinburgh lectures on this subject. Adam Smith, "Juris Prudence or Notes from the Lectures on Justice, Police, Revenue, and Arms" delivered in the University of Glasgow by Adam Smith Professor of Moral Philosophy, in *Lectures on Jurisprudence* 396, 398, R. L. Meed, D. D. Raphael, & P. G. Stein, eds. (Oxford: Oxford Univ. Press, 1978). The most significant—to his mind—component of police was "the opulence of a state," i.e., the wealth of a nation.

33. Blackstone, *Commentaries*, 4:176.

34. Ibid., p. 127.

35. Ibid., p. 162.

36. *Pennsylvania Coal Co. v. Mahon*, 260 U.S. 393 (1922).

37. Robert C. Post, "Between Governance and Management: The History and Theory of the Public Forum," *UCLA Law Review* 34 (1987): 1713.

38. Lon L. Fuller, *The Morality of Law* (rev. ed.) (New Haven, Conn.: Yale Univ. Press, 1969), pp. 207–17.

39. Friedrich Hayek, *The Constitution of Liberty* (Chicago: Univ. of Chicago Press, 1960).

40. Herbert L. Packer, *The Limits of the Criminal Sanction* (Stanford: Stanford Univ. Press, 1968).

41. See, e.g., Thomas M. Cooley, *A Treatise on the Constitutional Limitations Which Rest Upon the Legislative Power of the States of the American Union* (6th ed.) (Boston, Mass.: Little, Brown, 1890); Christopher G. Tiedeman, *A Treatise on the Limitations of Police Power in the United States Considered From Both a Civil and Criminal Standpoint* (St. Louis, Mo.: F. H. Thomas Law Book, 1886).

42. Thomas Jefferson, *Notes on the State of Virginia*, query xv (1781); Thomas Jefferson, *The Autobiography of Thomas Jefferson*; Thomas Jefferson, *A Bill for Amending the Constitution of the College of William and Mary, and Substituting More Certain Revenues for Its Support* (1779); see also Christopher L. Tomlins, *Law, Labor, and Ideology in the Early American Republic* (Cambridge: Cambridge Univ. Press, 1993), p. 36.

43. Thomas Jefferson, *A Bill for Proportioning Crimes and Punishments* §1 (1778).

44. See *Ruffin v. Commonwealth*, 62 Va. 790, 796 (1871) (felons as slaves of the state).

45. Note that the view of imprisonment as enslavement was neither unconsidered nor limited to the United States. See Cesare Beccaria, *Of Crimes and Punishments* §16 (imprisonment as enslavement), §30 (enslavement as punishment for theft); Immanuel Kant, *Rechtslehre* A199/B229 (same), A193–194/B222–224 (punishment as enslavement), B163 (same).

46. See Bruno Bettelheim, *The Informed Heart: Autonomy in a Mass Age* (New York: Free Press of Glencoe, 1960), p. 67.

47. Markus D. Dubber, "American Plea Bargains, German Lay Judges, and the Crisis of Criminal Procedure," *Stanford Law Review* 49 (1997): 547, 592.

48. Michael Köhler, *Strafrecht: Allgemeiner Teil* (Berlin: Springer, 1997); David A. J. Richards, "Human Rights and the Moral Foundations of the Substantive Criminal Law," *Georgia Law Review* 13 (1979): 1395; Gerald Dworkin, "Devlin Was Right: Law and the Enforcement of Morality," *William & Mary Law Review* 40 (1999): 927; R. A. Duff, *Trials and Punishments* (Cambridge: Cambridge Univ. Press, 1986); Paul Roberts, "The Philosophical Foundations of Consent in the Criminal Law," *Oxford Journal of Legal Studies* 17 (1997): 389, 405; *Personal Autonomy, the Private Sphere and the Criminal Law: A Comparative Study*, Peter Alldridge & Chrisje Brants, eds. (Oxford: Hart, 2001).

49. Cf. Herbert L. Packer, *The Limits of the Criminal Sanction* (Stanford, Calif.: Stanford Univ. Press, 1968), pp. 76–77. An omission may constitute such a manifestation as well, through the person's restraining herself from acting. What matters is the exercise of autonomy, not what form it takes. In the law of complicity—the imputation of one person's act to another—one might likewise distinguish between principal and accomplice by differentiating between the person whose autonomy was directly manifested in the criminal act (the principal) and the person whose autonomy is manifested indirectly, or constructively, through the principal's act (the accomplice). See, e.g., Claus Roxin, *Täterschaft und Tatherrschaft* 649, 7th ed. (Munich: C. H. Beck, 2000) (concept of *Tatherrschaft*, or "act dominion"); Wilfried Küper, "'Autonomie,' Irrtum und Zwang bei mittelbarer Täterschaft und Einwilligung," 1986 *Juristenzeitung* 219.

50. Punishment thus can be seen as the state's assertion that the offender's attempt to reduce her victim to an object of power, rather than a subject of rights, has failed. Cf.

G. W. F. Hegel, *Elements of the Philosophy of Right*, Allen W. Wood, ed., H. B. Nisbet, trans. (Cambridge: Cambridge Univ. Press, 1991), §99. In this sense, and only in this sense, attempt is the paradigmatic crime. In contemporary American doctrine, attempt is not a crime but the manifestation of dangerousness that calls for penal, and specifically, incapacitative treatment. See *Model Penal Code and Commentaries* (Official Draft and Revised Comments) §§3.01–5.07, at 323, 325 (1985); *People v. Dlugash*, 41 N.Y.2d 725 (1977); *Commonwealth v. Henley*, 504 Pa. 408 (1984).

51. See Jan Phillip Reemtsma, *Das Recht des Opfers auf die Bestrafung des Täters—als Problem* (Munich: C. H. Beck, 1999). This, I think, is the legitimate core of the idea of victims' rights. See Markus D. Dubber, *Victims in the War on Crime: The Use and Abuse of Victims' Rights* (New York: New York Univ. Press, 2002).

52. Uniform Victims of Crime Act (National Conference of Commissioners on Uniform State Laws) 4 (1992) (Prefatory Note); see Markus D. Dubber, "The Right to Be Punished: Autonomy and Its Demise in Modern Penal Thought," *Law & History Review* 16 (1998): 113; Herbert Morris, "Persons and Punishment," *The Monist* 53, no. 4 (1968): 475.

53. Joel Feinberg, *The Moral Limits of the Criminal Law*, vol. 3, *Harm to Self* (New York: Oxford Univ. Press, 1986), p. 34.

54. Similarly it has been argued that only voluntary acts may constitute intervening causes in the law of causation, though here the distinction between voluntary and intentional acts isn't always clear. See Glanville Williams, "Finis for Novus Actus?" *Cambridge Law Journal* 48 (1989): 391, 392 (discussing the doctrine of novus actus interveniens as a corollary of the "autonomy doctrine").

55. The Model Penal Code, for example, recognizes three negligence offenses: negligent homicide (§210.4), a type of assault (§211.1[1][b]; causing bodily injury with a deadly weapon), and a variety of criminal mischief (§220.3[1][b]; damaging property with "fire, explosives, or other dangerous means").

56. This consideration also applies to so-called strict liability crimes.

57. Paul G. Cassell, "Balancing the Scales of Justice: The Case for and the Effects of Utah's Victims' Rights Amendment," *Utah Law Review* 1373 (1994): 1416–17 (quoting Black's Law Dictionary, 1567 [6th ed., 1990]; emphasis added).

58. The autonomy of the "victim" of justified acts—say, the owner of the house set aflame to contain the oncoming fire storm—too finds recognition, in the provision that her rights not be violated except in circumstances where her harm is clearly less considerable than the harm avoided (passive autonomy), see, e.g., Claus Roxin, *Strafrecht: Allgemeiner Teil (Band I: Grundlagen—Der Aufbau der Verbrechenslehre)* §14 nos. 41 & 48, §16 no. 41 (Munich: C. H. Beck, 3d ed., 1997) ("principle of autonomy" in necessity), and in cases highlighting defendant's failure to obtain the victim's consent in some way (e.g., notice, consultation, voting, or the drawing of lots), see, e.g., *United States v. Holmes*, 26 F. Cas. 360 (E.D. Pa. 1842) (lifeboat); *The Queen v. Dudley and Stephens*, 14 Q.B.D. 273 (1884) (same).

59. See, e.g., Claus Roxin, Strafrecht: *Allgemeiner Teil (Band I: Grundlagen—Der Aufbau der Verbrechenslehre)* §13 nos. 2 & 70 (Munich: C. H. Beck, 3d ed., 1997); Lenckner,

in Schönke-Schröder, *Strafgesetzbuch* (25th ed., 1997) vor §§32 ff. no. 48; Knut Amelung, "Über Freiheit und Freiwilligkeit auf der Opferseite der Strafnorm," 1999 *Goltdammers Archiv* 182; Wilfried Küper, "'Autonomie,' Irrtum und Zwang bei mittelbarer Täterschaft und Einwilligung," 1986 *Juristenzeitung* 219; Alfred Göbel, *Die Einwilligung im Strafrecht als Ausprägung des Selbstbestimmungsrechts* (Frankfurt a.M.: Peter Lang, 1992).

60. *Model Penal Code* §2.11(1).

61. See, e.g., Wayne R. LaFave & Austin W. Scott, Jr., *Criminal Law*, 2d ed. (St. Paul: West Publishing, 1986), p. 481.

62. Feinberg, *Harm to Self*, chaps. 17–19; David A. J. Richards, *Sex, Drugs, Death, and the Law: An Essay on Human Rights and Overcriminalization* (Totowa, N.J.: Rowman & Littlefield, 1982); Gerald Dworkin, "Devlin Was Right: Law and the Enforcement of Morality," *William & Mary Law Review* 40 (1999): 927; Michael Köhler, "Freiheitliches Rechtsprinzip und Betäubungsmittelstrafrecht," *Zeitschrift für die gesamte Strafrechtswissenschaft* 104 (1992): 3 (drugs); Cornelius Nestler, "Constitutional Principles, Criminal Law Principles, and the German Drug Law," *Buffalo Criminal Law Review* 1 (1998): 661 (drugs).

63. In particular "crimes against personal autonomy" and "crimes against sexual autonomy." On the latter, see Tatjana Hörnle, "Penal Law and Sexuality: Recent Reforms in German Criminal Law," *Buffalo Criminal Law Review* 3 (2000): 638. See also Stephen J. Schulhofer, "Taking Sexual Autonomy Seriously: Rape Law and Beyond," *Law & Philosophy* 11 (1992): 35–94; Dorothy E. Roberts, "Rape, Violence, and Women's Autonomy," *Chicago-Kent Law Review* 69 (1993): 359; Note, "Feminist Legal Analysis and Sexual Autonomy: Using Statutory Rape Laws as an Illustration," *Harvard Law Review* 112 (1999): 1065; Sara Y. Lai & Regan E. Ralph, "Female Sexual Autonomy and Human Rights," *Harvard Human Rights Journal* 8 (1995): 201. That's not to say that it doesn't include many crimes that have nothing to do with autonomy. Also, note that this categorization may mislead one into thinking that sexual autonomy was not an aspect of personal autonomy and that autonomy is not an attribute of personhood.

64. See, e.g., Claire Finkelstein, "Positivism and the Notion of an Offense," *California Law Review* 88 (2000): 335 (outlining *constitutional* concept of crime on the basis of the harm principle); Joel Feinberg, *The Moral Limits of the Criminal Law*, 4 vols. (New York: Oxford Univ. Press, 1984–88); see also *Commonwealth v. Bonadio*, 490 Pa. 91, 96–98 (1980) (striking down sodomy statute as inconsistent with "the concepts underlying our view of the police power" as "once summarized . . . by the great philosopher, John Stuart Mill, in his eminent and apposite work, *On Liberty* [1859]"). For earlier invocation of Mill, see Note, "Limiting the State's Police Power: Judicial Reaction to John Stuart Mill," *University of Chicago Law Review* 37 (1969–70): 605.

65. For an interesting attempt to categorize criminal harm, see Andrew von Hirsch & Nils Jareborg, "Gauging Criminal Harm: A Living-Standard Analysis," in *Principled Sentencing*, Andrew von Hirsch & Andrew Ashworth, eds. (Oxford: Hart, 1992), p. 220.

66. Possession offenses today account for a far greater proportion of statutes, arrests, convictions, and penalties than is generally supposed. See Dubber, *Victims in the War on Crime*, pt. 1. For instance, by last count there were 153 possession offenses on the books

in New York, 115 of them felonies, and 11 that provided for a maximum sentence of life imprisonment. See also *Harmelin v. Michigan*, 501 U.S. 957 (1991) (upholding Michigan statute mandating life imprisonment without the possibility of parole for simple drug possession). In 1998 these possession offenses accounted for over 100,000 arrests, or about 18% of all arrests, roughly one third of which resulted in a prison or jail sentence. (By comparison, there were 60,000 arrests for all violent felonies *combined*.) One in every five prison or jail sentences handed out by New York courts that year was imposed for a possession offense. State of New York, Division of Criminal Justice Services, Possession Related Offenses New York State (Feb. 4, 2000) (on file with author). Also in 1998, *drug* possession offenses alone resulted in over 1.2 million arrests nationwide. U.S. Dep't of Justice, Bureau of Justice Statistics, "Estimated Number of Arrests, by Type of Drug Law Violation, 1982–99" (http://www.ojp.usdoj.gov/bjs/dcf/tables/salespos.htm).

67. *People v. Almodovar*, 62 N.Y.2d 126 (1984) (no justification as defense against "unlawful" possession charge); but see *United States v. Gomez*, 92 F.3d 770 (9th Cir. 1996) (self-defense as defense against felon-in-possession charge).

68. In fact, some jurisdictions recognize possession with intent to consume as a *mitigating* rather than an aggravating factor, especially when the drug possessed is marijuana (possession of quantities for personal use). See, e.g., N.Y. Penal Law §221.05 (marijuana).

69. Richards, *Sex, Drugs, Death*, chap. 4; Köhler, "Freiheitliches Rechtsprinzip"; Nestler, "Constitutional Principles"; see also Douglas N. Husak, *Drugs and Rights* (Cambridge: Cambridge Univ. Press 1992), chap. 2.

70. For a more detailed discussion of possession as a police offense, see Dubber, *Victims in the War on Crime*, pt. 1.

71. See Ted Conover, *Newjack: Guarding Sing Sing* (New York: Vintage Books, 2000), pp. 104–5 (contraband is defined in *Standards of Inmate Behavior* as "any article that is not authorized by the Superintendent or [his] designee.").

72. See N.Y. Penal Law §400.00(1)(a) (McKinney 2000 & Supp. 2001) ("of good moral character").

73. That's the idea behind "Project Exile," a federal-state project based on stringent federal gun possession laws that literally seeks to exile gun possessors from their communities by incarcerating them in remote federal prisons for extensive periods of time. Eric Westervelt, "Philadelphia's Crackdown on Criminals Who Possess Illegal Guns," *Morning Edition*, National Public Radio, March 23, 2000; see also William Clauss & Jay S. Ovsiovitch, "'Project Exile' Effort on Gun Crimes Increases Need for Attorneys to Give Clear Advice on Possible Sentences," *New York Bar Journal*, June 2000, at 35.

CHAPTER SIX

I owe thanks to Mel Eisenberg, Gillian Lester, Monique Marks, Erin Murphy, William Simon, Frank Zimring, and workshop participants at Berkeley, Columbia, and Buffalo. Some of this chapter also appears in my book *Democracy and the Police* (Stanford, Calif.: Stanford Univ. Press, 2008).

1. Markus D. Dubber, *The Police Power: Patriarchy and the Foundations of American Government* (New York: Columbia Univ. Press, 2005), p. xi.

2. Ibid.

3. On "the dominant view of police unions," see George L. Kelling & Robert B. Kliesmet, "Police Unions, Police Culture, and Police Abuse of Force," in *Police Violence: Understanding and Controlling Police Abuse of Force*, William A. Geller & Hans Toch, eds. (New Haven, Conn.: Yale Univ. Press, 1996), p. 191.

4. Edward Conlon, *Blue Blood* (New York: Penguin, 2004), p. 243.

5. See, e.g., David Laws & Martin Rein, "Knowledge for Policy and Practice," *Integrating Knowledge and Practice: The Case of Social Work and Social Science*, David J. Tucker, Charles Garvin, & Rosemary Sarri, eds. (Westport, Conn.: Praeger, 1997), p. 46.

6. See, e.g., Hans Toch & J. Douglas Grant, *Police as Problem Solvers: How Frontline Workers Can Promote Organizational and Community Change*, 2d ed. (Washington, D.C.: American Psychological Association, 2005), p. 81; Thomas J. Cowper, "The Myth of the 'Military Model' of Leadership in Law Enforcement," in *Contemporary Policing: Controversies, Challenges, and Solutions*, Quint C. Thurman & Jihong Zhao, eds. (Los Angeles: Roxbury, 2004), p. 113.

7. See, e.g., Gerald Frug, "City Services," *N.Y.U. Law Review* 73 (1998): 23, 81; Jerome Skolnick, "Neighborhood Police," *The Nation* (March 22, 1972): 372; Arthur L. Waskow, "Community Control of the Police," *Trans-Action* (December 1969): 4.

8. John Dewey, *The Public and Its Problems* (Chicago: Gateway Books, 1946), p. 217.

9. See, e.g., David Montgomery, *The Fall of the House of Labor: The Workplace, the State, and American Labor Activism, 1865–1925* (Cambridge: Cambridge Univ. Press, 1987), pp. 214–56.

10. See, e.g., Barbara Garson, *All the Livelong Day: The Meaning and Demeaning of Routine Work* (New York: Penguin, 1975), pp. 214–18; Mike Rose, *The Mind at Work: Valuing the Intelligence of the American Worker* (New York: Viking, 2004), pp. 142–47; John Fabian Witt, *The Accidental Republic: Crippled Workingmen, Destitute Widows, and the Remaking of American Law* (Cambridge, Mass.: Harvard Univ. Press, 2004), p. 109.

11. Dubber, supra note 1, at 3.

12. Frederick Winslow Taylor, *The Principles of Scientific Management* (New York: Harper & Brothers, 1911); see also, e.g., Frank Barkley Copley, *Frederick W. Taylor: Father of Scientific Management* (New York: Harper & Brothers, 1923).

13. See, e.g., Cynthia Estlund, *Working Together: How Workplace Bonds Strengthen a Diverse Democracy* (New York: Oxford Univ. Press, 2003), pp. 56–59.

14. Dewey, supra note 8, p. 217.

15. See, e.g., Harry Braverman, *Labor and Monopoly Capitalism: The Degradation of Work in the Twentieth Century* (New York: Monthly Review Press, 1974); Garson, supra note 10; William H. Simon, "Ethics, Professionalism, and Meaningful Work," *Hofstra Law Review* 26 (1997): 445, 447–57.

16. See, e.g., James Miller, *Democracy Is in the Streets: From Port Huron to the Siege of Chicago* (Cambridge, Mass.: Harvard Univ. Press, 1994); David Alan Sklansky, "Police and Democracy," *Michigan Law Review* 103 (2005): 1699, 1756–62.

17. See, e.g., David Jenkins, *Job Power: Blue and White Collar Democracy* (Garden City, N.Y.: Doubleday, 1973); Jane J. Mansbridge, *Beyond Adversary Democracy* (New York: Basic Books, 1980); Carole Pateman, *Participation and Democratic Theory* (Cambridge: Cambridge Univ. Press, 1970); Philip Selznick, *Law, Society, and Industrial Justice* (New York: Russell Sage Foundation, 1969).

18. See, e.g., Wellford W. Wilms, *Restoring Prosperity: How Workers and Managers are Forging a New Culture of Cooperation* (New York: Times Books, 1996); Mark Barenberg, "Democracy and Domination in the Law of Workforce Cooperation: From Bureaucratic to Flexible Production," *Columbia Law Review* 94 (1994): 753, 881–904; William H. Simon, "The Politics of 'Cooperation' at the Workplace," *Reconstruction* (1990): 18.

19. See Barenberg, supra note 18, pp. 870–79, 904–18; Simon, "The Politics of 'Cooperation,'" supra note 18, pp. 18, 20–21, 55–57.

20. See Simon, "The Politics of 'Cooperation,'" supra note 18, pp. 18–19, 59–61; Graham Sewell, "The Discipline of Teams: The Control of Team-Based Industrial Work Through Electronic and Peer Surveillance," *Administrative Science Quarterly* 43 (1998): 397. "Quality circles" are "periodic meetings at which small groups of employees are encouraged to discuss workplace issues and to make 'suggestions' to management." Simon, "The Politics of 'Cooperation,'" supra note 18, p. 18; see also, e.g., Wilms, supra note 18, p. 34.

21. See, e.g., Jerome H. Skolnick, *Justice without Trial: Law Enforcement in Democratic Society*, 3d ed. (New York: Macmillan College Publishing, 1994); Joseph Goldstein, "Police Discretion Not to Invoke the Criminal Process: Low-Visibility Decisions in the Administration of Justice," *Yale Law Journal* 69 (1960): 543; Sanford H. Kadish, "Legal Norm and Discretion in the Police and Sentencing Processes," *Harvard Law Review* 75 (1962): 904, 906–15; Charles A. Reich, "Police Questioning of Law Abiding Citizens," *Yale Law Journal* 75 (1966): 1161, 1164–70.

22. On Warren Court and Burger Court criminal procedure, see, e.g., Sklansky, "Police and Democracy," supra note 16, pp. 1736–41. For the argument for regulating the police by legislation, see, e.g., Craig M. Bradley, *The Failure of the Criminal Procedure Revolution* (Philadelphia: Univ. of Pennsylvania Press 1993). For suggestions that the police should be regulated through rules promulgated by police agencies themselves, see Kenneth Culp Davis, *Discretionary Justice: A Preliminary Inquiry* (Baton Rouge: Louisiana State Univ. Press, 1969), pp. 65, 95; Anthony G. Amsterdam, "Perspectives on the Fourth Amendment," *Minnesota Law Review* 58 (1974): 349, 380. On civilian oversight, see, e.g., Samuel Walker, *Police Accountability: The Role of Citizen Oversight* (Belmont, Calif.: Wadsworth, 2002).

23. See, e.g., Egon Bittner, "The Police on Skid-Row: A Study of Peace Keeping," *American Sociological Review* 5 (1967): 699–700.

24. See, e.g., Herman Goldstein, *Problem-Oriented Policing* (New York: McGraw-Hill, 1990), p. xii.

25. See, e.g., Egon Bittner, "The Functions of the Police: A Review of Background Factors, Current Practices, and Possible Role Models," *Aspects of Police Work* (Boston:

Northeastern Univ. Press, 1990), p. 89 (reprinting monograph originally published in 1970); William Ker Muir Jr., *Police: Streetcorner Politicians* (Chicago: Univ. of Chicago Press, 1977); James Q. Wilson, *Varieties of Police Behavior: The Management of Law and Order in Eight Communities* (Cambridge, Mass.: Harvard Univ. Press 1968).

26. Bittner, "The Functions of the Police," supra note 25, p. 131.

27. Ibid., pp. 148–49.

28. See, e.g., ibid., p. 153 ("Whenever police officers are furnished an opportunity to discuss their work problems around a conference table, they generally display a thoughtful approach that amazes outsiders. Naturally not all policemen contribute to discussions nor do all benefit from them. But in this respect they are not very different from teachers, some of whom might also not attend faculty meetings without much loss.").

29. Hans Toch, J. Douglas Grant, & Raymond T. Galvin, *Agents of Change: A Study in Police Reform* (New York: Wiley, 1975). A revised account of the study appears in Toch & Grant, supra note 6.

30. Goldstein, *Problem-Oriented Policing*, supra note 24, p. 28.

31. See, e.g., Wilms, supra note 18.

32. See Justin McCrary, "The Effect of Court-Ordered Hiring Quotas on the Composition and Quality of Police," *American Economic Review* 97 (2007): 318, 323.

33. See Conlon, supra note 4, p. 74 ("For cops, there was never any shortage of complaints, formal and otherwise: the crime reports we wrote were called complaints, and when the DA wrote up a charge, it was called a complaint, and when a civilian accused a cop of wrongdoing, it was also a complaint. We complained among ourselves, about bad food, hurting feet, lousy bosses, long hours, and little money. We complained about the sun and the rain. We did have a lot to complain about, within the Job and without, but some cops seemed to lose the power of speech altogether, except for complaining."); see also, e.g., ibid., pp. 284–85.

34. This is a major subject of Edward Conlon's recent memoir of his work as a New York City police officer. See, e.g., ibid., pp. 307–404.

35. See, e.g., Muir, supra note 25.

36. Conlon, supra note 4, p. 312.

37. See, e.g., Susan Ehrlich Martin, *Breaking and Entering: Police Women on Patrol* (Berkeley: Univ. of California Press, 1980); Muir, supra note 25.

38. See, e.g., Conlon, supra note 4, pp. 291–94, 322–30; Steven Maynard-Moody & Michael Musheno, *Cops, Teachers, Counselors: Stories from the Front Lines of Public Service* (Ann Arbor: Univ. of Michigan Press, 2003), p. 57. This, too, is a large theme of Conlon's book.

39. E.g., Jack Dunphy, "Betrayal, Not Bullets, Is What Cops Fear," *Los Angeles Times* (September 4, 2005): M3; see also "Report of the Rampart Independent Review Panel: A Report to the Los Angeles Board of Police Commissioners Concerning the Operations, Policies, and Procedures of the Los Angeles Police Department in the Wake of the Rampart Scandal" (Los Angeles, 2000), p. 55.

40. See Goldstein, *Problem-Oriented Policing*, supra note 24, p. 149.

41. See David L. Carter & Allen D. Sapp, "The Evolution of Higher Education in Law Enforcement: Preliminary Findings from a National Study," *Journal of Criminal Justice Education* 1 (1990): 59.

42. See ibid., pp. 62–63.

43. See Goldstein, *Problem-Oriented Policing*, supra note 24, p. 150.

44. *Jordan v. City of New London*, 2000 U.S. App. Lexis 22195 (2d Cir. 2000) (unpublished opinion); see also Mike Allen, "Help Wanted Invoking the Not-Too-High-IQ Test," *New York Times* (September 19, 1999): D4.

45. *Jordan*, supra note 44, p. 2.

46. Allen, supra note 44.

47. Ibid.

48. Ibid. (quoting New London Deputy Police Chief William C. Gavitt).

49. Ibid. (quoting Charles F. Wonderlic Jr.).

50. Taylor, supra note 12, p. 59.

51. Allen, supra note 44 (quoting Gilbert G. Gallegos, national president of the Fraternal Order of Police).

52. See, e.g., Conlon, supra note 4, p. 313 (discussing officers who "left the Job with the taste of ashes in their mouths").

53. See, e.g., Skolnick, *Justice without Trial*, supra note 21, pp. 57–62; William A. Westley, *Violence and the Police: A Sociological Study of Law, Custom, and Morality* (Cambridge, Mass.: MIT Press, 1970); Maureen Cain, "Some Go Forward, Some Go Back: Police Work in Comparative Perspective," *Comparative Sociology* 22 (1993): 319–20.

54. See, e.g., Skolnick, *Justice without Trial*, supra note 21, pp. 41–68.

55. See Michael G. Aamodt & Nicole A. Stalnaker, "Police Officer Suicide: Frequency and Officer Profiles," in *Suicide and Law Enforcement*, Donald C. Sheehan & Janet I. Warren, eds. (Washington, D.C., U.S. Dep't of Justice, 2001); Melissa J. Erwin et al., "Reports of Intimate Partner Violence Made Against Police Officers," *Journal of Family Violence* 20 (2005): 13; Erlend Hem, Anne Marie Berg, & Oivind Dkeberg, "Suicide in the Police—A Critical Review," *Suicide & Life-Threatening Behavior* 31 (2001): 224.

56. See, e.g., Akiva M. Liberman et al., "Routine Occupational Stress and Psychological Distress in Police," *Policing* 21 (2002): 421.

57. See Mary Ann Wycoff & Wesley K. Skogan, *Community Policing in Madison: Quality From the Inside Out* (Washington, D.C.: U.S. Dep't of Justice, 1993), p. 46.

58. See Todd Wuestewald & Brigitte Steinheider, "Shared Leadership: Can Empowerment Work in Police Organizations?" *The Police Chief* (January 2006): 48.

59. On Mill and Cole, see Pateman, supra note 17, pp. 33–44.

60. See Sklansky, *Police and Democracy*, supra note 16, pp. 1708–28.

61. See, e.g., Mansbridge, supra note 17; Pateman, supra note 17.

62. See, e.g., Herman Goldstein, *Policing a Free Society* (Cambridge, Mass.: Ballinger Publishing Company, 1977), p. 1.

63. See Muir, supra note 25, pp. 3–4, 79–80, 99, 119, 144, 268.

64. See, e.g., Skolnick, *Justice without Trial*, supra note 21, pp. 249–56; Byron Michael Jackson, "Leadership and Change in a Public Organization: The Dilemmas of an Urban Police Chief" (PhD diss., Univ. of California, Berkeley, 1979).

65. Muir, supra note 25, p. 253. All of the officers Muir studied were men. Oakland's police force at the time was 97% male; the nationwide figure was 98%. See Federal Bureau of Investigation, *Uniform Crime Reports for the United States* (1971), pp. 160, 249.

66. Muir, supra note 25, p. 253.

67. Ibid., p. 281.

68. Westley, supra note 53, p. xvii.

69. George E. Berkley, *The Democratic Policeman* (Boston: Beacon, 1969), pp. 29–39.

70. John E. Angell, "Toward an Alternative to Classic Police Organizational Arrangements: A Democratic Model," *Criminology* 9 (1971): 185, 187, 193–95; see also John E. Angell, "The Democratic Model Needs a Fair Trial: Angell's Response," *Criminology* 12 (1975): 379.

71. See, e.g., Peter B. Bloch & David Specht, *Neighborhood Team Policing* (Washington, D.C.: U.S. Dep't of Justice, 1973); William G. Gay et al., *Neighborhood Team Policing* (Washington, D.C.: U.S. Dep't of Justice, 1977); Lawrence W. Sherman et al., *Team Policing: Seven Case Studies* (Washington, D.C.: Police Foundation, 1973).

72. Jerome H. Skolnick & David H. Bayley, *The* New *Blue Line: Police Innovation in Six American Cities* (New York: Free Press, 1986), pp. 214–15.

73. See ibid., pp. 151–52; Toch & Grant, supra note 6, p. 100 n. 3.

74. The theme is entirely absent, for example, from a recent, otherwise balanced encyclopedia article on police and democracy by the sociologist Gary Marx, despite the fact that both Berkley and Muir appear in the bibliography. See Gary T. Marx, "Police Power," in *Encyclopedia of Democracy*, Seymour Martin Lipset, ed. (Washington, D.C.: Congressional Quarterly, 1995), p. 954, reprinted with revisions as Gary T. Marx, "Police and Democracy," in *Policing, Security, and Democracy: Theory and Practice*, Menachem Amir & Staley Einstein, eds. (Huntsville, Tex.: Office of International Criminal Justice, 2000), p. 35.

75. Compare, for example, Carole Pateman's influential argument for workplace democracy, published in 1970, supra note 17, with Jane Mansbridge's equally famous but much more qualified defense of the same ideal in 1980, supra note 17.

76. See David Alan Sklansky, "Not Your Father's Police Department: Making Sense of the New Demographics of Law Enforcement," *Journal of Criminal Law and Criminology* 96 (2006): 1209.

77. See, e.g., Robert M. Fogelson, *Big-City Police* (Cambridge, Mass.: Harvard Univ. Press 1977), pp. 239–42; Christopher Lasch, *The Agony of the American Left* (New York: Knopf, 1969), pp. 206–7; Jerome H. Skolnick, *The Politics of Protest* (New York: Ballantine, 1969), pp. 278–81; Walker, supra note 22, pp. 27–29.

78. See Sklansky, *Police and Democracy*, supra note 16, pp. 1771–74.

79. Kelling & Kliesmet, supra note 3, p. 193; see also, e.g., Toch & Grant, supra note 6, pp. 33–37; Albert J. Reiss, "Police Organization in the Twentieth Century," *Modern*

Policing, Michael Tonry & Norval Morris, eds. (Chicago: Univ. of Chicago Press, 1992), pp. 51, 68–72.

80. See Gary T. Marx, "When the Guards Guard Themselves: Undercover Tactics Turned Inward," *Policing and Society* 2 (1992): 151.

81. Kelling & Kliesmet, supra note 3, p. 193.

82. See, e.g., Max Lerner, *America as a Civilization: Life and Thought in the United States Today* (New York: Simon & Shuster, 1957), p. 433 ("The American is not overly impressed by police authority, considering the police officer as a badly paid job holder, not above being 'fixed' by a bribe.").

83. See Sklansky, "Police and Democracy," supra note 16, pp. 1708–28.

84. James Q. Wilson, *Thinking about Crime* (New York: Basic Books, 1975), p. xix.

85. See Skolnick, *The Politics of Protest*, supra note 77, pp. 286–88.

86. Reinhard Bendix, "Industrialization, Ideologies, and Social Structure," *American Sociological Review* 24 (1959): 613, 619–22, reprinted in Reinhard Bendix, *Work and Authority in Industry: Managerial Ideologies in the Course of Industrialization* (New Brunswick: Transaction, 2001), p. 434.

87. Skolnick, *Justice without Trial*, supra note 21, pp. 226–30.

88. Ibid., p. 11.

89. Ibid., pp. 6, 226–30; see also Jonathan Simon, "Speaking Truth and Power," *Law & Society Review* 36 (2002): 37, 40 (noting that "Skolnick saw the identification with the rule of law as the defining aspect of the police and a way to reconcile their fundamentally authoritarian character with the democratic society they were policing").

90. See, e.g., T. A. Critchley, *A History of Police in England and Wales, 900–1966* (London: Constable, 1967), pp. 35–57.

91. See, e.g., Brian Chapman, *Police State* (London: Macmillan, 1970), pp. 20–32; Peter K. Manning, *Police Work: The Social Organization of Policing*, 2d ed. (Cambridge, Mass.: MIT Press, 1997), p. 98.

92. Chapman, supra note 91, p. 51; see also, e.g., W. L. Melville Lee, *A History of Police in England* (London: Methuen, 1905), p. x.

93. On the role of "contrast-models" in democratic theory and political rhetoric, see William E. Connolly, "The Challenge to Pluralist Theory," in *The Bias of Pluralism*, William E. Connolly, ed. (New York: Atherton, 1969), pp. 3, 22–23.

94. It is unsurprising, in this light, that twentieth-century police states found themselves attracted to Taylorism, notwithstanding its aura of capitalist exploitation. See, e.g., Ronald Smelser, "How 'Modern' Were the Nazis? DAF Social Planning and the Modernization Question," *German Studies Review* 13 (1990): 285, 289–90; Joan A. Armstrong, Book Review, *Slavic Review* 44 (1985): 332.

95. Goldstein, *Problem-Oriented Policing*, supra note 24, p. 27.

96. See, e.g., Debra Livingston, "Police Discretion and the Quality of Life in Public Places: Courts, Commentators, and the New Policing," *Columbia Law Review* 97 (1997): 574–78.

97. John Thomas Delaney & Peter Feuille, "Police," in *Collective Bargaining in American Industry: Contemporary Perspectives and Future Directions*, David B. Lipsky & Clifford B.

Donn, eds. (Lexington, Mass.: Lexington Books, 1987), pp. 265, 301; see also, e.g., Stephen C. Halpern, *Police-Association and Department Leaders: The Politics of Co-Optation* (Lexington, Mass.: Lexington Books, 1974), pp. 93–99.

98. See Sklansky, "Not Your Father's Police Department," supra note 76.

99. See David Alan Sklansky, "Seeing Blue: Police Reform, Occupational Culture, and Cognitive Burn-In," in *Police Occupational Culture: New Debates and Directions*, Megan O'Neill, Monique Marks, & Anne-Marie Singh, eds. (Oxford: Elsevier, 2007), p. 19.

100. Simon, "Speaking Truth and Power," supra note 89, p. 40.

101. Skolnick, *Justice without Trial*, supra note 21, pp. 226–30.

102. See ibid., p. 11 ("In the abstract, the rule of law embodies rational restraints on authority as it defines criminal conduct. There must be specificity, clarity, prospectivity, and strict construction in favor of the accused. There must be procedural regularity and fairness, and so forth. In practice, however, such standards may not be clear"). Phrases like "and so forth" are quite typical in discussions of the rule of law.

103. Lon L. Fuller, *The Morality of Law* (New Haven, Conn.: Yale Univ. Press, 1964), p. 39.

104. See, e.g., Joseph Raz, "The Rule of Law and Its Virtue," in *The Authority of Law* (Oxford: Clarendon, 1979), pp. 210, 214; Richard H. Fallon Jr., "'The Rule of Law' as a Concept in Constitutional Discourse," *Columbia Law Review* 97 (1997): 1, 8 and n. 27; Margaret Jane Radin, "Reconsidering the Rule of Law," *Boston University Law Review* 69 (1989): 781, 785.

105. See Fallon, supra note 104, pp. 10–24.

106. Fuller, supra note 103, p. 81; cf., e.g., Jerome H. Skolnick & James J. Fyfe, *Above the Law: Police and the Excessive Use of Force* (New York: Free Press, 1993), p. xvi (arguing that "in a free society, especially in the United States, where police derive their authority from law and take an oath to support the Constitution, they are obliged to acknowledge the law's moral force and to be constrained by it").

107. Fuller, supra note 103, p. 39.

108. F. A. Hayek, *The Road to Serfdom* (London: Routledge, 1944), p. 54 (quoted in, e.g., Raz, supra note 104, p. 210); cf., e.g., Raz, supra note 104, p. 219 (noting that "the rule of law is often rightly contrasted with arbitrary power").

109. See Raz, supra note 104, at 210–11.

110. William Kornblum, "Drug Legalization and the Minority Poor," *Milbank Quarterly* 69 (1991): 415, 422.

111. See, e.g., Emily J. Sack, "Battered Women and the State of the Law: The Struggle for the Future of Domestic Violence Policy," *Wisconsin Law Review* 6 (2004): 1657.

112. See, e.g., Selznick, supra note 17, p. 29.

113. Tom R. Tyler, "Enhancing Police Legitimacy," *Annals of the American Academy of Political and Social Science* 593 (2004): 84, 94; see also, e.g., Tom R. Tyler, *Why People Obey the Law* (Princeton, N.J.: Princeton Univ. Press, 1990).

114. See William H. Simon, "Toyota Jurisprudence: Legal Theory and Rolling Rules Regimes," *Law and New Governance in the EU and the US*, Grainne de Burca & Joanne Scott, eds. (Oxford: Hart, 2006), pp. 37, 47–48.

115. This is the point stressed by Raz: the rule of law is a political virtue, but it is not the only political virtue, and sometimes it should yield. See Raz, supra note 104.

116. See, e.g., Michael E. Buerger, "The Limits of Community," in *The Challenge of Community Policing: Testing the Premises*, Dennis P. Rosenbaum, ed. (Thousand Oaks, Calif.: Sage, 1994), pp. 270–71; Frug, supra note 7, p. 81.

117. Walker, supra note 22.

118. See Cowper, supra note 6.

CHAPTER SEVEN

1. Markus D. Dubber, *The Police Power: Patriarchy and the Foundations of American Government* (New York: Columbia Univ. Press, 2005), pp. 158, 159, 163.

2. Bodo Pieroth, Bernhard Schlink, & Michael Kniesel, *Polizei- und Ordnungsrecht*, 6th ed. (Munich: Beck, 2004), pp. 23–24.

3. Ibid.

4. Ibid., pp. 16–17.

5. Marco König, *Trennung und Zusammenarbeit von Polizei und Nachrichtendiensten* (Stuttgart: Boorberg, 2005).

6. Ibid., p. 15.

7. Ibid., p. 28. "[Die Polizei] tritt dem Bürger grundsätzlich offen und nur ausnahmsweise verdeckt gegenüber; [Geheimdienste aber] begegnen dem Bürger grundsätzlich verdeckt und nur ausnahmsweise offen." (In the main, the Police confront the citizen openly; confronting him covertly is the exception. In the main, intelligence services encounter the citizen covertly, and only under exceptional circumstances do they confront him openly.)

8. Robert Harnischmacher & Arved Semerak, *Deutsche Polizeigeschichte* (Stuttgart: Kohlhammer, 1986), p. 33.

9. Ibid., p. 38.

10. Bernhard Schloer, *Vom Preußischen Polizeireicht zum Bayerischen Sicherheitsrecht* (Stuttgart: Boorberg, 1990).

11. StPO §110.

12. BVerfGE 65, 1, NJW 1984, 419.

13. Indeed, other European countries enacted legislation to regulate undercover policing, once the European Court of Human Rights began to treat abuses of undercover policing as violations of the fair trial guarantee written into the European Convention on Human Rights. *Luedi v. Switzerland*, 238 European Court of Human Rights (ECtHR) (ser. A) at 20–21 (1992); *Kostovski v. Netherlands*, 166 ECtHR (ser. A) (1989); *Underpertinger v. Austria*, 110 ECtHR (ser. A) (1986); *X. v. Belgium*, 16 Eur. Comm'n H.R. 2050 (1979); *Windisch v. Austria*, 186 ECtHR (ser. A) (1990); *Delta v. France*, 191 ECtHR (ser. A) (1990). See, e.g., Legge di giugno, 1990 n. 162, Art. 25(1), Art. 97; legge di dicembre, 1992 n. 356, Art. 12 quarter; 1998 n. 269(1), Art. 14 (Italy), and more recently, "Loi n° 2004-204 du 9 mars 2004 portant adaptation de la justice aux évolutions de la criminalité" (France).

14. Gesetz zur Bekämpfung der organisierten Kriminalität (Law to Fight Organized Crime), subseq. StPO §110a. Before these reforms, undercover policing was governed

through norms prohibiting undercover agents and informants from committing crimes or excessively encouraging others to do so. These norms have been elaborated through judicial decisions and scholarly commentary. Kempf, StV 1999, 128; Weiler, GA 1994, 561; Bruns, NStZ 1983, 49; Sommer, NStZ 1999, 48; Kinzig, StV 1999, 288; Stock & Kreuzer, *Drogen und Polizei*, 1996; Franzheim, NJW 1979, 2015; Seier & Schlehofer, JuS 1983, 52; Taschke, StV 1984, 178. These prohibitions were backed up by the principle of legality, which, in principle, mandated criminal prosecution of undercover agents who committed crimes undercover, even when the police violated the law for investigative purposes. The principle of legality also constrained covert tactics by prohibiting the police from tolerating law-breaking by targets. StPO §152, 163. Aside from enforcement of the principle of legality and the substantive norms, undercover policing had been regulated through guidelines issued jointly by state ministries of justice and the interior. Gemeinsame Richtlinien der Justizminister/-senatoren und der Innenminister/-senatoren der Länder über die Inanspruchnahme von Informanten sowie über den Einsatz von Vertrauenspersonen (V-Personen) und Verdeckten Ermittlern im Rahmen der Strafverfolgung, 15 RiStBV Anl. D (first issued in 1985 and amended in 1993 and 1994 to accord with the 1992 statute). The guidelines had imposed few limits on the types of crimes that agents could target and offered little guidance for how covert operations should be conducted.

15. That the owner voluntarily admitted an undercover agent into his home did not relieve agents of the obligation to obtain judicial approval in advance, assuming that the need for meeting in a private apartment could be anticipated. BGH 1997, NStZ 1997, 448; Roxin, StV 1998, 43.

16. König, *Trennung*.

17. StPO §110b.

18. A 1990 regulation envisaged just this sort of covert activity, by directing the police to undertake early-stage "proactive investigations" to collect the intelligence necessary to target specific milieus or individuals for repressive (evidence-gathering) stings. RiStBV Anl. E (1990).

19. Interview with German chief of covert policing unit, May 26, 2003. "There's an empty casino making huge profits. We send our guy in to find out, how is this possible? Where do they get their money? Who runs things? Who's the boss? Once we learn what crimes this place is sheltering, we can transform the investigation into an official evidence-gathering probe. Nothing changes in what we do; only now we've got the judge's permission." Interview with supervisor of German covert policing unit, May 17, 2004.

20. Interview with supervisor of German covert policing unit, May 19, 2004.

21. Repressive operations do this largely by generating "Lagebilder" and "Lageberichte"—sketches of criminal milieus—which the police compile from the systematic compilation and sifting of reports from repressive operations. Interview with German prosecutor, March 10, 2004.

22. Interview with German covert policing chief, May 27, 2003.

23. Interview with chief of German covert policing unit, March 8, 2004.

24. Interview with supervisor of German covert policing unit, May 27, 2003.

25. Interview with German prosecutor, May 22, 2003.

26. Interview with German prosecutor, May 23, 2003.

27. Interview with supervisor of German covert policing unit, May 27, 2003.

28. Interview with chief of German covert policing unit, June 2, 2003.

29. Interview of German judge, May 27, 2003.

30. Annette von Stetten, *Beweisverwertung beim Einsatz Verdeckter Ermittler* (Frankfurt: Lang, 1999), pp. 188–191.

31. Interview with German control officer, May 19, 2003.

32. Interview with German prosecutor, May 10, 2004; see also interview with German prosecutor, May 13, 2004, note 58.

33. Interview with supervisor of German covert policing unit, June 2, 2003.

34. Bremen (§ 35 PolG), Lower Saxony (§ 36a SOG), Saarland (§ 28 PolG), Saxony (§ 39 PolG). Interestingly, Schleswig-Holstein does not allow undercover investigations all together, due to the deceitful character (see also Bäurnler at https://www.datenschutz zentrum.de/material/themen/divers/lverwg30.htm).

35. Hamburg (prior approval, § 12 I 2 GesDatVPol), Hessen (briefing about ongoing investigation, § 6 V 7 SOG), Sachsen-Anhalt (approval, § 18 V 2 SOG), Thüringen (information if indicating commission of crime, § 34 III 4 PAG).

36. Baden-Württemberg (§ 22 III PolG), Bavaria (Art. 33 III Nr. 2 PAG), Berlin (§ 26 I Nr. 2 ASOG), Brandenburg (§ 35 I Nr. 2 PolG), Bremen (§ 35 I Nr. 2 and 4 PolG), Hamburg (§ 12 I Nr. 2 GesDatVPol), Hessen (§ 16 II SOG), Mecklenburg-Vorpommern (§ 33 II SOG), Lower Saxony (§§ 36a I, 34 I Nr. 2 SOG), Nordrhein-Westfalen (§ 20 I Nr. 2 PolG), Rheinland-Pfalz (§ 28 I Nr. 2 POG), Saarland (§ 28 I PolG), Saxony (§ 39 I Nr. 2 PolG), Saxony-Anhalt (§ 18 II SOG), Thüringen (§ 31 V PAG).

37. Interview with supervisor of German covert policing unit, May 26, 2003.

38. Interview with supervisor of German covert policing unit, June 2, 2003.

39. Ibid.

40. "If you stay in the preventive realm too long, you risk suppression of the evidence, and, at any rate, you've got no reason to stay in the preventive realm, because telephone tapping is only permitted once you've moved into evidence-gathering under the federal code," which governs the police in their repressive capacity. Ibid.

41. BKAG Art. 1. Two states do not permit the states to conduct undercover investigations in their crime-prevention capacities, in one case (Sachsen-Anhalt) because its state police laws did not provide for them, in the other (Saxony) because a state supreme court decision found such operations unconstitutional, absent adequate procedures for notifying targets after the fact. SächsVerfGH 1996 LKV 272.

42. Interview with supervisor in German covert policing unit, June 3, 2003.

43. Interview with supervisor of shallow-cover agents, May 12, 2004. "Once, it was our goal to get into a Turkish café through the target; our shallow-cover guy, whose family is from Turkey, gains entry into the scene through his target; he gets to know who goes to the café, who do they associate with, where do they talk about drugs, what cars do they drive, what phones do they use, where do they get their stuff. It's pure intelligence. When something is offered, he tells us about it. He hangs out, gets to know people, but he can't make buys. Because then it would have to go in the file. His job is to

give us a picture of that social scene; it helps us to identify 'hot spots' where drugs are being distributed, as an entry point into other possible operations." Ibid.

44. Interview with German prosecutor, May 21, 2004.

45. Interview with director of shallow-cover operations, May 12, 2004.

46. Interview with German control officer, May 19, 2004.

47. Interview with German prosecutor, May 19, 2004.

48. Interview with director of German shallow-cover operations, May 12, 2004; interview with supervisor in German covert policing unit, May 19, 2004.

49. Interview of German prosecutor, May 30, 2004. It is worth noting that this particular nonevidentiary use of undercover buys may be particular to the investigation of drug crimes, though these form an important nucleus of covert operations.

50. Interview with supervisor of German covert policing unit, March 8, 2004; interview with German prosecutor, March 9, 2004; interview with German prosecutor, March 19, 2004.

51. Interview with chief of covert policing unit, March 10, 2004.

52. Interview with German prosecutor, May 30, 2003.

53. Ibid.

54. Interview with German control officer, May 14, 2004.

55. Interview with supervisor of German covert policing unit, May 14, 2004.

56. Interview with former deep-cover agent (Germany), May 14, 2004.

57. Interview with German prosecutor, May 19, 2004.

58. Interview with German prosecutor, March 9, 2004.

59. Interview with supervisor of German covert policing unit, June 2, 2004.

60. Interview with supervisor of German covert policing unit, May 17, 2004.

61. Interview with German prosecutor, May 13, 2004.

62. Ibid.

63. Interview with supervisor of German covert policing unit, May 17, 2004.

64. Ibid.

65. Interview with German prosecutor, May 19, 2004.

66. Ibid.

67. StPO §110b.

68. Interview with German prosecutor, May 18, 2004.

69. Interview with German police officer assigned to drug unit, May 25, 2003. "Sometimes it's not even clear from the file that there were two informants and not just one," a judge confirmed. Interview with German judges, May 18, 2004.

70. Interview with German prosecutor, May 21, 2004.

71. Interview with chief of covert policing unit, March 10, 2004.

72. See Gary T. Marx, "Thoughts on a Neglected Category of Social Movement Participant: The Agent Provocateur and the Informant," *American Journal of Sociology* 80 (1974): 402.

73. Office of the Inspector General, U.S. Dep't of Justice, *The Federal Bureau of Investigation's Compliance with the Attorney General's Investigative Guidelines* (2005), p. 19 (http://www.usdoj.gov/oig/special/0509/final.pdf). In particular, the guidelines allow

the FBI to visit public places, attend public events, and surf the Internet for publicly available information, "even absent specific investigative predicates"; FBI agents were "empowered to scour public sources for information on future terrorist threats" and "will also be able to enter and observe public places and forums just as any members of the public might." Ibid., p. 189. Part 6, "Counterterrorism Activities and Other Authorizations," of the General Crimes guidelines allow activities "which can be carried out even in the absence of a checking of leads, preliminary inquiry, or full investigation," that is, without the particularized information ordinarily required for such investigative activities. Ibid., pp. 190, 196; General Crimes Guidelines Section 6.A.2. "The revised Guidelines permit attendance [for the purpose of detecting or preventing terrorism, or assessing a threat to national security] even if neither a preliminary inquiry nor a full investigation is open," so long as agents limit themselves "to matters observable and obtainable in a public forum. Undercover activity, surreptitious entry into a private gathering at these events, and certain other investigative techniques (e.g., consensual recording of conversations) are not permitted under this authority." Ibid., p. 198 (citing to September 1, 2004, Guidelines of the Counterterrorism Division).

74. Jim Dwyer, "Police Memos Say Arrest Tactics Calmed Protest," *New York Times* (March 17, 2006).

CHAPTER EIGHT

My thanks to Lindsay Farmer, Nicola Lacey, Stuart Macdonald, Alan Norrie, Suke Wolton, Lucia Zedner, two anonymous reviewers, and the participants in the Buffalo workshop for their comments and good advice.

1. Lindsay Farmer, "The Jurisprudence of Security: The Police Power and the Criminal Law," in *The New Police Science: The Police Power in Domestic and International Governance*, M. Dubber & M. Valverde, eds. (Stanford, Calif.: Stanford Univ. Press, 2006).

2. Markus D. Dubber & Mariana Valverde, "Perspectives on the Power and Science of Police," in Dubber & Valverde, supra note 1.

3. Markus D. Dubber, *The Police Power: Patriarchy and the Foundations of American Government* (New York: Columbia Univ. Press, 2005), p. 3.

4. Ibid.

5. Ibid., p. 4.

6. Ibid., p. 8.

7. Ibid., pp. 4–46.

8. See Dubber & Valverde, supra note 2.

9. Dubber, supra note 3, p. 4.

10. Ibid., p. 158.

11. Ibid., p. 211.

12. See, generally, Dubber & Valverde, supra note 2. For criticism, see Christopher Tomlins, "Conclusion, Framing the Fragments. Police: Genealogies, Discourses, Locales, Principles," in Dubber & Valverde, supra note 2.

13. Supra note 3, p. 159.

14. For an account see Elizabeth Burney, *Making People Behave* (Cullompton, UK: Willan, 2005).

15. For a brief comparison of the ASBO with American strategies, see Philip Heymann, "The New Policing," *Fordham Urban Law Journal* 28 (2000): 407.

16. CDA 1998 §1(4).

17. CDA 1998 §1(6).

18. ASBO terms are sometimes bizarre and their targets diverse. In addition to the nuisance neighbors and troublesome teenagers against whom ASBOs were initially promoted as a legal weapon, they have been used against prostitutes, alleged street drug dealers, political protestors, beggars, street drinkers, flyposters, and suicidal depressives. See the Case Studies section at http://www.statewatch.org/asbo/ASBOwatch.html.

19. CDA 1998 §1(7).

20. *R (McCann and Others) v. Crown Court at Manchester and Another* (2003) 1 AC 787.

21. CDA 1998 §1(10).

22. Although an equally significant aspect of ASBOs in practice is that they may also specifically prohibit conduct that is in any case a criminal offence, changing the grounds of its criminalization and the maximum penalties available, see *R v. Stevens, R v. H* (2006) 2 Cr App R (S) 453 CA.

23. Peter Ramsay, "What Is Anti-Social Behaviour?" *Criminal Law Review* (2004): 908, 920.

24. See, for example, Home Office, *A Guide to Anti-Social Behaviour Orders and Acceptable Behaviour Contracts* (London: Home Office, 2002), p. 11.

25. See Home Office, *Defining and Measuring Anti-social Behaviour*, Home Office Development and Practice Reports, 2004.

26. Andrew von Hirsch et al., "Overtaking on the Right," *New Law Journal* 145 (1995): 1516.

27. Although I have elsewhere argued that they can be read as a dispositional test of fault that is itself a vehicle of the threat assessment. For further discussion, see Peter Ramsay, "The Theory of Vulnerable Autonomy and the Legitimacy of the Civil Preventative Order," in B. McSherry, A. Norrie, & S. Bronnitt, eds., *Regulating Deviance* (Oxford: Onati International Series on Law and Society/Hart Publishing, forthcoming) and Ramsay, supra note 23.

28. This aspect is even more marked in proceedings for breach of an ASBO. By virtue of the order itself, the civil rights of this person have already been more or less precisely adjusted relative to the threat the person has been assessed as representing. See Ramsay, supra note 23, pp. 921–23. In consequence the person will be criminally liable for various kinds of conduct that another person who has not been assessed as representing the same threat will not be.

29. Ramsay, supra note 23, pp. 919–21.

30. Ibid., p. 917.

31. William Blackstone, *Commentaries on the Laws of England: Of Public Wrongs* (Chicago: Univ. of Chicago Press, 1979), p. 248.

32. Ibid., p. 249.

33. Ibid., p. 250.

34. Ibid., p. 253.

35. Ibid.

36. Ibid.

37. Dubber, supra note 3, p. 56.

38. Law Commission, *Binding Over*, Law Com. No. 222 (London: HMSO, 1994), p. 7.

39. Law Commission, *Binding Over: The Issues*, Working Paper 103 (London: HMSO, 1987).

40. *Stone's Justices Manual* (London: Butterworths, 2006), pp. 3–540.

41. Magistrates Court Act 1980, §115(3)

42. Lindsay Farmer, *Criminal Law, Tradition and Legal Order* (Cambridge: Cambridge Univ. Press, 1997), p. 114.

43. *R v. Howell* (1982) QB 416, 426.

44. *Hughes v. Holley* (1988) 86 Cr. App. R. 130, 139.

45. P. Tain, "Keeping the Peace," *Solicitors' Journal* 147, no. 28 (2003): 839.

46. Supra note 38, pp. 14–17.

47. CDA 1998, §1(1)(b).

48. *Aubrey-Fletcher ex parte Thompson* (1969) 53 Cr. App. R. 380.

49. Law Commission, supra note 38, p. 15.

50. Ibid.

51. Ibid., p. 30.

52. Ibid., p. 4.

53. Ibid., p. 41.

54. Ibid., p. 42.

55. *Redmond Bate v. DPP* (1999) *Criminal Law Review* 998.

56. *Foulkes v. Chief Constable of Merseyside* (1998) 3 All ER 705; see also *Percy v. DPP* (1995) 1 WLR 1382; *Selvanayagam v. DPP* (1996) JP Reports 155.

57. *Steel and Others v. UK* (1999) 28 EHRR 603, 637.

58. *Hashman and Harrup v. UK* (2000) 30 EHRR 241.

59. See *Stone's Justices Manual*, 3–540. The Home Office responded to the *Hashman* decision and the Law Commission report with a consultation document that recommended remodeling the bind over on the model of the ASBO (*Bind Overs: A Power for the 21st Century* (London: Home Office, 2003), p. 9).

60. Supra note 58, p. 257.

61. Ibid., pp. 257–58.

62. Moreover, the Court of Appeal has ruled that the prohibitions in the ASBO itself must be clearly stated if they are to be necessary to prevent future ASB by the defendant, see *R v. Boness and Others* (2006) 1 Cr. App. R. (S) 120.

63. Supra note 44, p. 137, citing Fitzgerald, J., in *Feehan v. Justices of Queens County* (1882) 10 LR Ir 294.

64. It has been argued that preventing offense is the purpose of the ASBO; see, generally, A. von Hirsch & A. Simester, eds., *Incivilities: Regulating Offensive Behaviour*

(Oxford: Hart, 2006). For a detailed argument on the relation of this interpretation to the argument presented here, see Ramsay, supra note 27.

65. Although the applicant authority does have to prove the presence of someone likely to be caused harassment, alarm, or distress, see *R (Gosport Borough Council) v. Fareham Magistrates Court* (2006) All ER (D) 267 (Nov) QBD.

66. See Ramsay, supra note 23.

67. Cited in S. Chakrabati, "Asbomania," British Institute of Human Rights Lecture (January 2006).

68. *Chief Constable of Lancashire v. Potter* (2003) EWHC 2272 (QB) 32, ¶¶44 and 46.

69. See also Tain, supra note 45.

70. Labour Party, *A Quiet Life* (London: Labour Party, 1995); Burney, supra note 14.

71. Elizabeth Burney, "Talking Tough, Acting Coy: What Happened to the Anti-Social Behaviour Order?" *Howard Journal* 41, no. 5 (2002): 341.

72. T. Blair, Speech on returning to 10 Downing Street, May 6, 2005, http://www.number10.gov.uk/output/Page7459.asp.

73. Home Office, *Respect and Responsibility: Taking a Stand Against Anti-Social Behaviour* (London: HMSO, 2003), p. 13.

74. Ibid., p. 13.

75. Ibid.

76. Ibid. (emphasis added).

77. Supra note 20, p. 806.

78. Ibid. (emphasis added).

79. Ibid., p. 835.

80. T. Blair, *Observer*, April 23, 2006.

81. See Frank Furedi, *Politics of Fear* (London: Continuum, 2005).

82. For a more detailed treatment of the axiomatic position of vulnerability in these theories, see Ramsay, supra note 27.

83. Anthony Giddens, *Where Now for New Labour?* (Cambridge: Polity, 2002), p. 17.

84. Anthony Giddens, *Modernity and Self-Identity* (Cambridge: Polity, 1991), pp. 75–80.

85. Ibid., pp. 40–47.

86. Anthony Giddens, *The Third Way* (Cambridge: Polity, 1998), p. 65.

87. Amitai Etzioni, *The New Golden Rule: Community and Morality in a Democratic Society* (New York: Basic Books, 1996), p. 21; Michael Sandel, *Liberalism and the Limits of Justice* (Cambridge: Cambridge Univ. Press, 1982), pp. 165–67.

88. On the ASBO specifically, see Roger Burke & Ruth Morrill, "Anti-Social Behaviour Orders: An Infringement of the Human Rights Act 1998?" *Nottingham Law Journal* 11, no. 2 (2002): 1. Just how far communitarians are prepared to go in requiring citizens to reassure the authorities can be seen in Amitai Etzioni, "Rights and Responsibilities 2001," in *The Communitarian Reader*, Etzioni et al., eds. (Lanham, Md.: Rowman & Littlefield, 2004), p. 196.

89. The term is borrowed from J. Anderson & A. Honneth, "Autonomy, Vulnerability, Recognition and Justice," in J. Christman & J. Anderson, *Autonomy and the Challenges to Liberalism: New Essays* (Cambridge: Cambridge Univ. Press, 2005).

90. Michael Kottow, "Vulnerability: What Kind of a Principle Is It?" *Medicine, Health Care and Philosophy* 7 (2004): 281, 284.

91. See, for example, "Anti-Social Behaviour Orders," http://www.liberty-human-rights.org.uk/issues/7-asbos/index.shtml (accessed July 19, 2007); Allison Brown, "ASBOs, Anti-social Behaviour, Crime Control and Social Control," *Howard Journal* 43 (2004): 203.

92. This relationship in ASB politics between the ubiquitous vulnerability of humans as such and the particular vulnerability of contingently disadvantaged individuals is particularly interesting from a theoretical point of view because it reverses the relationship between the two concepts of vulnerability as it is postulated in contemporary theories of justice and human rights. The theories envisage that ubiquitous vulnerability provides a rational basis for moral duties toward, or protection of the human rights of, the contingently disadvantaged and oppressed. See, for example, Onora O'Neill, *Towards Justice and Virtue: A Constructive Account of Practical Reasoning* (Cambridge: Cambridge Univ. Press, 1996), and Bryan Turner, "Outline of the Theory of Human Rights," in *Citizenship and Social Theory*, Bryan Turner, ed. (London: Sage, 1993).

93. As Kottow puts it, "Vulnerability, dignity and integrity are descriptions that lack an action-guiding norm, which is added by the ethical prescription of respect and protection." Supra note 90, p. 286.

94. Blair, supra note 80.

95. Supra note 20, pp. 813–14.

96. Ibid.

97. Supra note 73, p. 53.

98. Hobbes observes that the subjects of natural rights will be "diffident" of one another and "from this diffidence of one another, there is no way for any man to secure himselfe, so reasonable, as Anticipation." Thomas Hobbes, *Leviathan* (Harmondsworth, UK: Penguin, 1968), p. 184.

99. This description of anomia is drawn from Ralf Dahrendorf, *Law and Order* (London: Stevens & Sons, 1985), p. 21. It is interesting that Anthony Bottoms finds exactly this lack of expectation in the understanding of ASB revealed by surveys of residents of deprived neighborhoods in England. See A. Bottoms, "Incivilities, Offence and Social Order in Residential Communities," in von Hirsch & Simester, eds., supra note 64.

100. Giorgio Agamben, *State of Exception* (Chicago: Chicago Univ. Press, 2005), p. 51.

101. Ibid., p. 22.

102. David Garland, *The Culture of Control: Crime and Social Order in Contemporary Society* (Oxford: Oxford Univ. Press, 2001), and David Garland, "The Limits of the Sovereign State: Strategies of Crime Control in Contemporary Society," *British Journal of Criminology* 36 (1996): 445.

103. Garland (2001), supra note 102, p. 106.

104. Note though the difference between Garland's starting point and the official position on the ASBO. The Home Office observes that fear of crime may rise even though crime rates fall, see supra note 73. The Home Office nevertheless understands fear of crime as corrosive of public trust in the state, see text at supra note 97.

105. *Pace* R. Sullivan, "The Schizophrenic State: Neoliberal Criminal Justice," in *Crime, Risk and Justice*, Kevin Stenson & Robert Sullivan, eds. (Cullompton, UK: Willan, 2001), and Pat O'Malley, "Volatile and contradictory punishment," *Theoretical Criminology* 3, no. 2 (1999): 175.

106. Garland (2001), supra note 102, p. 134.

107. Garland claims too much when he writes that "for most people, crime is no longer an aberration or an unexpected, abnormal event." (Garland [1996], supra note 102, p. 446). It may well be that some offenses, such as burglary and offenses involving vehicles, cannot be described as entirely unexpected. Nevertheless, for "most people," the experience of crime, especially serious crime, remains infrequent, "abnormal" and an "aberration." For a fascinating discussion of the victimization data, see T. Hope & A. Trickett, "La distribution de la victimation dans la population," *Déviance et Société* 28, no. 3 (2004): 385. Garland's view, in this respect, seems to imply the normality of a vulnerability to others that is comparable to the view that underlies the ASBO.

108. Clifford Shearing & Jennifer Wood, "Nodal Governance, Democracy and the New 'Denizens,'" *Journal of Law and Society* 30, no. 3 (2003): 403.

109. Garland (2001), supra note 102, p. 202.

110. A theory founded in the work of Carl Schmitt, see Carl Schmitt, *Political Theology: Four Chapters on the Concept of Sovereignty* (Chicago: Chicago Univ. Press, 1985).

111. Garland (2001), supra note 102, p. 135.

112. Cf. Richard Sparks, "Perspectives on risk and penal politics," in *Crime, Risk and Insecurity*, Tim Hope & Richard Sparks, eds. (London: Routledge, 2000), p. 136.

113. Cf. Lucia Zedner, "Policing Before and After the Police: The Historical Antecedents of Contemporary Crime Control," *British Journal of Criminology* 46 (2006): 78.

114. Otto Kirchheimer, "In Quest of Sovereignty," in *Politics, Law and Social Change: Selected Essays of Otto Kirchheimer*, Frederic Burin & Kurt Shell, eds. (New York: Columbia Univ. Press, 1969), p. 191.

115. In respect of crime and fear of crime, see the evidence in Hope & Trickett, supra note 107.

116. Farmer, supra note 1.

117. Ibid.

118. In addition to the political theories mentioned in notes 83–88 supra, the very broad potential scope of the concept of vulnerability's application is suggested by Margrit Shildrick, *Embodying the Monster: Encounters with the Vulnerable Self* (London: Sage, 2002), p. 79, and Bryan Turner, "Forgetfulness and Frailty: Otherness and Rights in Contemporary Social Theory," in *The Politics of Jean-Francois Lyotard: Justice and Political Theory*, Chris Rojek & Bryan Turner, eds. (London: Routledge, 1998), pp. 25–26. As the other side of security, it can be detected in the influential discourse of human security. See, for example, Commission on Human Security, *Human Security Now: Pro-*

tecting and Empowering People (New York: Commission on Human Security, 2003). The concept of human security is widely recognized to represent a profound challenge to the claim of sovereignty to be the axiomatic norm of international relations and international law. See Gerd Oberleitner, "Human Security: A Challenge to International Law?" *Global Governance* 11 (2005): 185; Tara McCormack, "From State of War to State of Nature: Human Security and Sovereignty," in *Politics without Sovereignty*, Christopher Bickerton, Philip Cunliffe, & Alex Gourevitch, eds. (New York: UCL Press, 2007).

119. For a discussion in the context of counterterrorism see Lucia Zedner, "Securing Liberty in the Face of Terror: Reflections from Criminal Justice," *Journal of Law and Society* 32, no. 4 (2005): 507, 517–18.

CHAPTER NINE

I am grateful to Bernard Harcourt for his insights on this topic, and to Mariana Valverde and two anonymous reviewers for their insights and comments on this chapter. Research and writing for this chapter were supported by the Canadian Institute for Advanced Research, the Harry Frank Guggenheim Foundation, and the Social Sciences and Humanities Research Council of Canada.

Epigraph. Michel Foucault, *Sécurité, Territoire, Population: Cours au Collège De France, 1977–1978* (Paris: Seuil, 2004), p. 344.

1. John Merriman, *The Margins of City Life: Explorations on the French Urban Frontier, 1815–1851* (New York: Oxford Univ. Press, 1991); James Scott, *Seeing Like a State: How Certain Schemes to Improve the Human Condition Have Failed* (New Haven, Conn.: Yale Univ. Press, 1998).

2. Scott, supra note 1.

3. Michel Carmona, *Haussmann* (Paris: Fayard, 2000); Howard Payne, *The Police State of Louis Napoleon Bonaparte, 1851–1860* (Seattle: Univ. of Washington Press, 1966); Patrick Joyce, *The Rule of Freedom: Liberalism and the Modern City* (London: Verso, 2003), p. 149; Scott, supra note 1, pp. 53–63.

4. Jeanne Pronteau, *Edme Verniquet, 1727–1804* (Paris: Commission des Travaux Historiques, Ville de Paris, 1986); Anthony Sutcliffe, *Paris: An Architectural History* (New Haven, Conn.: Yale Univ. Press, 1996), pp. 67–69.

5. David P. Jordan, *Transforming Paris: The Life and Labors of Baron Haussmann* (New York: Free Press, 1995), pp. 34–37; Paul Rabinow, *French Modern: Norms and Forms of the Social Environment* (Chicago: Univ. of Chicago Press, 1995), p. 75.

6. Carmona, supra note 3; Françoise Choay, *Les Mémoires d'Haussmann* (Paris: Seuil, 2000), pp. 19–20. Circulation, for Haussmann, is also what underwrote and guaranteed political support for the project from the population itself—and Napoleon III was equally enamored with movement, and its centrality to a healthy and salubrious city. See Jordan, supra note 5, pp. 171, 295.

7. Jordan, supra note 5, p. 74; Rabinow, supra note 5.

8. Carmona, supra note 3, pp. 520–23.

9. Francis Lieber, *On Civil Liberty and Self-Government*, 2d ed. (Philadelphia, Pa.: J. B. Lippincott, 1891), p. 87.

10. See William Novak, *The People's Welfare: Law and Regulation in Nineteenth-Century America* (Chapel Hill: Univ. of North Carolina Press, 1996), pp. 117–18.

11. Joyce, supra note 3, pp. 35–56, 86–87.

12. Carl Smith, *The Plan of Chicago: Daniel Burnham and the Remaking of the American City* (Chicago: Univ. of Chicago Press, 2006); Daniel Hess, "Transportation Beautiful: Did the City Beautiful Movement Improve Urban Transportation?" *Journal of Urban History* 32 (2006): 511–45; Christopher Tunnard, "A City Called Beautiful," *Journal of the Society of Architectural Historians* 9 (1950): 31–36.

13. Hess, supra note 12, p. 535.

14. Ibid., p. 531.

15. City of Chicago, Committee on Police and Fire. 1992a. *Meeting Held on May 15, 1992*, appendix 1 of City of Chicago's Memorandum in Opposition to Defendant's Motion to Dismiss in *Chicago v. Avilar*, No. 93 MC1 376001 (filed May 10, 1993); City of Chicago, Committee on Police and Fire. 1992b. *Meeting Held on May 18, 1992*, appendix 2 of City of Chicago's Memorandum in Opposition to Defendant's Motion to Dismiss in *Chicago v. Avilar*, No. 93 MC1 376001 (filed May 10, 1993).

16. Debra Livingston, "Police Discretion and the Quality of Life in Public Places: Courts, Communities, and the New Policing," *Columbia Law Review* 97 (1997): 551–672; Richard Schragger, "The Limits of Localism," *Michigan Law Review* 100 (2001): 371–472.

17. Fran Spielman, "Daley Endorses Anti-gang Law; Rodriguez Wary," *Chicago Sun-Times*, May 20, 1992, p. 14.

18. Wesley Skogan & Susan Hartnett, *Community Policing, Chicago Style* (New York: Oxford Univ. Press, 1997), p. 22; Fran Spielman & Ray Long, "What Will Stop the Killing? Daley's Finger Points Nowhere; Issues Can't Be Dodged Any Longer," *Chicago Sun-Times*, October 18, 1992; Isabel Wilkerson, "Crack Hits Chicago, Along With a Wave of Killing," *New York Times*, September 24, 1991, p. A1.

19. City of Chicago, Substitute Ordinance, amending the Municipal Code of Chicago by adding a new Section 8-4-015 (June 17, 1992).

20. Mariana Valverde & Ron Levi, "Gobernando la comunidad, gobernando a través de la comunidad," *Delito y Sociedad: Revista de Ciencias Sociales* 22 (2006): 5–30.

21. Joyce, supra note 3, pp. 147, 155. On the police project in this context, see Markus D. Dubber, "The Victim in American Penal Law," *Buffalo Criminal Law Review* 3 (1999): 3–31; Markus D. Dubber & Mariana Valverde, "Perspectives on the Power and Science of Police," in *The New Police Science: The Police Power in Domestic and International Governance*, Markus D. Dubber & Mariana Valverde, eds. (Stanford: Stanford Univ. Press, 2006), pp. 1–16; John Merriman, *Police Stories: Building the French State, 1815–1851* (New York: Oxford Univ. Press, 2006); Novak, supra note 10.

22. *Chicago* v. *Morales*, 527 U.S. 41 (1999).

23. E.g., David Cole, "Discretion and Discrimination Reconsidered: A Response to the New Criminal Justice Scholarship," *Georgetown Law Journal* 87 (1999): 1059–93; Dan Kahan & Tracey Meares, "The Coming Crisis of Criminal Procedure," *Georgetown*

Law Journal 86 (1998): 1153–84; Tracey Meares & Dan Kahan, "The Wages of Antiquated Procedural Thinking: A Critique of Chicago v. Morales," *University of Chicago Legal Forum* 1998 (1998): 197–214; Debra Livingston, "Gang Loitering, the Court, and Some Realism about Police Patrol," *Supreme Court Review* 1999 (1999): 141–202; Dorothy Roberts, "Race, Vagueness, and the Social Meaning of Order-Maintenance Policing," *Journal of Criminal Law & Criminology* 89 (1999): 775–836.

24. Cf. Martha Nussbaum, *Hiding from Humanity: Disgust, Shame, and the Law* (Princeton, N.J.: Princeton Univ. Press, 2004), pp. 271–77.

25. Dubber, supra note 21; Markus D. Dubber, "Toward a Constitutional Law of Crime and Punishment," *Hastings Law Journal* 55 (2004): 509–71; Markus D. Dubber, "The New Police Science and the Police Power Model of the Criminal Process," in *The New Police Science: The Police Power in Domestic and International Governance*, Markus D. Dubber & Mariana Valverde, eds. (Stanford, Calif.: Stanford Univ. Press, 2006), pp. 107–44; Erik Luna, "The Models of Criminal Procedure," *Buffalo Criminal Law Review* 2 (1999): 389–535; Erik Luna, "Constitutional Road Maps," *Journal of Criminal Law and Criminology* 90 (2000): 1125–50, 1125; Schragger, supra note 16.

26. E.g., William Chambliss, "A Sociological Analysis of the Law of Vagrancy," *Social Problems* 12 (1964): 67–77; Caleb Foote, "Vagrancy-Type Law and Its Administration," *University of Pennsylvania Law Review* 104 (1956): 603–50; Bernard Harcourt, *Illusion of Order: The False Promise of Broken-Windows Policing* (Cambridge, Mass.: Harvard Univ. Press, 2001); Joe Hermer & Janet Mosher, *Disorderly People: Law and the Politics of Exclusion in Ontario* (Halifax: Fernwood, 2002); Gary Stewart, "Black Codes and Broken Windows: The Legacy of Racial Hegemony in Anti-Gang Civil Injunctions," *Yale Law Journal* 107 (1998): 2249–79.

27. Alan Hunt, "Police and the Regulation of Traffic: Policing as a Civilizing Process?" in *The New Police Science: The Police Power in Domestic and International Governance*, Markus D. Dubber & Mariana Valverde, eds. (Stanford: Stanford Univ. Press, 2006), pp. 168–84.

28. Michel Foucault, *Sécurité, Territoire, Population: Cours au Collège De France, 1977–1978* (Paris: Seuil, 2004), pp. 333, 344. All translations from *Sécurité, Territoire, Population* are mine.

29. Ibid.

30. Paolo Napoli, *Naissance de la Police Moderne: Pouvoir, Normes, Sociétés* (Paris: La Découverte, 2003).

31. Mark Neocleous, "Social Police and the Mechanisms of Prevention: Patrick Colquhoun and the Condition of Poverty," *British Journal of Criminology* 40 (2000): 710–26; Novak, supra note 10.

32. Foucault, supra note 28, p. 321.

33. Ibid., pp. 319–21, 330.

34. Ibid., pp. 321, 326.

35. I am grateful to Mariana Valverde for pointing out the connection between "splendor" and "prosperity" as it would be conceived of in the work of Adam Smith.

36. See also Mark Neocleous, "Theoretical Foundations of the 'New Police Science,'" in *The New Police Science: The Police Power in Domestic and International Governance*,

Markus D. Dubber & Mariana Valverde, eds. (Stanford: Stanford Univ. Press, 2006), pp. 17–41.

37. Foucault, supra note 28, pp. 327–28.

38. Ibid., pp. 328–30 (emphasis added).

39. Ibid., p. 330 (emphasis added).

40. Ibid., p. 330.

41. Ibid., pp. 330–32.

42. Ibid., pp. 330–33.

43. Ibid., pp. 333, 343; see also Joyce, supra note 3.

44. Ibid., p. 333.

45. Merriman, supra note 21, pp. 118–40. Cf. Foucault, supra note 28, p. 343.

46. Foucault, supra note 28, pp. 342–43.

47. Ibid., pp. 344–349.

48. Jane Gross, "A New, Purified Form of Cocaine Causes Alarm as Abuse Increases," *New York Times*, November 29, 1985, p. A1; Julie Jacobs, "Don't Rely on Gangs' Promises," *Chicago Sun-Times*, October 29, 1992, p. 37; Wilkerson, supra note 18.

49. Skogan & Hartnett, supra note 18, p. 22.

50. Wilkerson, supra note 18.

51. Don Hayner, "Laws Multiply as Neighborhood Fears Rise," *Chicago Sun-Times*, August 30, 1992, p. 26.

52. Robert Davis & William Recktenwald, "Angry Aldermen Target Gangs: Daley Backs City Council Call for Extra Police Powers," *Chicago Tribune*, October 24, 1991, p. 1.

53. Jim Casey, "City to Put More Cops on the Street: Killings Bring Pledge to Boost Foot Patrols," *Chicago Sun-Times*, April 9, 1991, p. 1.

54. Ray Hanania, "O'Malley Rejects Martin's Call to Ban Loitering," *Chicago Sun-Times*, April 13, 1991, p. 36.

55. John Kass & Sharman Stein, "Daley Weighs Racial Politics in Picking Police Chief," *Chicago Tribune*, April 12, 1992, p. 1; Skogan & Hartnett, supra note 18, pp. 20–37; Spielman & Long, supra note 18, p. 29.

56. Kass & Stein, supra note 55.

57. Albert Alschuler & Stephen Schulhofer, "Antiquated Procedures or Bedrock Rights? A Response to Professors Meares and Kahan," *University of Chicago Legal Forum* 1998: 215–44; Davis & Recktenwald, supra note 52.

58. Davis & Recktenwald, supra note 52, p. 1.

59. Ibid. The importance attached to street "corners" throughout the ordinance's history is noteworthy and echoes a fascination with "corners" and urban life that has equally occupied Chicago School sociology. See most notably William Foote Whyte, *Street Corner Society: The Social Structure of an Italian Slum* (Chicago: Univ. of Chicago Press, 1943) and Elliot Liebow, *Tally's Corner: A Study of Negro Streetcorner Men* (Boston: Little, Brown, 1967), and more recently picked up in Elijah Anderson, *A Place on the Corner* (Chicago: Univ. of Chicago Press, 1978).

60. Philip Franchine, "W. Side Raids Just the Start, Officials Say," *Chicago Sun-Times*, October 20, 1991, p. 20.

61. Chicago Neighborhood Organizations, *Brief Amicus Curiae of the Chicago Neighborhood Organizations in Support of Petitioner in Chicago v. Morales*, No. 97-1121 (filed June 1998) (1997) U.S. Briefs 1121, Lexis (Briefs), p. 20.

62. See supra note 15.

63. Cate Plys, "Leave It to Beavers to Shake Up the Status Quo," *Chicago Sun-Times*, June 11, 1999, p. 43.

64. Livingston, supra note 23.

65. Committee on Police and Fire, 1992a, supra note 15, p. 148.

66. Ron Levi, *The Constitution of Community in Legal Sites: A Study of Law, Crime and its Control* (SJD diss., 2003), Faculty of Law, Univ. of Toronto.

67. Committee on Police and Fire, 1992a, supra note 15, pp. 105, 65, 67.

68. Ibid., pp. 76, 50.

69. Livingston, supra note 23.

70. Schragger, supra note 16.

71. Spielman, supra note 17; Spielman & Long, supra note 18.

72. Kurt Andersen, "The City That No Longer Works," *Time*, December 17, 1984; John Lorinc, "The City That Really Works," *Toronto Life* 34, no. 14 (2000): 72–76, 78ff; Gerald Suttles, *The Man-Made City: The Land-Use Confidence Game in Chicago* (Chicago: Univ. of Chicago Press, 1990).

73. Robert Davis, "New Police Arrest Power Lights City Council Fuse," *Chicago Tribune*, June 18, 1992, p. 1; Livingston, supra note 23; Spielman, supra note 17.

74. Davis, supra note 73; Robert Davis, "Special Units to Police Loiterers: City Wants to Make New Anti-Gang Law Hold Up in Court," *Chicago Tribune*, June 19, 1992, p. 3; Spielman, supra note 17.

75. City of Chicago, Petition for a Writ of Certiorari to the Supreme Court of Illinois in *Chicago v. Morales* (filed January 2, 1998), pp. 3, 8.

76. Chicago Police Department, General Order No. 92-4, *Anti-Gang Loitering Ordinance*, August 7, 1992, appendix G of Petition for a Writ of Certiorari to the Supreme Court of Illinois in *Chicago v. Morales* (filed January 2, 1998).

77. Wayne LaFave & Austin Scott Jr., *Substantive Criminal Law*, updated by the 2003 pocket part (St. Paul, Minn.: West, 1986), §1.7; Wayne Logan, "The Shadow Criminal Law of Municipal Governance," *Ohio State Law Journal* 62 (2001): 1409–72.

78. E.g., Shawn Napier, "America Responds to Criminal Gang Activity; Taking Back Our Streets: A Critical Analysis of City of Chicago v. Morales," *Capital University Law Review* 29 (2002): 719–59; Kim Strosnider, "Anti-Gang Ordinances after City of Chicago v. Morales: The Intersection of Race, Vagueness Doctrine, and Equal Protection in the Criminal Law," *American Criminal Law Review* 39 (2002): 101–44. But see Logan, supra note 77; Schragger, supra note 16.

79. Committee on Police and Fire, 1992b, supra note 15, pp. 200–1.

80. Levi, supra note 66.

81. Cf. Markus D. Dubber, "Policing Possession: The War on Crime and the End of Criminal Law," *Journal of Criminal Law and Criminology* 91 (2001): 829–996; Stewart, supra note 26, pp. 2249–79.

82. Novak, supra note 10.

83. Ibid., pp. 123–24.

84. Ibid., p. 120.

85. Cf. Jennifer Coffin, "The United Mall of America: Free Speech, State Constitutions, and the Growing Fortress of Private Property," *University of Michigan Journal of Law Reform* 33 (2000): 615–49.

86. Ron Levi & Mariana Valverde, "Knowledge on Tap: Police Science and 'Common Knowledge' in the Legal Regulation of Drunkenness," *Law & Social Inquiry* 26 (2001): 201–28; Novak, supra note 10.

87. Supra note 76, s. 3(c). This restriction on police officers appears to have soon given way. Alschuler & Schulhofer report that by 1995 it seems that all Chicago police working in the designated enforcement areas considered themselves authorized to arrest individuals under the ordinance. Alschuler & Schulhofer, supra note 57, p. 244, n. 108.

88. Levi & Valverde, supra note 86. This knowledge heterogeneity is paralleled by the guidelines on what constitutes a "criminal street gang." Referring to "specific, documented and reliable information," the General Order lists the following as potential, though not exclusive, forms of knowledge that can be relied on: analysis of crime pattern information; observations of department members; witness interviews; interviews of admitted criminal street gang members; and information received from informants who have proven to be reliable. This carries through to the criteria for defining gang membership, which privileges police officers' on-the-job knowledge by requiring that gang membership "must be substantiated by the arresting officer's experience and knowledge of the alleged offenders" (Chicago Police Department, 1992, supra note 76). For more on the intersection between police science, law, and knowledge see Levi & Valverde, supra note 86.

89. Alschuler & Schulhofer, supra note 57, p. 233; Chicago Police Department, "Mayor Daley Hails Passage of Gang Loitering Ordinance," press release, February 16, 2000; *Chicago v. Morales*, supra note 22, pp. 49–50; Harcourt, supra note 26, p. 51.

90. Harcourt, supra note 26, pp. 104–6.

91. Peter Poulos, "Chicago's Ban on Gang Loitering: Making Sense of Vagueness and Overbreadth in Loitering Laws," *California Law Review* 83 (1995): 379–417, p. 384 n. 26.

92. *Chicago v. Youkhana*, No. 93-MC1-293363 (Illinois Cir. Ct., 29 September 1993), appendix E of Petition for a Writ of Certiorari to the Supreme Court of Illinois in *Chicago v. Morales* (filed January 2, 1998).

93. *Chicago v. Morales*, supra note 22.

94. With successful challenges both at trial and in the supreme court of Illinois, the decisions in *Chicago v. Youkhana* (1993, 1995) resulted in a reversal of the conviction of six other individuals originally convicted in *Chicago v. Morales* (1995) and a reversal of the conviction of fifty other individuals in *Chicago v. Ramsey* (1995; see *Chicago v. Youkhana* [1993] No. 93-MC1-293363 [Illinois Cir. Ct., September 29], appendix E of Petition for a Writ of Certiorari to the Supreme Court of Illinois in *Chicago v. Morales* [filed January 2, 1998]; *Chicago v. Youkhana* [1995], 277 Ill. App. 3d 101; *Chicago v. Morales* [1995],

No. 1-93-4039 [Illinois App., December 29], appendix C of Petition for a Writ of Certiorari to the Supreme Court of Illinois in *Chicago v. Morales* [filed January 2, 1998]; *Chicago v. Ramsey* [1995], No. 1-93-4125 [Illinois App., December 29], appendix D of Petition for a Writ of Certiorari to the Supreme Court of Illinois in *Chicago v. Morales* [filed January 2, 1998]). All the defendants in *Youkhana*, *Morales*, and *Ramsey* were then consolidated, 70 defendants in all, before the supreme court of Illinois in *Chicago v. Morales* (1997, 177 Ill. 2d 440 [Sup. Ct.]). The supreme court of Illinois found that the ordinance was an unconstitutional violation of due process, and it is this decision that was later appealed to the U.S. Supreme Court in *Morales* (1999), supra note 22.

95. Strosnider, supra note 78, pp. 112–26.

96. E.g., Robert Delchin, "The Gang's All Here: Anti-Loitering Laws in the Face of City of *Chicago v. Morales*," *Cleveland State Law Review* 48 (2000): 215–33; Aaron Mann, "A Plurality of the Supreme Court Asserts a Due Process Right to Do Absolutely Nothing in City of *Chicago v. Morales*," *Creighton Law Review* 33 (2000): 579–641; Strosnider, supra note 78; Matt Wawrzyn, "*Chicago v. Morales*: Constitutional Principles at Loggerheads with Community Action," *DePaul Law Review* 50 (2000): 371–419.

97. Foucault, supra note 28, p. 344.

98. See also Joyce, supra note 3; Schragger, supra note 16.

99. *Chicago v. Morales*, supra note 22, p. 60.

100. Ibid., pp. 60–62.

101. Ibid., pp. 63–64.

102. Ibid., p. 60; *Kolender v. Lawson*, 461 U.S. 352 (1983).

103. Morton Horwitz, "The Warren Court and the Pursuit of Justice," *Washington and Lee Law Review* 50 (1993): 5–13; David Luban, "The Warren Court and the Concept of a Right," *Harvard Civil Rights-Civil Liberties Law Review* 34 (1999): 7–37; Robert Weisberg, "Foreword: Criminal Procedure Doctrine: Some Versions of the Skeptical," *Journal of Criminal Law and Criminology* 76 (1985): 832–55.

104. *Chicago v. Morales*, supra note 22, pp. 62–63.

105. We can infer that what the majority is requiring are *individually discernible* harms, which must be *visible to an individual police officer* and which as a result must be both geographically and temporally proximate to the loitering that is taking place. The question of which harms count is thereby critical to the majority opinion, though never articulated as such. See, generally, Bernard Harcourt, "The Collapse of the Harm Principle," *Journal of Criminal Law and Criminology* 90 (1999): 109–94; Mariana Valverde, "The Harms of Sex and the Risks of Breasts: Obscenity and Indecency in Canadian Law," *Social and Legal Studies* 8 (1999): 181–97. This stems from the majority decision's purported focus on civil liberties, which leads it to neglect the possibility of a community harm by focusing solely on a temporally defined police-citizen encounter. Local communities, then, are not authorized to make decisions regarding harm, nor is harm a matter of scientific expertise—also in keeping with police epistemology. See Levi & Valverde, supra note 86.

106. *Chicago v. Morales*, supra note 22, p. 60.

107. Ibid., p. 63.

108. Ibid., pp. 60–64 (emphasis added).

109. Ibid., pp. 63–64.

110. Mariana Valverde, "Targeted Governance and the Problem of Desire," in *Risk and Morality*, Richard Ericson & Aaron Doyle, eds. (Toronto: Univ. of Toronto Press, 2003), pp. 438–58, at p. 438.

111. Nikolas Rose, *Powers of Freedom: Reframing Political Thought* (New York: Cambridge Univ. Press, 1999), p. 271.

112. Strosnider, supra note 78.

113. This emphasis on geographic targeting is gaining even greater significance through the emergence of geographic profiling within crime prevention programs; e.g., National Institute of Justice, "Geographic Profiling—NIJ's MAPS Program: Crime Mapping & Analysis Research," available at http://www.ojp.usdoj.gov/nij/maps/gp.html (accessed February 11, 2007).

114. *Chicago v. Morales*, supra note 22, pp. 53–54.

115. Ibid., pp. 56–57.

116. Ibid., p. 59.

117. Ibid., pp. 59–60.

118. Novak, supra note 10, p. 78.

119. Oyez Project, *Chicago v. Morales*, 527 U.S. 41 (1999), http://www.oyez.org/cases/case?case=1990-1999/1998/1998_97_1121 (accessed February 11, 2007).

120. Hunt, supra note 27.

121. Christopher Tomlins, *Law, Labor, and Ideology in the Early American Republic* (New York: Cambridge Univ. Press, 1993).

122. Markus D. Dubber, *The Police Power: Patriarchy and the Foundations of American Government* (New York: Columbia Univ. Press, 2005), p. 211.

123. Ibid., pp. 137–38.

124. Pat O'Malley, "Risk and Responsibility," in *Foucault and Political Reason: Liberalism, Neo-Liberalism and Rationalities of Government*, Andrew Barry, Thomas Osborne, & Nikolas Rose, eds. (Chicago: Univ. of Chicago Press, 1996), pp. 189–208.

125. *Chicago v. Morales*, supra note 22, pp. 73–74 (emphasis added).

126. Ibid., p. 97. The political theory underwriting Justice Scalia's invocation of police regulations is explicitly resisted by the plurality judges. In response, they note that when the Illinois speed limit was enacted, there were nearly 1.7 million citizens of Chicago, but only between 8,000 and 80,000 cars, concluding that "it seems quite clear that it was pedestrians, rather than drivers, who were primarily responsible for Illinois' decision to impose a speed limit." Ibid., p. 54, n. 21.

127. Ibid., p. 87.

128. Joyce, supra note 3, p. 98 (and see especially chap. 2, pp. 62–97, "The Water and the Blood of the City"). On the Paris sewers, see Donald Reid, *Paris Sewers and Sewermen: Realities and Representations* (Cambridge, Mass.: Harvard Univ. Press, 1991).

129. *Chicago v. Morales*, supra note 22, pp. 92–93.

130. Ibid., p. 93 (Scalia's brackets and emphasis).

131. Ibid., pp. 97–98.

132. Justice Thomas quotes Freund for the proposition that "the criminal law deals with offenses after they have been committed, the police power aims to prevent them.

The activity of the police for the prevention of crime is partly such as needs no special legal authority," Ibid., pp. 106–7, and Tiedeman's conclusion that "the vagrant has been very appropriately described as the chrysalis of every species of criminal. A wanderer through the land, without home ties, idle, and without apparent means of support, what but criminality is to be expected from such a person? If vagrancy could be successfully combated . . . the infractions of the law would be reduced to a surprisingly small number; and it is not to be wondered at that an effort is so generally made to suppress vagrancy." Ibid., p. 104, n. 4.

133. Ibid., p. 101.

134. Ibid., pp. 102–6; see also Dubber, supra note 122, p. 136.

135. *Chicago v. Morales*, supra note 22, pp. 101–2.

136. Ibid., p. 107; see also Dubber, supra note 122, p. 137.

137. *Chicago v. Morales*, supra note 22, pp. 107–8.

138. Ibid., p. 109; Dubber (2006), supra note 25, pp. 108, 118.

139. *Chicago v. Morales*, supra note 22, pp. 114–15 (emphasis added, internal citations omitted).

140. Max Weber, *The City* (Don Martindale & Gertrud Neuwirth, eds. and trans., Glencoe, Ill.: Free Press, 1958), p. 94.

141. Dubber, supra note 122, pp. 130–38.

142. Joyce, supra note 3, pp. 210–30.

143. Cf. Ibid., pp. 137–38.

144. See e.g., Loïc Wacquant & William Julius Wilson, "The Cost of Racial and Class Exclusion in the Inner City," *Annals of the American Academy of Political and Social Science* 501 (1989): 8–25. On the effects of incarceration and the punitive mobility it generates, see, e.g., Todd Clear, Dina Rose, Elin Waring, & Kristen Scully, "Coercive Mobility and Crime: A Preliminary Examination of Concentrated Incarceration and Social Disorganization," *Justice Quarterly* 20 (2003): 33–64; Dorothy Roberts, "The Social and Moral Cost of Mass Incarceration in African American Communities," *Stanford Law Review* 56 (2004): 1271–306 (especially pp. 1275–76).

145. Cf. Alschuler & Schulhofer, supra note 57; Cole supra note 23; Harcourt, supra note 26; Meares & Kahan, supra note 23.

146. Dubber, supra note 122, pp. 211–17.

147. City of Chicago, Amendment of Title 8, Chapter 4 of Municipal Code of Chicago by Repeal of Section 015 and Creation of New Sections 015 and 017 which Prohibit Loitering in Public Places by Criminal Street Gang Members, *Journal of Proceedings of the City Council* 25705–11 (February 16, 2000); Ernesto Palomo, "'The Sheriff Knows Who the Troublemakers Are. Just Let Him Round Them Up': Chicago's New Gang Loitering Ordinance," *University of Illinois Law Review* 2002: 729–60; Lawrence Rosenthal, "Gang Loitering and Race," *Journal of Criminal Law and Criminology* 91 (2000): 99–160; Gregory Washburn & Eric Ferkenhoff, "City Targets 86 Hot Spots for Gangs, Keeps List Secret," *Chicago Tribune*, August 23, 2000, p. 1.

148. City of Chicago, 2000, supra note 147, at §1.

Index

CRITICAL PERSPECTIVES ON CRIME AND LAW

David Alan Sklansky, *Democracy and the Police*

Markus D. Dubber and Lindsay Farmer, editors, *Modern Histories of Crime and Punishment*

Markus D. Dubber and Mariana Valverde, editors, *The New Police Science: The Police Power in Domestic and International Governance*

The authorized representative in the EU for product safety and compliance is:
Mare Nostrum Group
B.V Doelen 72
4831 GR Breda
The Netherlands

www.ingramcontent.com/pod-product-compliance
Lightning Source LLC
LaVergne TN
LVHW091516200926
848483LV00005B/426/J
* 9 7 8 0 8 0 4 7 5 9 3 2 8 *